BECOMING AN ART TEACHER

BECOMING
AN ART
TEACHER

JANE K. BATES
TOWSON UNIVERSITY

WADSWORTH
CENGAGE Learning

Australia • Brazil • Japan • Korea • Mexico • Singapore • Spain • United Kingdom • United States

Becoming an Art Teacher
Jane K. Bates

Education Editor: Dianne Lindsay

Assistant Editor: Tangelique Williams

Editorial Assistant: Keynia Johnson

Marketing Manager: Becky Tollerson

Project Editor: Trudy Brown

Print Buyer: April Reynolds

Permissions Editor: Joohee Lee

Production Service: The Book Company

Text Designer: Baugher Design Inc.

Copy Editor: Linda Purrington

Illustrator: David Ruppe, Impact Publications

Compositor: Thompson Type

Cover Designer: Baugher Design Inc.

Cover Photo: Baugher Design Inc.

For product information and technology assistance, contact us at
Cengage Learning Customer & Sales Support, 1-800-354-9706

For permission to use material from this text or product,
submit all requests online at **www.cengage.com/permissions**
Further permissions questions can be emailed to
permissionrequest@cengage.com

Library of Congress Control Number: 99053404

ISBN-13: 978-0-534-52239-1

ISBN-10: 0-534-52239-4

Wadsworth
10 Davis Drive
Belmont, CA 94002-3098
USA

Cengage Learning is a leading provider of customized learning solutions with office locations around the globe, including Singapore, the United Kingdom, Australia, Mexico, Brazil, and Japan. Locate your local office at: **international.cengage.com/region**

Cengage Learning products are represented in Canada by Nelson Education, Ltd.

To learn more about Wadsworth, visit **www.cengage.com/wadsworth**

Purchase any of our products at your local college store or at our preferred online store **www.ichapters.com**

Printed in the United States of America
12 13 14 15 16   16 15 14 13 12

DEDICATION

As we look at the title of this text, *Becoming an Art Teacher,* we can identify several key words. Certainly *teacher* is one. This book is, after all, about teaching. In addition, it is about what motivated many of us to become teachers: *art.* Perhaps the most important word, however, is neither teacher nor art, but *becoming.* Becoming implies movement toward a goal, growth, transformation. It suggests ongoing learning. Whether you are a preservice teacher, an accomplished artist, a veteran art educator, or a college professor, you are simultaneously a learner. This book was written in the hopes that it will support you wherever you happen to be and is dedicated to learners of all ages along the endless continuum of becoming.

CONTENTS

RECOGNIZING BATS AND WAYS TO AVOID THEM

EARLY in my career as an art teacher I quit my high school job, relocated, and, failing to find a high school position, accepted a job on the elementary level. I had no training to teach elementary art, so I simply did what the other art teacher in the school did.

Every October, she got out her bat patterns, Styrofoam "O's," and black paper. Every year the students in the third grade classes happily spent fifteen minutes tracing and cutting bat patterns, gluing on foam eyes, and stapling on strings. Then they spent the next twenty minutes flying their bats around the room and making bat noises.

I did this project my first year. I did it again the second year. After the first ten minutes of my second year of bat flying and noise making, I said to myself, "Why am I doing this?" Then I asked myself,

- Does this teach motor skills that most third graders don't already have?
- Does it teach anything about seeing and making judgments?
- Does it teach about the origins of Halloween?
- Is it creative?
- Does it engage the mind?
- Does it express something personal?
- Does it have any connection to the world of art?

I searched for some sound educational reasons for making bats. I found none. Before you plan an art experience, ask yourself, "Why am I doing this?" If your answer is

- To decorate the bulletin board before open house
- To make a Mother's Day gift
- To acknowledge a holiday with a table centerpiece . . . you may be inviting bats.

Bats come in many shapes and sizes and can be found in a variety of locations. Often they hang on refrigerators. Bats that are three-dimensional or too heavy to hang on refrigerators could be called "mantelpiece bats." They appear at all levels. Preschool art projects in which the teacher puts everything together and then lets the children put on the last dabs of glue are bats. High school painting courses that rely on stacks of nature magazines as subject matter for students to copy are bat-oriented. Any assignment that results in mindless activity, devoid of educational value, can be labeled as a bat. All of you have seen bats somewhere in your experiences, although you may not have labeled them as such. One of my colleagues lit up with recognition when he read this story and said, "I call my bats *turkeys*. You know, when the students trace around their hands, make the thumb into the head, the fingers into the tail feathers and add legs to the heel of the hand . . ."

This story is symbolic of what to avoid on your journey as an art educator. It also serves to introduce the intent of this book: to provide a path on which to learn the why's, what's, and how's of art education. *Becoming an Art Teacher* is designed for use in K–12 methods courses, taken by students as they progress through an art education program. Part I provides an introduction to the field, a model of art education on which this text is based, and strategies for planning units of study. It is intended to carry students to the point where they might begin teaching in preservice experiences. Parts II and III present issues, content, and strategies related to teaching and are intended to deepen students' understanding of theory and practice, as they gain more experience in the field. Part IV acts as a synthesis and prepares students to make transitions into teachers. The goals of the text are

- To present a view of art education that integrates philosophical, historical, theoretical, and practical aspects of teaching;
- To encourage students to retain their "artistic selves," using their own interests, inspirations, and art making as motivations for teaching;
- To teach art students how to think and act like educators, as they translate theory into practice;
- To provide models, methods, and experiences in the hopes that they will enlighten, inspire, and occasionally amuse others.

The writing of this book grew out of my need to organize and present the experiences, beliefs, and knowledge that have shaped me as an art educator. I spent twenty years teaching K–12 art in public schools across the United States. When I made the transition from "art teacher" to "university professor," I turned to resources in the field to guide me in my new role. I found references dealing with the history of art, the history of art education, the teaching of art from various perspectives, the meaning of art in the Western world, the meaning of masks in tribal societies, and one hundred things to make from a paper plate. I did not find what I sought—a practical guide to becoming an art teacher. I set out to bridge the gap between esoteric ivory tower jargon and recipes for how to make art from household junk.

My process was first to look within and to share with my students what I had learned as I journeyed down my path. Sharings came in the form of anecdotes, lecture notes, dialogues, and experiential activities. As interaction between my students and me developed, more questions were raised, more issues were addressed, and the road leading to "art teacher" became more clearly defined. Class notes became longer and turned into chapters, which in turn became the contents of this book. To present the anecdotes, I borrowed a device from the psychologist and educator Madeline Hunter called a "Birdwalk." It is a metaphor for deviating from the path, as a bird might wander from its path in order to explore the moment. My birdwalks deviate from the path through stories such as my bat-making tale. Their purpose is not to lead you astray, but to clarify where the path is. Whenever you encounter information bracketed by the illustration in the left margin, you know you are about to go on a birdwalk.

The subjects of these stories are not to be viewed as real people, but as models to whom I have given names. They symbolize what to embrace and what to avoid along your path. In addition to helping you remember where the path is, they ground theory in practice. They will remind you that this book grew out of real experiences with real students in real classrooms. Here I present the subjects of these stories, leaders who have shaped the field of art education, and myself in the hopes that all will engage your mind and heart, challenge your ideas, encourage your questions, prompt you to seek answers, and support you in becoming an art teacher who never has to resort to bat making.

ACKNOWLEDGMENTS

Some books spring fully formed from the heads of their authors. Others do not. This one fits into the latter group, emerging slowly, growing organically bit by bit from notes on yellow pads. This product is the result of more than ten years of notes, expansion, refinement, and the formulation of a philosophy that integrates the parts into a cohesive whole. Many have been instrumental in my process. First, I acknowledge Jack Taylor, my mentor at Arizona State University, whose knowledge, wisdom, and high energy teaching inspired me to move beyond teaching at the K–12 level to become a trainer of teachers. Second, I acknowledge the many K–12 teachers who have modeled excellent practice in the classroom and helped me define my path. Third, viewing teaching as a dance in which teacher and student take turns leading and following, I acknowledge the hundreds of students who have served as teachers for me. Of course, there are also numerous art educators who have shaped the field. Those who have been most influential in my development are introduced in the text. Additionally, I acknowledge those who have been so supportive in the production of this work. They include my colleagues at Towson University and my student assistants, especially Jane Wynn, whose dedication and expertise were invaluable in the development of the final manuscript. And finally, for manifesting a vision in concrete form, I acknowledge the following people associated with Wadsworth Publishing Company: Dianne Lindsay, education editor; Trudy Brown, project editor; Dusty Friedman, production service; Linda Purrington, copy editor; Norman Baugher, designer; and David Ruppe, artist.

I especially want to thank reviewers of this edition: Lynda E. Andrus, Kansas State University; David W. Baker, University of Wisconsin, Milwaukee; Ann Beiersdorfer, Xavier University; Shauna Castellaw, Lewis-Clark State College; Cynthia Colbert, University of South Carolina; Carol Edwards, Kennesaw State University; Linda Ganstrom, Fort Hays State University; Jacqueline Golden, University of Arkansas; Eugene Harrison, Eastern Illinois University; Elisabeth Hartung, California State University, Long Beach; Gregory W. Hawkins, Eastern Washington University; Howard Hull, University of Tennessee; Erik Nielsen, Southwest Texas State University; Lee A. Ransaw, Morris Brown College; Ralph Raunft, Miami University; Susan Shoaff-Ballanger, Truman State University; Marcia F. Taylor, The College of New Jersey; Betty Tisinger (professor emeritus), Virginia Commonwealth University; and Randy L. Waln, Montana State University, Northern. To all of the above I extend my deepest appreciation and say thank you.

A B O U T
T H E
A U T H O R

Growing up hasn't been easy. I was born and raised in Los Angeles, where I attended six elementary schools, two high schools, and two colleges, graduating from UCLA in 1964. The threads that connected the parts of my life were first my passion for art and then my passion for teaching art. I began teaching in 1965 in a high school thirty miles from where I lived.

After four years of driving to and from work on the freeway and totaling two Volkswagens in the process, I decided to explore life outside California. I applied to the Department of Defense and was sent to teach art in grades 7–12 on an army base in Würzburg, Germany. There I got married and the following year moved with my husband to his home in Rochester, New York, where I taught art in grades 7–12 in the inner city. After a year of serving as a "roving" teacher (transporting boxes of art supplies from the basement to the third floor), dealing with race riots, and driving in blizzards, we moved to someplace that was gentler, warmer, and had schools built on one level. I spent the next thirteen years in Scottsdale, Arizona, teaching art in grades 1–8. There I learned to avoid bats, earned a master's degree at Arizona State University, had two children, and eventually, tiring of telling children not to eat the paste, returned to Arizona State University for a doctoral degree. On graduation, I focused on my next goals: (1) going some place green, and (2) teaching on the college level. I began by accepting a position at Marshall University in West Virginia, where I stayed for two years. In 1986, I moved to Baltimore, Maryland, to teach at Towson University, my home today.

In support of my teaching, I regularly present at district, state, and national conferences; have written curriculum for the states of Arizona and Maryland; and have served as a consultant for museum education. I received awards as the Outstanding Art Educator of the Year in the state of Arizona and the Outstanding Art Educator of the Year in the Higher Education Division for the Eastern Region. At Towson University I direct the undergraduate and graduate programs in art education, mentor students through the writing of their master's theses, supervise student teachers, and teach the three-semester sequence of course work for which I wrote this text. As a teacher first and foremost, I welcome this opportunity to share in the becoming of those who have chosen art education as their field.

PART

PREPARING FOR TEACHING

PART I focuses on preparing for teaching. Chapter 1, "Exploring Our Roots," presents an introduction to philosophical and historical perspectives of art education, which provide a context for understanding issues and trends of today. A model of art education diagrams the philosophical stance embraced within this text. It is holistic in nature, integrating child- and subject-centered approaches, and presents art production at its core. Chapter 2, "Emphasizing Art Making," reflects the focus of our model and moves into the relationship between theory and practice. Models for teaching art production lay the foundation for teaching studio-centered units of study. Chapter 3, "Planning Verbally and Visually," moves into unit planning and support of written plans through visual planning. Chapter 4, "Progressing Through Planning Toward Teaching," illustrates how to move from the general in a unit plan to the specific, fleshed out in individual lesson plans, to teaching. These four chapters are intended to provide enough preparation for a student to walk into an introductory pre-service experience and begin to teach.

EXPLORING
OUR
ROOTS

Recognizing bats and bat-making experiences is not difficult. Agreeing on what constitutes sound art education theory and practice can be much more challenging—especially now. Art education today is a result of what we have chosen to embrace or to react against in our past. Presented here is a brief introduction—art education's beginnings in the United States, rationales for its existence within the general curriculum, and influences leading to where we are today. At any given time in our history we can see a relationship among the needs and values of society, the direction of general education in response to those needs and values, and the focus of art education as a particular aspect of general education. As needs and values have changed, art education has changed. This chapter explores the relationship diagrammed in Figure 1.1 and the movements that have developed since art was introduced into the general curriculum in the mid 1800s. Sections discuss (1) art to support society, (2) art to enhance the individual child, (3) art as a curricular discipline, (4) art education of the 1980s and 1990s, and (5) a vision for art education today.

Needs and values
of society

General education
fulfills needs and
reflects values

Art education
refines goals
of general
education

FIGURE 1.1
*Society, General
Education, and Art
Education Relationships*

ART TO SUPPORT SOCIETY

In the 1800s the general curriculum was designed to support the well-being of the social order. As a new country, the United States was focused on developing a strong, economically independent nation. Draftspeople and designers were needed to promote our Industrial Revolution. To address this need, art was taught as mechanical drawing. Three educators were particularly influential in promoting society-centered art education during the nineteenth century: William Bentley Fowle, William Minifie, and Walter Smith. William Bentley Fowle was a general educator who published *Common Schools Journal* (1842–1852), through which he promoted art as useful in developing drawing skills. Because of his efforts, drawing was first introduced in 1847 as a permissible subject at Boston English High School.

William Minifie was an architect who was hired by the public commissioners of Baltimore to teach drawing at Boys' High School during the 1840s and 1850s. Through a textbook on geometric drawing, he promoted drawing as a science rather than as picture making. Walter Smith was brought to Boston from England to be the Director of Art Education for the city and the State Supervisor of Drawing. He provided leadership in the development of art education in Massachusetts, which in 1870 passed the first law making drawing a required high school subject. He saw art education as a sequence of drawing lessons that were so clear and precise that non-art specialists could teach students to draw. His book *Teacher's Manual for Freehand Drawing and Designing* (1876) consisted of a series of graduated exercises in which students were required to copy geometric patterns of lines and shapes. This type of teaching, reflected by these early art educators, is called *closed-ended* instruction. Its purpose is to develop skills in working with tools, materials, and techniques.

The society-centered orientation has continued to be a thread throughout our history. It has been most visible when our nation has been most challenged. For example, during the depression of the 1930s "art for daily living" became a rationale for art education. The Owattona Project reflected this rationale in a program designed to help community members of Owattona, Minnesota make aesthetic decisions relevant to their daily lives. In the 1940s art education was used to promote the war effort. In the 1950s art education was used to develop creative thinking skills necessary to compete with the Soviet Union in the space race. In the 1960s "art for the social order" reflected the civil rights movement. Today some of what we see in art education reflects our concern with issues such as conservation of natural resources.

▼
ART TO ENHANCE THE INDIVIDUAL CHILD

The child-centered orientation developed in the 1920s as a reaction against the philosophy that education existed to serve the needs of the society at the expense of the individual. Goals and content for art education were derived from the developmental levels and needs of the child. The purpose of art education was seen at this time as promoting self-expression. Children were encouraged to experiment with materials and were allowed freedom to develop their intrinsic qualities through relatively unstructured art experiences.

One of the most influential and revolutionary educators supporting the child-centered orientation was John Dewey, the intellectual leader of the Progressive Movement from 1920 to 1940. Dewey believed the child was not merely a miniature adult in the process of becoming fully formed. He thought children needed types of experiences other than rote memorization of facts and closed-ended art instruction intended to develop mature artistic skills. He saw the task of education as providing environments that would encourage creativity and adaptation to real life situations. Dewey viewed the school as a place that allowed students freedom to make choices, to move around, and to solve problems.

Two important developments in art education grew out of Dewey's philosophy and the practices of the Progressive Movement—correlated art and art for self-expression. Correlated art activities were introduced in classrooms designed to reflect the outside world. Many teachers set up their rooms as small communities in which students were presented with problem situations to solve through cooperative efforts. Students produced murals, puppet shows, tabletop models, charts, displays, and bulletin boards. These activities all involved art. Art correlated with other subjects became a way of providing experiential learning, problem-solving opportunities, and freedom for self-expression.

During the Progressive Movement "art for self-expression" became the major rationale for art education. In seeking to provide experiences that encouraged problem-solving behavior and self-expression, educators replaced closed-ended instruction with other teaching strategies. The *open-ended* approach was used to develop skills in problem solving. Teachers presented a "problem" defined by a set of rules or criteria. Students were given opportunities to work within the criteria to solve the problem. Using this approach teachers recognized individual differences, a variety of problem-solving behaviors, and multiple "right" answers. An even less structured teaching strategy used to encourage self-expression was the *laissez-faire* approach. *Laissez-faire,* a French expression meaning "without interference or direction," is a teaching method that allows students maximum freedom to explore and experiment. Students are presented with a wide range of materials in order to discover how they can be used in self-expressive ways. The laissez-faire strategy was used to elicit the freshness and spontaneity intrinsic in children's artwork and to protect children from what was perceived as contamination by adult standards.

The child-centered orientation introduced by Dewey and practiced in the Progressive Movement has continued primarily through the work of another major figure in art education—Viktor Lowenfeld. Lowenfeld was an Austrian art educator who in 1939 fled before the Holocaust and came to the United States. Coming from a background in which he had contact with horrendous social conditions, Lowenfeld naturally aligned with the child-centered movement. He focused on the holistic nature of the child, considering physical, mental, emotional, and creative capacities. In *Creative and Mental Growth* (1947) Lowenfeld clearly reflected the philosophy of postwar times. Educators were concerned with making the world "safe for peace." Art was seen as a humanizing activity that was broadly therapeutic. Lowenfeld saw art as a vehicle for developing human creative capacities through freedom of expression. Through his teaching and writing, he has had an impact that endures to the present day.

▼
ART AS A CURRICULAR DISCIPLINE

Not long after the return to peace after World War II, America was shaken by the Soviets' launch of *Sputnik.* The approach adopted by general education was "back to basics." Engineers and scientists needed to be trained to compete in the space race. Art education that focused on freedom for self-expression was perceived as "soft" and lacking in substance. Mirroring the academization occurring in general education, art education of the 1960s began a major movement in the direction of content and structure. The focus started to shift from art taught through experiential studio activities in child-centered approaches to art presented as a "body of knowledge." Curricula with specific concepts and content were designed in an effort to place art as a discipline alongside math and science. This approach, referred to as *subject centered, content centered*, or *discipline based*, grew gradually over a twenty-year period and was formalized in the 1980s as DBAE (discipline-based art education).

▼
ART EDUCATION OF THE 1980s AND 1990s

DBAE developed into a major movement due in large part to the Getty Education Institute for the Arts. In the 1980s the institute, investigating art education practices throughout the country, found that despite the direction subject-centered approaches had begun to take, most programs remained heavily focused on studio production. One of its goals was to balance art making with the study of art in culture and as culture. This was accomplished by presenting art education as four interrelated domains or disciplines:

- *Art production*—focusing on art making
- *Art criticism*—focusing on perceiving and understanding visual qualities of art through the use of critical dialogue
- *Aesthetics*—focusing on the development of appreciation, personal taste, and knowledge of art's value as established within various times, places, and cultures
- *Art history*—focusing on art within the context of history and culture

The institute provided research, curriculum, and training to implement its philosophy and to fulfill what had become the number one goal of the National Art Education Association (NAEA): "All elementary and secondary schools shall require students to complete a sequential program of art instruction that integrates the study of art production, aesthetics, art criticism, and art history."

Although art educators in general may have supported this goal, many questioned implementation strategies. Educators critical of DBAE as it existed in practice made these observations:

- Some discipline-based approaches replaced art production as the primary focus with the study of art objects. This was referred to as *object-centered* art education because the main activity consisted of viewing and discussing objects, rather than making art. The approach was seen by some as a weakness, because studio experiences were viewed by many as the essence of art education.
- Some discipline-based programs were rigidly implemented through a formula in which domains were presented in a specific order with production addressed last. This structure restricted flexible integration and tended to de-emphasize art production.
- When art production was de-emphasized, students often created expressions modeled after the artwork they had studied, rather than exhibiting creative self-expression. Instead of making bat clones, they made Picasso, Matisse, or Mona Lisa clones.
- Art activities that were reduced to recreating expressions based on ideas of master artists tended to be product oriented. Rather than becoming involved in the experiential processes of art making, students were focused on producing end results. These were often judged on their resemblance to the original, rather than on the intrinsic worth of the experience.
- The majority of artwork presented for study when DBAE began was from Western cultures. Non-Western cultures were inadequately represented.
- When implementing DBAE, some school districts designed guides that specified particular artists to be presented at each grade level. This was seen as overly restrictive in program planning.
- Some advocates of DBAE avoided interdisciplinary planning, fearing integration with other subjects would diminish art education. Lack of connectedness was seen as a weakness.
- Some discipline-based art educators presented artwork and studio activities in ways that were inappropriate for the developmental levels of children and had little or no relevance to the lives of their students.

These criticisms were often well founded, well taken, and addressed. Art educators began experimenting with different ways to integrate child- and subject-centered approaches. A number of strategies were developed that shared these characteristics:

- They integrated art history, aesthetics, and art criticism with art production in ways that supported rather than devalued studio experiences.

- They addressed developmental levels and age appropriateness.
- They promoted self-expression and developed problem-solving skills.
- They were inclusive rather than exclusive, recognizing the connection of art to other subjects and to life in general.
- They developed reading, writing, and thinking skills.
- They provided a global perspective of art, presenting expressions representative of all cultures.
- They made connections between the values, ideas, experiences, and expressions of artists and of individual students.
- They were concerned with accountability and provided measures to assess learning in all domains of art education.

One way to gain an understanding of subject-centered art education and how it differs from child-centered is to compare texts in the field. Lowenfeld's *Creative and Mental Growth* is still popular today and considered by many to be the "bible" of child-centered art education. In contrast, a number of subject-centered student texts have been written in the last three decades of the twentieth century.

Selected examples, presented next, indicate the use of these texts at all grade levels:

elementary-level student texts
- *Adventures in Art* (a series of six texts) by Chapman
- *Art in Action* (a series of six texts) by Hubbard
- *Art: Meaning, Method and Media* (a series of six texts) by Hubbard and Rouse
- *Discover Art* (a series of six texts) by Chapman

middle-school–level student texts
- *A World of Images* by Chapman
- *Art: Images and Ideas* by Chapman
- *Art in Your Visual Environment* by Brommer and Horn
- *Art in Your World* by Brommer and Horn
- *Exploring Art* by Mittler and Ragans
- *Exploring Visual Design* by Gatto, Porter, and Sellack
- *Introducing Art* by Ragans, Mittler, Morman, Unsworth, and Scannell
- *Understanding and Creating Art* by Goldstein, Katz, Kowalchuk, and Saunders
- *Understanding Art* by Mittler and Ragans
- *The Visual Experience* by Hobbs and Salome

high-school–level texts
- *Art in Focus* by Mittler
- *Art Talk* by Ragans
- *Creating and Understanding Drawings* by Mittler and Howze
- *Discovering Art History* by Brommer
- *Themes and Foundations of Art* by Katz, Lankford, and Plank

The controversy over what to and what not to do increased significantly in the 1980s and 1990s with the emergence of DBAE. Teachers became consumed in healthy debate over purposes of art education, content of art education, and methods for delivering instruction. Some clung adamantly to child-centered art education, viewing DBAE as the enemy that substituted academic study of art for authentic self-expression. Others saw DBAE as offering much-needed content and structure. Still others adopted more holistic approaches, integrating positive aspects of both orientations. Regardless of where one stood along the child-subject–centered continuum, all were encouraged to move into the year 2000 providing opportunities for students at every grade level to connect with art through experiences in art production, art criticism, aesthetics, and art history.

This encouragement came in the form of the Goals 2000: Educate America Act, which identified the arts as core subjects equal in importance to the academics and mandated their teaching in grades K–12. The result of this law was the formulation of the National Visual Arts Standards (presented in full in Chapter 14). These identify what students should know and be able to do on completion of high school. They reflect the breadth of what is deemed important in art education today: ability to communicate through the arts, capacity to reflect on and assess art, knowledge of art within a variety of cultures and historical periods, and understanding of art's relevance to other subjects and life in general. Moving into the twenty-first century, we see as one of our strengths our diversity, the variety of voices and approaches addressing standards and demonstrating accountability in art education. The individuals introduced next illustrate this point.

ELLIOT EISNER

Elliot Eisner has been especially noteworthy as a supporter of DBAE. A writer, curriculum designer, and art educator at Stanford University, Eisner is an outspoken advocate for art as basic and provided us with a vision of what DBAE at its best might be. He has presented these rationales for teaching art:

- Art invites students to look carefully so that they might see.
- Art develops multiple forms of literacy that give students meaningful access to "cultural capital."
- Art provides children with opportunities to use their imaginations, to create multiple solutions to problems, and to rely on their own judgment to determine when a problem is solved.

In answer to the question posed in his 1987 article on DBAE, "Are the arts ornamental in our schools?" Eisner responded,

> [Art] is only ornamental if meaningful access to some of our most significant cultural achievements is a marginal educational aim. It is only ornamental if the kinds of mental skills fostered by work in the arts are tangential to the kinds of problems both children and adults encounter outside school. . . . The arts represent a form of thinking and a way of knowing. Their presence in our schools is as basic as anything could be. (p. 10)

HOWARD GARDNER

Eisner is not alone in his belief in the power of art education to develop multiple forms of literacy, encourage multiple solutions to problems, and promote multiple forms of intelligence. Howard Gardner is a psychologist and educator most noted for his research in multiple intelligences. Viewing human beings in a holistic way, Gardner identified eight forms of intelligence: (1) verbal/linguistic, (2) logical/mathematical, (3) body/kinesthetic, (4) visual/spatial, (5) musical/rhythmical, (6) interpersonal (person to person), (7) intrapersonal (awareness of self), and (8) naturalistic (relating to the world of nature). His interest in going beyond "verbal ability," most characteristically identified as "intelligence," led him into a long-term involvement: Project Zero. This was an investigation co-directed with David Perkins at Harvard University, studying the nature of understanding across disciplines, the origins of creativity, the development of thinking abilities, and the promotion of critical judgment. The project was inspired by and took its name from the answer to the question "What do we know about how humans learn in and through the arts?" (posed by the philosopher Nelson Goodman). The answer was "zero." Growing out of Project Zero, a group dealing specifically with the arts was developed—Arts PROPEL. This organization was formed to investigate, teach, and assess cognitive functioning through the arts. It is based in studio production and focuses on experiential processes of art making and performance. Emphasis is placed on creating and assessing a record of progress through the keeping of studio portfolios. This approach is significantly different from that of DBAE. However, many paths lead to common goals, as we may infer from this statement from Arts PROPEL:

> *The creation and production of art represents human achievement at its highest. Exercising hand, heart and mind together develops important mental skills such as symbol use, analysis, problem solving, invention and reflection . . . exactly the sort of independent intellectual activity that distinguishes thinkers, inventors and leaders.*

ELLEN DISSANAYAKE

In contrast to these two examples, consider the ideas of Ellen Dissanayake, an anthropologist who influenced the field with her view of art as "species centered." In *What Is Art For?* (1988), she presented art as a universal behavior and explored these ideas:

- Human beings have engaged in art behaviors since the earliest beginnings of our species.
- Art began when early humans were not only able to recognize something as "special," but deliberately set out to make something "special."
- "Making special" is behavior that elevates experiences and objects from the mundane, the everyday, and the ordinary.
- Our ancestors not only made "special" objects (such as tools) but also developed "special" or "controlled" behaviors (rituals) in order to ensure success.
- Because rituals have been and are still part of life in all cultures, we may view ritualistic objects not as examples of art for art's sake, but as *art for life's sake.*

Dissanayake also viewed art as basic, not so much because of its potential to teach about cultures or to develop intelligence, but because art making is intrinsic behavior of humankind. Delivering a keynote address at the 1991 convention of the NAEA, she stated,

> *Art is not confined to a small coterie of geniuses, visionaries, cranks and charlatans—indistinguishable from one another—but is instead a fundamental human species characteristic that demands and deserves to be promoted and nourished. . . . Art is a normal and necessary behavior of human beings that like talking, exercising, playing, working, socializing, learning, loving and nurturing should be encouraged and developed in everyone.*

PETER LONDON

Finally, let's turn to the work of Peter London—writer, art therapist, art educator, and a leading proponent of child-centered art education today. Much like Dissanayake, London defined art as "a category of human activity." In this process-centered orientation he urged art educators to go beyond "simply providing strategies to replicate, study, talk about and display . . . aesthetic amenities" (things in which we seek relief from or enhancement of everyday life). He viewed art education as a powerful instrument through which we may transform the quality of an individual's life from its current condition to a preferred and elevated one. In *No More Secondhand Art* (1989, p. 8), he described art in the service of transformation as functioning in these ways:

- Renewing and reaffirming the covenants between humankind and nature and between man and God
- Grappling with the ephemeral qualities of life and with our own mortality
- Marking significant times, places, and events
- Discovering the actual range of human possibilities
- Awakening us to higher levels of consciousness

In *Step Outside* (1994), London presented ways to translate these ideas into classroom practice. His approach, *community-based art education* (CBAE), begins with the experiences, knowledge, and curiosity the student brings into the classroom. From this central point in which interaction is based on what the student initially offers, the scope of experiences is widened to include the immediate environment outside the classroom, the larger school, the home and family, neighborhood, community, nation, and ultimately the globe.

These individuals were not selected because they represent all of art education. Some might argue that they may not even represent art education in the mainstream. Do we really have a "mainstream" today? Times have changed from the days in which art education was defined as drawing. As our profession has grown, we have become more inclusive and diversified. Today we are about many things. What Eisner, Gardner, Dissanayake, and London collectively represent is the richness of the tapestry. They were selected not only because each has delivered a significant message about the purpose and path of art education, but also because their messages are different.

The fabric of art education has been woven over a long period. At any given time those in the field have attempted to provide what was perceived as best within the context of general education and the larger society. These educators did not exist in a vacuum. Their ideas came from observations of human behaviors, perceptions of the world beyond the classroom, study of art and other fields, analyses of art education of the past, assessments of strengths and weaknesses of art education in the present, and visions of how we might guide individuals and society into the future. Table 1.1 on page 10 summarizes the development of art education, chronicling the progress of society-, child-, and subject-centered approaches.

▼
A VISION OF ART EDUCATION TODAY

Progressing from an introduction to "bat consciousness" to knowledge of events in our history and resulting trends in art education, you may understand how a number of rationales for the teaching of art have emerged. They include

- To ensure economic security
- To develop connections among people
- To support the social order
- To promote appreciation
- To develop trade skills
- For leisure time

- To teach moral values
- To gain skills for careers
- To support war efforts
- For spiritual unfolding
- To enhance daily living
- For personal and planetary transformation

TABLE 1.1
Selected Examples of Three Orientations in Art Education

TIME	HISTORICAL EVENTS AND INFLUENCES OF GENERAL EDUCATION	SOCIETY-CENTERED ORIENTATION IN ART EDUCATION
1870s	The Industrial Revolution promotes economic competition with Europe.	Mechanical drawing is introduced as the first art education to train boys to be draftsmen and designers in the Industrial Revolution.
1890s	Schools include vocational training to develop skills useful for children of immigrants.	Crafts—woodwork, metal work, sewing, weaving—are introduced to provide training in trades.
1900s	Education includes training in morals and values.	Art appreciation called "picture study" involves discussing religious subject matter of "famous paintings" to transmit moral values.
1920s	The Progressive Movement embraces Dewey's views that education should be experiential and promote self-expression.	
1930s	The Depression leads to financial and emotional stress.	"Art for daily living" becomes a rationale. Children are taught to make decorative and practical items to brighten home environments.
1940s	America fights World War II.	Art education is seen as a vehicle to support the war effort and focuses on making patriotic posters and mementos.
	World War II ends. Education seeks to make the world "safe for peace" through the development of creative capacities.	
1950s	The Soviets launch *Sputnik,* leaping ahead in the race to control space.	"Art for creativity" becomes a rationale to promote creative problem-solving skills needed in the space race.
1960s	The reaction to the Soviet Union's achievements in space is a back-to-basics movement. Education stresses academic excellence.	
	The civil rights movement and women's liberation movement promote multicultural awareness.	Art for the social order becomes important. Courses in black and Hispanic art are added to programs. The work of women artists begins to be introduced into art education curricula.
1970s	A counterculture develops, protesting the values of the establishment and the war in Vietnam.	
1980s	*A Nation at Risk* calls for educational reform.	
1990s	Education emphasizes standards, assessment, and accountability in the Goals 2000: Educate America Act.	Art education is mandated into law through the Goals 2000 Act.
	Technology furthers "the information age" and the development of a global society.	Art education incorporates technology to access and communicate information on a global scale.
2000s		

TABLE 1.1 *(continued)*

TIME	CHILD-CENTERED ORIENTATION IN ART EDUCATION	SUBJECT-CENTERED ORIENTATION IN ART EDUCATION
1870s		
1880s		
1890s		
1900s		
1910s		
1920s	Art is correlated with other subjects to promote experiential learning. Art education focuses on fostering self-expression and learning through experimentation and discovery.	
1930s		
1940s	Art is seen as a developmental activity to promote health and well-being. Experimentation with materials is encouraged for creative self-expression.	
1950s	Art as creative self-expression and experiential learning through manipulation of materials continues.	
1960s	Art as creative self-expression and experiential learning through manipulation of materials continues.	Art education is seen as "a body of knowledge" with discrete subject matter, concepts, and skills. Focus shifts from the art learner to art content. Art education reflects the academic orientation of general education.
1970s	Crafts are revived as an expression of individual creativity and as a protest against mass production and social conformity.	Art education continues to reflect an academic orientation and broadens to include the teaching of art concepts, perceptual skills, and historical content.
1980s	Arts PROPEL presents a studio-centered approach to promote cognitive functioning.	DBAE formalizes "art as a body of knowledge" into the four domains of art criticism, aesthetics, art history, and art production.
1990s	Community-based art education focuses on a studio-centered curriculum based on needs and interests of the child.	Discipline-based approaches offer K–12 sequential instruction in all four domains. Art education emphasizes art content, multicultural involvement, interdisciplinary connections, use of technology, standards, and assessment.
2000s		

- For culture refinement
- To gain access to cultural capital
- For art's sake
- To promote visual literacy
- To develop perceptual skills
- To develop cognitive skills
- To develop psychomotor skills
- To develop social skills
- To develop affective skills
- To promote self-expression
- To develop inquiring minds
- To promote enhanced experiencing of life

These rationales grew from society-, child-, and subject-centered orientations. Sometimes approaches considered to be polar opposites deliver the same message from different ends of a continuum. For example, DBAE places primary importance on the study of art within cultural contexts. As students study the art of others and relate what they are learning to themselves, they progress from the outside in, as diagrammed in Figure 1.2.

FIGURE 1.2
Outside-In Orientation

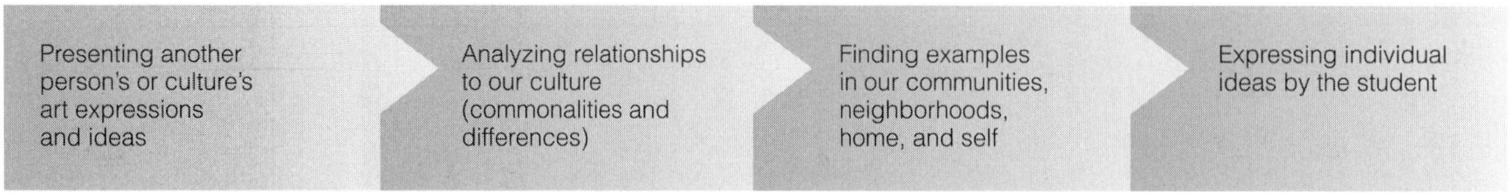

| Presenting another person's or culture's art expressions and ideas | Analyzing relationships to our culture (commonalities and differences) | Finding examples in our communities, neighborhoods, home, and self | Expressing individual ideas by the student |

Child-centered art education, in contrast, places primary importance on the intrinsic qualities of the learner. Students first look within to express themselves and then discover commonalities with others through shared ideas, experiences, and expressions. They learn from the inside out.

FIGURE 1.3
Inside-Out Orientation

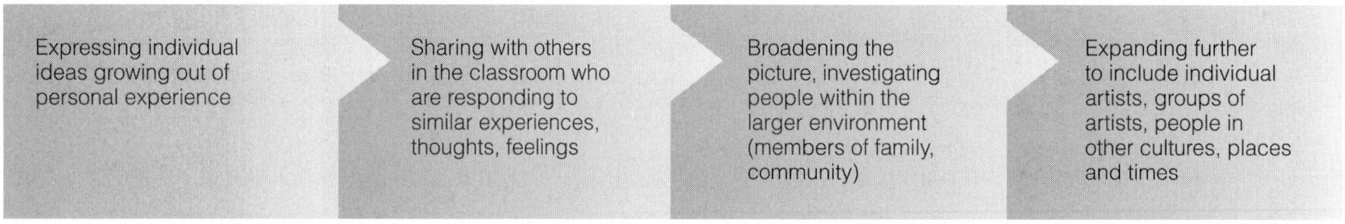

| Expressing individual ideas growing out of personal experience | Sharing with others in the classroom who are responding to similar experiences, thoughts, feelings | Broadening the picture, investigating people within the larger environment (members of family, community) | Expanding further to include individual artists, groups of artists, people in other cultures, places and times |

One approach begins with the general and progresses toward the particular, and the other proceeds in the opposite way. Although these are significant differences, there is an implied common message: "Art is a visual language that connects human beings, relating the inside to the outside and the outside to the inside."

Understanding the common messages, as well as the differences, is important. As we embark on our study of art education, we must articulate what we believe and define where we stand along the path. If we proclaim ourselves as followers of DBAE, we will move in one direction to deliver our message. If we align with child-centered art educators, we will move in a different direction. Another choice is to consider all of what is being offered and to design our own route selectively. The path presented in this guide is holistic, integrating ideas from multiple points of view. It is based on these beliefs:

1. Art is a visual language through which human beings speak to one another.

2. "Speaking the language" is synonymous with "creating art." Art production is of primary importance and should be emphasized above all else in studio-centered curricular designs.

3. The study of aesthetics, art criticism, and art history develops attitudes, skills, and knowledge that support the ability to "speak" (make) art.

4. Speaking and understanding the language of art involves connecting both the inside to the outside and the outside to the inside.
   a. Every unit of study should offer students opportunities to express their authentic selves in studio experiences intended to promote thinking and creativity.
   b. Every unit of study should include a historical referent to create a connection with the outside.
   c. We can move in either direction, progressing from the inside out or from the outside in to make connections.
5. The domains of aesthetics, art criticism, and art history should be presented in ways that explore "inside" and "outside" issues.
   a. Inside issues

   Aesthetics:
   - What do I like (in terms of art)?
   - How do I assign value to art?
   - Why is art important to me?

   Art criticism:
   - How do I understand and express myself through art?
   - What am I saying through my art?
   - How can I assess my own artwork?

   Art history:
   - How am I connected to others through my art?
   b. Outside issues

   Aesthetics:
   - What is art (as defined by people in different cultures, times, and places)?
   - Why is art valued by others?

   Art criticism:
   - How can I experience and understand the art of others?
   - What are others saying to me through their artwork?
   - How can I assess the art of others?

   Art history:
   - How does humankind express through art?
6. Art touches everyone. It both influences and is influenced by all of life. We can convey the importance of art as an integral aspect of human existence by presenting it within various contexts:
   a. Art as an expression of the authentic self
   b. Art as an expression of one's own culture
   c. Art as a universal expression of humankind
   d. Art as an expression of life in general

These points define a belief system illustrated in Figure 1.4. The model integrates the ideas into a cohesive whole. Notice that *art making* has been placed in the center, signifying its importance as the core of art education. On each side are influences informing art making. These "inside" and "outside" influences have been subdivided into aesthetics, art criticism, and art history to illustrate the supporting roles of these domains. The four additional categories—the authentic self, one's own culture, a global perspective, and life in general—present increasingly expanding contexts in which to explore art. Each outside category is connected to "art making" by double-headed arrows, illustrating that art both impacts and is impacted by everything else. Additionally, the parts of the model are connected by two concentric circles moving in opposite directions. The outside circle suggests that we can move from the outside in, progressing from "life in general" toward "the authentic self". The inside circle implies that we can also move in the opposite direction, progressing from "inside influences" toward "life in general".

FIGURE 1.4
Model of Art Education

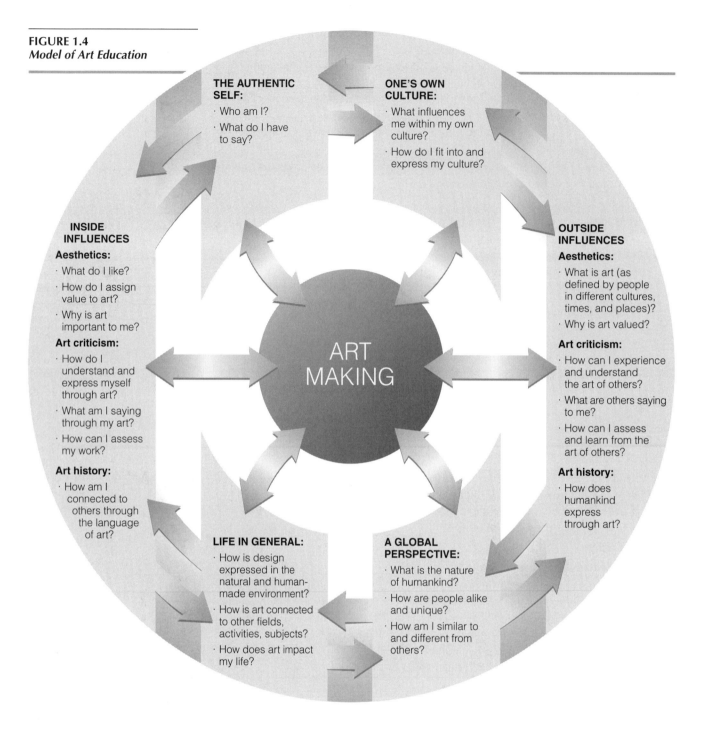

THE AUTHENTIC SELF:
· Who am I?
· What do I have to say?

ONE'S OWN CULTURE:
· What influences me within my own culture?
· How do I fit into and express my culture?

INSIDE INFLUENCES

Aesthetics:
· What do I like?
· How do I assign value to art?
· Why is art important to me?

Art criticism:
· How do I understand and express myself through art?
· What am I saying through my art?
· How can I assess my work?

Art history:
· How am I connected to others through the language of art?

OUTSIDE INFLUENCES

Aesthetics:
· What is art (as defined by people in different cultures, times, and places)?
· Why is art valued?

Art criticism:
· How can I experience and understand the art of others?
· What are others saying to me?
· How can I assess and learn from the art of others?

Art history:
· How does humankind express through art?

ART MAKING

LIFE IN GENERAL:
· How is design expressed in the natural and human-made environment?
· How is art connected to other fields, activities, subjects?
· How does art impact my life?

A GLOBAL PERSPECTIVE:
· What is the nature of humankind?
· How are people alike and unique?
· How am I similar to and different from others?

S U M M A R Y

The history of art education in America shows the relationships among art education, general education, and the larger society. At any given time in our history we can see a pattern: The rationales for art education, the content of art education, and even the strategies for teaching are a response to historical events and conditions, societal needs and values, and directions of general education.

Two rationales have given rise to two general movements: art to support society and art to enhance the individual child. The society-centered orientation appeared in the 1800s, responding to the needs of a growing nation. Art was seen as a vehicle for promoting societal well-being. Teaching focused on the building of skills through closed-ended instruction. The child-centered orientation began in the 1920s as a reaction against the lack of concern with individual growth and development reflected in the society-centered approach. The child-centered orientation, which grew out of the philosophy of John Dewey and the educational practices of the Progressive Movement, was carried forward by art educators influenced primarily by the writings and teachings of Viktor Lowenfeld. In the child-centered view, art education was seen as a means for promoting growth of physically, mentally, and emotionally healthy individuals. Open-ended and laissez-faire teaching strategies were used, relying heavily on free exploration with materials.

A third broad movement is a subject-centered approach in which art is taught as a curricular discipline. As in previous movements, this one responded to societal needs and perspectives in general education. In the 1960s a back-to-basics movement caused a reevaluation of art education. A shift from child- to subject-centered art education began, and art education was defined as "a body of knowledge." Over the next twenty years, the subject-centered approach was slow to take hold. Not until the 1980s did it emerge as a primary orientation in the form of discipline-based art education. DBAE integrates four domains of art education—art production, art criticism, aesthetics, and art history. It challenged beliefs and practices of child-centered educators and caused considerable controversy in the field. Its advocates supported it because it provided substance and taught students to understand and appreciate art as viewers through experiences in art history, criticism, and aesthetics. Critics argued that it was implemented in ways that de-emphasized art production, stifled creativity, and required students to engage in activities that were often developmentally inappropriate.

The last twenty years of the twentieth century were particularly rich in terms of diversity. Many art educators defined themselves as discipline-based and created their own subject-centered approaches to address criticisms of DBAE. A growing number of art educators embraced an alternative to DBAE in the form of community-based art education (CBAE). This group brought child-centered art education back with renewed strength, developing its curricular structure from the needs, values, interests, and energy of the individual learner. Regardless of where teachers stood philosophically, all were encouraged to move into the twenty-first century providing high quality art education defined by structure and content. This encouragement came in the form of the national Goals 2000: Educate America Act. This law mandated art education in grades K–12. As a result, National Visual Arts Standards were formulated. These stipulated what students should know and be able to do in art on graduation from high school. They reflect the breadth of what is deemed important today: the ability to communicate through the arts, the capacity to reflect on and assess art, knowledge of art within culture and history, and understanding of art's relevance to other subjects within the curriculum.

The vision of art education on which this book is based is holistic, integrating the strengths of various movements, approaches, and individuals. A model for art education illustrates how the subject-centered orientation (with its focus on the world of art outside the individual) and the child-centered orientation (with its focus on the learner) can be brought together in a synergistic whole. The vehicle used to connect the "outside" to the "inside" is art production. The model is studio centered, with aesthetics, art criticism, and art history used to support art making. As you progress through the book, you will discover chapter by chapter how this theoretical model becomes translated into practical application, addressing art in relationship to the authentic self, culture, a global society, and life in general.

WHY TEACH ART?

Scenario

Your principal has just told you that because of budget cuts art (and your position) may be eliminated from the school.

Directions

1. Present a convincing argument that art should stay by listing at least 10 rationales for the teaching of art to all students, 2. Indicate with an asterisk (*) the four rationales you believe are the strongest, and 3. Discuss each of the four in detail in the spaces provided below.

10 Rationales for Teaching Art:

Rationale 1:

Rationale 2:

Rationale 3:

Rationale 4:

EMPHASIZING
ART MAKING

Beginning with the premise that art making is central to art education, we turn first to the domain of art production. This chapter presents a view of those who will engage in art-making experiences (the students) and discusses the nature, purpose, and design of different kinds of productive activities. Sections include (1) artistic expression of children, (2) three types of studio activities: closed-ended, open-ended, and laissez-faire, and (3) teaching models to structure studio experiences.

▼
ARTISTIC EXPRESSION OF CHILDREN

To have an art-making experience, we need several components: (1) the art learner, (2) the actions or behaviors of the learner, and (3) the results of those actions—the art expressions. The starting point seems obvious: the students themselves, bringing in their excitement, interests, feelings, and needs. They serve as guides for where to begin in the design of studio activities. Because at this point you may have had limited experience with children, let's turn to someone who has shed light on the subject. Lowenfeld, in *Creative and Mental Growth,* influenced the field with his studies and theories on stages of artistic development and visual and haptic types of expression.

●
STAGES OF ARTISTIC DEVELOPMENT

In comparing art expressions of learners at different ages, Lowenfeld saw that children draw in predictable ways, going through defined stages, ranging from the free scribbles of 2-year-olds through deliberate mark making of adolescents. These stages are summarized and illustrated in Table 2.1 and Figure 2.1.

As you review Table 2.1, you may have questions, such as these:

- Are the stages universal? Do children everywhere express themselves in these ways?
- Should teachers simply accept artistic expressions of children as typical of a given stage and not interfere?
- Should teachers present skills and information that will carry students from where they are to higher levels of skill and/or understanding?

These are good questions that are not easy to answer. At one time it was generally accepted that all children go through these stages. As interest has increased in multicultural expressions, researchers have found that children in some non-Western cultures do not fit this model of development. In our Western culture, however, you will see drawing after drawing that you can identify as "normal" expression of each stage. It is important to have a stan-

TABLE 2.1
Stages of Artistic Development

STAGE OF DEVELOPMENT	AGE	CHARACTERISTICS OF STAGE
Scribbling Stage	2–4	Children make random marks, feeling the kinesthetic aspect of the experience. Mark making becomes a movement activity that develops motor coordination. As children gain control of their bodies, they move from random scribbles to horizontal and vertical scribbles to circular scribbles.
Preschematic Stage	4–7	Children advance from circular scribbles to their first attempts to represent objects in their environment. People are symbolized by a circular figure with arm and leg lines radiating from the head. Figures or objects float randomly on the page with little regard for size or placement.

Schematic Stage	7–9	Children move from representing objects as more or less circular shapes with appendages to using schemas or formulas.
		
		   Schemas are conceptual—they represent concepts or ideas of things and people, rather than realistic perceptions of individual objects. (For example, children often draw trees like lollipops regardless of how individual trees are actually perceived.) Children begin to develop ways to organize space. Objects are typically lined up along a ground line; the sky becomes a line across the top of the page; objects are seldom overlapped and space is relatively flat.
		
		   Drawings and paintings tend to be large, free, and spontaneous. Children are relatively uncritical of their own work and the work of others and they enjoy sharing.

Stage of Dawning Realism (the gang age)	9–12	Children continue to represent objects in schematic form. They become interested in detail and realism. Artwork gradually becomes small and tight. Children are much more aware of themselves and how they are perceived by their peers. They tend to be more inhibited. They become much more critical of themselves and their artwork.
Pseudonaturalistic Stage (the stage of reasoning)	12–14	Children become increasingly aware of surroundings and are concerned with realistic depiction of objects. They develop an interest in portraying depth and correct proportions. Although many children at this stage still represent the environment through schemas, they become increasingly interested in observational drawing (looking at objects and drawing what they see rather than drawing concepts or ideas of imagined objects). Students become even more critical of their work and may be embarrassed to share it.
Period of Decision (adolescent art in high school)	14–17	Mark making moves from an act of natural self-expression to a deliberate attempt to explore art processes and to create art products. Decisions become important as students choose how and to what degree they will involve themselves in making art.

dard for "normal." If you have no standard for normal, you will have trouble recognizing "special." "Special" may be a first grader whose artistic expressions consist primarily of scribbling. "Special" may also be a first grader who overlaps objects and creates foreground, middle ground, and background.

This understanding of what is "normal" and what is "special" brings us to the next issues: Should teachers accept students where they are? Should teachers give students skills and information to accelerate learning into the next stage? During the Progressive Movement there was a hands-off philosophy. Educators were willing to allow abilities of children to develop without much intervention. This laissez-faire approach was considered a healthy counterbalance to the restrictions of closed-ended instruction of earlier times.

Today many art teachers believe that adult intervention is a necessary part of the educational process. When we use language students can understand, present information in small bits through carefully sequenced step-by-step processes, and teach through a variety of experiential activities, students learn

FIGURE 2.1
Drawings Illustrating Stages of Artistic Development

Source: Lowenfeld. © 1982. *Creative and Mental Growth,* 1e. Reprinted by permission of Prentice Hall, Upper Saddle River NJ.

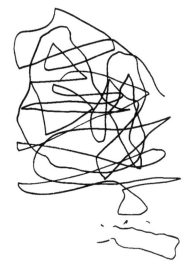

1. Scribbling Stage (2–4 years)

2. Preschematic Stage (4–7 years)

3. Schematic Stage (7–9 years)

4. Age of Dawning Realism (9–12 years)

5. Pseudonaturalistic Stage (12–14 years)

6. Period of Decision (14–17 years)

more at earlier ages. For example, many of you may not have encountered contour drawing until you were in high school. Art teachers now present contour drawing experiences to students in fourth and fifth grade. Most fourth and fifth graders do *conceptual* drawings, using schemas to represent objects. Contour drawing is a *perceptual* activity, involving looking at a specific object and drawing exactly what is seen. Are fourth and fifth graders capable of doing this? Yes. Will it change how they see and draw? Maybe. Will they continue to make schematic drawings? Probably they will, and by providing experiences beyond the schematic mode of representation, you may broaden your students' artistic repertoires and choices for self-expression.

▼ VISUAL AND HAPTIC MODES OF EXPRESSION

In addition to contributing a wealth of information on child art and child-centered art education, Lowenfeld also provided insight into two different modes of artistic expression—visual and haptic. In working with the partially blind, he discovered that some students took in information through what they could see, whereas others took in information through what they could feel. He called those who related primarily through their sense of sight *visual learners* and those who related primarily through their sense of touch, *haptic learners.* Branching out from the partially blind adult to fully sighted adults and children, Lowenfeld continued to test his theory. He found that at about age 12 many children begin to show a preference for how they take in and respond to information. Like any "theory," Lowenfeld's idea has been supported by some and rejected by others. The information in Table 2.2 is offered not as fact but as description of characteristics and behaviors observed by many teachers of art. These categories are not meant to serve as boxes into which to place students and their artistic expressions. Rather, they are presented to heighten your awareness.

Most people are neither exclusively visual nor haptic, but fall somewhere on a continuum between the two polarities. It is important to be sensitive to these two types, to recognize their characteristics, and to provide experiences to accommodate both styles of learning and expression.

TABLE 2.2
Characteristics of Visual and Haptic Types

THE VISUAL TYPE	THE HAPTIC TYPE
• Observes the environment through the sense of sight	• Feels the environment through the sense of touch
• Records what he or she sees from the point of view of an observer	• Interprets what he or she feels from the point of view of a participant
• Sees the whole without an awareness of the details	• Focuses on details, parts, textures
• Progresses from the general to the specific in creating compositions	• Progresses from the parts to the whole in creating compositions
• Is objective and emotionally detached	• Is emotionally involved, often using abstract imagery to suggest feelings
• Uses color objectively	• Uses color subjectively

FRED, an extremely visual student teacher, introduced a lesson to a group of eighth graders using the following strategy: In preparing students to create sculptures from blocks of plaster poured into half-gallon milk containers, he had them fold sheets of paper into four vertical areas and draw what they imagined the sides of their sculptures would look like in each. Tom quietly sat in the back of the room, ripping out sheets of paper from his notebook, folding each into four sections and attempting to draw lines that represented his idea. Clearly he had an idea; he was motivated to try to represent it as he had been told, and he was struggling. At the point at which the wadded failed attempts surrounding his desk were becoming noticeable to other students, he gave up and sat staring into space. After several minutes he came to and realized he was looking into an open cupboard with a bin labeled Plasticine. Quietly he got up, helped himself to some clay, and happily constructed a model of his envisioned sculpture.

The point is this: If we wish to advance our students' artistic expressions beyond where they would be without our intervention, we need to recognize and accept where our students are. Only by starting where students are can we lead them to their next steps. Lowenfeld's studies provide useful information that has helped teachers to recognize where students are artistically along their developmental paths.

▼
THREE TYPES OF PRODUCTIVE ACTIVITIES: CLOSED-ENDED, OPEN-ENDED, AND LAISSEZ-FAIRE

As we reviewed the historical development of art education, we saw that for the most part art production has been central in the teaching of art. The first art activities were *closed-ended*, intended to develop skills in working with tools, materials, and techniques. During the Progressive Movement, the *laissez-faire* approach provided freedom for individual exploration and self-expression. *Open-ended* instruction developed as a balance between the two, offering students broad structure, defined through general criteria, coupled with freedom to interpret in creative ways. The three types can be thought of as points along a continuum, as Figure 2.2 suggests.

Each type of activity has a place in teaching art production and can be used in appropriate or inappropriate ways. Table 2.3 provides guidance in making appropriate use of each.

FIGURE 2.2
*Closed-Ended–Open-Ended–
Laissez-Faire Continuum*

Closed-Ended, Open-Ended, and Laissez-Faire Activities

◄──►

Closed-ended
Provides maximum structure for skill development

Open-ended:
Provides a balance of structure and freedom for creative interpretation

Laissez-faire:
Provides maximum freedom for experimentation with media and processes

TABLE 2.3
Analysis of Closed-Ended, Open-Ended, and Laissez-Faire Teaching Activities

CLOSED-ENDED	OPEN-ENDED	LAISSEZ-FAIRE
Purposes		
• To build skills in working with tools, materials, and techniques	• To promote creativity and problem-solving skills • To promote understanding of art concepts • To develop skills in the creation of a work of art	• To motivate students through exploration of media and processes • To encourage self-expression for its own sake • To encourage discovery learning
Characteristics		
• There is maximum guidance from the teacher. • The teacher provides an example of what should be done. • Students follow the teacher's step-by-step instructions. • There is only one "right" answer and way to do the assignment.	• The teacher provides broad criteria and some guidance. • The teacher provides several examples of "right" answers. • Students must follow criteria and are allowed freedom for individual interpretation. • The activity may be process or product oriented.	• There is minimum guidance from the teacher. • Examples or criteria may not be needed or provided. • Students have freedom to explore and discover without having to meet preconceived expectations. • The activity is process oriented: exploration of media and processes is valued over making an art object.
Appropriate Uses		
• To introduce the use of new tools, materials, or techniques • To teach processes that require specific instruction	• To generate ideas • To learn skills, processes, and concepts necessary for creation of an artwork	• To introduce a new medium or process with which students experiment
Examples of Appropriate Activities		
• Draw cubes using the rules of one-point perspective as an introduction to the design of a cityscape. • Throw a 6" cylinder as an introduction to making wheel-thrown pots.	• Create designs illustrating different types of balance. • Create an artwork interpreting a theme explored by other artists.	• Explore the tactile properties of clay as an introduction to creating clay sculpture. • Experiment with color mixing to learn what variations can be made.
Typical Outcomes		
• All work looks alike. • Success is determined by how skillful the student is in using particular tools, materials, and processes.	• Each outcome is different. • Products reflect creative thinking as a result of individual interpretation of criteria.	• Although an "artwork" may result, the intention is to explore processes/media. • Success is determined by what the student discovers from the experience while engaging in the activity.
Inappropriate Uses		
• Closed-ended activities are inappropriate when used to make final products that are intended to be creative. • Closed-ended activities are inappropriate when there are multiple ways to demonstrate learning of a skill or concept.	• Open-ended activities are inappropriate when specific instruction in using tools and materials is required. • Open-ended activities are inappropriate in assignments that require one "right" answer.	• Laissez-faire activities can be inappropriate to teach skills and to promote creativity. (Skill development often requires instruction from the teacher. Creative behavior requires students to go beyond exploration of media and processes to solve problems.)
Examples of Inappropriate Activities		
• Paint a landscape by copying a picture from a nature magazine.	• Use the paper cutter to make as many 3" × 5" cards as possible from a 12" × 18" paper.	• Tell students to be creative! • Invite them to use any materials they want to make a picture for the art show.

As you read the information in Table 2.3, you may have thought, "I would never do anything as stupid as turning the students loose to cut up cards on the paper cutter." Often what is inappropriate may not seem so obvious, as Mandy's piggy bank experience in the Birdwalk below illustrates.

Analyzing Mandy's teaching strategy, we may identify a number of factors that contributed to what Mandy perceived as a "disaster."

- The classroom teacher viewed the purpose of the experience as creating a product. Mandy focused on the process of self-expression. Neither considered how to present activities in age-appropriate ways.

- In Mandy's attempt to turn clones into creative outcomes, she allowed students free rein. Rather than taking a teacher-directive stance, in which she could teach skills in handling a paint brush and applying paint, she took a laissez-faire position.

- Mandy not only overestimated the children's ability to apply paint to a three-dimensional surface, she underestimated the time required to achieve a level of quality she and the classroom teacher had envisioned.

In discussing what Mandy could have done differently, we will address four key issues in the teaching of art: (1) process versus product, (2) age appropriateness, (3) use of productive activities, and (4) sequencing.

PROCESS VERSUS PRODUCT

The process-centered orientation is one in which the experience of making art has intrinsic value, regardless of how the resulting artistic expression looks. The purpose of teaching is to build skills and to foster meaningful self-expression, as a teacher guides students through art-making activities. These activities may result in nothing more than experimentations in mark making, or they may produce powerful pieces that one might label as "works of art." Whether the outcome is short-lived and tossed in the wastebasket when the experience is over or framed and hung on the wall is not important. In the process-oriented approach the quality of the experience and resultant growth or learning are of value. In contrast, the product-oriented approach looks on the object created not simply as the by-product of an experience, but as having worth in and of itself.

PAPIER-MÂCHÉ PIGGY BANKS

Mandy was a recently graduated teacher who was familiar with "bat making." Early in her first year on the job, a first grade teacher came to her with a request. Would she devote an art period to allow children to paint the papier-mâché piggy banks they had made in her room? Reluctantly she agreed. The following week she watched child after child file into her room with identical papier-mâchéd milk cartons with legs. In her mind she saw bats and immediately jumped from the closed-ended products to what she thought would turn clones into individual creative expressions. She said to the students, "Be creative! Do anything you want to make your piggy banks different—stripes, flowers, designs." Then she put out all the colors she had and let them paint. They dove into the colors, mixing reds and blues and yellows and greens. They painted color on top of color, and by the end of the period all had completed their paint jobs. Mandy watched the students file out of the room at the end of the period, each with a dripping wet, muddy, brown pig.

AGE APPROPRIATENESS

In the teaching of art we provide both process- and product-oriented experiences. Students enjoy going beyond the point at which they simply experiment with ideas and media. They like creating and displaying products they view as works of art. However, without engaging in process-oriented experiences in which they learn to generate ideas, use tools, and experiment with techniques, the result might be muddy brown pigs. Muddy brown pigs point to a second issue—age appropriateness. Is it reasonable to expect that first graders have skills to produce well crafted papier-mâché sculptures? Might it be more appropriate to present process-oriented activities that focus on the building of skills rather than on the making of a product? Might a product-oriented papier-mâché experience be more appropriately geared for students in fifth grade? These questions will be answered with more fitting examples of process-oriented experiences at the first grade level and product-oriented experiences at the fifth grade level in discussions that follow.

USE OF PRODUCTIVE ACTIVITIES

The third issue is the use of productive activities. The classroom teacher inappropriately used closed-ended instruction to lead her students through a step-by-step procedure to copy her model. Mandy inappropriately used laissez-faire instruction to encourage students to embellish the clones with creative surfaces. Neither provided a structure that combined teacher-directed instruction with freedom for personal interpretation. The steps that follow illustrate how this product-oriented experience might be redesigned for students at the fifth grade level, integrating closed- and open-ended activities.

1. Provide a variety of materials from which to construct armatures—cans, milk cartons, boxes, paper towel tubes, jars, lids. Show students how to attach forms with tape and glue. Lead them through a short exercise in which they use these processes to attach forms (a closed-ended, process-oriented step).

2. Ask students to discuss how the armature materials might be used to create bodies, legs, eyes, ears, etc. Let students construct piggy (or any preferred animal) bank armatures, using their new skills (an open-ended procedure focused on the final product).

3. Lead students through the papier-mâché process (a closed-ended procedure focused on the final product).

4. During time in which papier-mâché layers are drying, present a painting exercise in which students review and practice painting skills and explore design possibilities (such as pattern and color schemes) to be used in embellishing the sculptures (an open-ended, process-oriented activity).

5. Have students paint their "animal banks" one solid color (a closed-ended experience focused on the final product).

6. Have students embellish the surfaces by painting designs on top of the base color (an open-ended experience focused on the final product).

SEQUENCING

The preceding list illustrates the fourth issue—*sequencing.* "Art" is not created by a single act. It grows from ideas, knowledge, and skills that develop over a period of time. During this period, bit by bit, experiences cause the coming together of behaviors that result in art products. Your ability to sequence activities that result in visual expressions (which may or may not be labeled as "products") is of vital importance in the teaching of art. The following section deals with how to do this.

▼ TEACHING MODELS TO SEQUENCE STUDIO ACTIVITIES

A *teaching model,* as used here, refers to a diagram that sequences steps to teach art processes or content presented within a unit of study. In this guide you will be introduced to models to teach art production, art criticism, aesthetics, and art history. This section begins with Figure 2.3, the first of three models presented within this text to guide students through art-making experiences. The model, adapted for use here from the original designed by Jack Taylor, is the product-oriented teaching model.

FIGURE 2.3
Product-Oriented Teaching Model: Structure
Adapted by permission of Jack J. Taylor.

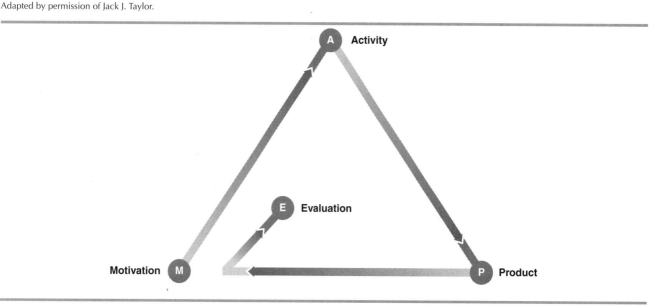

This model is designed to sequence experiences resulting in the creation of an art product. It is distinguished from other models used to teach art production by its triangular shape. To read the model, begin at the lower left-hand corner (motivation). This point provides a place to list everything you do or show to inspire students to engage in the art experience. From the motivation step, proceed to the apex of the triangle (activity). This step provides process-oriented experiences to prepare students to create the final product. The stage in which students create the product is at the third point of the triangle. The bottom line of the diagram completes the triangular shape and symbolizes a connection between the motivational experiences and the resulting art products. The last step, placed in the center of the model, is the evaluation procedure. The chart and sample applications in Figures 2.4 to 2.8 illustrate how to use the model in actual teaching practice.

FIGURE 2.4
Analysis of Product-Oriented Teaching Model

Steps of Model	Description of Step	Purpose of Step	Examples of Step
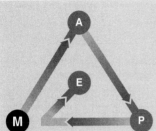	1. M = Motivation: presentation of stimuli to inspire students and introduce various activities.	· To instill the desire to participate in the lesson · To provide a direction or focus for the lesson · To set standards and expectations	· Objects in the environment · A still life display · Artworks done by fellow students, artists, the teacher · Stories, games, field trips, music, cultural themes and expressions
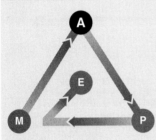	2. A = Activity steps: process-oriented experiences (closed-ended, open-ended, or laissez-faire) to give students opportunities to work with media and techniques and to explore ideas.	· To build skills in the use of specific tools, media, and processes · To explore art concepts · To generate ideas · To promote creativity · To prepare to make an art object	· Blend colors in a light to dark value range (closed-ended). · Explore what happens using wet-on-wet watercolor technique (laissez-faire). · Draw five different ideas for a poster advertising an issue (open-ended).
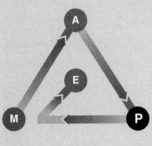	3. P = Product: procedures and/or criteria for creating an art product (Final assignments should be open-ended, providing broad criteria that allow students creative interpretation using previously acquired skills.)	· To create an art object · To provide tangible evidence of the learning that occurred as a result of experiences in the activity steps · To promote problem-solving behavior and creative thinking through open-ended assignments · To demonstrate skill in the production of self-expressive artwork	· Paint a still life using the following criteria: 1. Use a value range from light to dark. 2. Blend color to indicate volume and three-dimensional space. 3. Unify the composition thr the use of repeated color.
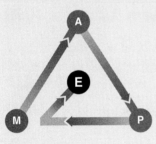	4. E = Evaluation: an assessment of the product based on success in fulfilling criteria.	· To determine the degree of success in meeting specified criteria · To determine the degree to which the class as a whole and individual students fulfilled the desired objectives · To guide the teacher (and students) in what to do next	· Display all work on the bulletin board · Review previously established criteria on the chalkboard · Ask students to focus on one criterion at a time, pointing out outstanding examples of: 1. Use of light and dark 2. Color blending 3. Use of repetition 4. Composition

FIGURE 2.5
Product-Oriented Model: Animal Pot

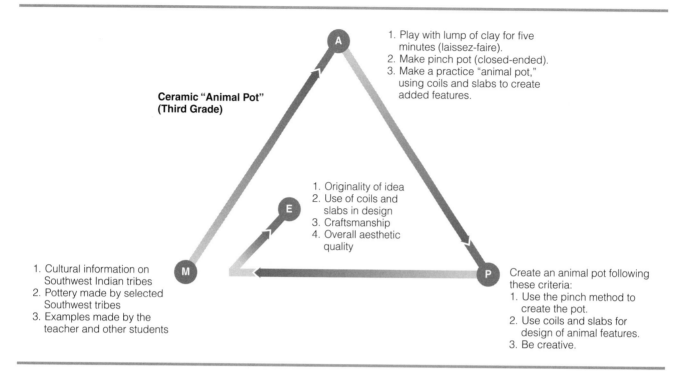

Ceramic "Animal Pot" (Third Grade)

A
1. Play with lump of clay for five minutes (laissez-faire).
2. Make pinch pot (closed-ended).
3. Make a practice "animal pot," using coils and slabs to create added features.

E
1. Originality of idea
2. Use of coils and slabs in design
3. Craftsmanship
4. Overall aesthetic quality

M
1. Cultural information on Southwest Indian tribes
2. Pottery made by selected Southwest tribes
3. Examples made by the teacher and other students

P
Create an animal pot following these criteria:
1. Use the pinch method to create the pot.
2. Use coils and slabs for design of animal features.
3. Be creative.

FIGURE 2.6
Product-Oriented Model: Papier-Mâché Bank

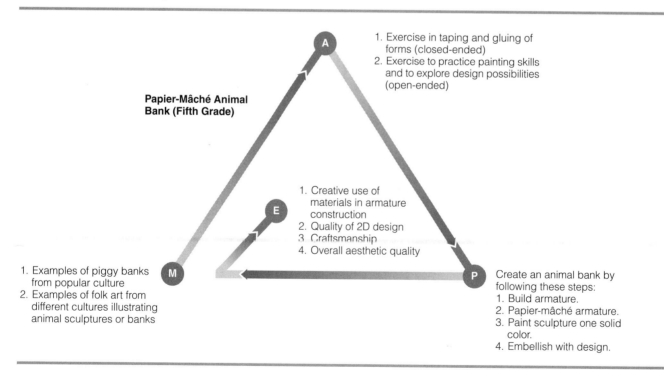

Papier-Mâché Animal Bank (Fifth Grade)

A
1. Exercise in taping and gluing of forms (closed-ended)
2. Exercise to practice painting skills and to explore design possibilities (open-ended)

E
1. Creative use of materials in armature construction
2. Quality of 2D design
3. Craftsmanship
4. Overall aesthetic quality

M
1. Examples of piggy banks from popular culture
2. Examples of folk art from different cultures illustrating animal sculptures or banks

P
Create an animal bank by following these steps:
1. Build armature.
2. Papier-mâché armature.
3. Paint sculpture one solid color.
4. Embellish with design.

FIGURE 2.7
Product-Oriented Model: Abstraction

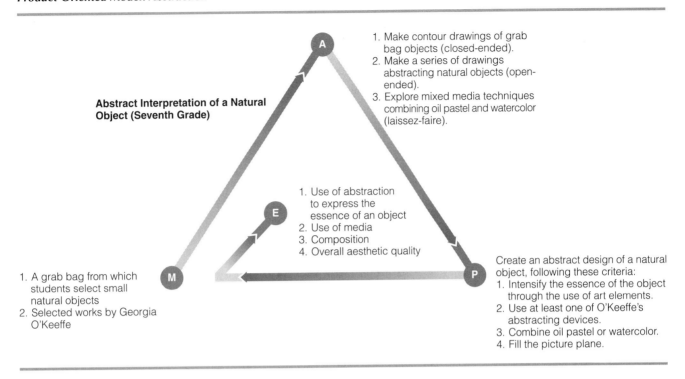

Abstract Interpretation of a Natural Object (Seventh Grade)

1. Make contour drawings of grab bag objects (closed-ended).
2. Make a series of drawings abstracting natural objects (open-ended).
3. Explore mixed media techniques combining oil pastel and watercolor (laissez-faire).

1. Use of abstraction to express the essence of an object
2. Use of media
3. Composition
4. Overall aesthetic quality

1. A grab bag from which students select small natural objects
2. Selected works by Georgia O'Keeffe

Create an abstract design of a natural object, following these criteria:
1. Intensify the essence of the object through the use of art elements.
2. Use at least one of O'Keeffe's abstracting devices.
3. Combine oil pastel or watercolor.
4. Fill the picture plane.

FIGURE 2.8
Product-Oriented Model: Still Life Painting

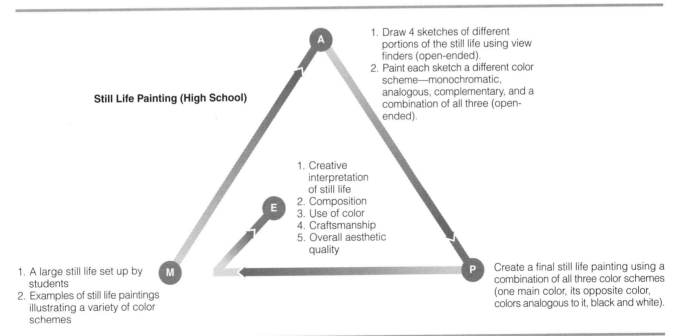

Still Life Painting (High School)

1. Draw 4 sketches of different portions of the still life using view finders (open-ended).
2. Paint each sketch a different color scheme—monochromatic, analogous, complementary, and a combination of all three (open-ended).

1. Creative interpretation of still life
2. Composition
3. Use of color
4. Craftsmanship
5. Overall aesthetic quality

1. A large still life set up by students
2. Examples of still life paintings illustrating a variety of color schemes

Create a final still life painting using a combination of all three color schemes (one main color, its opposite color, colors analogous to it, black and white).

As you can see, the product-oriented teaching model can be used to instruct students on any grade level in using any medium to portray any subject matter. The structure of the product-oriented teaching model is one that good teachers everywhere use. Although they may never have heard of productive art teaching models or seen this particular triangular diagram, they intuitively follow the steps of the model. Often, however, we see expressions that are not products of this model. Many of these products are bats. Bat making occurs when essential steps are eliminated from the model, as Figure 2.9 illustrates.

FIGURE 2.9
Bat-Oriented Model

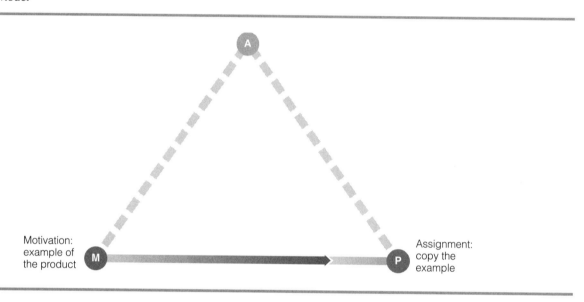

The visual representation of the bat-oriented teaching model is a straight horizontal line, similar to the straight horizontal line that appears on an electroencephalogram after a patient's brain activity has ceased. This analogy will remind you that the bat-oriented teaching model promotes mindless activity. As you look at Figure 2.9, ask yourself, "What's wrong with this picture?" Your answers might be

1. Because the activity step is missing, students have no opportunity to practice, build skills, or explore media, techniques, or ideas.

2. Because the assignment for the final product is closed-ended, students have no opportunity to be creative.

3. There is nothing on which to base evaluation except how closely the product resembles the teacher's example or the image being copied.

This section deals with how to remedy these problems through the use of the product-oriented teaching model. It presents strategies to lead students through experiences in which their end focus is on the making of products. Key points include

- Appropriate use of closed-ended, open-ended, and laissez-faire process-oriented experiences to prepare students to create final products
- Sequencing of art experiences
- Matching art experiences to the developmental levels of learners

- Differences between a product- and a process-oriented focus
- The open-ended nature of assignments for final products, intended to motivate problem solving and authentic self-expression

Although you may value the learning that takes place in the creation of art products, as well as the intrinsic qualities of the products themselves, you should not assume that all productive experiences need to culminate in the creation of a product. On the contrary, much of what we have done historically and continue to do (especially in child-centered orientations) is to focus on the experiential nature of art making—the processes and behaviors of students as they engage in art activities. In this process-centered view we are most concerned with developing skills and attitudes. These include capacities to take in information through the senses of sight and touch, manipulative and psychomotor abilities, thinking and problem-solving skills, abilities to express ideas and communicate with others, attitudes of self-worth, and appreciation of others and the visual world.

The student who enters a classroom in kindergarten or first grade at age 4 or 5 or 6 has not lived long enough or had enough life experience to have developed these skills and attitudes. It is up to us to shape their behaviors in positive ways, not by focusing on "what to make," but by focusing on "how to do things." Because of the developmental levels of young learners and their particular needs, process-oriented activities are most appropriate for students in primary grades. This does not mean that we never have students make final products. It simply means we place our emphasis on learning we perceive to be occurring through observation of art behaviors, rather than on evaluation of art products.

The second model addressed in this chapter, the process-oriented teaching model (see Figure 2.10), provides a structure for a sequence of art experiences that develops these behaviors. The experiences are used to teach the use of tools, media, and techniques; to build skills; to develop creative capacities; and to explore art concepts. The activities result in a series of sketches, visual ideas, exercises, or experiments that are not considered to be "final products," but evidence of processes with which students were engaged.

FIGURE 2.10
The Process-Oriented Teaching Model

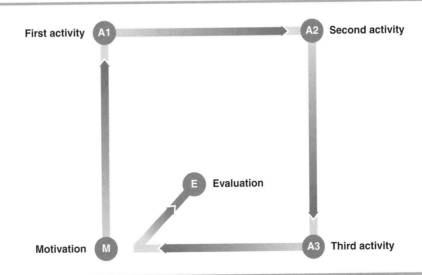

The process-oriented teaching model is designed as a square to differentiate it from the product-oriented teaching model. Each corner represents a *separate activity*, not individual steps within a single lesson. This format includes a motivation, followed by a sequence of three different art experiences, which may be presented over a number of days in a unit of study. One may, of course, also design process-oriented experiences that contain only one or two activities or more than three (as might be illustrated in a pentagon, hexagon, etc.). To illustrate the use of this model, let's refer back to the piggy bank project. I suggested that rather than focusing on the making of products, we might better serve first graders by building skills through process-oriented activities. Beyond the making of a piggy bank, this activity is about

- Developing manipulative skills
- Working in three dimensions
- Combining forms to create sculpture
- Solving problems
- Expressing the self in creative ways

The following sample application (see Figure 2.11) illustrates how these behaviors can be promoted through process-oriented experiences.

FIGURE 2.11
Process-Oriented Model: Sculpture Sequence

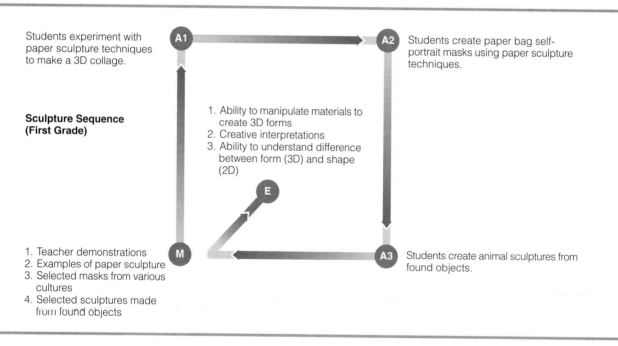

Students experiment with paper sculpture techniques to make a 3D collage.

Sculpture Sequence (First Grade)

1. Ability to manipulate materials to create 3D forms
2. Creative interpretations
3. Ability to understand difference between form (3D) and shape (2D)

Students create paper bag self-portrait masks using paper sculpture techniques.

1. Teacher demonstrations
2. Examples of paper sculpture
3. Selected masks from various cultures
4. Selected sculptures made from found objects

Students create animal sculptures from found objects.

In this sequence students focus on processes for creating sculptural forms, moving in the progression defined as follows:

LESSON A1

1. Students experiment to discover ways to create three dimensionality from flat paper (a five-minute laissez-faire activity).

2. Students follow a step-by-step procedure demonstrated by the teacher to learn specific sculpture techniques, such as fringing, curling, tabbing (a fifteen-minute closed-ended exercise).

3 Students use knowledge gained from free exploration and guided instruction to create a three-dimensional collage (a 20-minute open-ended activity).

4. Students share results and identify techniques (a five- minute closing).

LESSON A2

1. The teacher presents her example of the activity—a self-portrait paper bag mask using paper sculpture techniques learned in previous lesson. Students identify features on the mask and processes used to make them. They then discuss their own features and how they might be portrayed (a ten-minute open-ended discussion).

2. Students create self-portrait masks using paper scraps and other materials (yarn, buttons, etc.); paper sculpture techniques are emphasized to achieve 3D forms in facial features (a thirty-minute open-ended activity).

3. Students share their masks and view examples of masks from various cultures. They discuss use of materials and 3D aspects of their own and others' masks (a ten-minute sharing).

LESSON A3

1. Students are shown examples of animal sculptures made from scrap materials and found objects (Picasso's *Bull's Head*, made from a bicycle seat and handle bars, for instance). They discuss subject matter and use of objects (a ten-minute introduction).

2. Following the teacher's lead, students attach forms by gluing and taping objects together (a five-minute closed-ended activity).

3. Students create animal sculptures from scrap materials such as boxes, lids, tubes, jars (a twenty-five–minute open-ended activity).

4. Students share their animals, discuss use of materials, and compare their sculptures with sculptures made by other artists (a ten-minute closure).

The activities comprising these three lessons are significantly different from those in Mandy's piggy bank project:

- This sequence of lessons is not about creating an object; it is about exploring sculpture. Each lesson builds on the one before to lead students to an understanding of and ability to create form.

- Closed-ended and laissez-faire activities are used to support creative expression in open-ended studio activities.

- Because the experiences focus on the 3D aspect, students are not required to paint their sculptures.

- Teacher directedness is appropriate. Students learn from watching teacher demonstrations and then become self-directed in processes of manipulating paper, materials, and objects.

- The lessons focus on art-making behaviors (processes) involving manipulative skills, problem-solving activities, and self-expression. The content and teaching strategies support the development of these behaviors.

As the examples in Figures 2.12 to 2.14 illustrate, the process-oriented teaching model can be used to design experiences at all grade levels. It may be especially effective

- To develop skills in the use of media and techniques

- To enhance behaviors of students who lack the skills to produce "works of art"

- To allow flexibility for students to move through processes at individual rates (because the goal is not a completed product)

- To accommodate scheduling constraints when time does not permit the making of final products

FIGURE 2.12
Process-Oriented Model: Texture Sequence

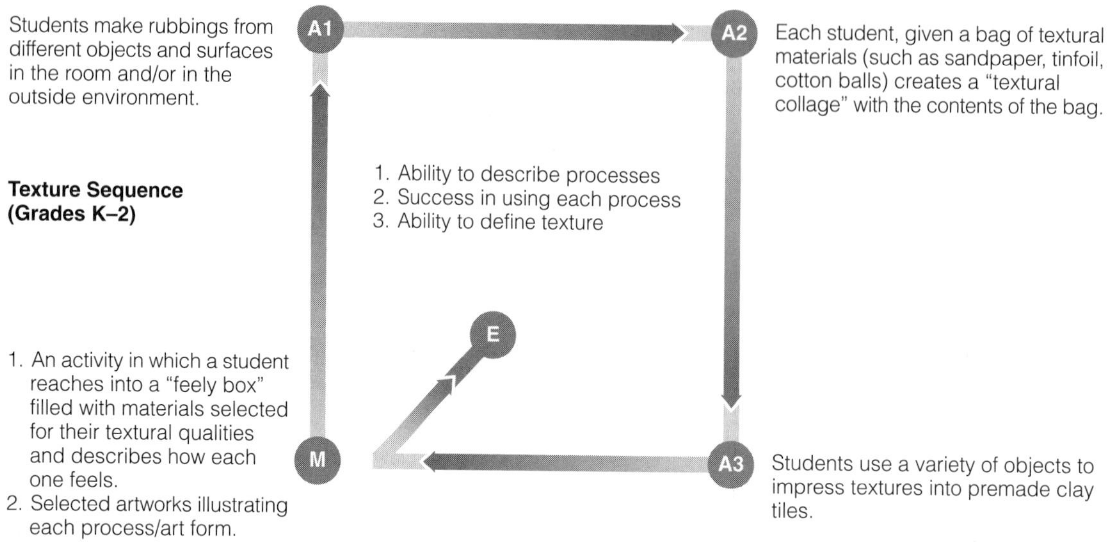

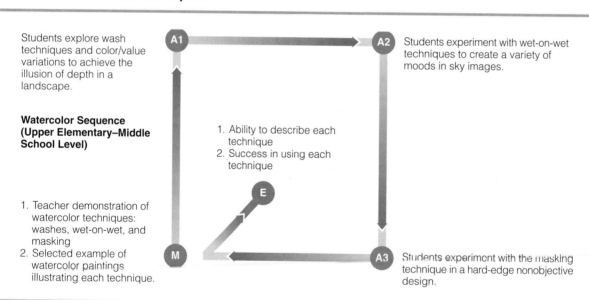

Students make rubbings from different objects and surfaces in the room and/or in the outside environment.

Texture Sequence (Grades K–2)

1. An activity in which a student reaches into a "feely box" filled with materials selected for their textural qualities and describes how each one feels.
2. Selected artworks illustrating each process/art form.

1. Ability to describe processes
2. Success in using each process
3. Ability to define texture

Each student, given a bag of textural materials (such as sandpaper, tinfoil, cotton balls) creates a "textural collage" with the contents of the bag.

Students use a variety of objects to impress textures into premade clay tiles.

FIGURE 2.13
Process-Oriented Model: Watercolor Sequence

Students explore wash techniques and color/value variations to achieve the illusion of depth in a landscape.

Watercolor Sequence (Upper Elementary–Middle School Level)

1. Teacher demonstration of watercolor techniques: washes, wet-on-wet, and masking
2. Selected example of watercolor paintings illustrating each technique.

1. Ability to describe each technique
2. Success in using each technique

Students experiment with wet-on-wet techniques to create a variety of moods in sky images.

Students experiment with the masking technique in a hard-edge nonobjective design.

FIGURE 2.14
Process-Oriented Model: Drawing Sequence

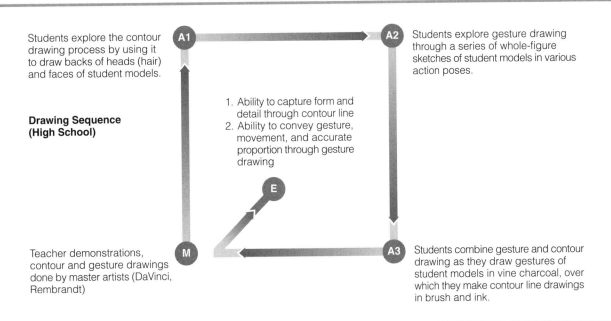

Students explore the contour drawing process by using it to draw backs of heads (hair) and faces of student models.

A1

A2

Students explore gesture drawing through a series of whole-figure sketches of student models in various action poses.

Drawing Sequence (High School)

1. Ability to capture form and detail through contour line
2. Ability to convey gesture, movement, and accurate proportion through gesture drawing

E

Teacher demonstrations, contour and gesture drawings done by master artists (DaVinci, Rembrandt)

M

A3

Students combine gesture and contour drawing as they draw gestures of student models in vine charcoal, over which they make contour line drawings in brush and ink.

These examples illustrate how this model can be used to explore (1) a studio area (sculpture), (2) an art element (texture), (3) an art medium (watercolor), and (4) art processes (contour and gesture drawing). Although the focus is on the exploration of processes, subject matter is specified. For example, in the watercolor sequence students are asked to explore the wash technique through landscape, wet on wet through sky images, and masking through nonobjective designs. Subject matter may be necessary to provide focus for the *what* while the students are exploring the *how*. After the first "oh's" and "ah's" expressed when red bleeds into yellow and makes orange, students may not know what to do next. In allowing them free rein to choose their own subject matter, you may be inhibiting their growth. Some students may be frustrated with "what to make," needing specific ideas. Some will do what they've always done, making familiar images that do not extend their thinking. Some may simply fool around with supplies and cause discipline problems. Do not confuse subject matter with final product. Subject matter simply provides a vehicle through which to explore processes.

S U M M A R Y

Child art can serve as an introduction to art-making behaviors and activities. Lowenfeld's stages of artistic development provide information about expressions typical of children in preschool through high school. Children begin art making as scribbling—a kinesthetic activity. Scribbles evolve from random marks into controlled directions. Circular scribbles turn into the first representations of figures. Children progress from drawing preschematic figures to drawing schemas or formulas representing objects in the environment. Through well-chosen studio experiences teachers can lead students from schemas into the creation of higher levels of expression and variety.

In addition to moving through stages of artistic development, students may express themselves either visually or haptically. Visually oriented students tend to be organized, neat, and clean. They have the detachment of an observer looking in on a scene. They express themselves well using realistic images in two-dimensional processes. Haptically oriented students may tend to be disorganized and are often viewed as messy. They feel things, experiencing the environment kinesthetically rather than visually. They do well with three-dimensional processes and express themselves from the viewpoint of a participant, often using abstract and emotional images. As art educators we need to provide experiences that address both types of expression.

Three types of activities are used to teach art production. *Closed-ended* activities develop skills in the use of tools, media, and techniques. They are the most structured and require the highest degree of teacher directiveness. In closed-ended activities there may be only one right answer or right way to do things. *Open-ended* activities promote problem-solving behavior, requiring students to interpret broad criteria in self-expressive ways. These experiences lead to multiple right answers. *Laissez-faire* activities allow students free exploration with art materials and processes. These experiences promote discovery learning and require the least amount of structure and teacher directiveness. All three types of activities should be used to teach different aspects of art making.

Closed-ended, open-ended, and laissez-faire activities can be sequenced through the use of teaching models. A teaching model is a visual diagram that provides structure for a sequence of lessons. The product-oriented teaching model provides structure for a sequence of experiences that leads to the creation of a final art product. The process-oriented teaching model provides structure for a sequence of process-oriented activities focusing on the building of skills and knowledge rather than on the making of products. Both models are useful at every level of teaching. Your understanding of them is important: They provide the structures on which you will build unit plans.

A. SEQUENCING ART EXPERIENCES THROUGH THE PRODUCT-ORIENTED TEACHING MODEL

Directions

Use the following product-oriented teaching model to structure a sequence of art experiences requiring 4–5 sessions. Begin with motivational activities followed by process-oriented activities. Indicate whether these activities are closed-ended, open-ended, or laissez-faire by placing a *C, O,* or, *L* after each. Move to an open-ended, product-oriented experience and conclude by listing criteria for assessment in the evaluation section.

Subject of lesson sequence:_____

Grade level:_____

The Product-Oriented Teaching Model

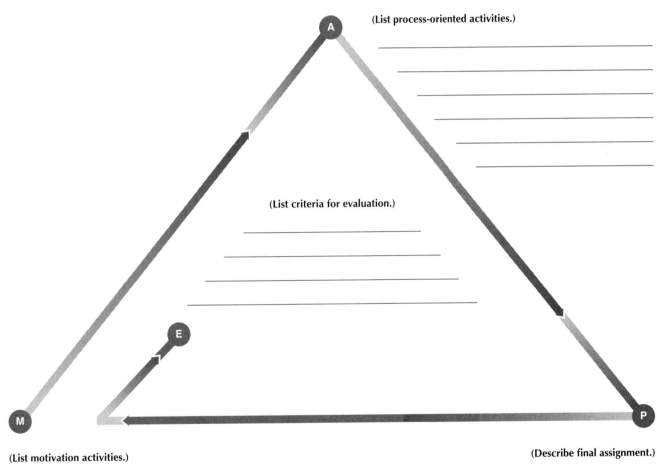

(List process-oriented activities.)

(List criteria for evaluation.)

A

E

M

(List motivation activities.)

P

(Describe final assignment.)

B. SEQUENCING ART EXPERIENCES THROUGH THE PROCESS-ORIENTED TEACHING MODEL

Directions

Use the process-oriented teaching model below to sequence three separate process-oriented art experiences designed to be taught over a 4- to 5-day period. These experiences may focus on use of (1) an art element or design principle, (2) a medium or technique, or (3) a particular theme or subject matter.

Subject of lesson sequence: _____

Grade level: _____

(Describe first activity.)

_____
_____
_____
_____
_____
_____
_____
_____

(Provide guidelines for evaluation.)

_____
_____
_____
_____
_____
_____
_____

(Describe second activity.)

_____
_____
_____
_____
_____
_____
_____

(List motivation activities.)

_____
_____
_____
_____
_____
_____
_____
_____

(Describe third activity.)

_____
_____
_____
_____
_____
_____
_____
_____

3

PLANNING
VERBALLY AND
VISUALLY

The teaching models presented in the last chapter provide a structure for planning. They can guide you in considering what to teach, how to motivate student involvement, how to select and sequence a variety of art-making experiences, how to balance the exploration of processes with the making of products, and what to look for in evaluating learning. As you move from the motivation point through successive steps in these models, you lay the foundation for what will become fully developed units of study.

This chapter is intended to extend your knowledge and skills from generating ideas in teaching models to planning units. This twofold process involves writing the unit plan ("verbal planning") and designing and creating visuals ("visual planning"). Verbal and visual planning are integrally linked, one supporting the other in a synergistic whole. Thus planning is not a linear process in which you begin with writing and end with making the final product. On the contrary, many teachers explore studio processes first to help them develop the written plan. They may move back and forth from ideas expressed in words to ideas as images, allowing the content and structure of a unit to emerge fluidly from the planning process, rather than from a predetermined set of steps. Although we know that verbal planning and visual planning are two entirely different kinds of processes, we recognize their interdependence and combine them in this chapter to underscore their connectedness. Because we cannot discuss them simultaneously, however, we begin with the verbal aspect—the unit plan—which will provide a context for addressing visual planning in the second half of the chapter. Sections include (1) planning verbally, (2) planning visually, and (3) integrating verbal and visual planning strategies.

▼
PLANNING VERBALLY

This section focuses on developing a unit of study through the process of writing. It (1) describes the component parts of a unit plan, (2) presents two sample units, and (3) provides strategies for writing a unit plan.

●
COMPONENTS OF A UNIT PLAN

A unit plan is a framework that binds a sequence of art experiences together. As the format in Figure 3.1 indicates, it includes the following six components:

1. Theme
2. Goals
3. Concepts
4. Cultural exemplar
5. Scope and sequence of art experiences
6. Evaluation procedures

FIGURE 3.1
Unit Plan Format

UNIT PLAN FORMAT

Unit Title

I. Theme and general description

II. Goals

III. Concepts

IV. Cultural exemplar

V. Scope and sequence of experiences

VI. Evaluation procedures

THEME

The theme serves as the foundation that integrates the individual parts of the unit. Ideas for themes can come from a variety of sources, such as subject matter, historical content, content from other subjects, studio areas, and styles of art, as indicated in the following box. For purposes of this discussion, we will identify *abstraction,* as exemplified through the work of Georgia O'Keeffe, as our theme on which to develop a sample unit plan.

Selected Examples of Unit Themes

Particular subject matter

- Still life
- Landscape
- Architecture
- Human figure
- Animals
- Fantasy

Any artist, school of art, period in art history, place, culture, or style of art

- Georgia O'Keeffe (artist)
- Cubism (school of art)
- Renaissance (period of history)
- Alaska (place)
- Cuna Indians (culture)
- Photorealism (style of art)

Universal attitudes or ideas

- Peace
- Brotherhood
- Environmental protection

Content from other subjects

- Heraldry (social studies)
- Light and color (science)
- Story illustration (English)

Any art element or design principle

- Color used to express emotion
- Contrast expressed through a variety of art elements
- Emphasis in poster design

Any studio process or medium

- Drawing
- Painting
- Sculpture
- Graphic processes (printmaking, photography, film making)
- Crafts

    Ceramics

    Jewelry

    Textiles

GOALS

Goals are general statements that identify purposes and describe long-term results or outcomes. Some educational systems have replaced the word *goal* with the word *outcome*. These terms address how a student will have grown as a result of participating in a unit of study. They answer the question "Why am I teaching this?" In providing answers, or goal statements, you may say, "I am doing this to enable students . . .

- To gain understanding of . . .
- To increase awareness of . . .
- To develop skill in . . .
- To develop appreciation for . . .
- To demonstrate ability to . . .
- To demonstrate knowledge of . . .

These phrases indicate knowledge, skills, and attitudes you expect students to demonstrate. Notice they are written to express what the student will do, not what the teacher will do. Once you have these beginning general phrases, you can complete the statements with information specific to a unit of study: "to demonstrate creativity using art elements . . . in the design of abstract images." This goal is written in two parts. The first part, "to demonstrate creativity using art elements," is broad enough to apply to any unit. The second part, "in the design of abstract images," focuses on the particular and indicates that this unit is about abstraction. This goal, dealing with development of studio skills, is a productive goal. Goals can be written to express outcomes in all four domains of art education. The following box illustrates goals for each domain in a unit on abstraction.

Selected Goals for a Unit on the Abstraction of Georgia O'Keeffe

- *Productive goals focus on learning to make art:*

  To demonstrate creativity using art elements *in the design of abstract images*

- *Historical goals focus on learning cultural/historical contexts of art:*

  To demonstrate knowledge of *Georgia O'Keeffe and her artwork*

- *Critical goals focus on learning to perceive, discuss, and evaluate visual characteristics of art:*

  To demonstrate understanding of visual characteristics of *abstract art*

- *Aesthetic goals focus on learning to appreciate art:*

  To develop appreciation for *abstract imagery* in one's own and others' works

---

CONCEPTS

Concepts reflect the cognitive information presented in the unit and answer the question "What will students understand about art?" Art concepts are general ideas applicable to art. No single words adequately express any art concept. To express a concept, you must convey the idea in a complete sentence. Concepts or ideas applicable to the word *abstraction* are provided in the following box.

Selected Concepts for a Unit on the Abstraction of Georgia O'Keeffe

- *Concepts can be vocabulary definitions:*

  Abstracting is a process of extrapolating or emphasizing the essential qualities of a thing.

  Abstract art uses nonrepresentational styles not intended to depict the natural world.

- *Concepts describe characteristics:*

  Abstract images have colors, lines, shapes, and/or textures that are used to exaggerate or intensify particular characteristics, qualities, or feelings.

- *Concepts describe purposes or functions:*

  Artists use abstraction to express ideas and to provide visual impact in their work.

- *Concepts convey information:*

  There are many different styles and degrees of abstraction.

- *Concepts provide cultural/historical information:*

  Georgia O'Keeffe was an artist who abstracted by using color, shape, size, and simplification.

Notice the order of the concepts listed in the preceding box. They tend to proceed from broad generalizations to more specific information. As the diagram on the left in Figure 3.2 illustrates, this structure provides a way of progressing from what is universally the case, to what is the case in selected contexts, to what is the case with individuals. Concepts may also be ordered in the opposite way, as the diagram on the right in Figure 3.2 illustrates.

FIGURE 3.2
Unit-Planning Continuum

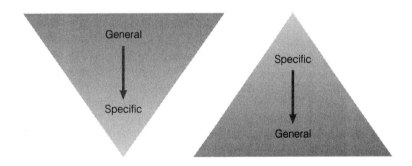

CULTURAL EXEMPLAR

A cultural exemplar is a cultural (human-made) object or group of objects that exemplifies a selected aspect of art. It is a key component of DBAE. Students are presented with art objects to learn about their significance in culture, to develop critical skills and visual literacy, and to gain appreciation for art in general. These are all good reasons for including cultural exemplars in a unit of study. Studio-based art educators also value the use of cultural exemplars. In addition to serving the functions identified by discipline-based art educators, cultural exemplars can send this message: Art is a visual language that connects the inside to the outside and the outside to the inside. Exemplars provide motivation for students' productive activities. Through exposure to the outside world, students go beyond themselves to learn from other artists. What they learn is not just about "other artists." They learn about themselves, as they reflect on what they have seen, develop ideas, expand their repertoires, and incorporate their new insights into authentic artistic expressions.

A cultural exemplar serves to connect students to something larger than themselves, larger than the studio activity, larger than the unit. It also serves as an example of one or more aspects of the studio experience in which students are engaged. A cultural exemplar may illustrate the following:

- An art form (drawing)
- A process (cross-hatching)
- A medium (charcoal)
- A subject matter (animals)
- A theme (love)
- An art element (color)
- A compositional device (focal point)
- A style (expressionism)

A cultural exemplar can be

- One work of art (*Starry Night*)
- Several works of art by one artist (selected works by Van Gogh)
- Works by several artists in a school of art or period in art history (Postimpressionists)
- Works by artists portraying the same theme or subject matter (landscape painters)
- Works by artists working with the same medium, technique, or art form (mask makers around the world)

A cultural exemplar can also be

- Clothing or wallpaper
- Cereal boxes or compact disc packages
- Neon signs, automobiles, or telephones

Any object presented as an example of design created by a human being can be considered a cultural exemplar. The questions you might ask in selecting an object are (1) What does this exemplify? (2) To whom am I presenting this exemplification? (3) Is this a clear example of what I intend to teach to this audience? The exemplars you select should relate as closely as possible to the studio experiences they are intended to support. For example, suppose you are teaching first graders about repeated pattern through gadget printing. What might you use to illustrate pattern in our culture and in the everyday environment? Examples of patterns on clothing and wallpaper design might provide a clear illustration. (You might save the Matisse interior scenes for a painting experience later.)

Although cultural exemplars are characteristically placed under the heading *motivation* when they appear in the structure of productive teaching models, they can be infused in a variety of places within a unit of study. The following box demonstrates placement in beginning, middle, and ending positions.

Flexible Placement of Cultural Exemplars in Three Studio Experiences

1. Unit sequence on assemblage
   a. **Show selected works by Joseph Cornell.**
   b. Lead students through process-oriented activities to explore symbolism, personal meaning, and placement of objects.
   c. Have students create final shadow box assemblages.
2. Unit sequence on abstraction
   a. Have students make realistic contour drawings of a natural object.
   b. Have students make a series of drawings abstracting the natural object.
   c. **Introduce Georgia O'Keeffe and several of her abstractions of natural objects.**
   d. Have students create final designs of natural objects, using some of O'Keeffe's abstracting devices.
3. Unit sequence on watercolor techniques
   a. Lead students through a discovery learning experience, experimenting with various watercolor processes.
   b. Have students use the processes in a series of paintings.
   c. **Show watercolors by selected artists using the various techniques.**

SCOPE AND SEQUENCE OF EXPERIENCES

The scope specifies how much will be included in a unit of study and the sequence specifies in what order experiences will be presented. A wide scope may be appropriate to provide general information in an introductory experience. A narrower scope will be more effective to provide in-depth learning. A scope and sequence can be designed from ideas generated in a teaching model. It will include motivational activities to introduce the unit, studio activities related to a cultural exemplar, and closing activities that allow for review and evaluation. The following box illustrates a sample scope and sequence for a unit on abstraction.

Sample Scope and Sequence for a Unit on the Abstraction of Georgia O'Keeffe

1. Students do contour drawings of small natural objects.
2. Students do a series of drawings abstracting natural objects.
3. Teacher introduces Georgia O'Keeffe and discusses her abstracting techniques.
4. Students explore media and processes using a combination of watercolor and oil pastel.
5. Students create final designs using abstraction to portray the essence of an object, employing at least one of O'Keeffe's devices.
6. Students evaluate work on specified criteria and compare and contrast their designs with O'Keeffe's work.

EVALUATION PROCEDURES

Evaluation is your assessment of your success in planning and teaching and your students' success in learning (demonstrating outcomes). Evaluation works best as an ongoing process. You should continually assess student behaviors, processes, products, understanding of concepts, and progress throughout a unit. Although you may pose specific questions to reflect goals and content of a particular unit, evaluation discussions at the end of a unit plan are generally broader than those focusing on individual lessons. You may structure unit evaluation procedures by posing questions and/or addressing content in four categories: (1) planning and teaching, (2) student behaviors, (3) art products, and (4) attainment of unit goals (productive, critical, aesthetics, and historical).

Evaluation questions for the unit on abstraction are suggested in the following box:

Evaluation Procedures for a Unit on the Abstraction of Georgia O'Keeffe

1. Reflecting on planning and teaching

   a. How effective was the scope and sequence in leading students to fulfill the goals?

   b. How effective were my teaching strategies in promoting student learning?

   c. What might be modified to improve planning and teaching?

2. Observing student behaviors

   a. How successful were students in using the process of contour drawing?

   b. How successful were students in generating a variety of ways to abstract an object?

   c. At what level were students engaged in exploring media and techniques and in creating the final product?

3. Assessing art products

   a. At what level did products reflect fulfillment of each criterion?

   b. Did products demonstrate that expected levels of skill development, problem solving, and personal interpretation had been met?

4. Determining whether unit goals were met

   a. Did behaviors and products demonstrate attainment of productive goals (development of skills in observational drawing; visual problem solving; and use of media, techniques, and art elements to convey intended effects)?

   b. Did oral discussions demonstrate students' understanding of concepts and information presented within critical, aesthetic, and historical domains (content on abstraction and Georgia O'Keeffe)?

SAMPLE UNIT PLANS

This section presents two sample unit plans. The first, "Abstraction of Georgia O'Keeffe," is a product-oriented unit developed from the product-oriented teaching model. It illustrates how the component parts of a unit may be structured into a cohesive whole. The second unit, "Pattern in the Everyday Environment," has been developed from the process-oriented teaching model. These two samples (in the following two boxes) may be used as models to develop units of study for students at all levels.

THE ABSTRACTION OF GEORGIA O'KEEFFE

I. Theme and General Description

    A. Abstraction is explored through a sequence of activities in which students (1) make realistic contour drawings of natural objects, (2) explore ways to abstract the objects, (3) experiment with media and techniques using watercolor and oil pastels, and (4) create a design of a small natural object, using abstraction to intensify its essence.

    B. Grade level: Seventh

    C. Time: Five 60-minute sessions

II. Goals

    A. To demonstrate perceptual awareness and skill in observational drawing (productive)

    B. To demonstrate manipulative and expressive skills through the use of oil pastel and watercolor (productive)

    C. To demonstrate creativity using art elements in the design of abstract images (productive)

    D. To demonstrate understanding of the characteristics of abstract art (critical)

    E. To demonstrate knowledge of Georgia O'Keeffe and her artwork (historical)

    F. To develop appreciation for abstract imagery in one's own and others' works (aesthetic)

III. Concepts

    A. Abstracting is a process of extrapolating or emphasizing the essential qualities of a thing.

    B. Abstract art uses nonrepresentational styles, not intended to depict the natural world.

    C. Abstract images have colors, lines, shapes, and textures that are used to exaggerate or intensify.

    D. Through the use of abstraction artists convey feelings and ideas and provide impact.

    E. There are many different styles and degrees of abstraction.

    F. Georgia O'Keeffe created abstractions through the use of color, shape, size, and simplification.

IV. Cultural Exemplar: selected abstract works by Georgia O'Keeffe

V. Scope and Sequence of Experiences

    A. *Session 1:* The teacher passes around a grab bag containing small natural objects. Students do contour drawings of objects selected from the grab bag.

    B. *Session 2:* Students do a series of drawings abstracting an object from the grab bag.

    C. *Session 3:* Georgia O'Keeffe is introduced. Students discuss how she used color, shape, size, and simplification in abstract images. Students experiment with media and processes, using a combination of oil pastel and watercolor.

    D. *Session 4:* Students begin final assignment: Using a natural object as subject matter, create an abstract design following these criteria:
- Intensify the essence of the object through the use of art elements
- Use at least one of O'Keeffe's abstracting devices
- Combine oil pastel and watercolor
- Fill the picture plane

    E. *Session 5:* Students complete assignment, critique the work on specified criteria, and discuss similarities and differences between O'Keeffe's and their works.

VI. Evaluation Procedures

    A. Assess effectiveness of written plans and teaching strategies in leading students to fulfill goals.

    B. Observe student behaviors to determine degree to which students were engaged in activities—contour drawing, abstracting, exploring oil pastel and watercolor, creating final products, oral discussions.

    C. Assess products, noting whether (1) criteria were fulfilled and (2) expected levels of skill development, problem solving, and personal interpretation were met.

    D. Review goals and ascertain whether studio processes, products, oral discussions, and student behaviors indicate fulfillment in productive, critical, aesthetic, and historical domains.

PATTERN IN THE EVERYDAY ENVIRONMENT

I. Theme and General Description

   A. Pattern in nature and in human-made objects
   is explored through three different processes:
   (1) printing with gadgets, (2) creating patterns
   through a folding and dyeing technique, and
   (3) making collages from patterned paper.
   B. Grade level: First
   C. Time: Four 60-minute sessions

II. Goals

   A. To demonstrate awareness and understanding of
   pattern in the everyday environment and in art
   (critical/historical)
   B. To demonstrate manipulative and expressive skills
   through exploration of pattern in studio processes
   (productive)
   C. To develop appreciation of pattern in one's own
   work, the works of others, and the environment
   (aesthetic)

III. Concepts

   A. A pattern is a repeated design.
   B. Patterns are all around us. They may be found in
   clothing, wallpaper, buildings, the bottoms of
   shoes, and in nature.
   C. Patterns can be made through printing
   processes.
   D. Patterns can be made through folding and dyeing
   processes.
   E. We can use premade patterns to create images.

IV. Exemplars

   A. Cultural exemplars of pattern illustrated in classroom objects such as brick walls and tiled floor
   and in clothing, wallpaper, and fabric
   B. Natural examples of pattern in plants and
   animals

V. Scope and Sequence of Experiences

   A. *Session 1:* Students are introduced to pattern in the
   natural and human-made environment. A variety of
   examples are shown and discussed. Students
   experiment first with creating repeated shapes
   through the process of gadget printing and then
   with a more structured process of creating regular
   pattern, using two or three colors and a variety of
   objects for printing—sponges, wood pieces, film
   canisters, foam rubber, etc.
   B. *Session 2:* Students continue to explore printing
   and pattern. They draw large animals and use gadgets to create patterns within them.
   C. *Session 3:* Students experiment with a fold-and-dye
   technique to create overlapping colors and patterns on paper. Students display work and review
   what they learned about patterns.
   D. *Session 4:* Students use patterned wallpaper, wrapping paper, and construction paper to create imaginary patterned landscape collages.

VI. Evaluation Procedures

   A. *Reflecting on planning and teaching:* Assess effectiveness of written plans and teaching strategies in
   leading students to fulfill goals.
   B. *Observing student behaviors:* Assess students' abilities to understand and use each process (printing,
   drawing, creating patterns through printing, folding
   and dyeing, and constructing collages).
   C. *Assessing products:* View products as vehicles to
   build skills in the use of materials and techniques,
   develop visual problem-solving skills, encourage
   authentic expression, and promote understanding
   of concepts and processes.
   D. *Determining whether unit goals were met:*
   Consider student behaviors, products, and
   comments during discussions to ascertain level
   of understanding of pattern and growth in
   manipulative/expressive skills.

UNIT-PLANNING STRATEGIES

As you review these sample unit plans, you might ask these questions:

- "Where do I start?"
- "How do I determine what to plug into each section of the plan?"
- "How do I develop the scope and sequence?"

The first step in designing a unit plan is developing a system that will allow you to generate ideas and see relationships. You need certain information to do this. Before you begin planning, ask yourself,

- What is the age, grade, and developmental level of the students with whom I will be working? (Picture the students sitting in class.)

- What types of experiences are appropriate for this population? (Picture the students working with processes and materials.)

- Where can I get ideas for art experiences that will be appropriate for these students?

Next, you might do some research. As you look through resources and as you have experiences in life and in art, ideas will occur to you. These may express in different forms:

- *Goal idea:* "I want to design an experience that will give my students an appreciation for African culture."

- *Concept idea:* "I want to design an experience in which my students learn that primary colors can be mixed to make secondary colors."

- *Cultural idea:* "I want to introduce my students to the work of Georgia O'Keeffe."

- *Process idea:* "I want to design an experience in which my students experiment with mixed media to achieve interesting visual effects."

- *Product idea:* "I want my students to make wind chimes."

You might visualize these ideas as existing along a continuum such as the following one.

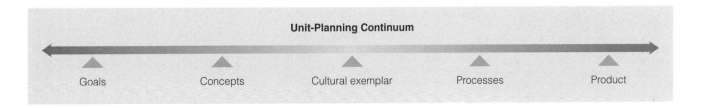

Unit-Planning Continuum

Goals   Concepts   Cultural exemplar   Processes   Product

This unit-planning continuum provides a structure for you to generate ideas and determine the relationships among the components. There is no "correct" place to start in planning a unit. You can begin with whichever idea you have first.

- *Product idea:* If you begin with an idea for an end product, ask yourself, "What educational value does this have? How will this enrich my students' lives? Why am I doing this?" These questions will provide you with goal statements and help you avoid bats. You can then determine what concepts the students will learn through the making of the product and what skills they will develop as they work with processes.

- *Goal idea:* If you begin with a goal, you might generate a list of activities that will enable students to demonstrate fulfillment of the goal. Analyze the activities to determine what concepts and processes you could teach through each. Then select the activities that appear to be the best choices to fulfill the goal.

- *Concept idea:* Your first idea may be a concept. You might generate a list of activities that could be used to teach the concept. Then you might ask yourself, "What is the educational value of each of these activities?" as a way of choosing the best activities to teach the concept.
- *Cultural idea:* Your first idea may be in the form of a particular artwork or works representing an artist or group of artists. In this case, ask yourself, (1) "Why am I selecting this work?" (2) "What concepts or processes can I teach through the work?" (3) How can my students most appropriately explore concepts and/or processes exemplified in the work?" (4) "How can they translate their learnings into authentic self-expressions?"
- *Process idea:* If your first idea is a process, you might think about (1) what students will learn by doing the process, (2) which artists have used the process, (3) which materials will be most appropriate, and (4) how to use the process as a criterion for a final product.

USING THE UNIT-PLANNING CONTINUUM

The unit-planning continuum provides a system for generating ideas without having to worry about structure. The three examples presented in Figures 3.3, 3.4, and 3.5 illustrate unit ideas that were developed from different starting points along the continuum.

FIGURE 3.3
Planning Continuum: Pattern

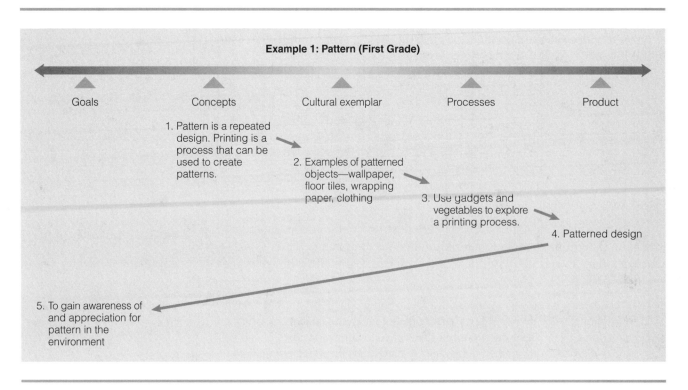

FIGURE 3.4
Planning Continuum: Masks

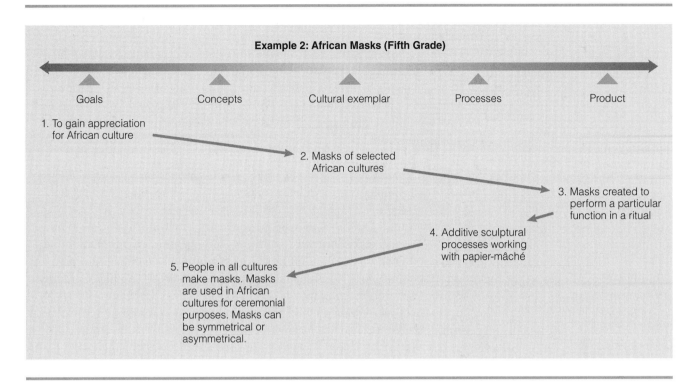

Example 2: African Masks (Fifth Grade)

Goals   Concepts   Cultural exemplar   Processes   Product

1. To gain appreciation for African culture

2. Masks of selected African cultures

3. Masks created to perform a particular function in a ritual

4. Additive sculptural processes working with papier-mâché

5. People in all cultures make masks. Masks are used in African cultures for ceremonial purposes. Masks can be symmetrical or asymmetrical.

FIGURE 3.5
Planning Continuum: Drawing

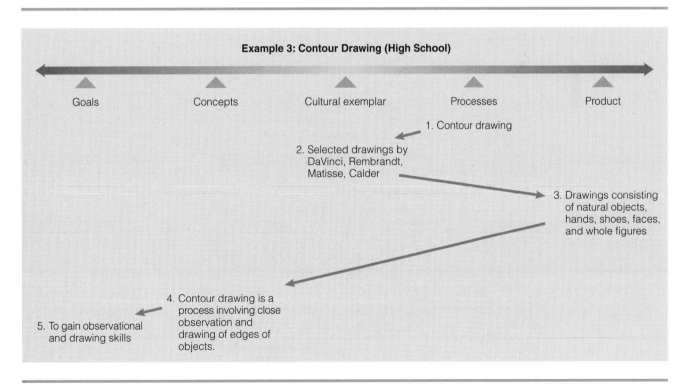

Example 3: Contour Drawing (High School)

Goals   Concepts   Cultural exemplar   Processes   Product

1. Contour drawing

2. Selected drawings by DaVinci, Rembrandt, Matisse, Calder

3. Drawings consisting of natural objects, hands, shoes, faces, and whole figures

4. Contour drawing is a process involving close observation and drawing of edges of objects.

5. To gain observational and drawing skills

▼ MOVING FROM THE PLANNING CONTINUUM TO A UNIT PLAN

The advantage of using the unit-planning continuum is that it lets you generate ideas in any order. You are not restricted to a linear progression of content. You can easily see relationships and fill in the details as they occur to you. Once you have completed all sections, you may realize you have a structure that resembles a unit plan. Notice the structure of the continuum laid out on a horizontal axis:

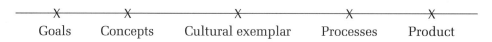

| Goals | Concepts | Cultural exemplar | Processes | Product |

It is very much like the progression, vertically illustrated, of a unit plan, defining in the correct order *goals, concepts,* and *cultural exemplar.* Through the process of fleshing out content in the continuum, you can create a large portion of the unit plan. Your next step is to translate what you have included under *processes* and *product* into procedures defined as the *scope and sequence.* Creating a scope and sequence requires that you design a linear progression of activities. The following box provides suggestions for how to do this.

Suggestions for Developing a Unit Scope and Sequence

1. Refer to activities included under *processes* and *product* in the unit-planning continuum.
2. List these activities along with additional ideas that will support goals, concepts, and the cultural exemplar in any order that occurs to you.
3. Indicate with an asterisk (*) the activities that seem the best.
4. Number the activities identified by an asterisk (*) in an order that seems most appropriate.
5. Rearrange the activities into the new order.
6. Determine whether transitional activities need to be included to guide students from one process to the next. Insert additional activities as needed.
7. Check to see that the scope and sequence includes appropriate beginning, middle, and ending activities.
8. Determine how much time will be needed to teach the unit. Add or eliminate activities if necessary to conform to a given time frame.

Having completed the sections of the unit plan that address goals, concepts, the cultural exemplar, and the scope and sequence, you may progress to the next step: introducing the plan in a few sentences. Summarize the content of the plan by identifying the theme and writing a general description. Finally, to complete the plan, include evaluation questions or procedures to guide you in assessing your planning and teaching and the success of your students in meeting unit goals.

▼
PLANNING VISUALLY

Can you imagine developing a unit similar to the one entitled "The Abstraction of Georgia O'Keeffe" (see p. 47) solely through the process of writing? If you are especially verbal and think linearly, you may be able to do this relatively easily. Most art teachers are visually oriented. They "think" in images. For this reason many make visuals as their primary planning process. Writing simply reflects what they have imagined in concrete form through visuals. Visual planning includes activities such as designing posters to illustrate ideas and procedures, doing demonstrations, selecting and presenting cultural exemplars, exploring media and techniques, and creating examples of assignments. Visual planning should be done along with written planning, prior to the actual teaching of lessons. You can use visual planning as a guide in writing and teaching processes. You also teach your students through the presentation of visual images. The following box lists reasons for making and using visuals.

Why Make Visuals?

- To support unit planning, lesson planning, and teaching
- To learn how to translate what you know as an artist into procedures to teach students
- To see through your students' eyes (as you explore processes from their perspective)
- To discover what will work and what will not
- To provide instruction and sequential steps in teaching studio activities
- To anticipate realistic time allotments for studio work
- To provide examples for visual learners
- To set standards for what you expect
- To model behaviors you want of students

The visuals you show your students for teaching purposes will vary widely. A visual can be a poster, a display, a work of art, a demonstration, or a natural or cultural object. Visuals include what you make, what your students make, and what you present through books, reproductions, slides, videos, and computer generated images. Using visuals in the teaching process is important in all subjects. Using visuals in teaching art is essential. People take in information through what they see, hear, and feel. Of the three modes—visual, auditory, and kinesthetic—the visual mode is dominant. More people learn most easily by seeing rather than by hearing or feeling. By using visuals we support what we tell students, what we ask them to read, and what we present in experiential activities. This section addresses how to design and use visuals to support the teaching/learning process. It includes (1) concept, process, and product visuals; (2) visuals to present cultural exemplars; and (3) technology applications in planning and teaching.

CONCEPT, PROCESS, AND PRODUCT VISUALS

Many of the visuals you will make will be in the form of posters that convey information. What you present can be categorized into three broad areas: information about (1) art concepts, (2) art processes, and (3) art products. This section discusses the purposes, design, and use of these types of visuals.

CONCEPT VISUALS

Concept visuals illustrate ideas. They may convey messages without words, expressing ideas entirely through design and content. Often, however, teachers reinforce ideas by combining simple written text with visual content, as the examples in Figure 3.6 illustrate. Because one concept can pertain to a number of lessons, concept visuals should be general enough to fit many different activities. For example, if you make a visual saying, "Flowers have geometric and organic shapes," you can use the poster only when flowers are the subject matter. If you make visuals illustrating what geometric and organic shapes are, you can use them for many lessons involving shape.

FIGURE 3.6
Concept Visuals Illustrating Types of Shapes

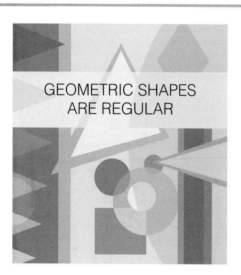 

The concept visuals in Figure 3.6 illustrate critical concepts (ideas about how we perceive the visual environment). In addition to illustrating critical concepts, we can also illustrate historical and aesthetic ideas. The fold-out display in Figure 3.7, illustrating multiple examples of O'Keeffe's work, may be thought of as a concept visual because it can be used to present cultural/historical information.

This type of visual can be a valuable teaching tool for a number of reasons:

- It allows students to compare and contrast images.
- Images might be attached with Velcro so that they can be removed for closer inspection.
- It can be set up on a table top or bulletin board as a portable display.

FIGURE 3.7
Concept Visual Illustrating a Cultural Exemplar

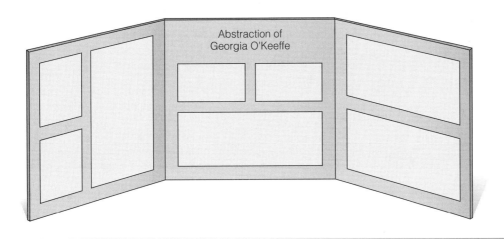

Abstraction of
Georgia O'Keeffe

PROCESS VISUALS

There are two types of process visuals, which serve different purposes:
(1) One illustrates *use of a particular process*—defining an image in contour
line, creating the illusion of depth through value variation or stippling, exploring watercolor techniques, blending with oil pastels, demonstrating ways to
abstract an image. (2) The other illustrates a *sequence of steps to complete a
procedure* (mixing plaster) *or to fulfill an assignment* (creating a relief print).
The first type of visual, shown in Figure 3.8, illustrates three different
processes one might use to abstract an image (modifying shapes, simplifying
areas, and altering proportions). The second type is exemplified by Figure 3.9,
"Progression of Steps in Creating a Design." This visual demonstrates a step-
by-step procedure moving from (1) using line to define contours, to (2) adding
interest through variation in line, to (3) embellishing through incorporation of
pattern. Process visuals can be created in a number of ways: They may simply
be a written list of procedures; they may communicate entirely with visual
images; they may combine visual and written information. Step-by-step procedures may be illustrated on a single poster or through a sequence of individual
posters. Many teachers present separate process visuals lesson-by-lesson as
steps within a procedure unfold in a unit of study.

FIGURE 3.8
Processes for Abstracting an Image

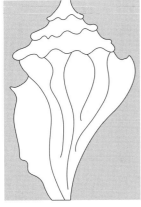

Draw realistic contours.

Modify shapes.

Simplify areas.

Alter proportions.

FIGURE 3.9
Progression of Steps in Creating a Design

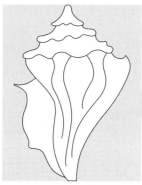

Step 1: Define contours. **Step 2:** Vary line quality. **Step 3:** Add pattern.

PRODUCT VISUALS

One of the ways you will prepare to teach is to do the studio assignments you plan to give to your students. These assignments will be both process- and product-oriented. Regardless of their nature, you should create examples before teaching to work out the best methods of presentation. These teacher examples can be thought of as product visuals. The making of a single example of an art product may teach you what you need to know about designing an assignment. Multiple examples, as displayed in the product poster in Figure 3.10, might serve your students better, however. By making several examples you can illustrate different problem-solving strategies and encourage a class to generate multiple right answers.

FIGURE 3.10
Teacher Examples: Abstract Interpretations of Natural Objects

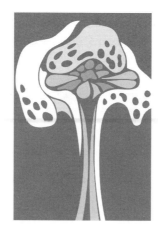

Shell Bone Leaves

Product visuals are made, first, to serve you in your learning process. Second, they are created to share with your students. As examples of creative outcomes (rather than closed-ended processes), they are not meant to be copied, but to inspire authentic self-expression. This is no easy task. Copying can be a perpetual problem. You can cut down on the amount of copying by using these strategies:

- Show multiple examples of an assignment; discuss how each example follows the given criteria; analyze how each piece solves the problem in a unique way.
- Show your teacher example(s) *after* students have begun work on final products.
- Prepare students to work on final products through the presentation of process-oriented activities, rather than through the showing of your example.
- Show ongoing student work throughout the studio experience to exemplify diversity.

You can also diminish the urge to copy (and strengthen your own teaching) by presenting your final product within the context of process visuals supporting its creation, as in the following diagram.

Progressing to a Final Product

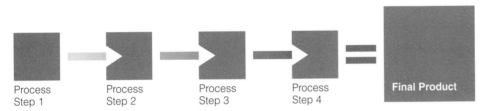

Viewing this diagram, you might assume that as a teacher you should start your visual planning by creating process poster 1 and work in a linear progression toward the creation of the final product. This system may work. It may also inhibit your creativity. This is not necessarily how artists create art. Many artists do not create by consciously stringing together a sequence of thoughts, behaviors, or procedures. They create as a result of being in a creative state, an internal place of feeling, inspiration, insight, spark. What this means for us as teachers/artists or artists/teachers is this: Perhaps the way to proceed is to go with our "artist" natures first, creating a work that has some intrinsic value to us, motivated by something either within or outside ourselves. Then we might look at the product of our "spark" and analyze how we got there. What skills did we have to possess in order to produce the piece? What knowledge or concepts did we employ? What steps in our development led us to the place where we were able to create this? The answers to these questions are the steps we will provide for our students through process-oriented activities. The progression in the following diagram illustrates how to begin with the final product and then work backward, analyzing the steps taken in its creation.

Progressing from a Final Product

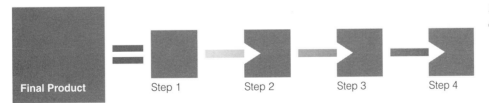

A big difference exists between the processes illustrated in each diagram. The first implies that art making can occur through a linear, logical progression of steps one might employ in solving a math problem. If you proceed in this way, you may create a predictable outcome. If you start from the other direction, allowing for expression to take form in a state where creative spark is more likely to occur, you may produce a much more inventive work.

As you think about whether your visuals are intended to be works of art, a sequence of procedures, or a presentation of a concept or cultural information, consider these words: *communicate, educate, motivate. Communicate* means sharing something with your students. *Educate* means providing new information. *Motivate* means instilling the intent to learn. As you make visuals, ask yourself, "How can I most effectively communicate? Does this communication teach the students something they don't already know? Will this motivate them to meet the desired goals?" The design of a visual is as important as the message it conveys. If lettering is not large enough to be seen from the back of the room, a poster will not communicate. If students are overwhelmed by the number of words on a poster, they will not read it. If the visual image is not interesting, it will not motivate. The following box provides suggestions for designing visuals.

Suggestions for Designing Visuals

• Print, as a general rule.

• Design your letters large and bold. Letters should be at least 2 inches tall and 1/4 inch thick. Use a color that contrasts with the background.

• Check to see that the words can be read from the back of the room. Experiment with several examples to determine what is the best for maximum readability.

• Use as few words as possible. The visual image is what attracts attention.

• Create a focal point. Posters that have an overall sameness tend to blend into the surroundings.

• Keep your designs simple, and limit the amount of information you present in a single poster. For example, make an individual poster for each art element rather than presenting information about all art elements on one poster. A series of posters on a theme can be very effective.

• Use a variety of media and techniques. You can use drawings in magazines and books by enlarging images on a copy machine. Use colored pencils or watercolor washes to add emphasis to black and white. Use an opaque projector to enlarge images from books onto poster board or banner paper. Cut letters and shapes from nonfading colored paper.

• Use a computer to generate words, designs, and print banner-sized visuals.

• Design your posters with the idea that they will be used to enhance the appearance of your room as well as to convey information. You might unify your room environment by using a common color scheme in your posters. Or you might use colors symbolically, for example, illustrating art elements on red and design principles on blue poster boards.

• Present yourself as an artist and teacher as professionally as you can through the visuals you create. Your visuals represent who you are to your students, fellow faculty, administrators, parents, and general public.

In addition to premade visuals, you will make on-the-spot visuals. These are demonstrations and are used to teach processes. They do not take the place of premade visuals but are often used in addition to process posters. There are a number of ways to demonstrate:

- A demonstration method that has become increasingly popular involves the use of the overhead projector. Many art teachers use overheads daily to project objectives and concepts, give instructions, and demonstrate studio processes. Using water-soluble markers, a paint brush, and water, you can actually paint an image on acetate film. Students view an enlargement of the image developing before their very eyes. You can also reproduce images on a copy machine and use a thermofax machine to make transparencies for an overhead projector.

- Some teachers keep easels with large pads of drawing paper in front of the room for demonstration purposes.

- Some use colored chalk especially made for chalkboards to attract attention and teach.

- Some have special demonstration corners or tables—areas in which students gather for a more relaxed, intimate view of "the artist at work."

Additional suggestions for demonstrating effectively are presented in the following box.

Suggestions for Doing Demonstrations

- Vary the ways in which you demonstrate. Work on a table or at an easel. Draw directly on the board. Draw on a large paper taped to the board. Draw on an acetate sheet on an overhead projector.

- Show students how to use processes and techniques, not how to make products or pictures of objects. For example, show students how to achieve a variety of textures, rather than how to draw a tree trunk.

- Demonstrate only as much as is necessary. You do not need to complete what you start.

- Make sure your students can see your demonstration. Draw large, using black magic marker, crayon, or charcoal rather than pencil. Gather the students around you if possible.

- If you feel unsure of your ability to do spontaneous demonstrations, you can use a paper on which you have already drawn lightly in pencil. As you quickly and confidently trace over the lines, you will impress your students with your ability to create art on the spot. You will also save time, because you will not have to think about how or what to illustrate.

- Think out loud as you demonstrate, giving students verbal as well as visual process instructions. Often students can learn more from watching your step-by-step demonstration and hearing your thinking processes than they can from simply viewing a premade example. They can ask questions about what they see or hear at any point in the process.

- Actively involve students in the demonstration process. You might ask them, "Is what I'm doing correct?" or "What should I do next?" One way to enliven a demonstration is to purposefully illustrate how *not* to do something or to leave out important steps. Watching "nonexamples" of what to do can be as informative and possibly much more entertaining than watching "how to do it correctly." You can also invite a student to work with you in demonstrating a process.

VISUALS TO PRESENT CULTURAL EXEMPLARS

In addition to the visuals you make, you will use a wide variety of visuals that already exist. Typical examples are real objects, printed reproductions of objects, slides, and videos. As we move forward in the twenty-first century, we will continue to experience the fruits of new technology. The students may have immediate access to the visual ideas and works of people anywhere on the planet. For purposes of this discussion, we will first address more traditional ways to explore the outside world and then describe ways in which teachers are using technology.

REAL OBJECTS

Sometimes we overlook the obvious. Real objects, whether they are art or simply things in the environment, are more concrete than pictures of objects. If you are teaching paper weaving, bring in an example of a woven fabric. Let your students feel it. Let them see real warp and weft threads. If you are teaching pottery, bring in some ceramic pieces or ask students to bring in examples of clay objects. Let your students know that there is a connection between what they learn and do in your art room and what exists as visual expression in the real world.

REPRODUCTIONS

Reproductions of all sizes—from postcards to door-sized posters—can be useful for a number of reasons:

1. You can keep the lights on when you show reproductions. Students are more likely to pay attention and you can monitor behavior more closely.
2. You can place several prints next to each other and make comparisons.
3. You can use them in experiential activities in which students become actively involved in seeing and learning about art. For example, you might ask a student to identify the focal point in three different prints and then create a design with a focal point using magnetized shapes on the board.

SLIDES AND OVERHEAD TRANSPARENCIES

Commercial slides produced to teach cultural content are plentiful and used by many art educators. Some teachers take their own slides of original art and of reproductions in art books to save on cost. By taking slides themselves, they can be more selective in choosing images to support particular units of study. Another good use of slides is to document studio work. Many teachers motivate and instruct by showing their own and students' work. You might consider doing this to document steps in a studio process, as well as to showcase excellent finished products. An alternative to slides are colored transparencies of artwork. These are becoming increasingly popular in commercially packaged materials and can also be made on color copy machines from reproductions in books and magazines.

BOOKS AND MAGAZINES

Books and magazines can be effectively used as resources conveying ideas and visual content. Many teachers, especially those following a discipline-based approach, use student textbooks or magazines such as *Scholastic Art*, in which they guide students to observe, read about, and discuss visual images. Some teachers show reproductions from books using an opaque projector.

Black and white images may be thermofaxed onto acetate sheets and shown on an overhead projector.

COMMERCIALLY PRODUCED PACKAGES

With the growth of discipline-based art education came an expansion of cultural resources available to art teachers. These materials come in many varieties. Some are packets of posters centering around a specific theme, such as family. Some kits or packages contain posters, videos, slides, and art games to motivate involvement in art history, criticism, and aesthetics. Many DBAE proponents view these as well worth the money. They work as visual packages focusing on a cultural exemplar. Child-centered and studio-centered advocates, who place greater emphasis on art production, have not viewed them so enthusiastically. Some have also viewed them as restrictive because the content is often selected to support a unit of study designed by someone else. Creative art teachers want to make their own decisions regarding whom to choose as exemplary artists, what to include, and how to put the pieces together. Commercially packaged units may or may not fit your student population, your curriculum content, or your particular time frame for teaching. They may do a good job presenting "the outside" (another artist or culture), while neglecting "the inside" (the individual student). In addition, they are expensive. Proceed with caution as you consider spending your art budget to purchase them. As a beginning teacher, you may be better served by building your own collection of visual resources. Some suggestions for how to do this are provided in the box that follows.

Suggestions for Building a Collection of Visual Resources

- Explore museums. Ask what is available as free literature. Visit museum stores. They often sell reproductions, postcards, slides, and books at reasonable prices. Introduce yourself to the museum education director. Find out what kinds of programs are offered to schools and what kinds of pre- and posttour materials are available.

- Look for art calendars and sale books in new and used book stores. (February–March is a good time to find art calendars on sale.)

- Look for old *Smithsonian, National Geographic,* and *Arizona Highways* in addition to other magazines on various subjects (sports, auto, nature, etc.) at rummage sales.

- Look through magazines, finding images you can use to illustrate concepts, processes, or subject matter. Mount, label, laminate, and file these pictures.

- Collect postcards of artwork used as advertising by art galleries.

- Ask the librarian at your school to donate books and magazines to the art room (such as old encyclopedias).

- Attend district, state, and national art conferences. Talk to vendors and sales representatives. Collect brochures and catalogues.

- Organize a filing system. Categories may include art elements, design principles, subject matter, artists, themes, processes, criticism, aesthetics, history, cultures. By using a filing system, you will become aware of what you have and what you need. You may be much more likely to acquire what you want if you have a system for organizing your resources.

- Wherever you go, whatever you see, whatever you read, think with your "teacher mind." You may be amazed at how much you are able to collect by consciously focusing on "visuals."

▼ TECHNOLOGY APPLICATIONS TO PLANNING AND TEACHING

Regardless of whether you choose to purchase commercial packages of visual materials or to create your own, you will use technology. The "information age" has challenged teachers to expand both curriculum content and teaching strategies. We take this opportunity to briefly discuss applications of technology in classroom settings: ways in which teachers are using technology in performing daily routines of classroom management, researching and presenting written information, presenting visual content, and teaching art production.

PERFORMING DAILY ROUTINES OF CLASSROOM MANAGEMENT

Routine management includes such activities as presenting morning announcements, giving instructions, taking attendance, and recording grades. "Smart classrooms," equipped with computers, VCRs, television monitors, and large-screen projection capabilities, can offer teachers and students more efficient and exciting ways of performing mundane tasks and interacting with one another. For example, students may role-play the part of a newscaster, presenting morning announcements over television. By using a computer and a television monitor, teachers can display unit goals, activities, criteria for assignments, process visuals—virtually any information that was once presented on an overhead projector or chalkboard. Some instructors have also replaced roll books and grade sheets with computer printouts.

RESEARCHING AND PRESENTING WRITTEN INFORMATION

Technology has also made acquiring and disseminating information much easier than in the past. "Surfing the Net" has for some replaced reading books. (The fact that the term "school librarian" has been replaced by "media specialist" reflects a shift in consciousness.) Many art educators have found computer technology extremely advantageous in researching information, preparing materials, and teaching. For example, they can

1. Access information from a computer terminal in a classroom or at home
2. Make connections among interrelated areas by visiting different web sites
3. Download content that can be used in written and oral presentations
4. Scan art images into reference materials for students
5. Create computer presentations (such as Power Point) to teach about artists, schools of art, periods in art history, or any other content applicable to art education
6. Teach students how to research and create their own presentations to share with their peers

Certainly one of the pluses of computer technology is the increased accessibility of information. This, however, can also cause a problem. Anyone can create a web site and post information, resulting in a wide range in quality.

Before assuming everything they find is informed and accurate, both teachers and students should check how current information is, credentials of authors, and bibliographical references.

PRESENTING VISUAL CONTENT

The presentation of visual materials often requires the use of technology. Much has changed in this area. The film strips and movies that were once standard audiovisual resources in schools are now almost nonexistent. Students in classrooms today are more likely to view a projection of an artist's studio or a current exhibition in a gallery or museum on the Internet. A teacher, using CD-ROMs and DVDs (digital video discs), can visually transport students to the Louvre. Videotapes on a multitude of artists, cultures, periods in art history, and studio processes are plentiful. Greater technology, however, does not necessarily result in better teaching. As teachers have been introduced to more sophisticated ways of presenting visual information, some have become so enamored of the technology itself that they have lost sight of their educational goals. Responding like children in a candy store, they have gone on and on sharing everything they could find on a topic. We must keep in mind that technology is the *medium*, not the *message*. As you use computers, videotapes, CD-ROMs, slides—any visual device—ask yourself these questions:

1. What is my goal in presenting this information?
2. How much is necessary in order to convey the message?
3. How can I select and integrate only what is necessary to support my goals?

You may find that, as in any presentation, more is not necessarily better, shorter may be more effective than longer, and active participation of students (through discussion, note taking, worksheets) is a key to effectiveness.

TEACHING ART PRODUCTION

One of the most exciting applications of technology is in the area of studio art. Entire curricula have been designed on the high school level in graphic design and computer art. Here, it is especially important that teachers address computer technology as a *tool*. Computers do not think, solve problems, and make "art." People make art through a sequence of steps that involves developing skills in the use of tools, techniques, and processes; generating ideas; experimenting with possibilities; and finally creating visual statements in intentional ways to communicate desired messages. (This is significantly different from simply pushing a button or clicking a mouse to create a symmetrical design and then labeling it "art.") To make art, students must be led to engage in a wide range of art-making behaviors. Whether this is done through the medium of a paint brush, a chisel, or a computer is not the issue. Teaching art through the use of a computer is not so different from teaching art using any other medium. You demonstrate how to achieve effects using software; present process-oriented activities (closed-ended, open-ended, and laissez-faire) to develop skills and knowledge; and give open-ended assignments that allow students to solve visual problems and demonstrate learning in self-expressive ways. The overriding point here is that technology in and of itself is not the substance of a new age, but a vehicle that, integrated wisely into educational practice, holds the potential to deepen understanding of art and expand possibilities for authentic artistic expression.

INTEGRATING VERBAL AND VISUAL PLANNING STRATEGIES

Looking back at the content of this chapter, you may begin to realize how extensive your planning needs to be. Visual planning can be even more time consuming than written planning. For most of us, it is also more fun. Facing the challenge of how to integrate the writing of a unit plan with the making of visuals, you might begin by referring back to the content and processes you had identified using a teaching model.

As you may recall, the unit "The Abstraction of Georgia O'Keeffe" began to take form like this:

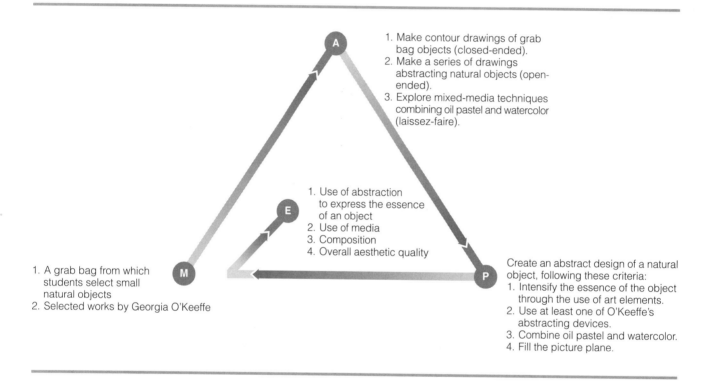

This diagram gives you the information you need to begin planning visually. Starting at the motivation step and working your way around the model, you can determine that you will need to do the following:

1. Collect small natural objects to place in a grab bag.

2. Show representative examples of O'Keeffe's work. This can be done by creating a large poster containing multiple small reproductions or showing large poster size reproductions, transparencies, or slides. You might also excerpt parts from a video, or a CD-ROM, or access images on the Internet.

3. Visually convey what contour drawing is. This might be done through an in-class demonstration and a premade visual comparing correct and incorrect drawing techniques.

4. Visually explain the process of abstracting. Again this may be done through a combination of in-class demonstration and a premade visual.

5. Demonstrate use of media prior to the laissez-faire activity.

6. Create at least one example of the final assignment.

7. Make a poster stating the criteria.

This may look like a lot of work. It is; however, remember the many purposes it serves. It

- Guides you in the writing process
- Prepares you to teach
- Provides the visual information you need as you expand your unit plan into individual lesson plans

Remember also that you will not use all these visuals in the first lesson of the unit. They will be introduced gradually as you progress through the unit. This integration of visual planning and written planning is further demonstrated in the next chapter, dealing with the expansion of a unit plan through individual lesson plans.

SUMMARY

In moving from a teaching model to a fully developed unit of study, you create units in two ways—through what you plan in writing and through what you plan visually. Verbal and visual planning have a synergistic relationship. The written aspect focuses on the design of a unit plan. This framework provides a structure for a sequence of art lessons. It includes these components.

1. The theme provides the foundation that integrates the individual parts of the unit and answers the question "What is my focus?"

2. Goals indicate what students should know and be able to do as a result of learning in the unit. They are statements of outcomes, providing answers to the question "Why am I teaching this?"

3. Concepts pertain to information about art that we present through activities in art production, art criticism, aesthetics, and art history. Concepts address the question "What cognitive information am I presenting?"

4. The cultural exemplar is one or more human-made object(s) presented to illustrate one or more aspect(s) of art. Objects may exemplify processes, media, subject matter, theme, composition, and/or concepts. They serve to link students "inside" expressions to the "outside" art world and answer the question "What can serve to illustrate content, processes, media, and/or concepts explored in studio production?"

5. The scope and sequence of experiences is the content of the unit. It provides a broad outline on which individual lessons will be based and answers the question "What experiences am I providing to lead students to fulfill goals?"

6. The evaluation procedures consist of processes you employ to ascertain your success in planning and teaching and your students' successes in learning. They include assessment of your own preparation, observation of student behaviors, and evaluation of products. These procedures address the question "Was the unit successful in leading students to fulfill goals?"

In addition to using teaching models and the unit-planning continuum to generate ideas for units, you can explore ideas visually. Concept, process, and product visuals are the posters or displays you create to teach concepts about art, to demonstrate studio processes, and to model assignments through your teacher examples. They are extremely important in planning: Through them you not only communicate visually to your students but also teach yourself how to teach. Teaching is not about *telling* students what to do; it is about *showing* them through your example. Presenting cultural exemplars also offers another opportunity to use a wide variety of visuals—postcards, posters, slides, videos, CD–ROMs, the Internet. The expansion of technology has significantly increased our access to visual images and our choices for how to present them.

Visual planning is for many art teachers the primary method for preparing to teach. Because they think visually, they focus first on their visual planning to support them later in writing a unit plan. Where you start your planning doesn't matter. What matters is that whatever method you use works best for you. Planning is a fluid process that may involve moving back and forth from words to images. The goal is to provide a general unit structure solid enough to move into your next steps—the planning of daily lessons and teaching.

A. EXPLORING AN IDEA FOR A UNIT OF STUDY

Directions
Use the unit-planning continuum to explore an idea for a unit of study generated in either the product-oriented teaching model or the process-oriented teaching model.

Planning Continuum

Goals	Concepts	Cultural	Processes	Product
———	———	———	———	———
———	———	———	———	———
———	———	———	———	———
———	———	———	———	———
———	———	———	———	———
———	———	———	———	———
———	———	———	———	———
———	———	———	———	———
———	———	———	———	———
———	———	———	———	———
———	———	———	———	———
———	———	———	———	———
———	———	———	———	———
———	———	———	———	———
———	———	———	———	———
———	———	———	———	———
———	———	———	———	———
———	———	———	———	———

B. DESIGNING VISUALS

Directions

Provide written information and drawings of posters to support ideas generated in the Planning Continuum.

A primary concept of the unit (write the concept in the space below).

A visual illustration of the concept (draw an idea for a concept poster in the box below).

_____

_____

_____

_____

_____

_____

_____

_____

_____

_____

_____

One or more posters to illustrate (1) a process or (2) a final product:

This illustrates: _____

PROGRESSING THROUGH PLANNING TOWARD TEACHING

Having progressed to the point of developing a plan for a unit of study supported by appropriate visual material, you are now ready for the next step: fine-tuning the unit plan through writing daily lesson plans. One function of lesson plans is to provide an expanded, detailed account of a unit's scope and sequence. A lesson plan is an outline, similar to a unit plan, that structures content presented within a single class period. The information within this chapter is intended to guide you from developing a unit plan to writing the first lesson plan to teaching the first lesson. Sections include (1) preparing to write a lesson plan, (2) lesson components and planning strategies, (3) expanding a unit plan through a sequence of lesson plans, and (4) moving from planning to teaching.

▼ PREPARING TO WRITE A LESSON PLAN

As you know by now, one does not dive into the planning process by beginning with the writing of a lesson plan. On the contrary, a lesson plan can be thought of as an end product, refining a progression of previous thought processes. Figure 4.1 illustrates a progression of steps to take in preparation for writing a lesson plan.

FIGURE 4.1
Steps to Take Before Writing a Lesson Plan

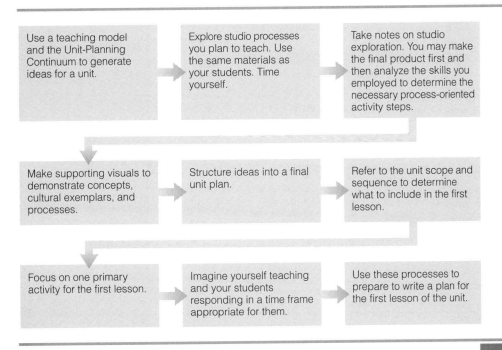

Use a teaching model and the Unit-Planning Continuum to generate ideas for a unit.

Explore studio processes you plan to teach. Use the same materials as your students. Time yourself.

Take notes on studio exploration. You may make the final product first and then analyze the skills you employed to determine the necessary process-oriented activity steps.

Make supporting visuals to demonstrate concepts, cultural exemplars, and processes.

Structure ideas into a final unit plan.

Refer to the unit scope and sequence to determine what to include in the first lesson.

Focus on one primary activity for the first lesson.

Imagine yourself teaching and your students responding in a time frame appropriate for them.

Use these processes to prepare to write a plan for the first lesson of the unit.

LESSON COMPONENTS AND PLANNING STRATEGIES

The procedures outlined in Figure 4.1 will help you discover if your idea is appropriate and teachable in one lesson. You may learn that your idea is inappropriate because it is too difficult for the intended age level. You may discover you have planned too much for one period. Or you may find that you are on track and ready to move on to the lesson plan. A lesson plan outline typically includes (1) goals, (2) objectives, (3) concepts, (4) visuals, (5) supplies and equipment, (6) teaching procedure, and (7) an evaluation. The structuring of these components is illustrated in the lesson plan format in the following box.

Lesson Plan Format

Title of Lesson

Grade Level or Course

   I. *Goal(s)*: purpose of the lesson drawn from unit goals

  II. *Objective(s)*: activity of students stated in behavioral terms

 III. *Concept(s)*: definitions of art terms and general art ideas presented as content of the lesson

 IV. Visuals

  V. Supplies and equipment

 VI. Teaching procedure

     Time allotment

     ____ to ____ A. Introduction
                  1. Review or transition from previous period
                  2. Motivation
                  3. Presentation of concepts/introductory activities
     ____ to ____ B. Instruction/demonstration
     ____ to ____ C. Work period
                  1. Supply distribution
                  2. Task analysis of student–teacher interaction
                  3. Clean-up procedures
     ____ to ____ D. Closure
                  1. Review of lesson
                  2. Sharing/critique of work

 VII. Evaluation (questions and/or procedures addressing the following)

    A. The planning/teaching process
    B. The meeting of objectives
    C. General behaviors of students
    D. The quality of work produced
    E. What to do for the next lesson

GOALS AND OBJECTIVES

Goals or outcomes, as you remember, answer the question "Why am I teaching this?" and reflect long-term learning. Lesson goals are the same as unit goals. More than one unit goal may apply to a lesson. Include only those goals that are pertinent, remembering that not all unit goals will be addressed in every lesson.

Objectives are different from goals. Objectives answer the question "What will students do to demonstrate that they are working toward fulfillment of a particular goal?" Objectives are observable behaviors. (The term *indicator* may also be used to refer to these behaviors.) The following box illustrates differences between goals and objectives.

Differences Between Goals and Objectives

Goals (Outcomes)

Characteristics of goals:

- Answer the question *"Why* do this?"
- Are written in general language
- Reflect long-term results
- May not be immediately verifiable

Examples of goals:

- To demonstrate creativity using art elements in the design of abstract images (productive)
- To demonstrate knowledge of Georgia O'Keeffe and her artwork (historical)
- To demonstrate understanding of characteristics of abstract art (critical)
- To develop appreciation for abstract imagery in one's own and others' works (aesthetic)

Objectives (Indicators)

Characteristics of objectives:

- Answer the question *"How* will students behave to demonstrate learning?"
- Specify particular behaviors
- Indicate what should happen on a daily basis

Examples of objectives:

- The learner will *draw* a series of sketches abstracting a natural object.
- The learner will *identify* the work of Georgia O'Keeffe when presented with abstract paintings of several artists.
- The learner will *describe* art elements and *analyze* design principles in selected abstract works.
- The learner will *discuss* reasons for appreciating abstraction in his or her own and O'Keeffe's works.

The verbs in the objectives are italicized because the verb is the word that indicates how students will behave. These behaviors can be categorized into two main groups: (1) how students will behave as makers of art, and (2) how they will behave as viewers as they respond to art. Objectives describing behaviors in the first group are called *productive objectives*. Productive objectives can be written to describe behaviors in closed-ended, open-ended, or laissez-faire activities:

- The learner will (TLW—a term used by Madeline Hunter) *draw* a natural object using contour line (closed-ended activity to develop perceptual and drawing skills).

- The learner will *explore* the use of watercolor and oil pastel in combination (laissez-faire activity to discover what color and textural variety can be achieved through the media).

- The learner will *create* an abstract image of a natural object, incorporating stylistic characteristics of Georgia O'Keeffe (open-ended activity to develop creative problem-solving skills).

As you can see, there is a range of specificity in the verbs, *draw* being the most specific and *explore* being the least specific. It is important that (1) the verb accurately describe the nature of the activity, (2) the activity is appropriate within the context of the unit, and (3) the behavior is verifiable. If you can look at a student and say, "Yes, this student is doing X," then you have written a verifiable objective. Phrases such as "become aware of" and "gain sensitivity to" are not verifiable. You cannot necessarily tell whether a student is aware or sensitive.

Objectives describing how students behave as viewers, as they respond to art, are called *response objectives*. Response objectives indicate what students will do as they talk or write about art in critical, aesthetic, and cultural experiences. Verbs applicable in these experiences are illustrated in the following objectives:

- The learner will *identify* objects in the painting *Peaceable Kingdom*, by Edward Hicks.

- The learner will *describe* variations in color in selected Monet landscapes.

- The learner will *analyze* how Matisse used pattern to unify his compositions.

- The learner will *interpret* meanings conveyed in Andrew Wyeth's *Christina's World.*

- The learner will *compare* and *contrast* shields from selected Oceanic cultures.

- The learner will *judge* which sculptures produced by students in the class are the most creative.

- The learner will *list* characteristics of Northwest Coast Indian art.

- The learner will *classify* selected paintings into schools of modern art.

- The learner will *discuss* purposes of and reactions to Pop Art.

- The learner will *write* a paragraph critiquing his/her own artwork.

You might think of objectives as steps students will take along a path to reach a goal. Many objectives may be designed in a sequence of lessons to accomplish one broad goal, as is illustrated in Figure 4.2. As you design objectives for a single lesson, state what the students will be doing as simply as possible. A studio activity can be expressed through a single objective. You need not specify all the steps of the procedure in separate objectives. If students will be engaged in more than one activity, such as a response and a production experience, state these in multiple objectives ordered to reflect the sequence of the lesson. Objectives can be written in a variety of ways, such as "The learner will . . . " (TLW), or as written on the chalkboard, simply "Today we will . . ."

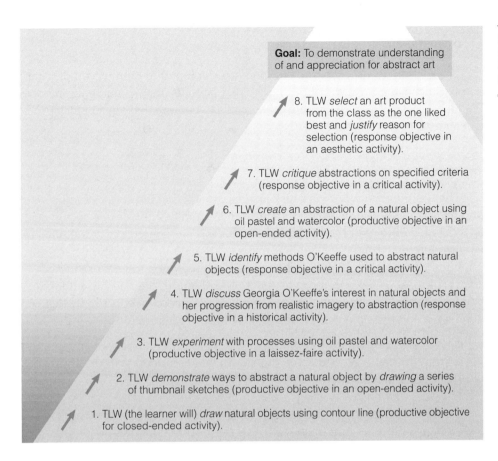

Goal: To demonstrate understanding of and appreciation for abstract art

8. TLW *select* an art product from the class as the one liked best and *justify* reason for selection (response objective in an aesthetic activity).

7. TLW *critique* abstractions on specified criteria (response objective in a critical activity).

6. TLW *create* an abstraction of a natural object using oil pastel and watercolor (productive objective in an open-ended activity).

5. TLW *identify* methods O'Keeffe used to abstract natural objects (response objective in a critical activity).

4. TLW *discuss* Georgia O'Keeffe's interest in natural objects and her progression from realistic imagery to abstraction (response objective in a historical activity).

3. TLW *experiment* with processes using oil pastel and watercolor (productive objective in a laissez-faire activity).

2. TLW *demonstrate* ways to abstract a natural object by *drawing* a series of thumbnail sketches (productive objective in an open-ended activity).

1. TLW (the learner will) *draw* natural objects using contour line (productive objective for closed-ended activity).

CONCEPTS

Lesson concepts are drawn from unit concepts. You may select concepts from your unit plan, or you may use unit concepts as guides to expand and express ideas in greater specificity. Write concepts in words your students will understand, rather than copying textbook and dictionary definitions. Suppose, for example, you are teaching second graders about the work of Henry Moore. You might translate a textbook definition of negative shape ("the area within and around objects") into "kiddie" language: A negative shape is a hole. When you present concepts, introduce new vocabulary (negative shape) in words your students will understand (a hole), and support these ideas with concrete examples (a Henry Moore sculpture with a negative shape). By translating textbook definitions into the language of your students, you can prepare yourself to successfully teach concepts.

VISUALS

Visuals include any visual aids you use to teach the lesson. They can be your own artwork, in-class demonstrations, work of other students, signs and posters you design to convey information, natural objects, or cultural exemplars. When planning to use a cultural exemplar, you need to know what is available before you write the lesson plan. Your list of visuals should reflect your research, specifying which artworks will be presented. Do not list visuals such as "examples of abstract painting." Be specific and selective, and include a few well-chosen examples to make your point.

SUPPLIES AND EQUIPMENT

The section on supplies and equipment is included to remind you of what you will need and how you should prepare. List tools, media, and equipment. Put an asterisk (*) next to anything that needs to be prepared ahead of time (such as thirty clay balls or twenty 4" × 4" pieces of paper).

TEACHING PROCEDURE

The teaching procedure is a task analysis specifying the step-by-step sequence you will follow to teach the lesson. You may think of this section as an expanded outline of the scope and sequence. The sequence may include (1) an introduction (which may contain reviews, transitions, motivations, or presentation of concepts), (2) instructions and demonstration, (3) a work period, and (4) closure. This section can be the most difficult to plan because it takes you from the theoretical realm of goals, objectives, and concepts to practical application. Suggestions for writing the teaching procedure follow:

1. *Design a general outline for the lesson.* Design a general outline including (a) how you will introduce the lesson, (b) what students will do during the work period, and (c) how you will close the lesson.

2. *Focus first on the primary aspect of the lesson.* Focus first on the section you consider to be the most important. This will vary according to where the lesson falls within the unit of study. If you are teaching the first lesson in a unit, the introductory section may be the most important. If you are in the middle of a unit, guiding your students through studio production, the work period will be most important. If you are teaching the last lesson in a unit, the closure will be the most important. Visualize what students will be doing and anticipate how much time will be required for this section.

3. *Establish blocks of time for each segment of the lesson.* Establish a block of time for the most important section. Then establish blocks of time for the other segments. Write the time blocks in the margin of your plan in real time (10:30–10:40), rather than in number of minutes. (If the time on your watch matches the time on your plan, you know you're on track.)

4. *Fill in the details.* Fill in the details of your teaching procedure, beginning with the introduction. Include only what is necessary. (Transitions, motivations, reviews, and demonstrations are not always necessary.)

5. *Consider reviews and transitions.* Include a review or transition from the previous period if it will help to guide students. If you have not seen your students in a week and they are in the middle of an activity, you may need to say, "Who can tell us what we did last week? This week we will . . ." If you saw your students yesterday, you may not need to say more than "You may get your materials and begin working." Don't waste time addressing what the students already know.

6. *Consider motivational strategies.* Include a motivation when your students need motivating. When you introduce any new unit, concept, medium, or technique, you will provide a motivation that will encourage your students to fulfill the objective of the lesson. A motivation can be anything that stimulates the intent to learn: your enthusiasm; a demonstration; a cultural exemplar; student participation in an activity; the novelty of using a new tool, medium, or technique; examples of artwork done by the students' peers; a preview of a final product. If your students are ready to start when they walk through the door, save your motivating introduction for another day.

7. *Describe how you will present the concepts.* The presentation of the concepts is not a repeat of the list of concepts provided earlier in the plan. The list of concepts indicates *what* you will teach; the presentation indicates *how* you will teach. In this section you will use visuals, do demonstrations, and provide experiential activities to present ideas. Include a script with specific questions and anticipated responses. You may preface statements in a dialogue with (T) or (S) indicating responses from teacher and students.

8. *Describe instruction and demonstration procedures.* Include what you will say and do in giving instructions and demonstrating processes. If you are introducing something new, instruction and demonstration are both necessary. (An exception to this is a laissez-faire activity in which you want students to discover on their own.) If you haven't seen your students in a week, instruction and demonstration are advisable. Instruction means telling your students what to do. Demonstration means doing something to model behavior. Do both together: *Tell* students what you are doing or what they should be doing *while you demonstrate.*

9. *Check for understanding through the inclusion of specific questions.* As you present concepts, historical information, and instructions, you may need to check for understanding. Just because your students are facing forward with their eyes open does not mean they are necessarily attending or understanding. Madeline Hunter developed a nonverbal signal system that enables a teacher to quickly check for understanding: Ask a yes/no question pertaining to the content or process you are teaching. (Do not ask, "Do you understand?") Ask all students to indicate the answer with signals such as thumbs up for yes, thumbs down for no, and a circle for "don't know." If you receive more wrong answers than right or more circles than thumbs, you will need to clarify or reteach the information. Checking for understanding is easy when students are doing studio activities. You simply note what they are doing and how they are doing it. Hunter's method is most appropriate when students are not actively engaged in a process, but sitting quietly watching and listening to you. Note in your lesson plan how you will check for understanding.

10. *Describe supply distribution.* Note in your lesson plan when and how you will distribute supplies. Note who the monitors are and what system you will use. Supply distribution may occur at various points depending on the nature of the lesson. Many teachers prefer to distribute supplies after they have demonstrated and given instructions. This procedure helps students to focus on what the teacher is saying and doing, rather than on how distracting they can be with the materials. If you are teaching a closed-ended activity in which you are modeling what to do, you will distribute supplies before the demonstration so that students can work with you. You may also prefer to distribute supplies at the beginning of the period if distributing them after the demonstration seems too time consuming or disruptive.

11. *Define the work period through a task analysis.* Write a task analysis detailing the student–teacher interaction during the work period. A task analysis is a list sequencing steps in a particular procedure. To guide you in the writing, review what you did and the notes you took as you explored media and processes in the preliminary planning stage.

12. *Specify cleanup procedures.* Specify when and how you will organize cleanup. You can anticipate cleanup taking five to ten minutes depending on the nature of the materials used. Write directions indicating what to do first, second, third, to avoid 30 children running around the room at once. Use a monitor system, and design some basic guidelines (such as, no more than three people at the sink at any one time).

13. *Include a closure.* End the lesson with a closure. In the closure you provide an opportunity for students to come full circle back to the beginning to gain understanding of what the lesson entailed. You may use a variety of strategies to close a lesson:

- Select students to share what they did or learned.
- Ask students to review concepts, vocabulary, historical information, or processes.
- Review the assignment and ask students to comment on how they met the objective.
- Involve students in a discussion in which they compare their works to a cultural exemplar.

Closure is the lesson component most often left out. The tendency of many beginning teachers is to let students work as long as possible in studio activities, conduct a frantic cleanup, and push one group of students out the door as the next is entering. This is not good teaching practice. Leave time for closure—even if it is only two minutes. You might combine closure with lineup as you dismiss students table by table to line up on the basis of answering review questions. Closure should involve active participation from students and provide opportunities to demonstrate learning.

EVALUATION

Evaluation questions and/or procedures at the end of a lesson plan are somewhat different from those at the end of the unit plan. Unit questions are broader, focusing on the fulfillment of goals. Lesson evaluation questions are intended to focus on what occurred during the period. There are a number of areas you might assess after the teaching of any lesson: (1) your process as you planned and delivered instruction, (2) objectives and students' attempts to meet them through their behaviors, (3) general behaviors of students, and (4) student work, reflecting understanding of assignments and ability to fulfill criteria. General questions to address each of these areas are provided next.

1. *Questions focusing on the teacher's success in planning and teaching:*
   - Was the lesson sequenced in a way that worked well to fulfill objectives?
   - Was sufficient time allotted for each activity?
   - Was the selected medium appropriate for the studio activity?
   - Was the teacher demonstration successful in guiding students to fulfill the objective?
   - What went well? What needs modifying? What should I do in the next lesson?

2. *Questions focusing on objectives and students' attempts to meet them:*
   - Did students fulfill the objective(s)?
   - Do objectives need to be modified for the entire class or for particular students to accommodate special needs?
   - Are lesson objectives likely to move students forward in fulfilling goals?

3. *Questions focusing on general behaviors:*
   - Were students interested in the content/process and motivated to do the assignment?
   - Did distribution and cleanup of supplies go smoothly?
   - How was behavior? work habits?

4. *Questions focusing on artwork:*
   - Does the artwork demonstrate understanding of concepts?
   - Does the artwork demonstrate that specified criteria were fulfilled?
   - Does the artwork demonstrate that objectives were met?
   - What is the general level of quality of the work?

▼ EXPANDING A UNIT PLAN THROUGH A SEQUENCE OF LESSON PLANS

To exemplify the relationship of lesson planning to unit planning, we return to the unit "The Abstraction of Georgia O'Keeffe." Content for each lesson is an expansion of the unit scope and sequence. Each lesson plan focuses on a different type of art experience:

Lesson 1 focuses on contour drawing, a closed-ended, process-oriented activity intended to promote observational and drawing skills.

Lesson 2 focuses on abstracting a natural object, an open-ended, process-oriented activity intended to promote creative thinking.

Lesson 3 introduces the cultural exemplar, the work of Georgia O'Keeffe, and provides time for experimentation with media in a laissez-faire activity.

Lesson 4 demonstrates moving from process-oriented activities to a final assignment in a product-oriented experience.

Lesson 5 exemplifies a unit closure, modeling a critique session in which students assess their own work and compare it to O'Keeffe's.

The sample plans that follow illustrate how you might flesh out a unit with individual daily plans, worksheet exercises, and supporting visuals. As you study the information in this unit packet, notice how theory and application come together in these ways:

- The broad unit plan provides a framework for a sequence of individual lesson plans.
- The basic lesson plan structure remains the same regardless of content.
- Lesson goals are drawn from and are identical to unit goals.
- The objectives specify behaviors students will demonstrate in one period as they progress toward fulfillment of the goals.
- Lesson concepts are either identical to or an extension of unit concepts.
- The work period is a task analysis reflecting how activities in the unit scope and sequence will be structured.
- Every lesson has a closure involving active participation of students.
- Every lesson plan includes an evaluation section for the teacher to address on completing the lesson.
- Each lesson is supported by at least one visual (either an in-class demonstration or a premade example).

THE ABSTRACTION OF GEORGIA O'KEEFFE

I. Theme and General Description

A. Abstraction is explored through a sequence of activities in which students (1) make realistic contour drawings of natural objects, (2) explore ways to abstract the objects, (3) experiment with media and techniques using watercolor and oil pastels, and (4) create a design of a small natural object, using abstraction to intensify its essence.

B. Grade level: Seventh

C. Time: Five 60-minute sessions

II. Goals

A. To demonstrate perceptual awareness and skill in observational drawing (productive)

B. To develop manipulative and expressive skills through the use of oil pastel and watercolor (productive)

C. To demonstrate creativity using art elements in the design of abstract images (productive)

D. To demonstrate understanding of the characteristics of abstract art (critical)

E. To demonstrate knowledge of Georgia O'Keeffe and her work (historical)

F. To develop appreciation for abstract imagery in one's own and others' works (aesthetic)

III. Concepts

A. Abstracting is extrapolating or emphasizing the essential qualities of a thing.

B. Abstract art uses nonrepresentational styles, not intended to depict the natural world.

C. Abstract images have colors, lines, shapes, and textures that are used to exaggerate or intensify.

D. By using abstraction, artists convey feelings and ideas and provide impact.

E. There are many different styles and degrees of abstraction.

F. Georgia O'Keeffe created abstractions through color, shape, size, and simplification.

IV. Cultural Exemplar

Selected abstract works by Georgia O'Keeffe

V. Scope and Sequence of Experiences

A. *Session 1:* The teacher passes around a grab bag containing small natural objects. Students do contour drawings of objects selected from the grab bag.

B. *Session 2:* Students do a series of drawings abstracting an object from the grab bag.

C. *Session 3:* Georgia O'Keeffe is introduced. Students discuss how she used color, shape, size, and simplification in abstract images. Students experiment with media and processes, using a combination of oil pastel and watercolor.

D. *Session 4:* Students begin final assignment: Using a natural object as subject matter, create an abstract design following these criteria:

- Intensify the essence of the object through the use of art elements
- Use at least one of O'Keeffe's abstracting devices
- Combine oil pastel and watercolor
- Fill the picture plane

E. *Session 5:* Students complete assignment, critique the work on specified criteria, and discuss similarities and differences between O'Keeffe's and their works.

VI. Evaluation Procedures

A. *Reflection on planning and teaching:* Assess effectiveness of written plans and teaching strategies in leading students to fulfill goals.

B. *Observation of student behaviors:* Assess the degree to which students were engaged in activities— exploration of media and processes, creation of the final product, oral discussion.

C. *Assessment of products:* View and discuss products as demonstrations that (1) criteria were fulfilled and (2) expected levels of skill development, problem solving, and personal interpretation were met.

D. *Fulfillment of unit goals:* Review goals and ascertain whether studio processes, products, oral discussions, and student behaviors indicate fulfillment in productive, critical, aesthetic, and historical domains.

LESSON 1: DRAWING A NATURAL
OBJECT IN CONTOUR LINE

I. Goal: To demonstrate perceptual awareness and skill in observational drawing

II. Objectives

TLW (The learner will) identify correct and incorrect examples of contour drawing (response behavior).
TLW draw several views of a natural object using contour line (productive behavior).

III. Concepts

A. *Contour* means edge.
B. Contour drawing is a drawing process involving the drawing of edges of objects in smooth continuous lines.

IV. Visuals

A. Demonstrations of correct and incorrect ways of doing contour drawing
B. Posters illustrating an example and a nonexample of contour line drawing

V. Supplies and equipment

A. A grab bag containing natural objects (pine cones, shells, leaves, seed pods, feathers, etc.)
B. 12″ × 18″ newsprint
C. Pencils
D. Audiotape and tape player

VI. Teaching procedure

Time allotment

10:00–10:05	A. Introduction
	1. T: "Who remembers what we did last week?"
(transition from previous period)	S: "We finished our imaginary landscape drawings."
	2. T: "Today we are going to do an entirely different kind of drawing. It does not involve drawing from imagination. It involves drawing exactly what you see."
	3. T: "How many of you think you are good at drawing? Raise your hands."
	S: Very few hands up.
	4. T: "Half of learning how to draw is learning how to see accurately. Today we will explore a process called contour drawing that will teach you to see and to draw better."
(presentation of concepts)	5. T: "The word *contour* means edge of a shape or form." Put *contour* = *edge* on the board.
	6. T: "Contour drawing is a special way of drawing in which you look very carefully at an object, and while you are following the outlines of the object with your eyes, you are drawing those edges on your paper."
10:05–10:20	B. Instruction/demonstration
(motivation)	1. T: "To teach you how to do contour drawing, I'm going to tell you the story of Sammy the Snail."
	2. Reach into a grab bag, take out a natural object, and tell the story of Sammy the Snail, who escaped from his fish tank to explore the world. As he was exploring

he came upon a huge object, which he crawled over, around, in, and out of, leaving his snail trail, a *contour line.*

3. Draw the object on the board (very large) while telling the story.

4. Ask students to describe the lines:
   a. They follow the edges of the object.
   b. They are very detailed, indicating careful observation.
   c. They are smooth and continuous.

5. Make two more drawings on the board, one of which is drawn using contour line and one that is not an example of contour line.

(check for understanding)

6. Ask students to indicate with thumbs up for yes, thumbs down for no, or a circle for "don't know," which are contour drawings and which are not.

7. Display posters illustrating an example and a non-example of contour line drawings (Figure 4.3).

10:20–10:55   C. Work period
(supply
distribution)

1. Pass around the grab bag and ask students to reach in blindly and select an object.

2. Monitor distributes paper and pencils.

(task analysis)

3. Instruct students to
   a. Place their objects in front of them and follow the edges with their eyes and their fingertips.
   b. Begin drawing slowly and carefully, following the edges of the objects.

4. Put on quiet music; ask for no talking.

5. Circulate among the students, giving individual help as needed.

6. When the first student completes a drawing, instruct students to make a second drawing of another view of the same object or of another object when each is ready.

7. Select three to four of the best drawings to show during the closure.

(cleanup)

8. Cleanup
   a. A monitor circulates with the grab bag to collect the objects.
   b. Table captains collect work in folders.
   c. Pencil monitor collects pencils.

10:55–11:00   D. Closure

1. Show examples of three to four of the best drawings.

2. Ask students why the drawings are good examples of contour drawing.

3. Ask students what they learned by doing contour drawing.

VII. Evaluation questions

   A. Were the teaching procedures and demonstrations successful in leading students to fulfill objectives?
   B. Were students able to correctly identify examples and nonexamples of contour drawing?
   C. Did the products demonstrate skill in observation and drawing?
   D. Were students able to successfully complete at least one contour drawing?
   E. How did the work period go? Did students get bored or frustrated?
   F. What should I do next period?

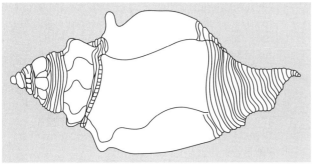

Example of contour line drawing

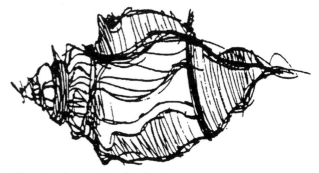

Example of noncontour line drawing

FIGURE 4.3
Visuals for Lesson 1
Contour lines

LESSON 2: ABSTRACTING FROM A NATURAL OBJECT

I. Goals

A. To demonstrate creativity using art elements in the design of abstract images
B. To demonstrate understanding of the characteristics of abstract art

II. Objective: TLW make four drawings of a natural object, abstracting the form in a variety of ways (productive behavior).

III. Concepts

A. Abstracting is extrapolating or emphasizing the essential qualities of a thing.
B. Abstract art uses nonrepresentational styles, not intended to depict the natural world.
C. Artists use colors, lines, shapes, and textures to create abstract images.
D. There are different ways of achieving abstraction: changing shapes, changing proportions, rearranging parts, simplifying, embellishing, cropping, etc.

IV. Visuals

A. Demonstrations made by the teacher on the chalkboard
B. Process poster showing ways to abstract an object

V. Supplies and equipment

A. Grab bag and contour drawings from Lesson 1
B. Abstraction worksheet
C. Pencils

VI. Teaching procedure

Time allotment	A. Introduction
10:00–10:10 (review)	1. T: "Who remembers what we did in the last lesson?" S: "We did contour drawings of natural objects." T: "What did you learn from doing contour drawing?" S: "To see more accurately and to draw exactly what we see."
(transition)	2. T: "Yes. In the contour drawing exercise you learned about the characteristics of your object through careful observation and drawing. Now we are going to intensify those characteristics through processes of abstraction." T: "What does *abstraction* mean?"

S: "To draw unrealistically."

(presentation
of concepts)

3. T: "Abstraction does involve unrealistic representation. Artists abstract intentionally to convey qualities, moods, feelings, and ideas. In the process of abstracting, artists may use colors, lines, shapes, and textures to exaggerate particular qualities of objects."

"Let's look at this sea shell, for example. What are some characteristics or qualities of this object?"

S: "It's a vessel; it's spiky; it has concentric growth patterns."

10:10–10:20   B. Instruction/demonstration

1. Teacher writes characteristics of the shell on the board as students identify them.

2. Students discuss ways the shell could be drawn abstractly to illustrate characteristics. (Enlarge the hole to portray its vessel-like quality; use only geometric shapes to exaggerate its spiky quality; add concentric lines to enhance its growth pattern, etc.)

(motivation)

3. Teacher illustrates these ideas on the board, abstracting the shell again and again as students identify various characteristics.

4. Teacher concludes the discussion by presenting the poster "Processes for Abstracting an Image" (Figure 4.4 on page 84) with labels on the bottom covered with pieces of paper. Students identify how each image has been abstracted. As they do so, the teacher reveals the answers.

10:20–10:55   C. Work period

(supply
distribution)

1. Monitors distribute drawings from last session and the abstraction worksheet (Worksheet 4.1).

2. Students select the grab bag objects they had last session.

3. Students use their natural objects and drawings from last session as references for the worksheet exercise. Teacher reads the worksheet directions and explains, modeling behavior as needed.

(task analysis)
(cleanup)

4. Teacher circulates among students to provide individual attention.

5. Students put away drawing supplies. A monitor collects grab bag objects.

10:55–11:00   D. Closure

1. Students place worksheets on the bulletin board and discuss various solutions to the problem "abstracting the essence of an object."

2. Monitor collects worksheets in a folder and gives to teacher.

VII. Evaluation questions

A. Were teaching procedures and demonstrations successful in leading students to fulfill the objective?

B. Were students able to generate a variety of ways to modify an object?

C. How successful were students at visually representing essential qualities through the use of abstraction techniques?

D. Were students able to complete the assignment?

E. How was behavior?

F. What should I do next period?

EMPHASIZING THE ESSENTIAL QUALITIES OF AN OBJECT THROUGH THE USE OF ABSTRACTION

Directions
1. Identify a quality or characteristic of your natural object and write it on line A of the first box. 2. Select a method of abstraction to intensify that characteristic and write it on line B. 3. Illustrate your idea. 4. Use this procedure in the remaining three boxes to explore other characteristics and abstracting methods.

Name:

1. A _____
   B _____

2. A _____
   B _____

3. A _____
   B _____

4. A _____
   B _____

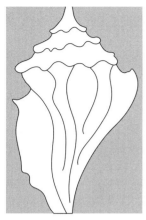
Draw realistically.

Modify shapes.

Simplify areas.

Alter proportions.

FIGURE 4.4
Visual for Lesson 2
Ways to abstract a natural object

LESSON 3: EXPLORING WATERCOLOR AND OIL PASTEL

I. Goals

   A. To develop manipulative and expressive skills through use of oil pastel and watercolor
   B. To gain knowledge of Georgia O'Keeffe and her artwork
   C. To demonstrate understanding of the characteristics of abstract art

II. Objectives

   A. TLW identify and discuss ways in which Georgia O'Keeffe used abstraction (response behavior).
   B. TLW explore processes and techniques using watercolor and oil pastel (productive behavior).

III. Concepts

   A. Abstracting is a process dealing with the representation of the essential qualities of a thing.
   B. Through the use of abstraction artists convey feelings and ideas and provide impact.
   C. There are many different styles and degrees of abstraction.
   D. Georgia O'Keeffe created abstractions through the use of color, shape, size, and simplification.
   E. Watercolor and oil pastels can be combined to achieve visually interesting effects.

IV. Visuals

   A. Prints of *Jack-in-the-Pulpit* paintings by O'Keeffe
   B. Concept poster containing reproductions of O'Keeffe's work
   C. Demonstrations of ways to use watercolor and oil pastel

V. Supplies and equipment

   A. Watercolors, brushes, water cans
   B. Oil pastels
   C. Scraps of white drawing paper for experimentation

VI. Teaching procedure

Time allotment
10:00–10:20
(review and check
for understanding)

A. Introduction

1. T: "What did we do last session?"
   S: "We did abstraction worksheets."
   T: "What do we do when we abstract?"
   S: "We change things from realistic to unrealistic."
   T: "Why do artists do this?"
   S: "To represent a different point of view or a particular idea or feeling."

2. T: "Yes. Now we are going to view the work of an American painter who was well known for portraying the essence of natural objects. She gave this advice to artists: 'Try to paint your world as though you were the first man looking at it.'"
   T: "Does anyone know who she is?"
   "She is Georgia O'Keeffe, and these are some examples of her work."

3. Teacher shows concept poster illustrating her style.
   T: "How did O'Keeffe portray the essence of objects? How did she abstract?" (Teacher helps students to focus by pointing to specific images.)
   S: "She made things appear bigger than life."
   S: "She intensified through the use of color."
   S: "She used simplification."
   S: "She painted closeup views of partial objects."
   T: "O'Keeffe began her exploration of abstraction much in the same way we did—by first drawing and painting realistically and progressing toward greater and greater degrees of abstraction. Most artists learn to draw realistically first before they move into abstraction. We can observe the progression of her style from realistic to more abstract by looking at a series she did."

4. Teacher shows prints of O'Keeffe's *Jack-in-the-Pulpit* series and asks for a student volunteer to place each one along a continuum ranging from most realistic to most abstract, as shown in the following illustration.

   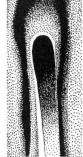

FIGURE 4.5
Visual for Lesson 3
Jack-in-the Pulpit *series*
by Georgia O'Keeffe

Most realistic

Most abstract

T: "As you can see, these images progress gradually from realistic to almost unrecognizable. Artists learn to design abstract images just as they learn to draw realistically. One way they learn is by drawing many variations of an object as we did in the last lesson. Another way is to experiment with art materials and processes. O'Keeffe used both watercolor and oil pastels. We are going to spend some time exploring what we can do with these media."

10:20–10:30 (demonstration)	B. Instruction/demonstration Teacher shows students how to 1. Create a variety of effects using watercolor washes, wet on wet, and dry brush 2. Blend oil pastels by overlapping colors 3. Combine oil pastel and watercolor to achieve a resist effect

10:30–10:55 (supply distribution) (task analysis)	C. Work period
	1. Monitors distribute supplies.
	2. Students experiment with the following processes:
	   a. Watercolor washes
	   b. Wet on wet
	   c. Dry brush
	   d. Blending oil pastels
	   e. Combining oil pastel with watercolor

(cleanup)	3. Monitors collect supplies.
10:55–11:00	D. Closure 1. Students review techniques O'Keeffe used to express the essence of objects. 2. Selected students share their experiments, discussing how their use of media and techniques express visual qualities. 3. As students are dismissed to line up, they place their work in a drying rack.

VII. Evaluation questions

    A. Were teaching procedures and demonstrations successful in leading students to fulfill objectives?

    B. Were students able to identify ways in which Georgia O'Keeffe abstracted forms?

    C. How successful were they in exploring processes and techniques?

    D. How was behavior?

    E. Could students discuss the visual qualities in their own work?

    F. Was there enough time?

    G. Recommendations for next period?

FIGURE 4.6
Visual for Lesson 3
Concept poster illustrating
selected O'Keeffe abstractions

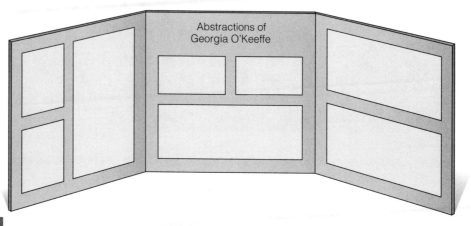

LESSON 4: CREATING AN ABSTRACT DESIGN

I. Goals

    A. To demonstrate creativity using art elements in the design of abstract images

    B. To develop manipulative and expressive skills through the use of oil pastel and watercolor

II. Objectives

TLW begin to create an abstract design of a natural object (productive behavior).

III. Concepts

    A. Objects can be abstracted through exaggeration, simplification, elaboration, and manipulation of line, shape, color, and texture.

    B. Watercolor and oil pastel can be combined to achieve visually interesting effects.

    C. Georgia O'Keeffe created abstractions by using color, shape, size, and simplification.

IV. Visuals

    A. Concept poster to review O'Keeffe's techniques

    B. Criteria poster for final assignment

V. Supplies and equipment

    A. Worksheets from Lesson 2 and pencils

    B. Scrap white drawing paper for experimentation

    C. 12" × 12" white drawing paper for final product

    D. Pencils, watercolors, brushes, water cans, oil pastels

VI. Teaching procedure

Time allotment	
10:00–10:15 (review and check for understanding)	A. Introduction
	1. T: "Who did we learn about last period?"
	S: "Georgia O'Keeffe."
	2. Teacher shows concept visual illustrating O'Keeffe's work.
	T: "What did we learn about her work?"
	S: "It's abstract."
	T: "How did she abstract?"
	S: "She used color, size, and simplification."
	T: "Why didn't she just paint things realistically?"
	S: "She wanted to intensify, express feelings, portray the essence of objects."
	3. T: "What did you learn through your exploration of oil pastel and watercolor last period?"
	S: "How to achieve interesting effects."
(transition)	T: "Do you think you could use some of these effects in an abstract design that portrays the essence of an object?"
	S: "Yes."
	B. Instruction/demonstration
	1. T: "Today we are going to begin a final design. You will be putting together what you have learned about contour drawing, abstracting, and experimenting with oil pastels and watercolor.

2. Teacher distributes worksheets on abstraction from Lesson 2 and explains that this exercise was practice for what students will be doing in the final assignment.

(motivation)

3. Teacher displays and explains final assignment/criteria poster:

FIGURE 4.7
Criteria poster

> Final Assignment/Criteria
> Using a natural object as subject matter, create an abstract design following these criteria:
>   1. Intensify the essence of the object through the use of art elements.
>   2. Use at least one of O'Keeffe's abstracting devices.
>   3. Combine oil pastel and watercolor.
>   4. Fill the picture plane.

4. Teacher explains procedure for the period.
   a. Students are given the option of working from their original objects and ideas generated on their worksheets or of selecting new objects.
   b. Teacher demonstrates thinking processes involved in moving from idea on the worksheet, to a sketch on scratch paper, to a drawing on the final paper.

10:15–10:55
(supply distribution)

C. Work period
   1. Monitors distribute worksheets from Lesson 2, grab bag objects, pencils, and scrap drawing paper on which to experiment with design possibilities and explore the use of oil pastels and watercolor.

(task analysis)

   2. Students do preliminary sketches on scrap drawing paper.
   3. When individual students are ready, they get materials from a supply table (12″ × 12″ white drawing paper, watercolors, oil pastels, water cans) and begin working on their final designs.
   4. Teacher circulates and guides students as needed.

(cleanup)

   5. Supply monitors collect oil pastels, watercolors, brushes, and cans and return them to the supply table.
   6. Folder monitor collects worksheet exercises and scrap papers (if not wet) in table folders.

D. Closure

10:55–11:00

   1. Students volunteer to hold up work in progress, sharing with entire class.
   2. Class members attempt to guess what object and particular quality is being portrayed.
   3. Students put work in drying rack as they line up for dismissal.

VII. Evaluation questions

A. Were the teaching processes effective in guiding the students?
B. How successful were students in moving from their worksheet drawings and/or natural objects to the design of their final works?
C. How creative were the final designs in terms of the use of abstraction to intensify particular qualities?

D. How effective was the use of oil pastels and watercolor?

E. Did the final designs reflect the criteria?

F. What needs to be addressed in the next lesson, as the students complete the assignment?

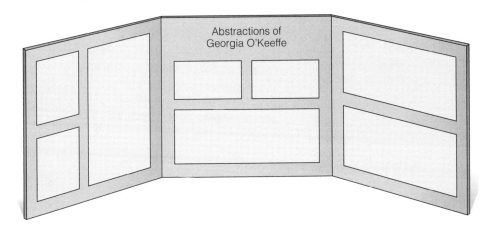

Abstractions of
Georgia O'Keeffe

FIGURE 4.8
Visuals for Lesson 4

1. *Concept poster illustrating selected O'Keeffe abstractions*
2. *Final assignment/criteria poster*

LESSON 5: LOOKING AT ABSTRACTION

I. Goals

A. To demonstrate creativity using art elements in the design of abstract images

B. To develop manipulative and expressive skills through the use of oil pastel and watercolor

C. To demonstrate understanding of the characteristics of abstract art

D. To demonstrate knowledge of Georgia O'Keeffe and her artwork

E. To develop appreciation for abstract imagery in one's own and others' works

II. Objectives

A. TLW complete abstract designs (productive behavior).

B. TLW critique works in terms of criteria (response behavior).

C. TLW compare student works with O'Keeffe's art (response behavior).

D. TLW share appreciations of work (response behavior).

III. Concepts

A. Abstracting is a process dealing with the representation of the essential qualities of a thing.

B. Georgia O'Keeffe created abstractions through the use of color, shape, size, and simplification.

IV. Visuals

A. Final assignment/criteria poster

B. Product poster displaying several teacher examples of the assignment

C. Several O'Keeffe prints not yet seen by students

V. Supplies and equipment

A. Designs begun last week

B. Scratch paper

C. Pencils, oil pastels, watercolors, water cans, brushes

VI. Teaching procedure

Time allotment   A. Introduction

10:00–10:10
1. Teacher presents final assignment/criteria poster and asks students to review guidelines.

(review)
2. Teacher presents product poster (Figure 4.8) and asks students to describe how each teacher example meets the criteria.

(motivation and check for understanding)
3. Teacher selects two to three samples of student work and asks students why each is successful.

B. Instruction

Teacher instructs students to follow criteria, as they complete the assignment. Emphasis is placed on elaboration of detail, use of media, filling the picture plane, creativity.

10:10–10:40   C. Work period

(supply distribution)
1. Monitors pass back work and distribute supplies.

(task analysis)
2. Students continue working on designs.

3. Teacher circulates and makes suggestions as needed.

4. As students work, teacher displays additional O'Keeffe paintings that students have not yet seen.

(10:30)
5. Students finishing early are asked to continue to explore abstraction by drawing or painting on another sheet of paper.

(10:35)
6. Students are informed they have five more minutes to work.

(cleanup)
7. Students are requested to place wet work on the floor under the bulletin board. Monitors collect supplies and clean tables.

10:40–11:00   D. Closure

1. Teacher refers students to final assignment/criteria poster, O'Keeffe prints, and their own work, asking them to respond to these questions:

a. "Which student works are the most creative in using abstraction to express the essence of an object? Why?"

b. "Which ones have used oil pastel and watercolor in the most effective ways? What do you like about them?"

c. "Which ones have used the space the most effectively and have the most successful compositions? Why?"

d. "Look at the prints on the bulletin board. These are additional paintings by Georgia O'Keeffe. Point out some abstracting devices she has used. Then point out images created by your fellow classmates that employ the same devices."

e. "Which of O'Keeffe's paintings do you like the best? Why?"

f. "Which of your classmates' paintings do you like the best? Why?"

g. "What do you like best about your own work?"

h. "What part of the unit did you enjoy most? Least?"

2. Teacher dismisses students to line up table by table as each group provides a different answer to the question "What did you learn from this unit?" (If this question is too broad to elicit meaningful responses, more specific questions may be asked:)

- "What is contour drawing? Why do you think we began a unit on abstraction with contour drawing?"

- "What do we do when we abstract something?"

- "Why might an artist choose to create abstract images rather than realistic images?"

- "Tell me three things you learned about Georgia O'Keeffe and/or her artwork."

- "How are we as artists similar to Georgia O'Keeffe?"

- "How are we different from her? From one another?"

VII. Evaluation questions

A. How well did planning and teaching support student learning?

B. How well did students fulfill lesson objectives and unit goals?

C. How well did products in general fulfill each criterion?

D. How was the closure? Were students able to answer questions and demonstrate understanding of their own work? O'Keeffe's work? The relationship between the two?

E. Suggested modification for future presentation:

F. What might be a direction for a follow-up unit?

Shell

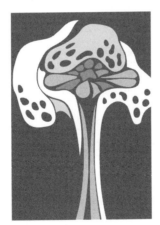
Bone

Leaf

FIGURE 4.9
Visuals for Lesson 5
1. *Product visual displaying three teacher examples of the final assignment*
2. *Poster defining assignment and criteria*
3. *Additional reproductions of Georgia O'Keeffe's work not previously seen by students*

▼ MOVING FROM PLANNING TO TEACHING

Your first plans will be quite long and detailed. They may look like scripts with dialogue and stage directions. There is a purpose for writing in this much specificity. Through this process you draw your intuitive knowledge to conscious understanding. These lesson plans do more than record what you will do in an art period. They provide a process and a format to teach yourself how to teach. The more experienced you become in teaching, the shorter your written plans can be. Eventually you may reach the point at which "planning" becomes a notation in a 2-inch square of a plan book. Today, however, reading through the unit package presented here, you may wonder if you will ever become proficient enough at planning to design an entire packet of materials comprising a unit of study. The question foremost in your mind might be "How do I get there?" The answer is "one plan at a time." This response reflects where we stand along the continuum that differentiates subject- from child-centered approaches to planning and teaching.

If we were 100 percent subject centered, we might define the purpose of education as "delivering information." Coming from this perspective, we might plan an entire unit, including all lessons and visuals, in detail before beginning the teaching process. We would cover the information in the time we had allotted, regardless of students' readiness or ability to meet objectives.

If, in contrast, we define the purpose of education as "prompting learning," we would create an entirely different relationship between planning and teaching processes. The position taken in this text is more centrally located along the continuum from subject-centered to child-centered, reflecting the purpose of education from the second perspective. Therefore, we do not recommend that you plan all lessons within a unit prior to its presentation. We suggest instead that you follow the procedure in the box.

Steps Defining the Relationship Between Planning and Teaching

1. Design a unit plan in general terms. List the primary activities in which students will be engaged day by day in the scope and sequence. Do not include specific objectives at this point.

2. Use the goals, concepts, and first activity in the scope and sequence as guides in writing the first lesson plan.

3. Write the first lesson in detail.

4. Read your completed lesson to yourself (or someone else). As you do so, envision yourself teaching and your students responding.

5. Make notes on 3″ × 5″ cards of what you will do and say in each section of the lesson. Include time annotations and key words that will trigger your thinking.

6. Practice teaching the lesson from your note cards. Make modifications on the cards if necessary.

7. Assume as you walk into the classroom that you have done everything you could possibly do to prepare yourself and that you are indeed ready.

8. Teach Lesson 1. (Begin by uttering your first words. The rest will follow.)

9. After teaching Lesson 1, use the evaluation questions or procedures at the end of the lesson plan to assess your effectiveness and student learning.

10. Write the second lesson plan to reflect whatever you ascertain the next step should be in the teaching/learning process, regardless of where your unit scope and sequence says you "should be."

11. Repeat this planning–teaching–assessing process, modifying your thinking as needed to prepare for each successive lesson, meet the needs of your students, and lead them toward fulfillment of goals.

As you can see, this process allows flexibility not possible in the first approach. It provides for a relationship between teacher and student in which leadership can be passed back and forth. In effect, it permits a teacher to say to students, "I have a plan for where to go (expressed through goals). I'm willing to listen to your feedback on how to get there (expressed through objectives)." Using this approach, you may discover that your anticipations match student performance and you can move on to the next activity in the unit scope and sequence, as planned. Or you may run into problems, such as these:

- You have underestimated the time required to build a skill (contour drawing) or to demonstrate understanding of a concept (how abstraction can express an essential quality of an object). You allow more time for completion of the unit.
- Your goal is appropriate, but the path toward the goal (the sequence of objectives) is rocky. You modify objectives.
- While working toward a solution to a visual problem or fulfillment of a goal, students suggest paths you had not considered. You expand your vision or criteria to allow for greater flexibility and diversity.
- The studio assignment is appropriate, but students cannot relate to the cultural exemplar. You provide alternate examples more relevant to your population.
- A fire drill disrupts your lesson. You devote two periods to what you had planned to present in one.

The more you can relate to students in real teaching situations, the better attuned to their capabilities, needs, and interests you will become. As a beginning teacher, you may know far more about teaching *art* than teaching *students*. The students will reflect back to you when you are on target and when you are not. Being sensitive to where your students are at any given point in a unit is far more important than adhering to what you have written on paper. Do not be afraid to deviate from your plan if the plan is not working. Do not be attached to the time and effort you have spent writing plans. They represent progress along your learning curve. They may change again and again as you learn to make connections between what you plan and what is possible and appropriate in practical application.

S U M M A R Y

Expanding a unit plan into a sequence of lesson plans involves several steps. Before the actual writing of the plan, (1) generate ideas using a teaching model and the unit-planning continuum, (2) explore studio media and processes you intend to present to students, (3) make supporting visuals, and (4) structure your ideas into a unit plan.

Next, consider the components of a lesson plan, some of which are identical to those of a unit plan. Unit and lesson goals, for example, are identical. Objectives are descriptions of verifiable behaviors that students are expected to demonstrate as they progress toward the fulfillment of broad, long-range goals. Concepts of a particular lesson are derived from unit concepts. They may be identical to unit concepts, or they may be expanded and written in greater detail. Visuals, supplies, and equipment specify what you will need to teach the lesson. The teaching procedure describes the process of teaching—how you will motivate and present concepts, what you will do to ensure that students meet objectives. This part of the plan expands a section of the unit scope and sequence. The last component, evaluation, provides questions and procedures to assess the teaching/learning process. The primary difference between unit and lesson evaluation questions is that the former focuses on meeting goals, whereas the latter focuses on meeting objectives.

A fully developed unit of study, integrating unit, lesson, and visual planning might thus contain

- The unit plan "The Abstraction of Georgia O'Keeffe"
- Lesson 1, "Drawing a Natural Object in Contour Line" (illustrating a closed-ended, process-oriented lesson intended to develop perceptual and drawing skills)
- Lesson 2, "Abstracting from a Natural Object" (illustrating an open-ended, process-oriented lesson intended to develop visual problem-solving skills)
- Lesson 3, "Exploring Watercolor and Oil Pastel" (modeling a laissez-faire activity and the introduction of a cultural exemplar)
- Lesson 4, "Creating an Abstract Design" (illustrating how to move from process-oriented activities to a final product-oriented assignment)
- Lesson 5, "Looking at Abstraction" (modeling a critique session and unit closure)

The following strategy integrates planning and teaching processes: (1) Move from the design of the visuals and unit plan to the writing of the first lesson plan; (2) stop planning; (3) teach the first lesson; (4) assess planning/teaching/learning; and (5) plan each succeeding lesson on the basis of what occurred in the previous lesson. This process heightens interaction between you and your students. Metaphorically, you are engaging in a dance in which you lead students in a particular direction. The roles of leader and follower may shift back and forth as you become more and more sensitive to your students' needs and interests. This is teaching at its highest. Planning prepares you to take your next step: moving into the classroom and asking your students to dance.

A. MOVING TOWARD GOALS THROUGH INDIVIDUAL OBJECTIVES

Directions
1. Refer to goals you generate in the unit-planning continuum or in a fully developed unit of study. 2. List one goal in each domain. 3. List two objectives that might be used to lead students toward fulfillment of each goal.

Productive goal:

Objective 1:

Objective 2:

Critical goal:

Objective 1:

Objective 2:

Aesthetic goal:

Objective 1:

Objective 2:

Historical goal:

Objective 1:

Objective 2:

B. WRITING A TASK ANALYSIS FOR AN ACTIVITY

Directions

Illustrate how you might move from a goal to an objective to a task analysis of an activity intended to fulfill the objective.

Unit goal:

Lesson objective:

**Task analysis of student–teacher interaction intended to lead students to fulfill the objective
(listed step by step as 1, 2, 3, etc.):**

PART 2

MOVING INTO THE CLASSROOM

PART II is intended to move you from the theoretical constructs of your plans into actual teaching in real classrooms. It deals with the "inside" aspect of our model of art education. It encourages you to focus on your students, as you create learning atmospheres, develop teaching strategies, and implement instruction to support optimal growth. Chapter 5, "Preparing for Your Students," discusses classroom environment, behavior management, motivational strategies, and connecting with your students. Chapter 6, "Teaching the Language of Vision," focuses on the form of visual language and presents strategies to teach the language through perceptual and productive activities. Chapter 7, "Promoting Creativity," continues the exploration of visual language, presenting it as a vehicle through which to express the authentic self. This chapter illustrates connections among cognitive functioning, expressive skills, and art making. Chapter 8, "Encouraging Reflection," addresses the role that critical capacities play in developing reflective behavior, intrinsic motivation, and artistic expression.

PREPARING FOR YOUR STUDENTS

As we progress, continuing to add pieces to the art education puzzle, you may notice that one section has taken form—the aspect of planning. Part I of the text presents a path leading from planning to teaching. We ended the last chapter by asking you to envision yourself walking into a classroom and teaching for the first time. Probably your first teaching experience will be in someone else's room. This chapter invites you to imagine what you might do in your own art room.

Moving into your own environment and teaching is more easily said than done. In the planning stage you deal primarily with your own thoughts and processes, envisioning yourself guiding students through art experiences. The minute you walk into the classroom, however, you are outnumbered—one among perhaps twenty-five or thirty others, each of whom may have his or her own agenda for what will happen. As arduous as planning is, it is only half of the picture. The other half is what you do with the plan, as you interact with live students in real classroom settings. The "TLW" ("The learner will . . . ") statements you have written in your lesson plans suddenly take on a reality as you attempt to lead Jimmy, Jamal, and Juanita down the path you have intended for them to go. This chapter is about moving from theoretical constructs on paper to actual teaching environments and practices. Sections include (1) creating the physical environment, (2) creating the emotional environment, and (3) getting to know your students.

▼ CREATING THE PHYSICAL ENVIRONMENT

You may have already envisioned your "ideal" job or "perfect" art room. You may have observed wonderful lessons taught in large, window-lined rooms with lots of storage space, multiple sinks, and incredible supply closets. Perhaps you thought, "Yes! This is what I want!" You may also have seen equally outstanding lessons presented in windowless trailers with crowded rows of desks, narrow aisles, and inadequate storage and display space. Art teachers teach in and with whatever is provided for them. At bare minimum it might be a cart wheeled from room to room. At best it could be a space that far exceeds anything you could imagine. The point to remember is that whatever space is provided is simply that—a space. It is up to you to create an aesthetic, functional environment.

● MAKING AN AESTHETIC STATEMENT

Perhaps most important to keep in mind as you are about to turn a space into an environment is this: You may spend a large portion of your life in this room; make it a place you feel good in. You will function in this setting day after day, week after week, possibly year after year, sharing the best of yourself with your students. Create a place for yourself and for them that makes an aesthetic statement, feels nurturing, and optimizes learning. Teachers in a wide variety of situations have done this in a number of ways. Some suggestions are listed here:

- *Consider the use of color.* Color can be used to establish a mood, add interest, or unify a space. Often art teachers are able to alter old spaces or help design new ones through choice of color. You might be able to select the wall color(s) or color and type of cabinets. You can enliven walls by painting border designs in a unifying color scheme. Color used in posters or bulletin board papers and edging can also become a unifying element.

- *Consider the use of wall space.* Do not overcrowd. Too many images on a wall defeat their purpose. Students will not be able to see the trees for the forest if the forest is too thick. Posters, artwork, cultural exemplars—any type of visual needs space around it in order to stand out. Overcrowded spaces may overstimulate students and be perceived as confusing and claustrophobic. More is not necessarily better.

- *Consider the use of windows.* You may or may not want light and the outside world coming in. Windows can elicit a feeling of space and airiness or be a distraction. Teachers whose windows face busy streets have used the space as a bulletin board, hanging work on permanently closed blinds. Some teachers make or select their own curtains or window treatments. If you intend to show slides in a window-lit room, you will need to darken the space. Think about the aesthetic, psychological, and functional aspects of windows as you design your environment.

- *Consider the use of bulletin boards and display cases.* In addition to using these to teach about and display art, they can be used to enhance the aesthetic environment. At the beginning of a school year before student work is available, many teachers create large, colorful bulletin boards relating to a unit theme. This can be an excellent way to introduce yourself to new students and to showcase your skills.

- *Present yourself as an artist.* Consider displaying your personal artwork in your room. Students expect art teachers to create art. Let them know they are right. A way to motivate their interest in making and viewing art and to enhance their appreciation of you is to share your work as part of the aesthetic environment.

- *Display visually interesting objects.* Visually interesting objects can be natural (rocks, bones, shells, feathers, twigs, honeycombs, sunflowers) or human-made (bicycle wheels, machinery parts, tools, hats, shoes, gloves, mannequins). They can be stored in cases or on the tops of cupboards. Their purpose is to inspire curiosity and investigation of the visual world, to teach design concepts, to serve as still life, and to provide atmosphere as "neat stuff."

- *Invite students to be co-creators of and participants within the environment.* Encourage students to be actively involved in the design and maintenance of the space. For example, in older rooms students might paint designs on cabinets or walls. Many teachers provide warmth within an environment and encourage students to take responsibility by bringing in plants and even animals (such as hamsters or fish) for which students care. Some high school teachers have large rooms that advanced students divide into individual studio areas. Students can take a hand in creating an environment at any age. Through co-creation they can make a space theirs and demonstrate appreciation by acting responsibly within it.

- *Use the environment to reflect your art program.* Consider what best reflects your program or philosophical orientation and express your values through the design of the visual environment. Teachers who view the study of art objects as the core of art education may reflect their programs primarily in displaying works by master artists. Studio-centered art educators will reflect their orientation by exhibiting student work. Using the perspective of this text, you might display work that connects the inside to the outside. A unit of study may be showcased by exhibiting a wide range of solutions to a studio problem along with the exemplar that created the connection to the outside.

DESIGNING A FUNCTIONAL SPACE

Creating a space in which you and your students like to spend time because it looks and feels appealing is only one consideration. An equally important step is designing a space that works. Like the creation of the aesthetic environment, the design of the physical space is a personal matter. There are many right answers and what works for one may not necessarily work for another. The points that follow provide guidance for what to consider in setting up a well-functioning art room.

- *Consider seating arrangement.* Ascertain the largest number of students you will accommodate and provide enough seating for all. Many teachers prefer to seat students at tables. Group seating can be advantageous because it supports cooperative learning (a teaching strategy in which students work together to share ideas, solve problems, and perform tasks). Working on studio activities at tables also promotes healthy sharing. Teachers who do not have tables may put individual desks together to create groupings of four to six students. One desk may serve as the "supply desk." The type of furniture and its arrangement will depend on the nature of your courses and your students. Advanced high school classes may have easels or drawing benches placed around a central modeling stand or still life display. What is most important is that the seating meet the needs of your students as they engage in various art activities.

- *Consider traffic flow.* The space between the seating is equally important. Think about entering and exiting the room; creating enough space between groups; traffic patterns as students get supplies, sharpen pencils, use the sink, and store work. Leave as much space as possible for students to move and work comfortably. Some teachers, given large enough rooms, create special areas for different activities. For example, they may design quiet corners for individual art activities and reading or create a space through the use of an area rug on which students sit for class discussions and sharing of artwork. Envision the kinds of art activities engaged in by the students and the spaces they will need for optimal performance.

- *Consider the placement of your desk.* Even if your desk is nothing more than a surface on which you keep your plan book, you will have some area that is yours. The location of your "teacher space" is important because it sends psychological messages. If you put your students in rows facing you at your desk in the front of the room, you are sending these messages: "I am in charge. I am your leader. You will follow me and do as I say." (This is how teaching may have looked when art education consisted entirely of closed-ended instruction intended to build skills.) If you group students at tables arranged around the room, allowing individuals to face one another, and place your desk in a corner, you will send an entirely different message. Here are some points to consider when deciding where to place your desk:

  1. You will not teach from your desk. You will teach standing up as you present ideas, write on the board, do demonstrations, and circulate among students.

  2. Where you position yourself in the room and how you deliver instruction will depend on the nature of particular art activities. When you present a closed-end lesson, you will be teacher-directive and stand in the "front" or center of the room to model behavior. When you present a discovery learning activity, you may simply blend into the surroundings as you stand back and watch.

3. Because you will not be sitting at your desk to teach, you can place your desk in a position where you can unobtrusively observe students at work. You need to see them; they don't need to see you.

- *Consider storage and maintenance of equipment and supplies.* Analyze optimal ways to store and distribute materials. Do not arrange supplies in alphabetical order. (You may end up with brushes on one end of the room and paints on the other.) Group similar materials together. Decide which materials should be out in the open or readily available to students in labeled cupboards and which need to be under lock and key (potentially hazardous and expensive materials). Teachers have various methods for storing, distributing, and keeping track of art supplies. Some distribute and collect everything themselves; some select monitors to be responsible; some allow students free rein and expect each individual to be completely self-sufficient. You will design a system that is appropriate for the ages and the developmental levels of your students and that supports you in your preference for order or tolerance of chaos. Many teachers design devices to keep track of supplies. These include blocks of wood with holes to store brushes and pegboard paneling on which images of tools such as scissors have been stenciled under hooks for hanging. By using these storage devices, you may eliminate the need to count everything. The holes or empty spaces tell you that supplies are still out.

- *Consider methods for storage and distribution of artwork.* A typical art teacher interacts with 150 students a day, each of whom is working on some project that needs to be stored in the room. Having a method to keep track of work is extremely important. Most teachers use folders or portfolios. If students are arranged at tables, each table may have a portfolio into which student folders are placed. If students are arranged in rows, teachers may make row portfolios. Each student should have an individual folder for his or her work. Every student should be able to easily locate work because it is stored in a way that reflects a particular seating arrangement within a class. Teachers use a number of ways to identify seating arrangements of students and their work. Some tape symbols to tables; others hang symbols from the ceiling above each group. These symbols might be numbers, colors, art tools, master artists, or schools of art. Folders are then identified and stored according to seating labels (blue table, Miró table, Impressionist table, etc.). In addition to supplying each individual with a folder and each group of students with a table portfolio, maintain a labeled drawer or cupboard space for each class. As obvious as this seems, some beginning teachers do not realize the importance of using a system. By the end of their first month they have added to the overall confusion by cluttering their space with unidentified piles of papers. Make sure you have created a system *before* your students arrive.

▼ CREATING THE EMOTIONAL ENVIRONMENT

We may define the physical environment as the space itself and the objects within the space. In attending to aesthetic and functional aspects, teachers create a setting. They design an inviting ambiance, organize the tables, supply enough chairs, provide whatever is necessary for students to engage in activities. All this is background for what happens when teacher and students come together in an educational experience. An educational experience is about transmitting attitudes, values, ideas, skills, and knowledge from one human being to another. For this to happen in a qualitative way, students need to be physically comfortable. They also need to be emotionally comfortable. They need to feel they are part of a system that supports them; they need to feel visible; they need to feel good about being an individual. In any educational environment, teachers should address these needs. In an art room, where we prize the affective domain, encourage the feeling nature of human beings, cherish each child's uniqueness, and promote creative expression, we must be most attentive to creating a positive emotional environment. What does this mean? To some it may mean anything from soothing music to pizza parties. We will focus here on classroom management and motivational strategies.

CLASSROOM MANAGEMENT

Classroom management involves creating a physical and emotional structure that supports teaching and learning. As we have previously noted, there are multiple ways to do this. Every teacher has his or her own way of leading, encouraging, and modifying behavior. Classroom management is best learned by managing a classroom. Reading, by itself, will not prepare you. Nevertheless, outstanding teachers share some strategies that can serve as guidelines:

- *Set boundaries for behavior.* Boundaries, defined by rules for behavior, give students a framework in which to perform. Students know that if their behaviors are within the limits, they are doing what is expected of them. They are more likely to feel good about themselves and safe. Students who feel safe are more open to education, to asking questions, to taking risks, to expressing themselves creatively. Students also feel safer when they know that people who are not operating within the boundaries will be attended to. Some general rules that set boundaries for behavior are (1) Attend class on time, (2) Be considerate of others, (3) Raise your hand to speak, (4) Follow directions, (5) Put forth your best effort, and (6) Be responsible for your work space. Notice that these rules are stated in positive terms and are very broad. A few general guidelines such as "be considerate" and "follow directions" can be more effective than long lists of specific rules.

- *Clearly communicate expectations.* By setting boundaries, you provide a safe learning atmosphere in which students work day after day. In addition to setting these general rules, you can promote specific behaviors by clearly communicating expectations. You can do this in the following ways:

  1. Apprising students of the objective (TLW, the learner will, . . .) translated into ordinary language
  2. Doing demonstrations and modeling behaviors
  3. Showing examples of what students are to do
  4. Checking for understanding
  5. Telling students where they should be by the end of a session

  The clearer you are in your own mind about what you want students to do, the more clearly you can express your expectations to them. Students who understand what is expected are more likely to behave in ways that meet objectives.

- *Acknowledge students for working within the boundaries and meeting expectations.* One way to modify the behavior of students who are out of line is to acknowledge students who are working within the boundaries. "I like the way the students at Table 5 are sitting up straight and ready to be dismissed" affirms positive behavior and gently reminds those who need to be more attentive.

- *Focus on behavior, not on character.* By establishing general rules for classroom conduct and giving clear instructions for a particular lesson, you enable yourself to assess a student's behavior instead of his or her character or personality. Rather than sending the message "You are a bad person because you are talking out in class," you can send the message "You have broken an agreement and need to change your behavior." This message might be sent by simply asking, "Were you being considerate of others when you talked out in class?"

- *Intervene in the least confrontive way.* Students do not like to be reprimanded or embarrassed. Do not make a big deal over little things. (Save your energy for the big things.) Often you can modify a student's behavior through your body language. Making eye contact, putting your finger to your lips, or moving within close proximity of a student can be enough to curb disruptive behavior. If you need to isolate a child from the rest of the group, do it quietly. Avoid confronting a student in front of the class. A private talk out in the hall or at lunch may be more effective than demeaning a student in the midst of his or her peers.

- *Suggest positive behaviors to replace negative ones.* Students who are behaving in ways that are not likely to fulfill objectives—playing with supplies, passing notes, staring into space—may need to hear more than "Stop that!" Redirect inattentive behavior by telling students what positive actions they should be taking instead.

- *Create a system to deal with infractions.* Asking a student who is talking out in class, "Are you being considerate of others?" may be an effective disciplinary measure. It probably won't work to stop a fist fight. Sometimes teachers need to go beyond reminding students about classroom rules. You will need to set up consequences to deal with disruptive behaviors. Simple systems tend to work better than elaborate ones. It is possible to spend so much time at the board recording names and checks and minuses of "bad" students that you significantly decrease your teaching time with "good" ones. You will need to decide what "bad" behavior looks like. Art teachers may view students who talk with their tablemates about what they are making and get up to sharpen their pencils as acting appropriately. Classroom teachers, in contrast, may view these behaviors as disruptive. Questions to ask yourself as you decide whether a student is violating boundaries or simply exhibiting healthy exuberance are these:

  1. Is this student preventing me from teaching effectively?

  2. Is this student preventing other students from optimal learning?

  3. Is this student doing something potentially hazardous to self, others, or the general classroom environment?

  If your answer is yes to any of the previous questions, you must take action. This might be (1) conferring privately with the student, (2) separating the student from others in the room, (3) removing the student from the classroom, or (4) calling a parent. Because disruptions will occur in various degrees, you will need to design consequences to match a range of infractions. Whatever you decide to do, make sure you are in compliance with school policy.

- *Enforce your discipline system consistently and fairly.* Set consequences that are realistic and doable. Do not make idle threats. Follow through with actions you have established as part of your system. Do not bend the rules for "good" students, while treating the more "challenging" ones more harshly.

- *Encourage students to monitor their own behaviors.* An art room is a small community in which students interact. Like any community, its healthy functioning depends on the well-being of its members. Classroom rules and monitor systems in which everyone has a role can be used for more than simply maintaining the physical environment. When students are given responsibilities for the functioning of a space, they are more likely to see the space as theirs. As they develop a sense of ownership, they act in responsible ways and may influence their peers to do the same.

- *Keep your perspective as you view the big picture.* Most people enter the teaching profession because they like to interact with learners. They assume that children are intrinsically good, open to learning, and teachable. Certainly this view is a much better starting place than assuming children are basically wild, unruly, and in need of "training." We could spend years reading books and taking courses on how to modify negative behaviors. Sometimes in our classrooms we focus an inordinate amount of energy on a few who are missing the mark, while ignoring the majority that is doing exactly as we had planned. Remember to praise students, tell them when they are on track, and spend more time acknowledging the positive than reprimanding the negative. For your own emotional health, as well as for the sake of your students, every once in a while you might simply stand back and observe what is going *right.*

MOTIVATIONAL STRATEGIES

A large part of creating a healthy emotional environment and managing behavior is dependent on the ability to motivate. *Motivate* can be defined as instilling the desire to learn. This is an important definition to keep in mind as we examine motivational strategies. Teachers use a number of techniques to motivate students. They give positive reinforcement to promote appropriate behaviors and use negative reinforcement to extinguish undesirable ones. Positive reinforcements may be in the form of "star charts" on which stars are placed for good behavior, point systems, candy, and pizza parties. Negative reinforcements may be in the form of checkmarks in grade books, missed recesses, and trips to the principal's office. Consider these kinds of reinforcers. Do these strategies instill the desire to learn? They may motivate actions focused on winning a prize or avoiding punishment—extrinsic rewards, delivered from the outside. They do not for the most part instill the desire to learn because students view the learning in and of itself as intrinsically valuable.

A considerable amount of research has been done on motivational strategies and extrinsic reward systems. An overemphasis on extrinsic rewards implies an educational model that views children as objects to be manipulated rather than as learners to be engaged. Evidence suggests that the more people are extrinsically rewarded for doing something, the less likely they are to continue doing it. They cease to view their behavior as intrinsically worthwhile and instead attribute it to being rewarded. A teacher can actually erode a student's intrinsic motivation by acknowledging accomplishments in ways that are viewed as superficial or meaningless. We should not train students to work for gold stars and candy bars or to avoid behaviors for fear of checkmarks. Many teachers at all grade levels, in an attempt to send messages about the intrinsic worth of individuals and the value of art education, adamantly refuse to dangle goodies in front of students. They are able to maintain excellent classroom control because they do instill the desire to learn. Although strategies for promoting intrinsic motivation vary, some general guidelines are helpful:

- *Know your students.* Art teachers do not simply teach the subject of art. They teach the subject of art *to learners.* To intrinsically motivate your students, you must know what is motivating to them. Make a point of getting to know who they are, where their interests lie, what is happening in their subculture. Relate art to their world as you lead them to see connections between the two.

- *Plan for and encourage authentic expression.* Construct units of study carefully to lead students beyond mere skill development, beyond exercises in which they learn how to create the illusion of depth or provide balance within a composition. Certainly we need to teach these skills because this is how we increase abilities to "speak" visually. Once we have taught the language, however, what are we encouraging students to say? Are we asking them to simply mimic someone in the outside world who sounds good (or paints well), or are we asking them to use their newly developed skills to make statements of their own? What better way to promote motivation that is intrinsic (coming from within) than to encourage students to create expressions that come from within?

- *Provide opportunities for students to share what they communicate through their art.* In addition to motivating students through open-ended assignments that engage the mind and heart, teachers motivate by providing opportunities to share thoughts and emotions expressed in art products. In every unit of study you should plan enough time for a closure in which students share their works and the meanings behind them. This sharing goes beyond judging products on specified criteria to assess quality. It is about connecting with others. In these discussions students learn that their art, what they say through their art, and they themselves have intrinsic value.

- *Be sensitive to feedback.* If we view motivated behavior as "turned on," we may view its opposite as "turned off" or bored. Be sensitive to feedback from your students. If they are participating eagerly, they are probably motivated. If they are fidgeting, talking with one another, passing notes, or simply staring blankly into space, they may be bored. Beginning teachers often make the mistake of thinking they have to convey everything they know about a subject, or present an entire overview of a unit before starting the first activity, or show as many examples as possible to make a point clear. Often less is more. Your students will let you know this as they exhibit a variety of unmotivated behaviors. Rather than slapping them with an extrinsic negative reinforcer (a missed recess), change your own behavior. Stop what you are doing that is turning them off and find a way to turn them back on, to re-instill the desire to learn. Your own change of behavior might be

1. Concluding the introductory lecture and beginning the studio activity

2. Involving students in active participation through a dialogue

3. Changing your position or voice quality

4. *Showing* what you want students to do as well as *telling* them

Good teachers take cues from their students. They instill intrinsic motivation through their teaching, rather than controlling through a reward and punishment system.

- *Set high but attainable standards and expectations.* Students are sensitive enough to know how you perceive them. Those who are viewed as high performers tend to exhibit behaviors leading to high-quality performances. Students who are viewed as dull, ill behaved, and "bad" tend to live up to that perception. Developing intrinsic motivation has to do with instilling feelings of self-worth. Motivate your students to do their best by clearly communicating what you are asking of them and by expecting that they will deliver it at a high level of quality.

- *Infect your students with your own motivation.* One of the most powerful ways to motivate others is to be a motivated person. Share your enthusiasm for making art, for viewing art, and for encountering beauty in the environment. Let your students experience you as turned on to them, to teaching, to learning, and to having art in your life.

- *Build specific motivations into lessons.* In addition to using general motivational strategies, you will design specific motivations for various kinds of art experiences. Each time you present a new activity in a unit of study, you will introduce it through a motivation. In reviewing the unit "The Abstraction of Georgia O'Keeffe," notice the motivations used within the sequence of lessons:

Lesson 1. The "Sammy the Snail" demonstration and the grab bag motivated students to explore the contour drawing process.

Lesson 2. The teacher's interaction with students, as she visually translated their ideas for abstracting an object on the chalkboard, motivated creative problem-solving behavior.

Lesson 3. The presentation of O'Keeffe's work and the experimentation with the media itself were motivational.

Lesson 4. The criteria established for the final assignment were designed to motivate thinking and self-expression.

Lesson 5. The teacher's sharing of her interpretations of the assignment was intended as a motivation. The class discussion at the end motivated students to share ideas, intentions, and artwork.

Instilling the desire to learn is not easy. It can involve intrinsic motivation, extrinsic motivation, positive reinforcers, negative reinforcers, pressure you apply to students to modify their behaviors, ways you change your own teaching to heighten involvement, general guidelines, and specific strategies. *How* you teach will influence motivation. *What* you teach will also influence willingness to participate. Students will not be motivated by content and assignments to which they cannot relate. As you prepare yourself to move into the classroom, think not only about how you want to be, but what you want to present. What kind of activity might you design as you follow the first guideline for intrinsic motivation (know your students)?

▼
GETTING TO KNOW YOUR STUDENTS

The most effective way to motivate is through activities that are perceived as valuable. To lead students through intrinsically valuable experiences, a teacher must be connected to the degree that she knows what students view as worthwhile. Moving from the theoretical arena of book learning and written plans into the classroom, you may encounter hundreds of students, letting you know in their own ways what is important to them. This initial introduction is a significant event. It marks the point at which you start to build the connection that will enable you to know your students. It is the beginning of a dialogue between you and them. Sometimes you will take the lead and encourage them to follow. At other times, you will provide opportunities for them to lead you down the pathways of their interests, values, and experiences.

As you enter a teaching situation on the first day of a school year, you may want to orchestrate an experience that allows students optimal opportunity to let you know who they are. You will need to think about what kinds of art activities promote what kinds of behaviors. If you begin with a closed-ended activity, you will learn how well students follow directions and demonstrate a skill. If your students start with a laissez-faire activity, they may reveal their ability to explore media and processes. Neither of these activities allows students to interpret ideas. Open-ended experiences have the greatest potential to promote sharing between you and your students. They are based on a conversation you initiate by posing a problem defined through broad criteria. Students respond by interpreting the criteria in individual solutions. In presenting their answers, they are taking their first steps in revealing themselves, in allowing you to know who they are.

In addition to selecting the most appropriate type of activity to encourage students to share about themselves, you will need to consider another issue. It concerns how to implement this idea: Art is a visual language that connects the inside to the outside and the outside to the inside. Should you begin the conversation by presenting the outside (a cultural exemplar) and asking students to respond to a theme or idea you have illustrated through someone else's work? Should you begin with the inside (the students) and then connect what they have done or said to others? As you plan for any activity, lesson, or unit, ask yourself: "Why am I doing this?" Your answer will guide you in selecting the optimal kind of experience to meet your goal. If your goal is to provide an opportunity for students to share who they are, perhaps the place to start is with them.

What might you present on the first day of school to students you had never met? Rather than starting with a long unit of study, you might begin with a short activity in which students have opportunities to reveal their individual personalities. A standard assignment for the first day of school is the design of a name tag, personal folder, or portfolio for artwork. Criteria may incorporate the use of lettering, design, images, or symbols. As a teacher observes students in the creation and sharing of these products, he can learn a great deal about a class. Because of their self-revealing nature, these expressions serve in the broadest sense as self-portraits. A number of assignments can encourage students to create "self-portraits." The activity presented in the box illustrates how to use the process of guided visualization to motivate self-expression. (Guided visualization involves leading students on an imaginary journey in which they have adventures and see images in their minds' eyes.)

Procedure to Introduce a Guided Visualization: A Trip into Space

1. The teacher turns off the lights and asks students to sit in a relaxed position with their eyes closed.

2. She tells this story: "It's several hundred years in the future. The human-made environment is in shambles and the natural world has become increasingly polluted. People have given up on conservation of the planet and have turned their attentions to colonization of space.

   "You are sitting in a classroom with others like you—the most creative minds in the arts and sciences. Someone looks out the window and says, 'Let's get out of here. Let's go into space—start over on a new planet.' The others agree and with proper arrangements you find yourself in a space craft speeding toward some unknown destination.

   "Everyone was so excited to leave Earth that no one bothered to take the next step—investigating habitable environments. Although you have no idea where you are going, you have unshakable faith that you will be guided to the perfect planet. And suddenly it appears—a beautiful orb surrounded by iridescent clouds of pink, lavender, and turquoise. In unison, everyone cries, 'That's it.'

   "You land—and just in time, because you are out of fuel. As you jump onto the soil, you scream in horror. Those beautiful iridescent clouds were a facade, a sham, a camouflage for the reality beneath—a world much like Earth, but even more polluted and ugly.

   "As you peer through the dense atmosphere, you notice some creatures coming toward you. Are they biological lifeforms? Robots? Who knows? They look like humans but act like machines. They are dressed in identical gray uniforms. They communicate in clipped, monotone, unintelligible sounds and move in a predictable, mechanical way.

   "As you stand wondering what to do, someone says, 'We need to discuss this.' Back inside your craft each person begins to comment:

   "'We're out of fuel. We can't go back. We have to stay here.'

   "'These inhabitants are all like robots and we can't communicate with them.'

   "'Maybe we can communicate with them. Maybe we can tell them about ourselves—without words—through visual symbols.'

   "'What should we tell them?'

   "'Let's tell them that we're different from them. They are clones of someone or something. We are individuals, different from one another, unique. How can we convey this idea?'

   "'We could start by making signs or visual displays representing ourselves and what is unique about each one of us.'

   "'Great idea. What should we put on them?'

"'I'll tell you,' volunteers someone. 'Close your eyes, listen to me, and envision images in your mind. Picture your name printed or written in a way that reflects you. It could be printed in straight, bold letters or written in soft, flowing cursive lines, or any other way that suits you. Imagine colors, lines, shapes, and textures that reflect your tastes.'

"'What designs or patterns do you envision? Can you see symbols or objects that tell about your life, experiences, values?'

"'Who are you and how can you convey your uniqueness to these creatures? Take a moment to let the images of your name, designs, and objects float through your mind's eye, before opening your eyes on the count of three. One, two, three.'"

3. The teacher turns the lights on and gives the assignment: "Design a "name plaque" to introduce yourself to the inhabitants of this planet. It can be two-dimensional, three-dimensional, or a combination of both. Include your name and any other designs, symbols, or objects that represent you, your life experiences, values, and personality."

4. With only these instructions, students begin by generating ideas on scrap paper. They then work with an assortment of materials provided by the teacher to fulfill the assignment.

5. In the final session students introduce themselves through their name plaques, discussing their designs as symbolic representations of themselves.

The purpose of this activity is to provide an opportunity to watch students in action as they behave in various ways to interpret the story, use materials, solve problems, and express themselves. Through careful observation a teacher may discover how and to what degree students demonstrate the following:

- Creative ability
- Skill in craftsmanship
- A tendency toward haptic expression (more three-dimensional, tactile, and emotional)
- A tendency toward visual expression (more two-dimensional and representational)
- A focus on the story
- A focus on the self
- Time and effort spent on the assignment
- Visual communication skills
- Verbal communication skills
- Involvement in life–interests, values, experiences

How you introduce yourself to your students and provide opportunities for them to teach you about themselves is, of course, up to you. This activity, as it is presented, may work for you and your students. Some students, however, may need more guidance than the minimal direction suggested here. The point is to encourage students to be as self-directive as possible so that they may reveal themselves to you. You need to design safe ways for your students to lead you, as they participate in open-ended, self-expressive experiences. The more clearly you see the relationship between your own teaching and your students' behaviors, the more effectively you will be able to both lead and follow. The stronger you become as a leader, the better you will be at instilling intrinsic motivation. The greater the motivation, the smoother the classroom management. The smoother the classroom management, the better all can attend to teaching/learning processes. It's all really quite simple!

S U M M A R Y

Moving beyond the planning stage into the classroom introduces us to the importance of the physical environment. Teachers who have their own spaces often spend a considerable amount of time and energy personalizing them. As teachers turn a space into an environment conducive to teaching and learning art, they consider aesthetic as well as functional factors. Both are important for optimal physical well-being of students and teachers.

Supporting emotional growth in a learning environment is also a primary concern of teachers. Classroom management techniques address how to establish general rules for classroom decorum, set boundaries for behavior, and deal with infractions. A large part of managing behavior involves the ability to keep students motivated. Extrinsic motivations (rewards and punishments) are used by many teachers and may work up to a point. When overused, however, they can cease to be effective because students place emphasis on the winning of a prize, rather than on expressing themselves and learning for its own sake. Intrinsic motivations (those coming from within each individual learner) are far more effective and much preferred. To intrinsically motivate students, a teacher must know what is motivating to them. She must have sufficiently connected to her students to know how they will respond to an activity. One of the most effective ways to get to know a population of students is through the use of open-ended assignments. These might be thought of as conversations initiated by the teacher through the presentation of general criteria and responded to by the students through their individual answers. Open-ended problems such as "A Trip Into Space" can be especially well suited to initiate a conversation, promote sharing among students, and facilitate a teacher's understanding of her students at the beginning of a school year.

A. DEVELOPING BEHAVIORAL GUIDELINES

Directions

In the space below draw an idea for a poster on which you have listed guidelines for positive behaviors. Integrate symbols or visual images along with written text.

B. GETTING TO KNOW YOUR STUDENTS

Directions

Generate four "ice-breaking" activities you might use on the first day of school that will provide opportunities for you to know your students, your students to know you, and your students to know each other.

1.

2.

3.

4.

TEACHING
THE LANGUAGE
OF VISION

6

Having considered how to create an environment for art learning and begin conversing with students, we may next consider what messages we want to convey. These messages might be about the nature of visual expression. What does it look like? How do we use it? How can we learn to "speak visually," manifesting our ideas and feelings in concrete form? This chapter addresses these questions, exploring the language of vision and strategies to teach it in grades K–12. Sections include (1) defining the language of vision, (2) approaches to teaching the language, (3) sample activities to develop visual language skills, and (4) presenting visual concepts visually.

▼
DEFINING THE LANGUAGE
OF VISION

Perhaps the easiest way to understand visual language is to relate it to verbal language. As a child learns to speak, he or she begins by uttering sounds, which later become words. These words have meaning—they refer to people, things, places, directions, actions, qualities, emotions. They also have labels—*pronouns, proper nouns, common nouns, prepositions, verbs, adjectives* and *adverbs, expletives.* Children learn to use words to communicate ideas long before they are able to categorize them into parts of speech. They know that *bounce* describes the action of a ball hitting and leaving the ground without knowing that the word is a verb. Given opportunities, children develop visual language in a similar manner. They begin with mark making—scribbling—which can be likened to uttering sounds. These marks become the images through which children "speak." Their visual language has its own equivalent to the parts of speech: the elements of art—color, shape, line, and texture. Children use these naturally, without having knowledge of labels, definitions, or concepts. Just as they may shout simply to hear their own voices or run to experience the feeling of movement, they begin to use the language of vision solely for the experience of making and observing a line or a blob of color or a shape.

This is just the beginning. In a short time children learn to string words together to create phrases. These phrases become sentences, which are ordered in written language into paragraphs. Eventually students can be led to sequence paragraphs into compositions. In learning the language of vision, children parallel this progression. They use colors, shapes, lines, and textures to express themselves. As their cognitive skills develop along with their manipulative and expressive skills, they learn to identify and define these elements for the purpose of using them in more intentional ways. They may learn, for example, that yellow and red are warm colors, while they are experimenting with color mixing to make "color phrases." They then may combine "visual phrases" into compositions. Just as students create written compositions from arrangements of parts of speech, they create visual compositions from arrangements of art elements. These arrangements or relationships are called *principles of design.*

If we believe that visual expression can have intrinsic value to every individual and that visual language, like verbal language, can be taught, we must address the teaching of art as seriously as we address the teaching of English. We must start in kindergarten to provide opportunities for students to express visually and continue from there—week after week, semester after semester, year after year. We may begin by encouraging a 5-year-old to explore color, as she paints at an easel equipped with large paper, half-inch brushes, and margarine tubs of tempera. As we follow this child through twelve years of education, we might find her as a high school senior, still exploring color, as she stands at an easel, now equipped with canvas and oils, painting an expressionistic self-portrait. Few art educators would dispute the need to address art elements and design principles in the teaching of visual language. Considerable controversy exists, however, over how to present our language and build skills in its usage.

▼
APPROACHES TO TEACHING THE LANGUAGE
▬

As artists and students of art education, you are familiar with art elements and design principles. Did you ever wonder who identified these or where they originated? Arthur Wesley Dow created a design theory based on how we perceive the visual world. In his effort to comprehend what made a successful work of art, he cited composition, created through elements and principles of design. In 1899 he identified line, value, and color as art elements, and opposition, transition, dominance, subordination, repetition, and symmetry as design principles. His influence might best be appreciated by viewing the work of one of his students—Georgia O'Keeffe. In college O'Keeffe encountered Dow, who taught her to look beyond her subject matter—flowers, shells, bones, hills, buildings—to their visual components—organic form, positive and negative shape, light and dark, color. When she said, ". . . try to paint your world as though you were the first man looking at it . . . ," she was talking about seeing qualities inherent in the form of objects. When we describe objects in terms of color and shape, repetition and symmetry, we are discussing formal qualities. For years the study of formal qualities—elements and principles of art—has been the major component of courses on two- and three-dimensional design at the college level. It has not been so evident in K–12 art education. This is because child- and subject-centered art educators have approached the teaching of visual language from different perspectives.

●
A CHILD-CENTERED PERSPECTIVE
▬

All art educators may define what they do as teaching art to students. Those who come from a child-centered stance look to the nature of the learner to determine what and how to teach. They have provided guidelines for teaching visual language developmentally. The following ideas can guide you in designing age-appropriate activities to promote visual language skills.

- Human beings learn most effectively through participation. To motivate students to learn visual language, actively involve them in expressing visually. The essence of art education, especially for those who are just beginning to find their "visual voices," lies in process-oriented studio experiences.

- When students first begin to speak visually, their "voices" have not yet fully developed. They are in the process of gaining large and small motor skills. They will need to be shown various ways to hold drawing instruments, to dip a brush into paint, and then wash it out in water (banging it on top of the can is not an option), which fingers to put into the holes of scissors, and how to place paper at the back of scissors for most effective cutting. What we do primarily in the early years is to develop manipulative skills through the use of art materials.

- Students gain manipulative skills gradually. In teaching the language of vision, consider not only what medium or process will enhance understanding of color, shape, line, and texture, but what will be most appropriate to support students' natural development. Suggestions to build skills in using art elements at the primary level follow:

  Color. To develop skills in using color, select media and activities for maximum exploration of color—paints and painting. Finger paint (which can be made by adding liquid starch to tempera) is an effective medium to experience color and color mixing. Provide large surfaces on which to paint with big brushes. You might, for example, draw around students lying on banner paper and have them create life-sized self-portraits, painting in the details. Or you might group students in cooperative learning experiences to paint murals on sheets of banner paper. Working with students at this age, think "large," "spontaneous," "paint," "color." (Addressing these same students six years later in middle school, you might think "small," "tight," "well-planned," "colored pencils" to support their desire for control.)

  Shape. To develop awareness of and skill in using shape or form, provide opportunities to create with shapes. Kindergartners can combine premade shapes and forms into collages and assemblages. They can also cut their own shapes. Shapes intended to be circles, squares, and triangles may look like amorphous blobs to you; do not be deterred. This experience may be the students' first attempts at using scissors. Remember that you are teaching processes intended to develop manipulative and expressive skills. The minute you begin to think "product," you may be tempted to create "bats." (Avoid saying to yourself, "The students couldn't possibly cut these hearts out. I'll just provide the precut pieces for them to glue together in their valentines.")

  Line. To develop skill in the use of line, provide media with which to represent objects in linear form. Two-dimensional materials may include crayons, markers, oil pastels, and print-making instruments, such as cardboard edges and strings. Three-dimensional materials may be twigs, drinking straws, dowel rods, yarn, or any other object capable of being used as a line.

  Texture. To develop understanding of texture, have students feel textures, describe textures, and use textured materials in their artwork. The sequence of experiences exploring texture in the process-oriented teaching model in Chapter 2 includes the following activities: (1) making rubbings of textured materials, (2) creating a textured collage, and (3) impressing forms into premade clay tiles to make textures. This example will remind you that several process-oriented activities related to any art element (or design principle) can be sequenced into a unit of study.

- Children learn visual language by working with age-appropriate materials and processes. However, even if these support their developmental stages, the path to understanding art elements is not direct. Primary-level students do not think in terms of art elements. They think in terms of *objects.* If you ask first graders to describe images in their landscape paintings, they might identify houses, trees, and ground. They are as likely to say, "I painted squares, rectangles, and horizontal lines" as they are to tell you, "I speak in nouns and verbs." How then do we enhance their understanding of visual form? We begin where they are—at the concrete level. We provide subject matter to which they can relate—family, home, animals, places, vacations, holidays, play time, toys, pets, seasons—objects and ideas they may interpret in self-expressive ways. Then we lead them to a level that is more abstract: an understanding that a number of objects in their world—the sun, a ball, Christmas tree ornaments, polka dots—are all a particular shape called a *circle.* We use their own experiences in art making and their own artistic expressions, as well as works of master artists, the natural environment, and everyday objects as vehicles to build an understanding of visual qualities. As students learn to describe objects in terms of visual characteristics, they can be led to more intentional use of formal qualities.

- At the same time children are painting images of trees and learning that trunks might be rectangles, or rough textures, or mixtures of light and dark colors, they are arranging their images on surfaces. They may begin by painting a ground line on which they place a row of trees. These arrangements are their first compositions, created from placing art elements (lines, shapes, and colors that represent trees) into relationships called *design principles.* It is not possible to work with art elements separately from principles of design. As soon as more than one line, shape, or color is placed on a page, a relationship is formed. Students use design principles along with art elements from the very beginning in developing visual language. As they make rows of trees, they can be introduced to the principle of repetition. Understanding that repetition means "over and over again," they can be taught that "pattern is a design created from repeating shapes."

For many years, child-centered art educators approached the teaching of visual language primarily through experiential activities focused on exploration of materials and processes. Students were allowed to develop language abilities at their own rates. For the most part, visual language defined by art elements and design principles was addressed indirectly. In some cases art educators led students to an understanding of the form of the language through studio experiences. In other instances, however, teachers did not go beyond simply encouraging visual expression through manipulation of materials. Students did not advance to the point at which they consciously used elements and principles, and art education was attacked as lacking substance.

This criticism led to a more academic approach to teaching art, reflecting the back-to-the-basics movement in general education in the 1960s. At this time the focus of art education began to shift from the art learner to the subject of art. Curriculum guides provided evidence that art had substance in the form of specific content and concepts. Just as child-centered art educators contributed to our understanding of the art learner and age-appropriate experiences, subject-centered art educators provided insight about the content of art and how to present it conceptually.

A SUBJECT-CENTERED PERSPECTIVE

The subject-centered approach that began in the 1960s developed slowly over a twenty-year period. In the mid 1980s it became much more visible, in the form of DBAE. Art concepts defining ideas in the domains of art criticism, aesthetics, art history, and art production became the focus of many curriculum guides. Figure 6.1 illustrates common concepts about art elements. Italicized words indicate vocabulary that might be new to students.

Because discipline-based approaches expanded aspects of art education dealing with the understanding and appreciation of art objects, teaching about the form of visual language—art elements and design principles—became especially important. Students were introduced to vocabulary, definitions, and concepts with which to demonstrate their knowledge of visual design.

Art elements can be defined as the basic visual components of all natural and human-made objects. They are things—squares, lines, surfaces. Most guides and textbooks identify shape, color, line, and texture as art elements. Some also include form, space, and value. Resources that do not present these last three as separate elements categorize form as the three-dimensional aspect of shape, space as the negative aspect of shape, and value as a property of color dealing with lightness and darkness.

Design principles and concepts pertaining to them are also found in many curriculum guides. They are generally defined as relationships created by art elements working together in a composition. The key word is *relationships.* They are not things and cannot be identified by pointing to a particular object and labeling it as "an orange square." To understand design principles, one must focus on an entire composition to see the relationships among the parts. Different guides and textbooks often present relationships having the same or similar meanings expressed through a variety of terms. Table 6.1 and Figure 6.2 indicate commonly used terminology and concepts relating to design principles.

TABLE 6.1
Design Principles

1. CONTRAST **OPPOSITION** **VARIETY**	These terms refer to *differences* in a composition. They may imply *abrupt changes* from white to black, small to large, or smooth to rough, for example.
2. TRANSITION **GRADATION**	These terms refer to *gradual changes* in a composition—from white to gray to black or from small to medium to large, for example.
3. SYMMETRY **BALANCE** **PROPORTION**	These terms refer to *distribution of visual weight* in areas of a composition.
4. RHYTHM **MOVEMENT** **REPETITION** **PATTERN**	These terms refer to *repeated elements* that move the eye through a composition.
5. EMPHASIS **DOMINANCE** **CENTER OF INTEREST** **FOCAL POINT**	These terms refer to *importance* of one object or area in a composition over other objects or areas that are subordinate to it.
6. HARMONY **UNITY**	These terms refer to *cohesiveness* in a composition.

FIGURE 6.1
Sample Concepts Pertaining to Art Elements

Shape, Space, Form	· A shape is an area enclosed by a line.

· A shape is an area enclosed by a line.
· All natural and human-made objects are made of shapes.
· *Basic shapes* include the ▢, △, ○, and ▭.
· *Geometric shapes* are regular. They can be constructed through the use of mathematical formulas.
· *Organic, amorphous,* and *irregular* are words used to describe shapes that are not derived from mathematical formulas.
· Organic shapes are found in nature.
· Shapes can be different colors, sizes, and textures.
· Shapes can be combined to create other shapes.
· *Positive shapes* are shapes of solid objects.
· *Negative shapes* are shapes of the spaces within, between, and around solid objects.
· A hole is a negative shape.
· Space can create the illusion of depth on a two-dimensional surface.
· Space can be created through line (as in linear perspective).
· Space can be created through color variation in hue, intensity, and value (as in atmospheric or aerial perspective).
· A three-dimensional shape is called a *form*.
· Form can be created by combining shapes.
· Form is used to achieve three dimensionality in sculpture.
· Form corresponds to the dimension of depth in three-dimensional objects.
· Form can be illustrated on a two-dimensional surface through the use of line, color, value, and texture.

Color

· Color is the absorption and reflection of light on a surface.
· White is the reflection of all colors.
· Black is the absorption of all colors.
· The spectrum contains the primary colors (red, yellow, and blue); secondary colors (orange, green, and violet); and tertiary colors (red-orange, yellow-orange, yellow-green, blue-green, blue-violet, and red-violet).
· Colors and their relationships within the spectrum can be represented on the color wheel.
· *Warm colors* are variations of red, orange, and yellow.
· *Cool colors* are variations of green, blue, and violet.
· *Properties of color* are ways in which color varies: *hue, value,* and *intensity.*
· *Hue* is the name of a color—red-orange, orange.
· *Analogous* means related. Analogous colors are next to each other on the color wheel and have one color in common. (Blue-violet, blue, blue-green, and green are analogous because they all contain blue.) *Analogous color schemes* contain *variations of related hues.*
· *Value* is the lightness or darkness of a color—pink, red, maroon.
· *Tint* is a light value of a color—pink is red plus white.
· *Shade* is a dark value of a color—maroon is red plus black.
· *Tone* is a gray value achieved by mixing a color with black and white.
· *Monochrome* means one color. A *monochromatic color scheme* contains *light and dark value variations of one color.*
· *Intensity* is the brightness or dullness of a color.
· All colors on the color wheel are of maximum intensity. Nothing can be added to them to make them any brighter, but colors can be made to appear brighter by placing them next to dull colors.
· A dull color is one that has been mixed with the color opposite it on the color wheel.
· Gray can be made by mixing opposite colors (red-green, orange-blue, or yellow-violet).
· *Complementary* means opposite. A complementary color scheme is one in which two colors opposite one another on the color wheel have been used in combination (red-green, orange-blue, yellow-violet) to create variation in *intensity.*

Line

· All natural and human-made objects can be defined by lines.
· *Contour lines* define edges of objects.
· Lines have specific properties: length, width, direction, texture.
· Lines can be continuous, broken, or implied.
· Lines can be used to convey textural qualities.
· Lines can be used to create variations in value.
· Lines can convey dimensionality.
· Lines have expressive qualities.
· Lines provide direction in a work of art.
· Lines can imply movement in a work of art.

Texture

· *Texture* means surface quality.
· All natural and human-made objects have texture.
· We perceive *real* or *actual textures* through our sense of *touch.* They are *tactile:* We *feel* surfaces that are bumpy, scratchy, soft, slimy.
· We perceive *implied* or *simulated textures* through our sense of *sight.* They are *visual:* We *see* surfaces that *look* bumpy, scratchy, soft, slimy.
· Textures have expressive qualities.
· Texture can be conveyed through use of line, color, and shape.

FIGURE 6.2
Sample Concepts Pertaining to Design Principles

Contrast	· *Contrast* means differences in a composition.
	· Any art element used in opposition can provide contrast.
	  1. Color: red-green
	  2. Shape: geometric-organic
	  3. Line: vertical-horizontal
	  4. Texture: rough-smooth
	· Contrast can create variety in artwork.
	· Contrast can create movement in a composition.
	· Contrast can create emphasis in an artwork.
	· Contrast varies in works of art depending upon the degree of differences within compositions. (Some works have high contrast; some have low contrast.)

Balance	· *Balance* means visual weight in a composition. · Balance can be achieved through the use of color, line, shape, or texture. · Balance can be achieved through a combination of art elements. (A large gray square can balance a small red dot.) · *Symmetrical balance* is equal and the same on each side, forming a mirror image. (A tree on one side of a composition is repeated on the other side.) · *Asymmetrical balance* is equal and different on each side. (A large figure on one side of a composition may be balanced by two small figures on the other side.) · *Radial balance* radiates from a central point (rays from the sun, petals from a daisy's center, spokes from the hub of a wheel). · Balance exists in natural and human-made objects. · Many works of art deal with balance. · Some artworks are designed to be purposefully out of balance to create tension.

Emphasis	· *Emphasis* means the importance of one part in comparison to other parts in a composition.
	· Emphasis can exist in a composition as an area or as a specific object.
	· Emphasis can be achieved through:
	  1. Size relationships
	  2. Contrasting elements
	  3. Position in a composition
	  4. Movement directed toward a focal point
	· Any art element or combination of art elements can provide emphasis.
	· Emphasis attracts attention to a *dominant* area.
	· Areas that are not dominant are *subordinate* to the dominant area.
	· *Focal point* and *center of interest* are terms used to describe an area of emphasis.
	· Not all designs have emphasis. (A patterned wallpaper design may contain contrast, rhythm, and balance, but not emphasis.)

Figure 6.2 further defines and explores sample design principles through concepts related to each.

The concepts in Figures 6.1 and 6.2 contribute to the "body of knowledge" that has provided substance to K–12 art education. Although educators may not question the content itself, many have found fault with how it has been presented in subject-centered approaches. As DBAE gained strength, a number of teachers became more involved in addressing the response aspects of art education. Rather than teaching the language of vision through art making, they developed visual literacy primarily through study of art objects. Knowledge may have been demonstrated, not through students' art products, but in written form—on exercises, worksheets, reports, and tests. The push to demonstrate knowledge and to prove accountability in presenting substantial content has led in worst-case scenarios to teaching by requiring students to define lists of vocabulary on exams, "proving" their visual literacy.

Few would argue about the need to be accountable for developing visual literacy. The point is to illuminate the pitfalls when the pendulum swings too far in any one direction. Child-centered art educators can be only marginally effective in developing visual language if they do not go beyond exploration of media and processes. Subject-centered art education suffers when visual literacy is addressed primarily by talking or writing about characteristics of others'

FIGURE 6.2 *(continued)*

Rhythm	· *Rhythm* means movement or repetition of elements in a composition.
	· Rhythm can exist through repetition of one element or a combination of elements.
	· Rhythm directs the eye from one part of a composition to another.
	· Rhythm can create moods and emotions:
	  1. Horizontal rhythms may suggest relaxed, quiet states.
	  2. Vertical rhythms may suggest stability, formality, importance, alertness.
	  3. Diagonal rhythms may suggest movement, excitement, agitation.

Pattern	· *Patterns* are designs created by repeated motifs (repetition of dots, stripes, symbols, etc.). · Patterns can be *regular:* Motifs are *repeated in a predictable way.* · Patterns can be *random* or *irregular:* Motifs are *not repeated in a predictable way.* · Patterns can *alternate* (dot, square, dot, square). · Patterns exist in many natural objects: animals, plants, ground formations. · Patterns exist in many human-made objects: clothing, floor tiles, wallpaper, toys, artwork. · Artists use pattern to create design, embellish objects, and express ideas in works of art.

Transition	· *Transition* means gradual change in a composition.
	· Transitions can be achieved through changes in hue, value, intensity, shape, line, and texture.
	· Transition can be created through a series of images, such as the following:
	  1. Gradual change in direction
	  2. Gradual change in shape
	  3. Gradual change in size
	· Transitions connect parts of a composition.
	· Transitions can provide movement in a work of art.

Unity	· *Unity* pertains to *wholeness* or *oneness.* · Unity in art refers to ways in which the *parts work together to create a harmonious composition.* · Artists consciously consider the use of unity, creating purposefully harmonious or inharmonious compositions. · Unity may be achieved through repetition of art elements. · Unity may be achieved through use of design principles.

art objects. Focusing on the positive aspects of child- and subject-centered approaches, we can be guided in how to most effectively teach the language of vision. From a child-centered perspective, we may be directed to do the following:

- Look to the art learner for cues in designing developmentally appropriate activities.
- Present information actively, using strategies to encourage experiential learning.
- Use studio experiences as the primary vehicle for teaching the language.
- Lead students to embrace the language as "theirs" by using their own expressions to teach visual vocabulary.

From a subject-centered perspective, we may be directed to do the following:

- Teach art concepts.
- Proceed from the idea that the ability to create art is "taught," not "caught." (Adult intervention can move students beyond where they might be simply exploring art making on their own.)
- Support different learning modalities by providing opportunities to enhance visual literacy both as makers and as viewers of art.
- Enrich students' visual vocabulary by exposing them to outside artists.
- Relate the "outside" to the "inside" to help students internalize the use of the language in self-expressive ways.

SAMPLE ACTIVITIES TO DEVELOP VISUAL LANGUAGE SKILLS

Many educators today, recognizing the contributions of both child- and subject-centered approaches, have found a middle ground from which to present the language. Consider where you might feel most comfortable along the continuum from child– to subject-centered. How will you introduce art elements and design principles? What conceptual information will you present? How will you support learning through studio experiences? How will you lead students to learn by viewing and discussing art? The following box provides guidelines for teaching visual language, followed by sample K–12 activities you may use as models (Tables 6.2 and 6.3).

A Procedure for Developing Visual Language Skills

1. Identify a component of visual language you wish to present in a unit of study—either an art element or a design principle.

2. Decide what information to present about the art element or design principle. Write this in the form of a single concept.

3. Design an activity to present the concept in a concrete way, involving students in experiential learning. This may be thought of as "concretizing concepts." You may wish to begin with a *perceptual* experience (as modeled in the following samples), in which students respond as viewers, seeing or touching and discussing visual qualities of objects.

4. Provide a studio activity in which students explore the concept in their own work. This activity, intended to develop skill in the use of visual language, should be open-ended and process-oriented.

5. Present a cultural exemplar to illustrate the concept and provide a connection between the students and the outside world.

6. Be flexible in designing experiences. The order in which concepts, cultural exemplars, and activities are presented may vary from one experience to the next. There are no formulas for how to "concretize concepts."

7. Determine how to integrate the presentation of the concept and supporting activities into a unit of study. (You may design process-oriented units by combining several activities, or you may use the activities in Tables 6.2 and 6.3 as preliminary steps in preparing for product-oriented experiences.)

After reading through the sample activities on the following two pages, you may think to yourself, "Got it! I can do this." Yes, you can . . . and teaching visual language through "concretizing activities" can be more difficult than it appears on the surface. The story of Bill in the Birdwalk on page 123 illustrates this point. What went wrong with Bill's presentation?

First, Bill was doing a one-man show. Because he didn't ask for audience participation, the activity was not experiential. Second, he identified his concept as "color" and assumed he needed to be thorough in presenting the subject. Third, he thought if he could be impressive with one piece of information, he could be five times as impressive with five pieces of information. "Color" is not a concept, and many concepts presented in a single lesson may simply indicate lack of focus and cause confusion. Remember the advice given by Bill's teacher: *Count to one.* Introduce only one new piece of information at a time, adding bit by bit to students' previously gained skills and knowledge.

TABLE 6.2
Activities to "Concretize Concepts" About Art Elements

ART ELEMENT: TEXTURE
CONCEPT: THINGS IN NATURE HAVE DIFFERENT TEXTURES—SMOOTH, BUMPY, SCRATCHY, HARD, SOFT, ETC.
"CONCRETIZING" ACTIVITY INTENDED FOR USE IN GRADES K–2:

1. Take students outside to collect natural objects such as leaves, twigs, stones, pine cones, mud, grass, etc. (You might "plant" these objects in an area if they are not readily available on school grounds.) Have students share their findings—identifying objects, feeling objects, and describing surfaces (perceptual activity).
2. Explain that the words students are using to describe how their objects feel are words for *textures*. All these objects found outside in nature have textures—some are smooth, some are rough, etc.
3. Put students in groups to work together on the ground to design "creations" from their natural materials (studio activity).
4. Introduce Andy Goldsworthy, an artist who creates designs in natural settings from objects such as twigs, leaves, ice, and rocks. Show photographs of Goldsworthy's work, and ask students to identify natural materials, describe how materials might feel, and discuss how their work is similar to his (perceptual activity).

ART ELEMENT: SHAPE
CONCEPT: GEOMETRIC SHAPES ARE FOUND IN EVERYDAY OBJECTS AND IN WORKS OF ART.
"CONCRETIZING" ACTIVITY INTENDED FOR USE IN GRADES 3–5:

1. Have students look around the room and identify objects that have geometric shapes—tiles, clock, pencil sharpener, etc. (perceptual activity).
2. Show students examples of work by artists who composed with geometric shapes: Mondrian, Klee, Stella, Vasarely. Have them identify shapes in the artwork (perceptual activity).
3. Ask students to identify similarities between objects in the room and artwork. Present the concept (perceptual activity).
4. Have groups of three to four students select, paint, and combine large precut cardboard shapes to create large-scale wall designs (similar to Stella's early work).

ART ELEMENT: LINE
CONCEPT: LINE QUALITY CAN EXPRESS DIFFERENT FEELINGS IN LETTERING STYLES.
"CONCRETIZING" ACTIVITY INTENDED FOR USE IN GRADES 6–8:

1. Have students bring in words cut from magazines that have different lettering styles. Put the words on the bulletin board, and ask students to describe how specific line qualities express particular feelings. Have students compare the meanings and use of the words with visual qualities of the styles (perceptual activity).
2. Introduce the concept of how graphic designers use lettering styles to send messages psychologically, and discuss.
3. Have students generate a list of qualities about themselves. Then have them create a design by repeating their names over and over, using different lettering styles in each name to portray different qualities of their personalities (studio activity).

ART ELEMENT: COLOR
CONCEPT: THE ILLUSION OF SPACE CAN BE CONVEYED THROUGH INTENSITY OF COLOR.
"CONCRETIZING" ACTIVITY INTENDED FOR USE IN GRADES 9–12:

1. Have students look outside or view colored photographs of landscapes and describe what color changes they see as they focus farther and farther out into the distance: Objects in the foreground are brighter and more contrasting; objects in the background are duller and less contrasting (perceptual activity).
2. Introduce the concept. Show color studies by Joseph Albers to illustrate how color can be used to create the illusion of advancing or receding into space. Present the work of Robert Indiana to illustrate use of high-intensity opposite colors to create a pulsating color effect (perceptual activity).
3. Have students do a series of three color studies in which they use opposite colors to create intensities that advance, recede, and pulsate (studio activity).

TABLE 6.3
Activities to "Concretize Concepts" About Design Principles

DESIGN PRINCIPLE: BALANCE
CONCEPT: RADIAL BALANCE HAS LINES, SHAPES, OR COLORS THAT SHOOT OUT FROM A CENTRAL POINT.
"CONCRETIZING" ACTIVITY INTENDED FOR USE IN GRADES K–2:

---

1. Present images of objects that have radial balance—bicycle wheels, flowers, snowflakes, rose windows—and ask students to identify them (perceptual activity).
2. By pointing or gesturing, lead students to discover how these objects are alike. After students have discovered the similarity and stated the concept in their own words, introduce the term "radial balance." Ask students to supply more examples of objects with radial balance and illustrate them on the board (perceptual activity).
3. Have students explore radial balance by gluing precut construction paper shapes onto paper plates (studio activity).

DESIGN PRINCIPLE: RHYTHM
CONCEPT: RHYTHM EXISTS IN MUSIC AND IN ART.
"CONCRETIZING" ACTIVITY INTENDED FOR USE IN GRADES 3–5:

---

1. Play music that has a strong rhythm. Have students stand up and stamp their feet, move their bodies, or clap to the sound (perpetual activity).
2. Present the concept by explaining that students were moving to the rhythm of the music. Ask students if they might "draw" or paint rhythm while listening to music.
3. Place students into groups of three to four at tables with large sheets of banner paper and (a) colored markers, (b) colored chalk, and (c) tempera paint. Play three selections of music with different rhythms. Have students visually interpret each, using the progression of media suggested and then compare rhythms created with each medium (studio activity).
4. Introduce paintings by Kandinsky, explaining that he also painted to music and created visual rhythms. Ask students to suggest what kinds of music might accompany various paintings and why. Have them compare similarities between their works and Kandinsky's (perceptual activity).

DESIGN PRINCIPLE: TRANSITION
CONCEPT: TRANSITION IS A SLOW CHANGE FROM ONE FORM TO ANOTHER.
"CONCRETIZING" ACTIVITY INTENDED FOR USE IN GRADES 6–8:

---

1. Show a video of claymation (a form of animation done in modeling clay), such as the movie *Closed Mondays* and the California Raisins commercials. Ask students to describe how the images change (perceptual activity).
2. As students explain the process of something slowly transforming from one form into another, identify the process as transition. Explain that transition in claymation occurs through a gradual change in the *form* of three-dimensional objects. Show works of M. C. Escher to illustrate transition in shape.
3. Have students make a series of drawings showing a character or object making a transition from one shape to another. Then have them create a sequence of three-dimensional sketches in modeling clay, illustrating the same transition in form (studio activity).

DESIGN PRINCIPLE: EMPHASIS
CONCEPT: EMPHASIS CAN BE ACHIEVED THROUGH THE USE OF SIZE, POSITION, CONTRAST, AND/OR DIRECTION (ELEMENTS LEADING THE EYE TOWARD THE EMPHASIZED AREA).
"CONCRETIZING" ACTIVITY INTENDED FOR USE IN GRADES 9–12:

---

1. Present examples of still life paintings that contain obvious areas of emphases, and ask students to discuss how emphasis was achieved in each (perceptual activity).
2. Set up a still life of uniform objects spray-painted white, exemplifying lack of emphasis. Ask students to discuss ways the still life could be modified to create emphasized areas (perceptual activity).
3. Have students create paintings of the still life, modifying their interpretations to show emphasis in their compositions (studio activity).

A S BILL was beginning to demonstrate how effectively he could "concretize" concepts in his art education methods course, he walked up to the board and confidently drew a wavy line. Then he sectioned off the line and added numbers. He explained that these numbers indicated frequencies that could be translated into colors in a spectrum. Then he presented a prism and discussed how light is refracted. Then he brought out a color wheel and indicated primary, secondary, and tertiary colors. Next he demonstrated how to mix colors. As he was launching into a demonstration on mixing tints, tones, and shades, he finally looked at his audience. Seeing the glazed expressions, he stopped in midsentence and said, "I think I blew it."

The instructor smiled, nodded knowingly, and said, "Bill, let me tell you a story: My first year of teaching I shared a room with Mrs. Green. I walked into the room one day when Mrs. Green was explaining monochromatic color schemes as one color plus black and white. As she finished her explanation she saw John, the football team captain, lumber by her with his paint tray—on which he had carefully arranged red, orange, blue, green, purple, and black and white. Drawing herself up to her full 5-foot height and thrusting her index finger into his face, she bellowed, 'One color! CAN YOU COUNT TO ONE?'"

▼ PRESENTING VISUAL CONCEPTS VISUALLY

In addition to "counting to one," presenting concepts visually and actively involving students in viewing and responding to visual information are keys to effective teaching. This section presents strategies to present visual concepts visually.

- *Laminated images to teach composition.* One way to encourage class participation is through the use of board work. You might involve students in activities in which they arrange images on a chalkboard. Images can be shapes or representational objects cut from colored construction paper or magazines. You can laminate them and attach masking tape to the back (or magnetic tape if you have magnetized boards). Students can arrange the pieces to explore compositions. This teaching technique can be very effective because the pieces can be easily moved around, students can be used in the demonstration process, the imagery is clearly visible, and students are likely to pay attention to what their peers are doing at the board. Suppose, for example, you are presenting a landscape lesson on foreground, middle ground, and background. You might make plants and animals of various sizes, such as the ones in Figure 6.3a. One student might draw an area in which to place these objects, whereas another arranges them to illustrate the illusion of depth through size relationships.

- *Laminated shapes to teach design principles.* Just as images of objects (trees and animals) can be laminated and used for board work, examples of shapes, colors, lines, and textures can be used on the board to teach various concepts. The images in Figure 6.4 illustrate how random shapes can be arranged on a board to demonstrate the design principles rhythm, emphasis, and balance.

FIGURE 6.3
Objects to Be Arranged in a Space   ***Arrangement Within the Space***

(a) Individual objects to be placed into a landscape space on the chalkboard

(b) Objects arranged into a landscape space, illustrating placement to convey foreground, middle ground, and background

FIGURE 6.4
Use of Laminated Shapes to Illustrate Design

Random shapes

Arrangement of shapes to illustrate rhythm

Arrangement of shapes to illustrate emphasis

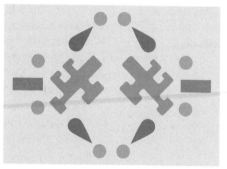

Arrangement of shapes to illustrate balance

- *Reproductions with acetate overlays.* Another activity that can be used to promote skills in seeing and designing compositions involves students in drawing on clear plastic sheets taped over reproductions. Suppose, for example, that you want your students to become aware of basic shapes in architecture. You could present a

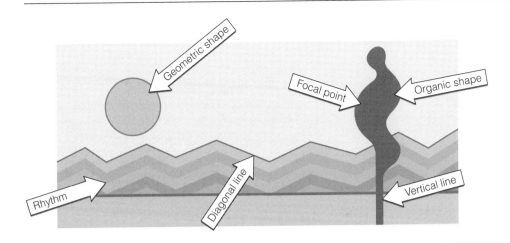

FIGURE 6.5
Using Vocabulary Arrows to Identify Formal Properties

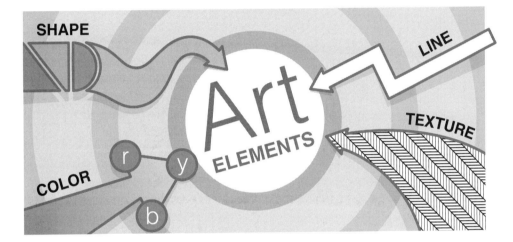

FIGURE 6.6
Visual Illustration of Art Elements

poster or photograph of buildings over which you have taped an acetate sheet. Have students use water-soluble markers to trace the basic shapes they find in the picture. The tracings can be wiped off and the picture reused.

A similar exercise using slides projected onto banner paper can be used to teach composition. Students can draw lines on the paper to illustrate the structure of the projected drawing or painting. For example, they might draw lines indicating movement or outline an area of emphasis.

- *Vocabulary arrows.* Another method to teach composition, as well as to reinforce vocabulary, is through the use of laminated vocabulary arrows. These arrows can be used to indicate art elements and design principles on reproductions of paintings, drawings, sculptures, craft items, buildings, etc., as illustrated in Figure 6.5.

- *Bulletin boards and display cases.* We often think of bulletin boards and cases as display spaces for final products. They can also be used as teaching tools, providing directions and information. By displaying concepts, historical information, and processes, as well as products, you can demonstrate art education content. For example, you might include signs that describe an assignment, give cultural background, or explain how a concept was used. At the beginning of the year when you lack current student work, you might design a teaching bulletin board that illustrates a concept, as in Figure 6.6.

FIGURE 6.7
The Language of Vision

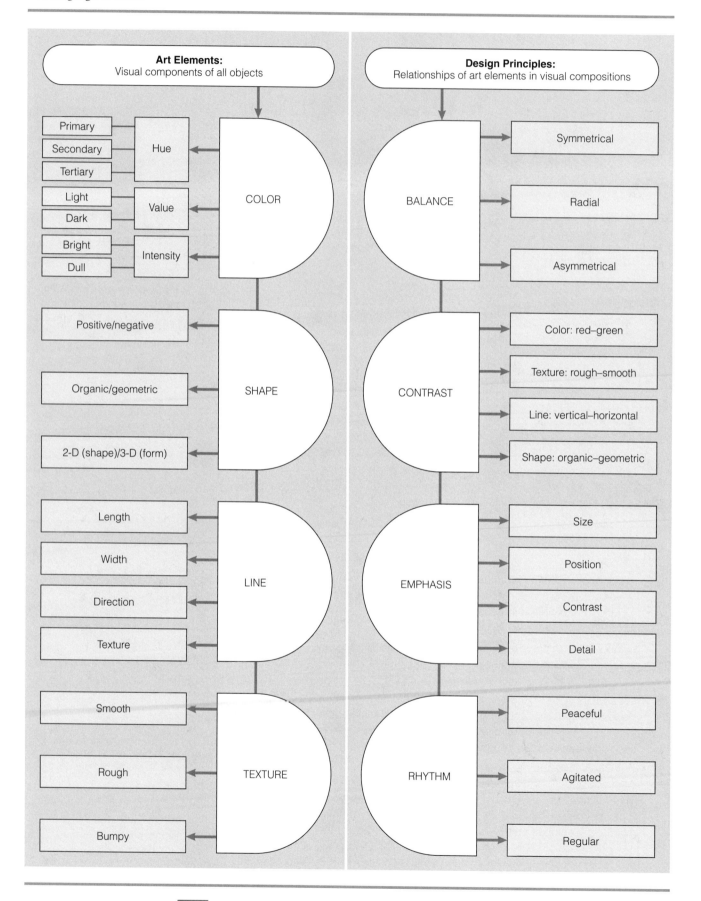

The teaching of visual language is not something you "get through" and then go on to something else. You will address art elements and design principles at every grade level, deepening understanding year by year. Figure 6.7 summarizes information about visual language. Each box contains a word about which multiple concepts can be formulated. Every concept might be presented individually in separate art activities. We build visual language skills over a period of time, much as English teachers build verbal skills. The goal is not to produce large groups of students who go out into the world as professional artists (or writers, using verbal language), but to enhance each individual's quality of life through heightened ability to express and take in information visually.

S U M M A R Y

To understand the language of vision in grades K–12, one can begin by comparing it with verbal language. Scribbling may be likened to uttering the first sounds. In developing their "visual voices," children move from random mark making to representing their world in schematic form, to organizing schema in compositions. As they progress, they can be introduced to terminology to discuss the language of vision. Just as we teach students about the parts of speech so that they may use verbal language in more conscious ways, we teach about "visual parts of speech" or art elements. We also lead students to understand how they use art elements in compositional relationships called *design principles.*

There are various approaches for teaching visual language. In the past child-centered art educators developed visual literacy through art-making activities in which children were encouraged to find their "visual voices" largely by manipulating and exploring materials and processes. Although in some cases students were led to understand how they used art elements and design principles to create visual form, in many cases they were not. In an effort to provide substance, appear "basic," and demonstrate accountability for teaching content, subject-centered art educators became more involved in addressing formal qualities of art. Art elements, design principles, and concepts pertaining to them became the focus of many curriculum guides. By the 1980s and 1990s some discipline-based approaches had become so academic that students were taught about visual language primarily by analyzing it in the works of master artists, studying vocabulary and concepts, and demonstrating knowledge through written tests. The pendulum had swung 180 degrees, from a "soft" experiential to a "hard" academic approach.

Recognizing the need for balance and the strengths in both child- and subject-centered approaches, this text presents a central position midway between the two. This path supports art making, rather than art criticism as the primary vehicle for developing understanding of visual language. It presents art elements and design principles as tools to develop higher levels of consciousness in using the language expressively. To teach concepts pertaining to visual language through active learning strategies, concepts are "concretized" through processes in which students

1. are introduced to a concept about an art element or design principle,

2. observe and discuss how the concept manifests in visual form, and

3. explore the concept in studio experiences.

All the activities discussed here may be viewed as process-oriented experiences for building visual language skills necessary to take the next step: using the language to express something personal, authentic, meaningful, and creative.

A. DESIGNING ACTIVITIES TO "CONCRETIZE" CONCEPTS ABOUT ART ELEMENTS

Directions

1. Select three art elements (one for each grade level). 2. Identify a specific grade within each level and write an age-appropriate concept. 3. Design a perceptual activity (seeing, feeling, or moving, and discussing) and a studio activity (using art materials), and identify a fitting cultural exemplar.

Art Element:_____   **Elementary Grade:**_____

Concept about Art Element:

Perceptual Activity:

Studio Activity:

Cultural Exemplar:

Art Element:_____   **Middle School Grade:**_____

Concept about Art Element:

Perceptual Activity:

Studio Activity:

Cultural Exemplar:

Art Element:_____   **High School Grade:**_____

Concept about Art Element:

Perceptual Activity:

Studio Activity:

Cultural Exemplar:

B. DESIGNING ACTIVITIES TO "CONCRETIZE" CONCEPTS ABOUT DESIGN PRINCIPLES

Directions

1. Select three design principles (one for each grade level). 2. Identify a specific grade within each level and write an age-appropriate concept. 3. Design a perceptual activity (seeing, feeling, or moving, and discussing) and a studio activity (using art materials), and identify a fitting cultural exemplar.

Design Principle:_____   **Elementary Grade:**_____

Concept about Design Principle:

Perceptual Activity:

Studio Activity:

Cultural Exemplar:

Design Principle:_____   **Middle School Grade:**_____

Concept about Design Principle:

Perceptual Activity:

Studio Activity:

Cultural Exemplar:

Design Principle:_____   **High School Grade:**_____

Concept about Design Principle:

Perceptual Activity:

Studio Activity:

Cultural Exemplar:

PROMOTING CREATIVITY

Having addressed the development of visual language, we move on to our next challenge: encouraging students to express something worth communicating. This involves moving students from the place of knowing how to create the illusion of objects receding into space to using this information to say something personal, particular, unique. What we guide students to express in visual form are answers to the questions "Who am I? What do I value? What do I have to say?" Students may be led to answer these questions in one of two ways: (1) They may start by looking at the work of other artists and use it as a springboard from which to launch into ideas and expressions of their own; or (2) they may start by expressing their own internal impulses, feelings, and ideas and then continue their journeys, discovering others creating expressions deriving from similar impulses, feelings, and ideas.

Whether students are led from the outside in or the inside out is not important as long as the results reflect thinking and authenticity. How do we develop behaviors that lead to these results? We provide opportunities for students to interpret ideas, to solve problems, and to go beyond the ordinary. As in the development of visual language skills, the promotion of creativity has been approached in a variety of ways for a number of reasons. This chapter explores rationales and strategies for developing creative behaviors. Sections include (1) creativity in the context of art education, (2) characteristics of creative behaviors, (3) strategies to promote creative behaviors, and (4) the creative problem-solving teaching model.

▼ CREATIVITY IN THE CONTEXT OF ART EDUCATION

As we look at the historical development of art education, we notice that promoting creative behavior has emerged as a rationale at particular times in our history. It appeared first as a reaction against closed-ended instruction in the society-centered orientation. During the Progressive Movement, John Dewey was especially influential in developing teaching strategies to promote creative behaviors. Believing that the school environment should be a microcosm of the real world, Dewey placed students in problem-solving situations similar to those they might encounter in real life. As they worked through the solving of problems, students developed thinking skills. When laissez-faire and open-ended activities became part of art education, students were encouraged to explore, experiment, and develop their creative capacities. As the child-centered orientation continued through the influences of Lowenfeld and other art educators of the 1940s and 1950s, creativity was viewed more as an ability to be self-expressive than as a process to solve problems.

International events in the 1950s brought about a change in the way the creativity was promoted. The Soviets launched *Sputnik*. U.S. engineers and scientists were needed to compete in the race for space, and the rationale in art education shifted from art for self-expression to art for developing problem-solving skills. Art education was seen to be of instrumental value because it could develop the kind of thinking Americans needed. After U.S. astronauts landed on the moon, some criticized the view that art should be taught because of its instrumental value rather than its intrinsic worth. Art for the development of problem-solving skills became less popular as a rationale. In decades from the 1960s to the 1990s, the back-to-the-basics movement and the focus on teaching of concepts also diminished the position creativity had once held in art education.

Today art educators express mixed views about the promotion of creativity. Some DBAE proponents, emphasizing the academic study of art over studio production, do not view the development of creative behavior as a primary goal. They focus on increasing understanding of art in the continuum of history. They provide connections, pointing out how artists have borrowed or "appropriated" ideas, images, and compositions from their predecessors in different times, places, and cultures. They may espouse the view "there is nothing new under the sun." Some art educators not only introduce appropriation in art history, but they also build on it in art production. Presenting images from the outside, they encourage students to interpret the ideas of others in statements of their own. Under the guidance of creative teachers who promote problem solving, students may produce works that reflect self-expressive forms and novel solutions. In other cases, however, students have not been required to go beyond mimicking. In the act of imitating someone or something outside themselves, they may simply go through the motions of producing objects reflecting neither personal connection, investment of the self, nor evidence of creative thinking.

These resulting student artworks, as well as the philosophical perspectives and teaching strategies that produced them, have caused a renewed interest in the promotion of creativity among studio-centered, child-centered, and community-based art educators. These teachers, linked through their emphasis on art production, view the essence of art education as promoting expression of the self through art-making behaviors. Although some may agree that "there is nothing new under the sun," they also acknowledge that a row of lollipop trees on a green line representing the ground may be new to its creator. Child-centered educators may stand back and watch students reinvent what has already been created in the outside world. These statements, which often do reflect personal connection, investment of the self, and evidence of creative thinking, are in no way diminished by the fact that others have made similar statements. On the contrary, by starting with the inside and then expanding into the outside, educators make connections that help students understand art as a universal language.

One group of art educators today that emphasizes production, begins with the inside, and focuses on the development of creative capacities is Arts PROPEL. Since the mid 1980s this group, influenced primarily by Howard Gardner's work in multiple intelligences, has collaborated with the Educational Testing Service and the Pittsburgh Public Schools. Arts PROPEL works with middle and high school students in the areas of music, imaginative writing, and visual art. Via a teaching model comprised of three components—production, perception, and reflection—students are led to develop productive skills, discriminative abilities, and reflective powers necessary to promote growth of artistic intelligences. Artistic intelligence is about modes of thinking, ideas, and how those ideas manifest in form as a dance, a musical composition, a poem, or a painting. All these expressions are connected through common characteristics relating to creativity.

▼ CHARACTERISTICS OF CREATIVE BEHAVIOR

When we say a particular student or artwork is "creative" we often mean that the student or work is different from what we consider to be "average" or "normal." Creative people and work produced by them possess qualities that are special. The psychologist E. Paul Torrance, who has significantly contributed to our understanding of creativity through his studies, reflected this idea when he said, "It takes courage to be creative: Just as soon as you have a new idea, you're in the minority of one." As the fields of psychology and education have advanced, researchers have become increasingly interested in determining what is special about creative people. They have determined that "creative" people have certain characteristics that enable them to generate ideas that "ordinary" people do not consider. The characteristics identified by Torrance are (1) fluency, (2) flexibility, (3) originality, and (4) elaboration.

FLUENCY

Fluency involves the ability to generate many ideas. One way to develop fluency is to present a theme and ask students to list as many examples of the theme as they can. For example, suppose your students are preparing to draw compositions of small natural objects. You might ask them to list all the natural objects they can think of in one minute. Lists from students with low and high fluency might look like those in Table 7.1.

To measure the degree of fluency displayed by each student, count the number of responses generated by each. The low-fluency student would receive a score of 4; the high-fluency student, a score of 12.

FLEXIBILITY

Flexibility involves the ability to generate ideas that go in many directions. The terms *flexible* and *divergent* are synonymous in this context. A diagram of flexibility or divergent thinking is illustrated in Figure 7.1.

Highly flexible people can see many possibilities. If they are doing something that isn't working, they let it go and try something else. They are able to generate a wide variety of responses and easily embrace alternatives. To illustrate the difference between fluency and flexibility, let's return to the problem.

FIGURE 7.1
A Diagram of Flexibility

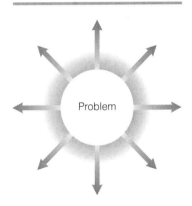

TABLE 7.1
Example of Low versus High Fluency

Low-Fluency Student	High-Fluency Student
Flowers, leaves, shells, rocks	Shells, twigs, lichen, bark, pine cones, cotton balls, leaves, rocks, insects, lizards, weeds, grass

TABLE 7.2
Example of Low versus High Flexibility

Low-Flexibility Student	High-Flexibility Student
Daisies, pansies, daffodils, roses, tulips, irises, dandelions, lilies, hibiscus, peonies, azaleas, jasmine	Shells, snails, bark, seed pods, seaweed, bones, insects, fish, weeds, lichen, feathers, rocks

Suppose two more students, one with low flexibility and one with high flexibility, made responses like the ones recorded in Table 7.2.

By counting the number of responses, you can determine that both students are equally fluent: Each list contains 12 items. Now look at the content in each list. To determine the degree of flexibility, count the number of categories into which responses fall. The number of categories for the low-flexibility student is one—all responses fall under the category of flowers. To determine the score for the high-flexibility student, look for relationships and cluster responses. You might create the following categories: (1) types of animals living on land, (2) types of animals living in water, (3) plants living on land, (4) plants living in water, (5) geologic formations, (6) parts of animals, and (7) parts of plants. Using these particular categories, you would give the high-flexibility student a score of 7. As you can see, it is possible for a student to be high in fluency and low in flexibility. This characteristic can be especially visible with middle school students who become proficient at drawing particular images—horses, for example. Students at this age often develop schema for drawing favorite objects and stay safe by using the schema over and over again in a way that can stifle creativity. As art teachers, we can design experiences that will develop flexibility in solving problems not only in art, but in life, as the Birdwalk below illustrates.

The exercise that follows presents an opportunity for you to test your flexibility. Solve the problem in the dot diagram on the next page, following these directions: Connect all nine dots, (1) by drawing only four straight lines, (2) without lifting your pencil, or (3) back-tracking on a line. You may need to experiment with solutions in multiple drawings of this configuration. The key to solving the problem is in remembering what flexibility means: the ability to change (from something that doesn't work to something that might work better). If you have difficulty doing the problem, it may be because you see the nine-dot configuration with a fixed perimeter. You might have assumed that

FLEXIBILITY: TURNING ROADSIDE TRASH INTO A FUNCTIONAL OBJECT

ONE day Nancy's car ran out of gas on her way to school. She pulled off the road and eventually flagged down a man who had a gas can. Although he had gas to give her, she could not get it from the can into her tank without a funnel. She began searching the area for trash—pieces of paper, discarded coffee cups, bits of tinfoil, or Styrofoam—whatever she could find, and fashioning it into a receptacle that would serve as a funnel. Her helper, watching her change junk on the roadside into a functional object, finally said, "You must be an art teacher." Nancy looked at him in amazement and said, "How did you know?"

He said, "I can tell by how creative you are in putting things together."

you had to stay within the perimeter. If you did, read the directions again. Do they say that you must stay within the perimeter of the nine dots? The way to solve this problem is to go beyond the nine dots.

"Going beyond the nine dots" may be viewed as a metaphor, reminding you of what you might do to encourage flexibility:

- Ask students to notice the constraints they place on themselves that are not inherent in a given problem.
- Encourage students to assess situations and change directions if something is not working.
- Promote a willingness to take risks to go beyond what students normally do.
- Motivate students to expand their repertoires.
- Develop students' visions to see alternatives.

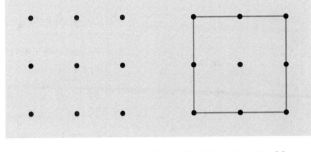

Solving the Nine-Dots Problem

ORIGINALITY

Originality involves the ability to produce clever or novel responses. It is often the result of both fluency and flexibility. Students who can generate many ideas in a wide variety of categories have more options from which to select their responses to a problem. To illustrate how fluency and flexibility support originality, let's return to the drawing assignment. The following procedure might be used to promote unusual responses:

1. List as many small natural objects as you can think of in one minute (fluency).
2. Categorize the objects into themes. A theme might be visual attributes (spiky, organic, patterned); objects (seed pods, leaves, twigs, insects); locations where objects are found (underground, garden, desert, sea), etc. (flexibility).
3. Continue expanding ideas by generating more categories for themes and more objects within each theme (fluency and flexibility).
4. Rank your themes and objects from most common (signified by 1) to most unusual (signified by 4).
5. Select the three most unusual objects as the subject matter of your drawing (originality).

ELABORATION

Elaboration involves the ability to expand, develop, and embellish products. The process of elaboration is what transforms a creative idea into a work of art. Elaboration is the degree of completion or amount of detail in a work. Just as flexibility is related to divergent, the terms *elaboration* and *convergent* both refer to a synthesis of ideas expressed in an art product. A diagram of elaboration or convergent thinking might look like Figure 7.2:

You might have students that are highly fluent, flexible, and original that lack the discipline and/or skills to follow through with elaboration. These students may fill several sketch books with "ideas" and half-finished drawings that are never developed into completed works of art. You might encourage these students to slow down. Praise them for their high degree of fluency, and ask them to select one or two ideas to work into finished art products. However, you may also have students who are quite content to work on the same drawing for weeks on end. These students sometimes do not know when enough is enough. A product may be only half as successful as it had been the week before because it became so overworked. You might help these students

FIGURE 7.2
A Diagram of Elaboration

Solution to the problem: Art Product

by asking them to do twenty 1-minute gesture drawings (quick, loose drawings conveying gesture or movement, rather than details of a form). Students at both extremes can be helped with the elaboration process through your careful design of criteria. For example, in the drawing problem, you might ask students to represent each object from a different viewpoint:

1. One as if you were looking at it from across the room (unfocused or simplified)
2. One as if you were looking at it at your desk (normal detail)
3. One as if you were looking at it under a strong magnifying glass (extreme detail)

This criterion could help both types of students use elaboration successfully. The student who, left to his or her own devices, will not elaborate on anything is pushed to elaborate in the magnified image. The student who elaborates to the point where it ceases to be effective is pushed to leave at least one object purposefully vague or simple, strengthening the composition through the use of contrast, emphasis, and subordination.

▼
STRATEGIES TO PROMOTE CREATIVITY

The word *creative* does not describe a single behavior, but a number of behaviors characterized by fluency, flexibility, originality, and elaboration. Creativity is a composite of behaviors that we can teach, just as we can teach students to see, to draw, or to mix colors. In promoting creative behaviors, we focus on cognitive aspects of art making. We encourage students to develop thinking skills, as we present problems to solve through visual expression. We can begin in kindergarten and continue to challenge students at progressively higher levels, as they develop cognitive, manipulative, and expressive abilities. This section presents strategies to promote creative thinking in grades K–12 in discussions on the following topics: (1) use of art media, (2) open-ended assignments, (3) brainstorming, (4) webs to develop thinking skills, and (5) Bauhaus teaching approaches.

●
USE OF ART MEDIA

You were introduced to the characteristics of creativity through a sample problem in which students were asked to (1) list as many small natural objects as possible in one minute, (2) categorize the objects into themes, (3) rank the categories/objects from least to most original, and (4) create a composition of the three most unusual objects. At what grade might students be capable of this level of problem solving? The answer depends on the degree to which students had been led in previous experiences to develop skills in thinking, using art materials, and creating compositions. Some students might be ready to tackle this assignment in middle school. Even art majors on the high school level, however, may not get beyond the first step without having had opportunities to develop these skills from kindergarten on up.

How do we begin with a 5-year-old? How do we know what is appropriate, possible, effective? Once again, we look to the nature of the child for answers in developing creative behaviors. Young art learners develop fluency, flexibility, originality and elaboration in the same way they learn to "speak" visually— through the manipulation of media and exploration of processes.

FLUENCY

Young art learners tend to be very direct and spontaneous. They have no need to draw images in pencil before beginning a painting. They do not make preliminary plans, sketching ideas before creating a work. Neither do they generate multiple ideas and select the best one to use in a finished product. Process-oriented, they simply express—quickly, easily, without laboring over what to say or how to say it. A kindergartner in a painting activity might produce six or seven pictures in a single art period. He is exhibiting a characteristic of creativity—fluency. One way to develop fluency is to motivate students with age-appropriate subject matter and simply allow them to explore it through a series of spontaneously created expressions.

FLEXIBILITY

Flexibility, or the ability to move in a number of directions, can also be developed through the use of materials and processes. When students paint at easels with wide paint brushes, they create one kind of expression. When they draw with crayons, they make marks differently. The expressions created with drawing and painting tools are different yet again from those made with modeling clay. How a child thinks when she (or he) pokes into clay is different from how she thinks when she builds a construction from blocks. As a child shifts from thinking on paper, to thinking with clay, to thinking "poking in," to thinking "building on," she is developing flexibility.

ORIGINALITY

To develop originality, we encourage students to generate ideas that are theirs—not ideas they have borrowed from children sitting next to them, remembered from a billboard or television commercial, or copied from the work of another artist. One way to encourage original thinking is to pose problems in the form of ideas that students can interpret in self-expressive ways. For example, rather than asking a student to draw a picture of an animal with pattern (i.e., an object that could be expressed by reproducing Tony the Tiger), present an idea, theme, or scenario: "You are on your first trip to the zoo. Monkeys are chattering, birds are squawking, seals are diving in and out of the water. Everything seems to be going fine, when suddenly, out of the corner of your eye you see . . . (fill in the blank by responding in visual form)."

ELABORATION

One way intelligence levels and degrees of creativity are ascertained in young learners is by analyzing their drawings. Although bright, creative youngsters may progress through the same developmental stages at the same rate as the average population, their drawings are often significantly different. A depiction of the self produced by an average preschooler might be a circle with four lines radiating from it to represent arms and legs. An image produced by a highly creative preschooler may be a similar circle with the same four lines, in which the child has included additional circles and lines to represent hands, feet, fingers, toes, ears, and hair. This ability to provide detail is elaboration. You can develop elaboration skills in a number of ways. For example, in a self-portrait lesson, you might encourage students to include all facial features, hair, body parts, details on clothing, etc. In a landscape assignment, you might ask students to fill the entire space or to work back into images to create details. You might provide mixed media, such as paint, crayons, and cut paper, for students to use as they create layers, depth, and interest in a composition. Materials such as beans, buttons, yarn, raffia, and feathers can be used to embellish two- and three-dimensional expressions. As students learn to elaborate, they go from making generalized forms to using a rich vocabulary of visual materials and elements.

OPEN-ENDED ASSIGNMENTS

As you consider how you might develop creativity through activities appropriate for the full range of K–12 students, remember this key term: *open-ended*. Open-ended assignments, both process- and product-oriented, are specifically intended to promote thinking. They present a "problem" defined by broad criteria. As students work within the criteria, they are challenged to think. This is because the criteria (what is stated) supply only a small percentage of the motivation. The major portion is what is left unstated, requiring each individual to fill in the blanks with his or her unique interpretation. Appropriately designed open-ended assignments can challenge students from kindergarten through college level, as the Birdwalk below illustrates.

As this story implies, open-ended assignments should result in artwork in which the *differences outnumber the similarities*. Criteria should be carefully

BUILDING ON THE UNSTATED

IT WAS a cold, gray day in the first week of February. Students were sitting in a college methods class in art education, learning about teaching art to young people. As the period came to a close, the instructor gave a homework assignment defined by these criteria:

- Make a valentine entirely out of hearts.
- Use only paper.
- Include a three-dimensional aspect.
- Go beyond "the nine dots."

The following week Jack came into class with his Valentine and in a disgruntled manner plopped it onto the table. It was a 12″ × 18″ piece of paper folded in half so that it could be placed in a standing position. On each side of the fold he had pasted some hearts of various sizes and colors. "This was the most boring assignment I ever had. What a waste of time!" At this point, Sally chimed in, "I hated this assignment too. I especially hate Valentine's Day—so trite, so pink and white with little candy hearts and doilies. I started making something really traditional and as I worked, I got madder and madder. After I took a break, I noticed the last criterion. Then I made this fish out of hearts created from paper pulp."

"I made a hanging mobile of a biological heart with veins and arteries, " said Trish.

"I made a lantern out of some tissue paper. Let me show you how light shines through with a candle inside," said Joe.

"I made a series of nesting heart-shaped boxes out of woven paper. The smallest box contains a special Valentine's gift," said Marge.

"I missed the point," said Jack, as he threw his 12″ × 18″ sheet of construction paper into the trash can.

selected to promote rather than inhibit creative interpretation. The next time you visit a school, look at the displays and bulletin boards in the hallways and art rooms. Very often you will see products resulting from what was intended to be a creative assignment. See if you can determine what the criteria were by noticing the similarities. Perhaps all the works are painted using a monochromatic color scheme or they all contain an area of emphasis. Then look for diversity. How different are they? Do they all look like they may have been modeled after some teacher's sample? Is degree of craftsmanship the most obvious difference, or do they reflect as a total group a high degree of fluency, flexibility, originality, and elaboration?

BRAINSTORMING

Brainstorming is a technique for solving problems. Many teachers use a variety of brainstorming strategies to elicit responses to open-ended problems. Brainstorming may be done orally (through class discussions), verbally (through writing processes), or visually (through representation of ideas in a two- or three-dimensional medium). You have already been introduced to some brainstorming techniques in this guide. (The worksheet "Abstracting the Essence of an Object" in the unit "The Abstraction of Georgia O'Keeffe" is an example of a visual brainstorming exercise.) The activities illustrating fluency and flexibility, in which students were asked to list natural objects, categorize them, and then generate additional categories and objects, are also examples of brainstorming. Brainstorming may be considered as any activity in which students generate a number of responses in answer to a problem that may be solved in multiple ways.

As students develop cognitive skills and knowledge necessary to generate multiple responses, they can brainstorm. For example, children in kindergarten can identify and classify objects according to color or shape. Developing thinking skills along with perceptual and expressive skills in art education, we can challenge students to go farther and farther out "beyond the nine dots." However, because students are often in academic situations in which they are required to demonstrate learning by supplying "the correct answer," they may not come to art class prepared for brainstorming activities. The following procedures demonstrate how to facilitate brainstorming behaviors by progressing from whole-class activities, to small-group exercises, to individual work.

ORAL BRAINSTORMING WITH AN ENTIRE CLASS

1. Present a problem: "You are a scientist who has been approached by an alien from another planet. The alien tells you that he is also a scientist and has come to study animal life on Earth. He asks you to tell him about the features of animals here. You begin telling him . . ."

2. Ask students to think of as many different features as they can in an effort to describe Earth animals.

3. Ask students not to judge whether an answer is "good." Any answer that falls within the category *animal features* is acceptable and can be contributed. Tell students they have one minute in which to respond.

4. Begin the process by writing *fangs* and *toenails* on the board.

5. Appoint a timekeeper. Ask students to call out answers. Write all answers on the board or list suggestions using an overhead projector. Continue the process until the timekeeper calls time.

VISUAL BRAINSTORMING WITH SMALL GROUPS

1. Divide the class into groups at separate tables. Give each group a large sheet of paper and pencils for all group members.

2. Continue with the scenario: "The alien scientist now has a list of words relating to animal features. Because he still has not seen an Earth animal, however, these words are meaningless."

3. Ask students to recall to themselves the list of animal features developed during the oral brainstorming activity. Tell them that as a group they are to draw as many animal features as they can in three minutes. These may be features mentioned in the previous discussion or new ones. As a student thinks of a feature, he or she is to state it to the group and then begin drawing. Other students may state additional features and draw immediately thereafter, not waiting for the first to finish. Students are to think of and draw as many features as possible within the allotted time.

4. Set the timer and instruct students to begin.

5. Stop students after three minutes. Ask the group to appoint a scorekeeper to count responses. Duplicate responses do not count. After each scorekeeper has counted answers, he or she calls out the number of responses followed by the list of features.

6. Declare the group with the most responses as the winner.

VERBAL/VISUAL BRAINSTORMING WITH INDIVIDUAL STUDENTS

The previous exercises can prepare students to engage in brainstorming on individual bases. This can be done in written form, visual form, or both. A combination often works well because some students think more easily in words, whereas others think better in pictures. A simple way to promote brainstorming is to have students fold newsprint into sections and then draw responses in each area. You can also design reproducible brainstorming sheets. These teacher-designed formats, such as the sample that follows (Worksheet 7.1), provide a structure while allowing freedom to explore possibilities. Although you may think of these exercises as typically being done in two-dimensional processes, you might also give students Plasticine clay with which to explore ideas three-dimensionally. (Remember to encourage haptic along with visual expression.)

Regardless of the content explored and the particular teaching strategies used in brainstorming exercises, the process can be defined by these general guidelines:

- A "problem" is presented.
- Students are asked to generate ideas to solve the problem.
- Spontaneity and speed are encouraged.
- Quantity is stressed, not quality.
- Ideas are not to be judged.

Students may remember these rules, as well as the characteristics of creativity, through this acronym:

D = defer judgment

O = original, out of the ordinary, outrageous, outside the nine dots

V = vastness of responses (fluency and flexibility)

E = elaboration of ideas, embellishment of detail

CREATIVE CREATURES

Scenario

The alien scientist now thinks he has an understanding of Earth animals. He is in the process of recording his information (below) when he becomes ill. He knows he will not be able to finish his research and he requests that you complete his notations by drawing two more examples of Earth animals. Not wanting to upset him, you complete his worksheet and show it to him before faxing more accurate representations to scientists on his home planet.

5 Animal Features

stripes

claws

fangs

spines

scales

Animal 1

Name: _____ *Dinotigefish* _____

5 More Animal Features

Animal 2

Name: _____

5 More Animal Features

Animal 3

Name: _____

WEBS TO DEVELOP THINKING SKILLS

A *web*, as in spider web, may be thought of as an organizational structure providing pathways or links to make connections. The most prominent example of "web" today may be the World Wide Web, which links information on the Internet. This should not be confused with webs that art teachers have been using since long before the Internet. Webs in art education are visual organizers used to facilitate thinking. Different types of web structures promote different kinds of thinking skills. Three types especially useful to art teachers are thematic, sequential, and compare and contrast.

THEMATIC WEB

A thematic web is a diagram, similar to the one in Figure 7.3, used in brainstorming activities to promote fluency and flexibility. The center of the diagram contains the problem "How can you use a tennis shoe to create an armature for a papier-mâché sculpture?" The areas radiating from the circle provide spaces to record possible solutions: (1) add wheels to turn it into a land vehicle; (2) add a propeller to make a helicopter; (3) create a figure to be set inside, turning it into a bed or a mummy case; (4) add features to turn it into an animal; (5) turn it into a Pop Art planter; (6) turn it upside-down and use the sole as a road or runway for miniature vehicles; (7) slit the toe, turning the shoe into a giant "Jaws" shark; and (8) create a house for the "old woman who lived in a shoe."

SEQUENTIAL WEB

Just as thematic webs are used to promote divergent thinking, sequential webs are used to develop linear thinking. Sequential webs, to which you have been introduced previously in the form of process visuals, are flowcharts, providing structure for a sequence of steps. To encourage students to solve problems through a linear thinking process, you might present starting and ending points along a continuum, as diagrammed:

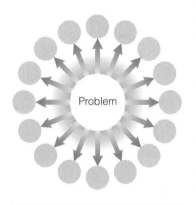

FIGURE 7.3
Sample Thematic Web

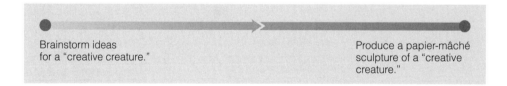

You might then ask students to fill in a sequence of steps to arrive at the goal. As students generate responses, you may construct a sequential web similar to the one in Figure 7.4:

FIGURE 7.4
Sample Sequential Web

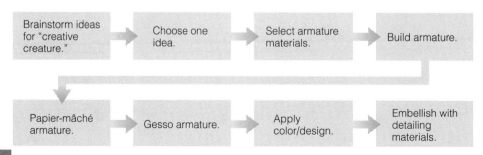

We often provide these steps in our visuals for students, solving problems through our own thinking processes. As students develop cognitively and artistically, we can encourage them to be progressively self-directed. The activity of developing sequential webs can be especially beneficial to students who have no blueprints, who are, in the truest sense of the word, original in their thinking and art-making behaviors.

COMPARE-AND-CONTRAST WEB

A compare-and-contrast web is a structure borrowed from the fields of math and logic called a Venn diagram. Its purpose is to promote thinking through the analysis of similarities and differences between two objects, processes, or themes sharing common characteristics. It is represented as two circles (or ovals) overlapping in the center (Figure 7.5).

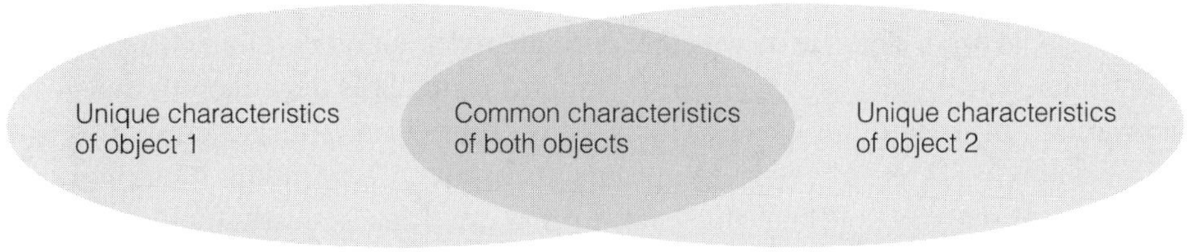

Unique characteristics of object 1

Common characteristics of both objects

Unique characteristics of object 2

FIGURE 7.5
Sample Compare-and-Contrast Web

This web can be especially useful to encourage students to respond in creative ways to the presentation of a cultural exemplar. For example, you might follow these steps in introducing an assignment for a fantasy landscape painting:

1. In the center of the diagram write the criteria, indicating common characteristics that will be shared by all student works and a cultural exemplar (a Rousseau painting):

   a. Representation of a place
   b. Inclusion of foliage
   c. Inclusion of at least two animals interacting in some way
   d. Fantasy-like quality
   e. Choice of one main color to explore in terms of hue, value, and intensity

2. Present a Rousseau painting illustrating ways *one particular artist* met the general criteria.

3. Ask students to identify these ways and as they do so, write responses in an outside area of the diagram.

4. Ask a student to generate ways in which he might fulfill the same criteria differently from Rousseau. Write his responses in the opposite outside portion of the diagram.

The result of this activity might look like Figure 7.6.

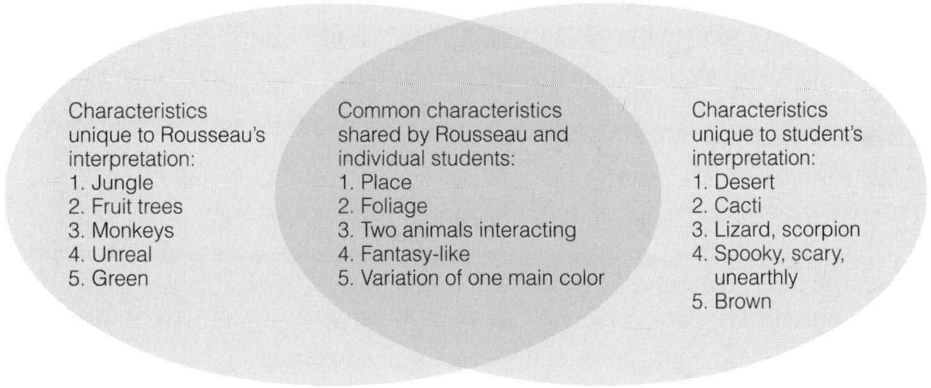

Characteristics unique to Rousseau's interpretation:
1. Jungle
2. Fruit trees
3. Monkeys
4. Unreal
5. Green

Common characteristics shared by Rousseau and individual students:
1. Place
2. Foliage
3. Two animals interacting
4. Fantasy-like
5. Variation of one main color

Characteristics unique to student's interpretation:
1. Desert
2. Cacti
3. Lizard, scorpion
4. Spooky, scary, unearthly
5. Brown

FIGURE 7.6
Compare-and-Contrast Web Illustrating Particular Ways to Meet General Criteria

As students develop this web, they can be led to understand that both Rousseau and they themselves are following the same criteria interpreted in individual ways.

BAUHAUS TEACHING APPROACHES

Art educators today who focus on the development of creative behaviors use a variety of strategies to stretch thinking. Brainstorming worksheets and webbing exercises are just two examples. Another kind of problem-solving activity that has become increasingly popular is one borrowed from the Bauhaus. The Bauhaus was an art school in Germany from 1919 to 1933 that emphasized the teaching of applied design. Its major goal was to combine the technological expertise of engineers with the aesthetic sensitivity of artists in the design of beautiful, functional objects for mass production and consumption. Bauhaus designers were interested in reflecting the function of an object through its aesthetic appearance. Their idea was to eliminate extraneous details and express functionality through elegant simplification of form. This approach to design is expressed in the Bauhaus saying "form follows function." Design courses typically included (1) use of a variety of tools, techniques, and media to explore attributes of materials; (2) emphasis on formal qualities in aesthetic and functional expression; and (3) situations in which students worked in groups to brainstorm ideas and arrive at a variety of solutions.

Because Bauhaus students were involved in the design of functional items, such as tables, chairs, and coffee pots, their objects were assessed in two areas: on functional criteria and on aesthetic criteria. In judging the quality of a coffee pot, for example, an instructor might first determine the degree to which it is functional: Does the pot hold liquid? Can liquid be poured from the spout? Does the top stay on when the vessel is held in a pouring position? Is the handle comfortable to hold? Is it cool enough to grasp when the pot is filled with hot coffee? No matter how beautiful it is, if it does not work, it is not a successful coffee pot. In assessing aesthetic criteria, an instructor might judge the elegance and simplicity of the form, surface detailing, color, and texture. These are characteristics relating to design qualities—use of art elements and principles to compose the perfect visual statement reflecting "essence of coffee pot." Functional and aesthetic criteria such as these have been used for years in college design courses to promote creative problem solving (CPS).

Today students from elementary through high school levels are asked to solve problems much like those presented in the Bauhaus. A typical activity involves the design of a functional, aesthetic package for a light bulb. The following boxed list presents a procedure for leading students through this process.

Procedure for a CPS Activity: Design a Light Bulb Package

1. Put students into groups of two to three, and give each group a light bulb, a rubber band, a brown lunch bag, a pair of scissors, a 6″ × 6″ piece of cardboard, and one sheet of newspaper.

2. Tell the students they are to design a package for a light bulb. To test the packaging, each packaged light bulb will be dropped from a 10-foot height.

3. Tell the students their packages will be judged on two criteria: (a) ability to protect the light bulb from damage (functional criterion) and (b) unusual design of the package (aesthetic criterion).

4. Give the students twenty minutes to create the packages.

5. Judge the aesthetic quality first. To do this, have each group display its package with a sheet of paper next to it. Instruct each student to rate each package by giving one to three points for degree of originality. Each group can then add up the points received for its package to determine the aesthetic score.

6. Test the functional aspect of the package by dropping each light bulb from a ladder top into a wastebasket. Unwrap the package to determine if the light bulb is still intact. Then plug unbroken light bulbs into a socket to see if they work.

7. Declare the winner as the functioning light bulb with the highest aesthetic score.

The light bulb package is simply one example of a problem-solving activity challenging students to generate multiple solutions. It serves as a model you may follow in (1) defining a problem through functional and aesthetic criteria, (2) providing for experimentation with materials and processes, and (3) judging solutions. Additional ideas you might implement at various grade levels follow:

- Design a structure to hold a shoe 6 inches off the ground using a variety of small pieces of paper, paper clips, scissors, and markers. Assess quality on (1) ability to support a shoe and (2) most unusual design (elementary level).

- Design a flying machine capable of protecting a raw egg enclosed within it from breaking when flown from a second-story window. Assess quality on (1) ability to protect the egg, (2) distance of flight, and (3) most unusual use of materials selected by individual students (middle school level).

- Design a structure from drinking straws intended to support a red brick one foot off the ground. Assess quality on (1) ability to support a brick and (2) simplicity of form and elegance of linear element (high school level).

▼
THE CREATIVE PROBLEM-SOLVING TEACHING MODEL

The ideas just presented may be viewed as experiments or open-ended, process-oriented activities. The creative problem-solving teaching model (Figure 7.7, the third model presented within this text to address art making), provides a structure on which to build an entire unit of study. Like the triangular product-oriented teaching model, the CPS model includes a motivation, a process-oriented activity step, and a final product. However, it differs from the product-oriented model in that the process-oriented activity step (CPS) is focused specifically on generating multiple solutions through brainstorming. In addition, no evaluation step is included. Rather, evaluation is implied through the criteria defining the problem. See the following box.

A Practical Application of the Creative Problem-Solving Teaching Model

The diamond shape of this model symbolizes problem-solving processes. At the top point the problem, defined through criteria, serves as the motivation. The problem may involve the creation of a functional item, in which case both functional and aesthetic criteria need to be stipulated. The model may also be used to promote problem solving in the creation of non-functional items, in which case aesthetic criteria alone will suffice. From the presentation of the problem, we move to the CPS step placed in the widest area of the model. This step (equivalent to the activity step in the product-oriented teaching model) is intended to promote divergent thinking, requiring students to demonstrate fluency and flexibility. Brainstorming in this step can be done in a

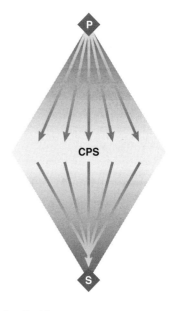

P = Problem
The problem is presented as the *motivation*. Specific criteria are given to motivate problem-solving behaviors.

CPS = Creative Problem Solving
This is the *process-oriented activity step*. Here students generate *multiple ways to solve the problem*, as they brainstorm and work with materials and techniques.

S = Solution
The *solution* is the *final product*, arrived at by synthesizing ideas generated in the CPS activity.

FIGURE 7.7
Creative Problem-Solving Teaching Model

number of ways. Students may draw ideas, construct three-dimensional models, or make a variety of "sketches" using different materials to ascertain which media and processes work best. Ideas generated in this step converge at the bottom of the model in the solution step, where students demonstrate elaboration skills in the creation of an original art product.

The steps that follow illustrate a practical application of the model in the unit "Symbolic Fish Kites" (fourth grade level).

I. Presentation of the Problem:

  A. The unit begins with an introduction to Japanese kites.

  B. Japanese carp kites are presented as the cultural exemplar. (These are wind sock–like kites, designed as carps, hung from bamboo poles. Although they were originally flown in front of houses to announce the birth of boys—the carp is a symbol of strength and virility—their use has become more generalized in modern times. Today they are used to honor both boys and girls in a celebration called the Children's Festival.

  C. The motivating problem is defined:
    Design a fish kite to fly in front of your house on your birthday in celebration of yourself.
    Follow these criteria:

      1. Include three patterns that visually symbolize your personal qualities.
      2. Use a color scheme that reflects your personality.
      3. Be creative in designing the shape and details of your kite.
      4. Include your name and birth date somewhere on your kite.

II. Presentation of CPS Activity:

  A. Instruct students in making a fish pattern by drawing a design on a folded sheet of 12″ × 18″ paper. Ask them to cut out the pattern to make a fish, as shown in the diagram.

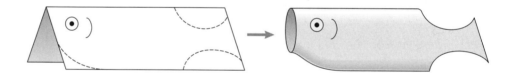

  B. Present a brainstorming activity in which students generate as many ideas as possible in two minutes to modify the basic pattern. Record responses in a thematic web on the board: lengthen the fish, fatten the fish, change the shape of the body and/or tail, add fins, add teeth, make gills, stripes, spots, spikes, etc.

  C. Provide students with materials—construction paper, tissue paper, glue, scissors, markers—with which to make at least three sketches for the final product. Each sketch must vary in shape, design, and lettering style.

III. Presentation Leading to the Solution:

  A. Ask students to refer to the sketches they created in the CPS activity. Tell them they may either select the design they like the best to use in the construction of the final product or use the best ideas from several sketches in creating a new composite fish like Figure 7.8.

  B. Using a sequential web, instruct students in how to progress from the sketch stage to the creation of a final product.

  C. Provide an opportunity for students to display and discuss products, hanging kites from poles in an outdoor exhibit.

  D. Use a compare-and-contrast web to guide students in analyzing similarities and differences between Japanese carp kites and their own products.

FIGURE 7.8
Composite Fish

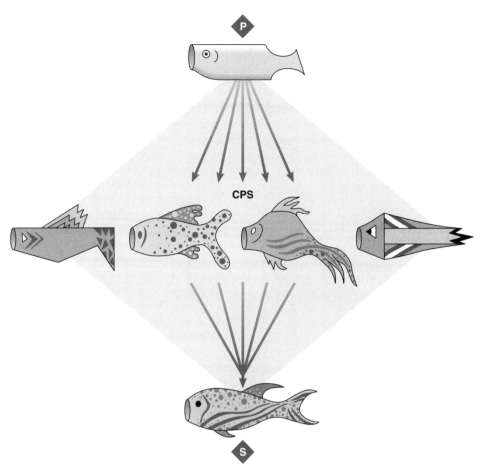

FIGURE 7.8
Composite Fish

S U M M A R Y

The development of creative behaviors is a rationale that has gone in and out of favor in the history of art education. Creativity was not particularly valued as long as society-centered art education focused on skill building through closed-ended exercises. Child-centered approaches of the past and present have placed more emphasis on self-expression and creative development than subject-centered approaches. Today art educators most likely to promote creativity are those emphasizing a studio-centered approach. Most noteworthy among this group is Arts PROPEL, focusing on the growth of artistic intelligences.

As studies in the fields of psychology and education have demonstrated, creativity is not something people either have or lack depending on genetic factors. Creativity is a group of characteristics that can be developed through problem-solving experiences. These characteristics include (1) fluency (the ability to think of many ideas, (2) flexibility (the ability to think divergently, generating responses in different categories), (3) originality (the ability to generate unusual or novel responses), and elaboration (the ability to think convergently, providing detail in a single solution). Just as "bats" are presented as a metaphor for mindless activities devoid of any challenge to solve problems, the nine-dots exercise is presented to illustrate problem-solving behavior. "Going beyond the nine dots," as illustrated in the diagram at the right, can be viewed as a metaphor for creative problem solving.

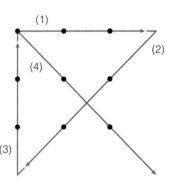

Solution to Nine-Dots Problem

When considering strategies to promote creativity in grades K–12, one of the most important factors to consider, especially in designing experiences for young learners, is age-appropriateness. As students are led to interpret ideas using a variety of art materials and processes, they develop creative capacities. Vehicles to develop problem-solving skills include open-ended assignments, brainstorming activities, webs, and Bauhaus-type exercises. The creative problem-solving teaching model provides a structure on which to develop a unit of study. Intended specifically to develop problem-solving behavior, the model guides students though a three-step process. Step 1 presents a problem as the motivation. Step 2 involves creative problem-solving activities in which students experiment with materials and techniques and generate multiple ideas to solve the problem. In step 3 students create solutions in the form of their art products. Practical application of the model is demonstrated in the unit "Symbolic Fish Kites." This unit illustrates how to put the pieces together—combining a cultural exemplar, an open-ended assignment, brainstorming, a CPS activity, and webs. The goal is to move beyond exploration of media and processes, beyond skill development, into the realm of personal interpretation and meaning in self-expressive works of art.

A. SEQUENCING STUDIO ACTIVITIES THROUGH THE CPS TEACHING MODEL

Directions
1. Select a grade level. 2. Use the CPS teaching model to structure a studio experience: Define the problem through specified criteria, describe what students will do in the CPS activity, and describe what students will do to create the solution.

Grade Level:_____

State the problem, and specify the criteria defining it.

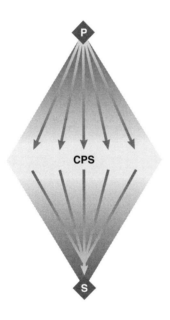

Describe the CPS activity, in which students generate multiple solutions to the problem through a brainstorming exercise.

Describe what students do to move from the CPS activity to the creation of the final solution.

B. DESIGNING A BRAINSTORMING WORKSHEET

Directions

1. In the space below design a brainstorming worksheet to be used in the CPS activity step described on the previous worksheet. 2. Include instructions for *visual* and/or *verbal* responses from students.

ENCOURAGING
REFLECTION

One of our goals in art education is to promote growth—perceptual, affective, cognitive, creative, expressive—by engaging students in art experiences. We have discussed strategies to promote skill development, self-expression, creative thinking, and authentic responses. All this is about what we as teachers do to affect students. In addition to growing as a result of motivation from the outside, students learn from the inside. They grow by observing their own processes, behaviors, and products. They reflect on what worked, what didn't, and what to do next time. Reflective behavior is a large part of the creative process and an important component in the growth of all individuals. Within the context of art education, reflective activities may encourage students to contemplate such questions as "What am I communicating through my art?" and "How well have I expressed myself?"

Students are not likely to analyze their behaviors, assess their work, or ask these questions unless we present opportunities to do so. These opportunities need to be built into units of study, providing time to reflect on experiences and accomplishments. Reflective activities can be used to "come full circle" in a unit, creating closure for both students and teacher. Processes involve returning to the beginning of a unit—the broad goals supported by specific objectives— and comparing what was intended with what actually occurred. As a teacher, you will continuously assess behaviors and products to determine whether goals and objectives have been met. This chapter focuses on how to lead students to reflect on experiences and assess their own processes and products. Sections include (1) reflecting on art behaviors, (2) assessing art products, and (3) engaging in critical dialogue.

▼ REFLECTING ON ART BEHAVIORS

By reflecting on their behaviors, students may connect actions to outcomes, take active roles in their growth, and find meaning and value in their experiences as "artists." One way to promote reflection is to get students talking at the end of an activity or unit. Well-posed questions can motivate students to think about what they learned and did. The problem with relying solely on oral communication, however, is that the most outspoken students are more likely to participate, whereas the least verbal may be most reticent. You have no way of knowing what may be happening in the minds of silent students. Because our goal is participation from *all* students, many teachers provide for written feedback. They design *reflection sheets* to guide students to think about how they met specific objectives.

In designing reflection sheets, keep in mind that students will engage in various kinds of art behaviors. Reviewing the continuum of closed-ended to open-ended to laissez-faire approaches (see Figure 8.1), we are reminded of the variety of processes in which students become involved to create art.

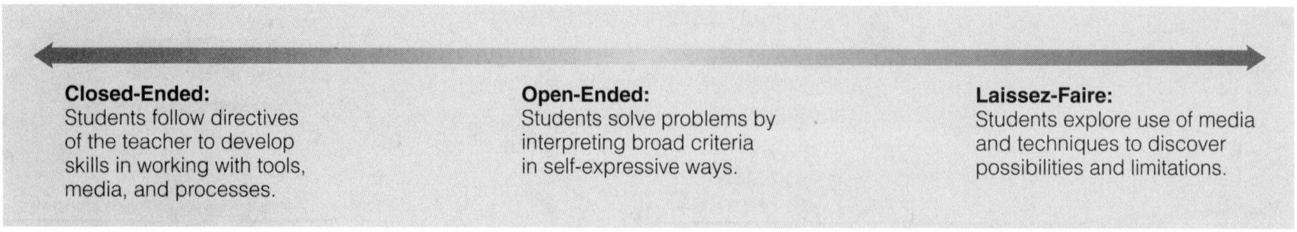

← Closed-Ended: Students follow directives of the teacher to develop skills in working with tools, media, and processes.

Open-Ended: Students solve problems by interpreting broad criteria in self-expressive ways.

Laissez-Faire: Students explore use of media and techniques to discover possibilities and limitations. →

FIGURE 8.1
Closed-Ended, Open-Ended, Laissez-Faire Behaviors

A reflection sheet may tell students of the purpose of a particular activity or ask them to supply the purpose. It should also ask students to analyze their processes or behaviors in attempts to meet lesson objectives. You can design different generic forms on which students provide feedback about closed-ended, open-ended, and laissez-faire experiences; or you can tailor forms to reflect specific assignments. To illustrate possibilities in designing reflection sheets, let's return to the unit "The Abstraction of Georgia O'Keeffe," presented in Chapter 4. This unit consists of the following process-oriented activities:

1. A closed-ended exercise intended to build perceptual and drawing skills (contour drawing)

2. An open-ended exercise intended to promote problem solving (abstracting a natural object)

3. A laissez-faire exercise intended to promote investigation of media and processes (exploring oil pastel and watercolor)

Time permitting, a teacher might use reflection sheets to conclude each of these experiences. The samples that follow illustrate both specific and generic forms applicable to this unit and include the following:

1. Worksheet 8.1: Sample Reflection Sheet for a Closed-Ended Activity: "How Skillful Am I at Contour Drawing?"

2. Worksheet 8.2: Sample Reflection Sheet for an Open-Ended Activity: "Abstracting a Natural Object"

3. Worksheet 8.3: Generic Reflection Sheet for an Open-Ended Activity

4. Worksheet 8.4: Generic Reflection Sheet for a Laissez-Faire Activity

HOW SKILLFUL AM I AT CONTOUR DRAWING?

Directions

Assess your ability to use the contour drawing process by answering the following questions. Use the boxes at the right to record checkmarks and points.

	Yes	No	Points
1. I looked mostly at my object, not at my drawing. Give yourself (a) 5 points if you looked at the object the entire time, (b) 4 points if you referred to your drawing occasionally, (c) 3 points if you referred to your drawing half the time, and (d) 1 point if you rarely looked at your object.			
2. I used long, smooth, continuous lines as I drew. Give yourself (a) 5 points for drawing the object in one long continuous line, (b) 4 points for lifting your drawing instrument occasionally, and (c) 3 points for using many short lines.			
3. I looked carefully, noticing and drawing lots of details. Rate yourself from 5 (highest) to 1 (lowest) on your ability to observe and draw details.			
4. I took a risk by using ink rather than pencil. Give yourself 4 bonus points for the use of a pen.			
5. I refrained from erasing. Give yourself 2 bonus points if you did not erase.			
6. I made corrections by redrawing rather than erasing. Give yourself 1 bonus point for redrawing.			
7. I chose to draw a difficult view of my object (such as a front view or foreshortened angle). Give yourself 5 to 1 points for the difficulty of the angle you chose.			
8. I drew more than 1 view. Give yourself an extra point for each additional drawing you did.			
9. I did my best. Give yourself 5 to 1 points for the effort you put forth in this exercise.			
10. I accomplished the objective (to draw at least one view of a natural object using contour line). Determine how successful you were in demonstrating your ability to do contour drawing by rating yourself from 5 to 1.			
TOTAL number of points:			

ABSTRACTING A NATURAL OBJECT

1. The objective for this activity was to demonstrate creativity by designing four abstract images of a natural object.

2. The natural object I selected was _____

3. I abstracted my object by exaggerating certain qualities. The qualities I chose to exaggerate were

A._____ B._____ C._____ D._____

4. I exaggerated to intensify the essence of my object by doing the following:

A. In drawing 1, I exaggerated the quality _____

by _____

B. In drawing 2, I exaggerated the quality _____

by _____

C. In drawing 3, I exaggerated the quality _____

by _____

D. In drawing 4, I exaggerated the quality _____

by _____

5. The design I like best is number _____ because _____

_____

_____

_____

_____

6. On a 5 (highest) to 1 (lowest) scale, I rate my level of creativity as _____ because _____

_____

_____

_____

_____

_____

GENERIC REFLECTION SHEET FOR AN OPEN-ENDED ACTIVITY

Name: _____

1. The objective of this activity was to

_____

_____

2. The criteria defining "the problem" were

a. _____

b. _____

c. _____

d. _____

3. I solved the problem by doing the following:

_____

_____

_____

_____

_____

4. My solution is/is not creative because

_____

_____

_____

_____

5. The grade I believe I have earned for this activity is _____

because _____

_____

_____

_____

_____

GENERIC REFLECTION SHEET FOR A LAISSEZ-FAIRE ACTIVITY

Name:_____

1. The purpose of this activity was to _____

_____

_____

2. The materials I used were _____

3. The processes or techniques I explored were _____

4. As I did this activity, I learned, discovered, gained ideas about the following:

_____

_____

_____

_____

_____

_____

_____

_____

_____

_____

_____

_____

_____

5. I thought this activity was_____

   (fill in the blank with an appropriate word or phrase—*really interesting, lots of fun, a great experience, a waste of*

   time, boring, etc.) because _____

_____

_____

6. The grade I believe I have earned for this activity is _____

   because _____

ASSESSING ART PRODUCTS

Notice that in these sample exercises students were not asked to comment on the quality of their work. These worksheets were designed to focus on *process*. Students were asked to reflect on their actions, as they developed skills, generated ideas, and explored media. By doing so, students readied themselves to engage in creating "works of art." Reflection sheets designed for product-oriented experiences may also include questions about processes and the unit itself. In addition, they focus on the art product, asking students to make judgments about the quality of their work. Worksheet 8.5 on page 159, "Specific Product-Oriented Reflection Sheet" (Unit Reflection Sheet: 'The Abstraction of Georgia O'Keeffe') models structure and content appropriate for a unit closure. It is divided into three sections. The first reminds students about their ideas, intentions, and processes. The second shifts attention to the product. Students review the criteria defining the assignment and make judgments based on their works' reflection of each criterion. The third section focuses on the unit in general.

Many teachers design similar forms for use at the conclusion of a unit of study. They may walk students through critical thinking processes, demonstrating how to use the forms. After completing reflection sheets, students may tape them to the backs of their works so that teachers can compare actual products with students' perceptions. Before returning work to students, teachers may then use the forms themselves to record their own assessments. By using well-designed reflection sheets and receiving sensitive guidance from teachers, students can begin to look at their own processes and artwork, pondering questions such as "What motivated me to express this idea? What was I trying to communicate? How well did I say it?"

These questions can be answered at one level by reflecting back to the specific criteria defining a particular studio problem. As students gain experience in art making and critical thinking, they develop a wider perspective, however. High school art majors, for example, can be encouraged to look beyond particular criteria defining a specific assignment to *general* criteria applicable to a variety of studio problems. These criteria (which can be remembered as the four *C*'s) are (1) content, (2) creativity, (3) composition, and (4) craftsmanship.

- *Content* involves message or meaning. It is about expressing the "inside," the authentic self. It has to do with communicating something worth saying, evoking thoughts and feelings, impacting the viewer. Meaningful content is most likely to result when students are encouraged to access the personal, interpreting open-ended assignments in self-expressive ways.

- *Creativity* is closely related to content in that it also deals with self-expression. The focus goes beyond expressing the self, however, to expressing the self in novel ways. Creativity is about fluency, flexibility, originality, and elaboration.

- *Composition* involves the use of visual language to communicate intended messages. It focuses on the *form* of the image, as expressed through *art elements* and *design principles*.

- *Craftsmanship* involves using tools, media, processes, and techniques. The focus is on skill development, as reflected in well-made art products.

Worksheet 8.6, the "Generic Product-Oriented Reflection Sheet," provides a structure in which specific and general criteria are combined. Whether you are designing such a form for students at a high level of experience or for "budding artists" in third grade, consider developmental levels. The idea is not to overwhelm students with written work, but to facilitate their growth through appropriate critical activities. Even young art learners can convey something in writing about the content of their works. You might design reflection sheets asking students to tell what their works are about, as modeled in Worksheet 8.7, "Interpreting Your Artwork." Through this process of interpreting meaning, students themselves become connected to their works and help us as teachers to understand their products as authentic self-expressions. Worksheets 8.5, 8.6, and 8.7 provide models you can use in designing forms for students at various cognitive and artistic levels.

UNIT REFLECTION SHEET:
THE ABSTRACTION OF GEORGIA O'KEEFFE

A. Read the questions below and fill in the blanks.

1. The natural object I selected to work from was _____

2. The quality that attracted me to this object was _____

3. I attempted to intensify this quality by _____

4. The characteristic(s) that my abstraction shares with O'Keeffe's work is (are)

   _____

5. The qualities that make my work unique are _____

   _____

6. What I like most about my work is _____

   _____

7. If I could change anything in my work, I would _____

B. Assess the quality of your work by recording a score of 5 (highest) to 1 (lowest) on fulfillment of each criterion.

	Student Score	Teacher Score
1. Intensify the essence of the object through the use of art elements.	☐	☐
2. Use at least one of O'Keeffe's abstracting devices.	☐	☐
3. Combine oil pastel and watercolor.	☐	☐
4. Fill the picture plane.	☐	☐
5. Overall assessment of aesthetic quality.	☐	☐

C. Comment on the unit in general:

1. What were your most important learnings? _____

2. What did you enjoy most? _____

3. Do you have any suggestions to improve the unit? _____

GENERIC PRODUCT-ORIENTED REFLECTION SHEET

Directions
A. Describe the assignment.
B. List the specific criteria defining the assignment and judge your work on each criterion by recording a 5 (highest) to 1 (lowest) score.
C. Judge the quality of your work on each general criterion with a 5–1 score and support your judgment with an explanatory statement.
D. Provide a general statement, commenting on level of involvement, work habits, and results.

A. Description of Assignment:

B. Specific Criteria (list below):	**Student Score**	**Teacher Score**
1.	☐	☐
2.	☐	☐
3.	☐	☐

C. General Criteria:	**Explanatory Statement:**		
1. Content:		☐	☐
2. Creativity:		☐	☐
3. Composition:		☐	☐
4. Craftsmanship:		☐	☐
5. Overall Aesthetic Quality:		☐	☐

D. General Statement by Student:

Teacher's Comments:

INTERPRETING YOUR ARTWORK

1. What was the assignment for this art activity?

2. Describe what your artwork is about, what you were trying to say, or what it means to you:

3. How do you feel about your work? Do you like it? Why or why not? Does it say what you intended to communicate? Why or why not?

▼ ENGAGING IN CRITICAL DIALOGUE

Written reflection sheets should not take the place of oral discussions. On the contrary, class sharing is what prepares students to make assessments in written form. Through sharing and discussion of products, students learn from one another. They communicate ideas, model behaviors, and contribute to the synergy of the group. In addition, oral discussions are important because not all students possess a level of reading, writing, and cognitive skills needed to communicate effectively on paper. Every student can, however, be encouraged to share his or her work and to say something about intention and/or meaning. This section focuses on strategies to promote sharing and critical thinking in oral discussions.

Guiding students to share perceptions and judgments about their own and others' artwork can be challenging—either because everyone wants to participate at once or because no one wants to participate at all. Primary-level students generally like to share experiences, talk about their work, and tell their classmates what good jobs everyone has done. Middle school students tend to hunker over their work in the hope that no one will see it, and may believe they will die of embarrassment if they have to show their creations. The teacher, standing between these two extremes, must design sharing strategies to avoid absolute chaos on the one hand and sullen silence on the other. The strategies presented in the following boxes illustrate approaches used by art teachers on elementary through high school levels.

Suggestions for "Show and Tell" at the Primary Level

1. Have all supplies cleaned up and students sitting quietly before sharing begins.

2. Select a small group of students to share each art period. You may use a number of methods to choose students:

    a. Select students at one table, rotating tables each week.

    b. Ask for one student to volunteer (or choose one student) from each table.

    c. Call on students in alphabetical order.

3. Keep track of who shares and provide opportunities for all to participate during the semester.

4. Ask students to share by stating what their works are about, what they were trying to say or do, what they like about their works.

5. If time permits, ask the audience to respond to work by sharing comments ("I like . . . because . . .").

6. Keep sharing short. A five-minute closure is sufficient at this level.

A Strategy for Sharing Artwork with Elementary-Level Students

This procedure may be used to reinforce understanding of objectives and to promote perceptual skills and critical thinking.

1. At the conclusion of a studio activity, have students clean up and leave their artwork on the tables.

2. Select one student to state the objective of the lesson in his or her own words: "Today we were to . . ."

3. Have the student quietly circulate in the room, tapping the shoulders of four students whose works best meet the objective.

4. Ask the four selected students to stand in front of the class and display their art.

5. Ask members of the class to make comments about each work, sharing what they like and pointing out how each piece met the objective *in a different way.*

6. Select a different student each week to choose artwork. Ask that students whose work has not been recently chosen be selected for discussion each week.

Praise, Question, Polish (PQP)

PQP can provide a nonthreatening way to give and receive feedback on strengths and weaknesses of works.

1. Three-quarters of the way into a studio activity, ask students to find partners with whom they are willing to share and discuss their work. Choose one student as your partner, and model the PQP procedure:

   a. Clarify the assignment and criteria: "The assignment was to create a landscape using tissue collage. The criteria were to suggest mood through the use of color and to include a focal point."

   b. Begin the assessment with *praise* for meeting a criterion and for achieving quality in a particular aspect: "These reds and oranges make me feel warm. You really did well in suggesting the hot intensity of the desert through the color scheme."

   c. Find an aspect of the work that is not so successful. Pose your negative assessment in the form of a *question*: "I know we were supposed to create a focal point. I'm having trouble finding one in your composition. Can you tell me where it is and what you did to create it?"

   d. Let your partner respond to the question: "I tried to make this mountain the focal point by making it bigger than the other objects."

   e. Offer a suggestion for how to improve or *polish* the work: "I see what you mean. Perhaps if you used a darker value of brown, the mountain would stand out more."

   f. Allow your partner to respond: "Thanks. That's a great idea. I could also add more detail to the mountain. I'm ready to get back to work now!"

2. Have students assess one another's work in partners using the PQP procedure.

3. After the exercise allow students to continue to work and act on "polishing" strategies their partners or they themselves contributed.

Conducting Critique Sessions with an Entire Class

This procedure can be used with students who have had enough experience with one another and with giving and receiving critical comments to feel comfortable sharing with an entire class.

1. Display all work together three-quarters of the way into a studio experience.

2. Review the criteria of the assignment on the board.

3. Ask students to focus on one criterion at a time as they praise works and offer "polishing" suggestions.

4. After specific criteria have been discussed, ask students to select the works they judge as superior in general criteria: (a) content, (b) creativity, (c) composition, (d) craftsmanship, and (e) overall aesthetic expression. Have them defend their choices.

5. Ask students, as they feel comfortable, to offer additional polishing suggestions.

These strategies are presented as vehicles to (1) increase perceptual awareness, (2) develop critical capacities, (3) express appreciation, and (4) promote growth in art making. Through these activities students connect with others and develop skills to evaluate work. As they become increasingly discerning and articulate as critics, they develop their potentials to grow as artists.

CRITIQUE SESSION

A GROUP of advanced high school students was just getting ready for a critique session when it was interrupted by visitors from a local college. The visitors, all preparing to be art teachers, were participating in a field experience and had come to observe. They were greeted warmly and told to get ready for the show. High school students were hanging their works on the bulletin board. First the teacher labeled tables as A, B, C, D, and F. She then reviewed the criteria for the assignment. Next she asked students to remove someone else's work from the board and place it on the A, B, C, D, or F table to indicate its quality. After all artwork had been placed, students walked around, viewing each table's collection. If a student believed a work had been misplaced, he (or she) could move it to another table as long as he could justify his opinion. The students began moving pieces, pointing out deficiencies in works and in others' opinions. The art education students stood in the back, watching in stunned silence. At one point a college student cornered a high school student and said, "This is the most brutal thing I've ever seen. You must hate it!"

"Hate it?" responded the high school student. "This is the most fun we have all year! This class has more scholarship winners than all the schools in the community put together. Do you know why? It's these critiques! This might look brutal to you, but to us it's just a little friendly support."

Besides illustrating the relationship between art criticism and art production, this story reminds us of the wide range of activities appropriate for various populations. The strategies we use to promote growth in high school seniors vying for art scholarships are not the same as those we use with first graders. As in designing written reflection forms, we structure critique sessions to meet the needs of students. We take them from where they are at any given point and gradually lead them toward higher levels of vision and expression. Some guidelines for how to do this are presented in the following box:

Suggestions for Leading Critique Sessions

- Treat beginning-level students, no matter what their ages, gently, by focusing on what they did right.

- Design guidelines for behavior that create a safe atmosphere for sharing (such as being respectful of others' works and opinions).

- Motivate students to want to participate by beginning with activities that are easy, nonthreatening, fun, and helpful.

- Model what to do and say.

- Lessen the fear of sharing by having students share first with a friend and then with students at a table, before sharing with an entire class.

- Structure sessions to promote positive attitudes, encouraging students to view critical remarks as suggestions to further growth.

- Balance a discussion of weaknesses by pointing out strengths.
- Encourage students to self-evaluate as they assess strengths and weaknesses of their own works.

S U M M A R Y

Reflection can be considered as any oral or written process in which students look back on what they did and what they produced to meet goals and objectives within a unit of study. It is an aspect of art criticism dealing with the "inside." As students are given opportunities to contemplate what they did, why they did it, how well they did it, and what value it has to them, they develop an understanding of how they express through art. Making art and discussing art in critical experiences are synergistically related. As we lead students to see, interpret, and make judgments, we promote behaviors they will internalize and use as artists. Our goal is to support growth in art making through the development of critical capacities. Strategies to develop reflective behaviors, include (1) reflecting on art behaviors, (2) assessing art products, and (3) engaging in critical discussions.

One way to promote critical thinking is through oral discussions presented at or near the conclusion of studio activities. These may be as simple as five-minute show-and-tell "sharings" with kindergartners, or they may be hour-long critique sessions at the high school level. Their length and intensity are dependent on the developmental and experiential levels of students. Teachers begin "lightly" with young students, presenting short exercises focusing on the positive. Gradually, as students develop perceptual, cognitive, and critical skills, they can engage in discussions at progressively higher levels.

At a point midway through the elementary years, most students have gained sufficient reading, writing, and thinking skills to discuss their works on paper. A combination of written and oral activities can work well. Through class discussions students share perceptions and ideas and model critical thinking for one another. Written exercises in the form of reflection sheets provide opportunities for every student to actively engage and give feedback. Process-oriented experiences, not intended to result in a final product, may be explored through reflection sheets focusing on behaviors (objectives). Their structure and content vary to emphasize differences in closed-ended, open-ended, and laissez-faire activities.

Reflection sheets for product-oriented experiences may also include questions about behaviors and the meeting of objectives. Primarily, however, they ask students to assess their artwork by determining a level at which criteria were met. Two sets of criteria may be used in judging the quality of artwork. Specific criteria are those guidelines defining a particular studio assignment. General criteria are broad enough to be applicable to any product-oriented assignment. Four identified here are content, creativity, composition, and craftsmanship:

- *Content* involves message or meaning. It is about expressing the "inside," the authentic self. It has to do with communicating something worth saying, evoking thoughts and feelings, impacting the viewer. Meaningful content is most likely to result when students are encouraged to access the personal, interpreting open-ended assignments in self-expressive ways.

- *Creativity* is closely related to content in that it also deals with self-expression. The focus goes beyond expressing the self, however, to expressing the self in novel ways. Creativity is about fluency, flexibility, originality, and elaboration.
- *Composition* involves the use of visual language to communicate intended messages. It focuses on the *form* of the image, as expressed through *art elements* and *design principles.*
- *Craftsmanship* involves using tools, media, processes, and techniques. The focus is on skill development, as reflected in well-made art products.

As students mature artistically, they can use these general criteria. Using reflective exercises, they may expand their views of art; increase their appreciation of art; develop their skills as art makers; and contribute in general to their perceptual, cognitive, and expressive development.

A. DESIGNING A REFLECTION SHEET FOR A PROCESS-ORIENTED ACTIVITY

Directions

Design a reflection sheet for a specific process-oriented experience included in a unit of study you have developed. Refer to the sample reflection sheets in this chapter as models in creating a form for a closed-ended, open-ended, or laissez-faire activity.

B. DESIGNING A CLOSING WORKSHEET
FOR A UNIT OF STUDY

Directions

Design a closing worksheet for a unit of study you have developed. Include opportunities for students to reflect on 1. their ideas, intentions, and processes; 2. the meeting of particular and/or general criteria in the creation of an artwork; and 3. the unit in general. (You may use the reflection sheet designed for the Georgia O'Keeffe unit as a model.)

EXPANDING INTO THE OUTSIDE

Part III adds yet another dimension to our model of art education. This section focuses primarily on content illustrating art's connection to the outside world. Chapter 9, "Embracing Diversity," deals with art as a reflection of humankind, providing strategies to explore cultures beyond one's own environment, culture within one's own environment, and connections between the two. Chapter 10, "Making Interdisciplinary Connections," examines interdisciplinary planning, providing guidance for integrating art into the general curriculum. The content of this chapter reflects these concepts: Art touches everyone. It both influences and is influenced by all of life. Chapter 11, "Focusing on Art Criticism and Aesthetics," and Chapter 12, "Presenting Art History," examine strategies to present cultural exemplars in greater depth. These chapters provide teaching models addressing processes and content to increase students' knowledge and appreciation of art. This information supports the view that the study of the "outside" enhances the "inside." Through the study of art, students enrich their visual vocabularies, connect with others, and perceive what they are doing within a wide context of expressions. All this helps students to validate their ideas and to affirm themselves as makers of art.

EMBRACING DIVERSITY

As we continue our exploration of art and how to teach it, we look to the world outside the child, outside the classroom. Seeing from a wider perspective, you may come to understand and to lead your students to understand that all peoples express through the language of vision. You may recall Dissanayake's statement (1991): "Art is not confined to a small coterie of geniuses, visionaries, cranks, and charlatans—indistinguishable from one another—but is instead a fundamental human species characteristic." We can convey this message by presenting art as cultural expression. We can lead students to understand how art is an extension of themselves within their own culture. We can encourage students to view other cultures, not only to learn about others, but also to become more sensitive to themselves. By comparing their own culture to others, students gain awareness of diversity, particularity, uniqueness. They also increase their awareness of commonalties, universal characteristics, and art expressions that reflect our connectedness as a species. This chapter models how to heighten awareness of the "inside" by contrasting it with the "outside," focusing on the teaching of multicultural art education. Sections include (1) multiculturalism within the context of art education, (2) multicultural unit planning, and (3) flexible approaches to planning.

▼ MULTICULTURALISM WITHIN THE CONTEXT OF ART EDUCATION

We will begin by looking at values of the larger society, as reflected in general education and refined in art education. Although Americans have referred to their nation as a "melting pot," written history for the most part has presented culture from the perspective of one particular group—that of the white, European male. Not until the 1960s and 1970s, in response to the civil rights movement and the women's liberation movement, did curriculum content reflect our culture through a broader lens. At this time courses in black and Hispanic studies and women's studies began to be offered. Concurrently art education, in what was a society-driven approach, began to present the art of women and non-Western peoples. The "melting pot" began to be replaced by the "patchwork quilt" as a metaphor for American culture.

The move, in the 1960s and 1970s, toward multiculturalism to promote ethnic pride and support a pluralistic society was not particularly strong. Emerging subject-centered approaches were more concerned with presenting academic content than in celebrating diversity. Art continued to be presented primarily from a Eurocentric perspective. This was especially true of early DBAE practices. In their presentation of art as culture, discipline-based educators of the 1980s relied heavily on the art history texts of the time. Most of these began with Paleolithic images in the caves of France and Spain and progressed chronologically through Europe and America. Their structure did not invite exploration of non-Western cultures nor did the labels they used to clump together art outside the mainstream—"naive," "primitive," and "folk." With a strong focus on the study of art objects, DBAE proponents attracted particular attention to the historical content they were presenting. By the 1990s many of these art educators, the content of their courses, and their resources were attacked as being narrow and stereotypical, representing neither global perspectives, nor art on earth. The emphasis we see today on multicultural art education is in part a reaction against DBAE practices of the past.

As we move forward in the twenty-first century, we see additional factors that have contributed to today's multicultural emphasis. We are experiencing an expanded consciousness—one that embraces diversity rather than builds boundaries, one that makes connections rather than maintains separateness. In the last half of the twentieth century, people witnessed the following: the tearing down of the Berlin Wall and the Iron Curtain; increased emigration and immigration; travel to anywhere on the planet in the space of a single day; instant global communication; Earth captured in photographs taken from space; humans landing on the moon; advances in astrophysics stretching exploration from our planet, out to our solar system, and beyond into the visible universe. Our perceptions of Earth have changed. Our planet is appearing increasingly smaller, and we, its inhabitants, are appearing to become closer together. Certainly our students will continue to experience themselves as connected in and to the world to a degree far greater than previous generations. As a culture growing up with television, videos, CD-ROMs, and the Internet, they have access to a much wider scope of information and hold the potential to become leaders in global society. To not embrace the entire globe, to not address multiple cultures seems as ludicrous as to represent the entire population of Earth from the perspective of one dominant people, culture, or geographical area. The question is not "whether to" but "how to."

Educators of the 1990s have contributed to our insights into how and how not to address multiculturalism. They have begun by defining terms. The term *multicultural* has been used in reference to cultures, subcultures, and expressions outside what is perceived as the dominant culture (white, Eurocentric, industrialized, male). Addressing our multiethnic population within the United States, we use the term to refer to expressions of those whose ancestries are non-European: Native Americans, Hispanics, African Americans, and Asian Americans. As we have become more and more globally oriented, the term has broadened. Today we use *multicultural* to reflect individual diversity on earth. It embraces men and women, young and old, tribal and industrialized peoples, folk artists and fine artists, and racial, ethnic, regional, religious, and socioeconomic groups all over the planet. This broad connotation serves art educators well. We can define the word by analyzing its component parts: *multi-* means more than one; *culture* refers to commonalities that bind a people together—shared heritage, beliefs, customs, traditions, values, artistic expressions. A "multicultural experience," therefore, loosely defined, is one in which we compare our students' lives and art within the context of their own culture to the lives and art of members of another culture. Through multicultural experiences, we guide students to learn about others and themselves, as they compare and contrast commonalities and differences. We set the stage to explore "inside" and "outside" aspects of our model of art education. But this is more easily said than done. A number of issues have arisen concerning how to optimally address both aspects. Three important considerations are discussed next: (1) how to present other cultures, (2) how to relate other cultures to our own culture, and (3) how to provide for meaningful experiences.

HOW TO PRESENT OTHER CULTURES

Years ago teachers used to address "other cultures" through presentations on "Indians," "Africans," and "Orientals." Well-meaning though they may have been, they were promoting stereotypes through these generalized, superficial approaches. As we have become more conscious of our planet and its inhabitants, we are more sensitive to individual cultures. Every group of people, every society, every culture has particularities. We need to present others in ways that reveal the authenticity of their expressions and that celebrate their particularities. The following suggestions can guide you in how to do this:

- *"Count to one."* Focus on one people at a time. For example, by addressing the Ashantis by themselves, rather than as "Africans," you can avoid generalizing and stereotyping all Africans as having "typical characteristics." Instead, you reveal ways in which one particular culture is unique, special, and different from neighboring peoples in Africa and people in the United States.

- *Point out similarities and differences of like peoples.* In some situations you may explore a geographical area (the Southwest United States, for example) and present several peoples within the region (the Navajos, Zunis, and Hopis). Avoid overgeneralizing; point out commonalities among the cultures, but also point out differences.

- *Do research.* Prepare yourself to present any culture as accurately as possible. Just as we promote integrity in our students by encouraging authentic expressions, we must act with integrity in presenting the lives, values, and artistic expressions of others. Make an effort to adequately inform yourself. You can choose what to share, of all you have learned, with your students. Factors such as students' ages and developmental levels, a topic's relevance to your unit of study, and time constraints will guide your selections.

- *Present "sensitive" issues sensitively.* As advanced technology has brought about the information age, we are now more than ever before in a position to enrich our own and our students' lives through knowledge of others' cultures—their values, beliefs, spiritual practices, and art-making experiences (which may be quite different from ours). Art educators who explore such aspects of art in and as culture sometimes do so at the risk of having their intentions misunderstood. Questions that can provide clarity and direction in the teaching of sensitive issues are these:

  1. What are other cultures' beliefs and values, and how do they use art to express them?

  2. Is a given art expression, especially one dealing with sacred beliefs, human rights, and political views, appropriate to present to our students?

  3. If, in the teacher's judgment, some artwork is not appropriate, what should be excluded, and why? If the teacher believes some such artwork is acceptable, for what reasons and for what populations of students is it most appropriate?

  4. How can we present sensitive materials in ways that illustrate their purpose and value within another culture?

  5. How can we provide bridges between another culture and our own culture, showing why the study of such materials may have value to our students?

  6. How can we make clear that when we teach about the art of other cultures, we are not asking students to adopt the beliefs, values, religious practices, or artistic expressions of others? For example, in presenting the spiritual practices guiding the performing of Navajo sandpainting, we are not asking our students to embrace the Navajo gods or belief system.

Some art educators enthusiastically confront these issues, whereas others avoid them. Whether you feel comfortable exploring sensitive issues and artwork may depend on your population of students, their community, and its openness to diverse ideas and aesthetic expressions. Another factor may be your definition of art. Is art simply a decorative object that ornaments a room? Can art be a political poster, a mural expressing the horrors of war, a ritual mask used in a spiritual ceremony? As multiculturalism has expanded, so have many individuals' views of art. Art educators have found ways to present different kinds of art expressions created by a wide range of peoples to serve a variety of functions within their cultures. The key to doing this successfully is research. By presenting art within an anthropological context, teachers have avoided accusations such as "teaching witchcraft."

The Navajo sandpainting unit that follows was especially designed to illustrate the presentation of sensitive materials, modeling how to

1. Do in-depth research on a culture, including spiritual practices, and present information as anthropological study.

2. Validate the use of "a spiritual object" as a cultural exemplar by placing it within its context of everyday life activities.

3. Discuss levels of meaning of symbolic objects within and outside a particular culture.

HOW TO RELATE OTHER CULTURES TO OUR CULTURE

Returning to our definition of multicultural, we are reminded that *multi-* means "more than one." The packages we design in multicultural units consist of two parts: an "outside" part, representing the other culture(s) and an "inside" part, representing the students' own lives and culture. This is an important concept that has been only marginally addressed in practices of the past. When DBAE was criticized as being narrow and Eurocentric, many educators broadened their scope to include multicultural exemplars. A wide variety of resources in the form of poster packets, slides, and videos appeared on the market. Many of these materials are excellent and may save a considerable amount of research time. However, their primary focus is on the "outside." Individual instructors must use these resources in creative teaching strategies that connect with the "inside." Teachers who ask students to appropriate the style, imagery, and/or content of another culture by mimicking its expressions may not be addressing their students' own lives and culture. For example, allowing students to copy Navajo symbols will not necessarily encourage them to consider symbolism as universal visual communication or to invent symbols meaningful to themselves. Such experience is therefore not multicultural. Because it does not lead the student inside both his or her own culture as well as into the focus culture, asking the student to consider and compare and contrast, such an experience is only "monocultural." *The essence of multicultural education lies in illuminating connections among cultures.* Procedures for relating the "outside" to the "inside" follow:

- *Present artistic expressions of other peoples within the context of their own cultures.* Discuss factors such as (1) why a piece was made, (2) what function or purpose it served, (3) who made it, (4) how it was made, (5) what materials were used, and (6) what happened to the object after it was created and used. Students should be presented with this information for these reasons: (1) Many non-Western people define, make, and use "art" in ways that differ from ours. Without understanding cultural contexts, students will not fully appreciate and connect with art as expressions of a people. (2) Art objects from different cultures are often made using materials and processes that we cannot use with our students. So we substitute age-appropriate materials and processes for traditional methods and media. This has resulted in making Kachina dolls from toilet paper tubes, a practice that has been criticized by art educators, artists, and others interested in preserving the integrity and authenticity of cultural art expressions. The problem is not the use of toilet paper tubes. It is failure to present cultural background through which students are led to understand authentic Hopi Kachinas as representations of sacred beliefs. The problem is trivializing the expressions of others by removing these objects from the cultures in which they were created and presenting them as if they could be reproduced using any old scrap materials. This is not to say that art is not and cannot be made from scrap. Many examples of art, including sacred images, are intentionally created from scrap as part of the inventive aesthetic statement. What we are referring to is the dominant culture trivializing a subordinate culture through insensitive presentations of expressions and experiences.

- *Move from the particular of an "outside" culture to universal expression.* Lead students from the specific cultural context of an art object to examine the bigger picture. Invite them to explore whether this cultural expression might be a particular example of a universal theme or common human behavior. For instance, totem poles, created by Northwest Coast Native American cultures, are representations of lineage used in ceremonies to celebrate family affairs. Rather than viewing totem poles as simply carved logs depicting animal and human forms, students can place them within larger contexts of universal expression, viewing them as (1) representations of family, (2) symbolic depictions of personal qualities, or (3) special objects used to celebrate people and events.

- *Move from the universal back to the particular of the "inside" (the students' own interpretations).* Guide students to move from a universal theme (family heritage) as exemplified by another culture (in totem poles) to self-expressive interpretations of the theme. This can be done by analyzing possible differences between students' interpretations and interpretations of the exemplifying culture. Differences may be expressed in a number of ways—through subject matter, content, style, materials, and/or processes. Using a thematic web, students may explore this problem: "How might I represent the theme family lineage through a personal/family totemic structure different from those created by Northwest Coast Native American cultures?"

HOW TO PROVIDE FOR MEANINGFUL EXPERIENCES

"Monoculturalism" masquerading as "multiculturalism" is one problem we have witnessed in our effort to expand into the outside. Another problem deals with lack of connectedness or sensitivity to our own populations of students. Again and again you have been encouraged to look to your students to discover who they are, what motivates them, and how to most effectively educate them. The outside cultures and exemplars we select must have meaning to them. Presenting African exemplars to an African-American population of students is not enough to create a relevant connection. "What," one might ask, "does a tribal society in Africa have in common with inner-city black teenagers dealing with issues such as poverty, broken homes, substance abuse, and crime?" Beyond skin color, very little connection may exist. Critics of multicultural practices remind us that African Americans are not Africans, and Mexican Americans may never have stepped foot in Mexico. Our students live in this country, create their own subcultures, and develop attitudes and values arising from life in families and neighborhoods here. This is not to say that there is no African or Mexican influence within African-American or Mexican-American populations; certainly there is. It is simply to point out that living in an American culture is a different experience from living in an African or Mexican culture. We can lead students to explore similarities and differences, rather than simply to mimic expressions of an outside culture. Moreover, we must be as sensitive to our own students as we are to the outside peoples we study. Suggestions for creating meaningful connections follow:

- *Go beyond skin color, race, religion, nationality, and gender as the primary reason for selecting an artist.* We do not need to abandon African exemplars because they are too far removed from culture within this country. We need to make curricular choices that are relevant to our students and to select exemplars that will most effectively support our units of study. Let's explore this idea using a hypothetical inner-city African-American population. Imagine designing an experience to engage students in a cooperative effort in which they share ideas, solve problems, create authentic expressions, enhance the school property, have fun, and promote neighborhood pride. The experience might involve creating murals on inside and/or outside walls of the school, reflecting aspects of school life, neighborhood, and culture. What exemplars might most effectively support this experience?

  1. Houses of the Ndebele people living in Southern Transvaal of South Africa are fitting. They are painted exclusively by women, who create bright, bold, geometric designs. They are not suggested because they are expressions of an African culture (or women), but because they are magnificent examples of murals, which just happen to be created by African women. These murals can provide a connection between our African-American students and the Ndebele people because of their relevance to the unit. They also serve as a motivation to learn about another culture, inviting students to explore artistic expressions, values, beliefs, lifestyle, and political/social struggles.

  2. Expressions of Mexican muralists—Jose Clemente Orozco, Diego Rivera, and David Alfaro Siqueiros—might be another choice. Again, these artists are selected not because they are Hispanic, and therefore qualify as non-Western, but because they have created large, powerful images of their own culture that can serve as models in exploring the African-American culture here.

  3. A third choice may be drawn from works of African-American artists, such as Faith Ringgold, Jacob Lawrence, William Johnson, and Romare Bearden, who are particularly well known for their portrayals of ethnic life in narrative images depicted in quilts, paintings, murals, and collages.

  4. Yet another choice may be to stay closer to home, presenting expressions of selected graffiti artists, representing a multiethnic subculture in our own urban centers.

  Notice these choices develop from the inside out, beginning with our own population as a guide in what and whom to explore in the outside world.

- *Look to the population of your own students for multicultural exemplars.* We do not need to transport students all the way to Africa to have multicultural experiences. Our schools are filled with multiethnic populations. Remembering the analogy of the patchwork quilt, we have only to step out into our communities to find examples of multicultural expression. Objects from our students' own families can serve as exemplars to illustrate diversity within culture.

- *Help students see their own cultural expressions and the expressions of others as the "patches" in the "patchwork quilt of humanity."* Whether we address multiculturalism by visually transporting students to another continent or by asking them to explore their own neighborhoods, we can provide meaningful connections by addressing diversity within universal themes and human conditions. By understanding the universal, we find meaning in the particular.

- *Keep the "art" in "art education."* Multicultural experiences have often been used as vehicles to transmit information about history, geography, sociology, and politics. Those who oppose using art education in this instrumental way ask, "Where has the 'art' in 'art education' gone?" Although we can teach such content through art, we can ask, "Is this what we are all about?" From the perspective of this book, the answer is no. Our primary intent is to enhance self-understanding and expression through art experiences supported by connections with the outside world.

▼ MULTICULTURAL UNIT PLANNING

This section suggests strategies to move from theory into practical application. First, it discusses components of a multicultural unit. Second, it illustrates how to progress from (1) a unit plan to (2) a teacher's outline for an introductory lesson to (3) a packet of materials designed for student use.

● COMPONENTS OF A MULTICULTURAL UNIT

A multicultural unit typically includes (1) an introduction to a selected culture, (2) a focus on an art form presented as the cultural exemplar, (3) productive experiences, and (4) a closure. Each of these components is examined here.

I. Introductory Lesson on a Selected Culture

A lesson introducing a culture should provide students with a broad view of the people, their beliefs and values, their lifestyle, and their art-making activities. The following suggestions are intended to help you organize this information.

A. *Start with art.* To introduce a people, begin with a presentation of art forms reflecting their culture. This strategy reinforces art (rather than geography or history) as the primary focus. Show real objects if available. Select examples from books, slides, posters, videos, and compact discs. As your students view a variety of art objects, address the following:

1. Purposes or functions of art objects within the culture
2. Materials and processes used in fabrication
3. Cultural themes or ideas expressed
4. Value of the objects to the culture of origin
5. Stylistic similarities among the objects

B. *Establish a geographical connection.* By presenting artwork visually, you can motivate students to want to know more about the people and their origins. At this point you may bring out a map and introduce information about the land and its effects on the culture and art. To illustrate where the culture is in relation to where we are, you might present a map activity in which students pinpoint where they live with a "You are here" flag, and where the culture exists with another identifying flag. Colored yarn can be connected to each flag to illustrate distance between the two locations. Next you might show pictures of the land and its natural resources. Focus on connections between the land and its influence on the following:

1. Lifestyle
2. Housing
3. Clothing
4. Art forms

C. *Introduce information about the people.* This information may include the following:

1. Family and/or social structure
2. Daily life/economy
3. Beliefs, ceremonies, rituals
4. Art-making activities

D. *Conclude with a compare-and-contrast activity.* Have students analyze similarities and differences between the other culture/art forms and their own culture/art forms.

II. Focus on a Particular Art Form as the Cultural Exemplar

After presenting a general overview of the people and their representative art forms, you may select one of those art forms as the cultural exemplar to explore in depth. In this aspect of the unit you move from the historical domain (in which you present the culture) to the critical domain (in which you focus on visual characteristics of the exemplar). At this point you may present several examples of the selected art form and discuss the following:

A. Use of media and processes
B. Subject matter
C. Thematic content/meaning
D. Style and formal qualities

This information can be presented in visual and oral form and reinforced through the use of packets of materials designed for student use. (The sample student packet that follows illustrates how to present such information, translating research into content appropriate for students. Because these packets can be lengthy and costly to reproduce, you may supply each table with one packet and have students take turns reading aloud in cooperative learning experiences.)

III. Productive Experiences

A multicultural unit, like any other unit, can be developed from teaching models. You may select the product-oriented model, the process-oriented model, or the creative problem-solving model, as shown in Figure 9.1. As is evident in these examples, a primary concern is in moving students from the study of an "outside" cultural exemplar to the creation of authentic "inside" expressions. Here are some reminders.

• Motivate students to participate in studio activities by presenting assignments and exemplars that are relevant to them.
• Remember the difference between multicultural and monocultural.
• Help students understand the relationship between the particular and the universal.
• Using thematic webs and other brainstorming strategies, encourage students to explore ideas.

FIGURE 9.1
Teaching Models Illustrating Multicultural Content

(a) Product-Oriented Model

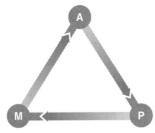

M = Tibetan mandalas
A = Each student (1) identifies and sketches a significant life event and (2) represents the event through 3–4 symbols.
P = Students create personal mandalas using symbols.

(b) Process-Oriented Model

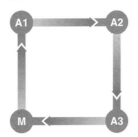

M = Japanese sumi-e painting
A1, A2, A3 = Students explore processes and brush strokes and create sumi-e–like paintings of subject matter indigenous to their own surroundings.

(c) Creative Problem-Solving Model

P = Create a personal transformation mask inspired by masks of Northwest Coast Native American cultures.
CPS = Students generate multiple ideas for mask designs.
S = Final masks

IV. Closure

As in any unit, a multicultural unit concludes with activities in which students demonstrate an understanding of concepts and share studio work. It should provide an opportunity for students to compare and contrast their expressions with those of the selected culture. This might be done through a compare-and-contrast web, illustrated in Figure 9.2. Through this webbing exercise, students may explore how two different groups of people (themselves and the other culture) interpreted a theme defined by criteria in a studio problem. More importantly, they may develop understanding of our connectedness as human beings through universal art expressions and our diversity as individuals within the realm of the universal.

FIGURE 9.2
Multicultural Compare-and-Contrast Web

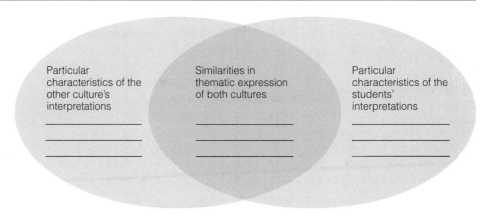

Particular characteristics of the other culture's interpretations

Similarities in thematic expression of both cultures

Particular characteristics of the students' interpretations

Moving from theory to practical application, we provide models of (1) a multicultural unit plan, (2) a teacher's outline for an introductory lesson, and (3) a student packet, presented consecutively in the boxes that follow.

NAVAJO SANDPAINTING

I. Theme and General Description

A. This unit introduces students to Navajo culture, focusing specifically on sandpainting. Students create sandpaintings interpreting the theme "harmony" through a figure, symbolic object(s), and/or designs representing harmonious relationships within their culture.

B. Grade level: Middle school

C. Time: approximately eight 50-minute sessions

II. Goals

A. To develop an understanding of humankind's connectedness through exploration of a universal theme: harmony within people, society, and nature (historical domain)

B. To develop understanding and appreciation of one culture's (the Navajos') expression of the theme in the form of sandpainting (historical and aesthetic domains)

C. To demonstrate understanding and appreciation of similarities and differences between Navajo art and culture and our art and culture (historical, critical, and aesthetic domains)

D. To demonstrate skill in the use of materials and processes in the creation of a sandpainting (productive domain)

E. To demonstrate ability to design and discuss visual composition created through the arrangement of art elements—color, line, and geometric and/or organic shape (productive/critical domains)

III. Concepts

A. All cultures express ideas and beliefs through art.

B. Many non-Western peoples use art in their daily lives as part of rituals and ceremonies.

C. The Navajos use the ritual of sandpainting to reinforce harmony within people, nature, and the universe.

D. Ritual sandpaintings performed by medicine men in ceremonies called *ways* are designs considered to be visual prayers. They are used to heal or bless a person, object, place, or event, thus helping to maintain harmony within the natural and spiritual worlds.

E. Sandpaintings transmit myths through simplified images and symbols of the universe, natural and supernatural phenomena, plants, animals, and people.

F. Ritual sandpaintings are sacred and are not shared with the outside world.

G. Permanent sandpaintings, made for sale, are similar in style and subject matter to ritual sandpaintings but do not have the same images, meanings, and power as those performed by medicine men.

H. Both ritual and commercial sandpaintings share these stylistic characteristics: (1) incorporation of symbols, (2) linear in quality, (3) use of simplified geometric and organic shapes, (4) symbolic use of color, and (5) predominant use of radial and symmetrical balance.

IV. Cultural Exemplar

Selected examples of traditional Navajo sandpainting designs from *Navajo Sandpainting Art* (Joe and Bahti, 1978)

V. Scope and Sequence of Experiences

Day 1: Introduction

A. Teacher introduces Navajo art in a visual and verbal presentation, using the teacher's outline of an introductory lesson.

B. Teacher focuses on sandpainting as the cultural exemplar (using additional visuals and student packets).

Day 2: Process-oriented activity 1

A. Teacher models "painting with sand" (sprinkling sand onto a glued surface).

B. Students experiment with the process. (Through this experimentation students become aware of the quality of the sand and the degree of detail they can achieve. They may use a number of different materials to simulate the ground-up, colored rock of traditional Navajo sandpainting: white sand colored with liquid tempera, corn meal dyed with food coloring, aquarium sand. Sand can be adhered to a variety of surfaces including boards, cardboard, and sandpaper.)

Day 3: Process-oriented activity 2

A. Students review information in their packets, focusing on the sandpainting of *Mother Earth* and *Father*

NAVAJO SANDPAINTING (continued)

Sky, which serves as a motivation for the final assignment.

B. Students explore ideas for the final assignment (a sandpainting depicting a figure, symbol, or design representing harmony within their culture) by creating designs from geometric and organic cut construction paper shapes. (Using this process, students will be more apt to simplify, stylize, and design images that can be readily translated into sandpaintings.)

Days 4–6: Focus on the final product

A. Teacher reviews assignment, shows his or her teacher example, and reads a paragraph interpreting its content (presented in the student packet).

B. Students create final products, working from ideas explored in cut paper sketches.

Day 7: Completion of studio and written work

A. Students finish sandpaintings.

B. Students write paragraphs interpreting their designs.

C. Students complete a unit worksheet (in student packet).

Day 8: Unit closure

A. All students share designs and interpretive paragraphs with table mates. Each table grouping selects one person to share his or her sandpainting and paragraph with the entire group.

B. All students display artwork on tables and circulate from table to table to view work.

C. Students comment on work produced and compare and contrast it with examples of traditional Navajo sandpaintings.

VI. Evaluation Procedures

A. Reflection on planning and teaching

1. How effectively did the introductory lesson and the student packet convey information about Navajo art and culture?

2. Did the process-oriented studio activities adequately prepare students to create final sandpaintings?

3. Was there enough time?

B. Observation of student behaviors

1. Did students demonstrate understanding of similarities and differences between Navajo art and culture and their art and culture?

2. Discuss levels at which students engaged in each activity (generating ideas, "painting with sand," designing images, creating final products). What was most successful? Did they experience any frustrations or problems?

C. Assessment of art products
Discuss products in general terms:

1. Creative interpretation of the theme (harmony)

2. Use of line, shape, color, balance, contrast to create composition

3. Use of materials and processes (craftsmanship)

4. Fulfillment of particular criteria

D. Fulfillment of unit goals

1. Did behavior and products demonstrate attainment of productive goals (ability to interpret a universal theme in a self-expressive product; ability to use media and processes to create a well-crafted, aesthetic work)?

2. Did oral discussions, interpretive paragraphs, and worksheets demonstrate attainment of critical, historical, and aesthetic goals?

Teacher's Sample Outline for an Introductory Lesson: Navajo Art and Culture

I. Traditional Art Forms of the Navajo People

The Navajos, like many tribal people, produce art in the form of functional objects for daily living and ritual objects for ceremonial use. In the last few decades the Navajos have also supported their economy through the sale of art and craft items, including decorative paintings, permanent sandpaintings, rugs, jewelry, baskets, and pottery. Much of what we see today outside the Navajo reservation has been made specifically for commercial purposes.

A. Weaving

The Navajos are especially well known for their high-quality weaving. Woven items include clothing, shoulder blankets, saddle blankets, ponchos, sashes, hair cords, leggings, and rugs. Woven designs have a wide variety of color and line in geometric motifs and symbols. Navajo weavings are prized by people in many cultures and are exhibited in leading museums throughout the world.

B. Silversmithing

The Navajos learned skills in silversmithing from their neighbors in Mexico and lapidary from other Native American tribes in the U.S. Southwest. Navajo silversmiths were the first to combine silver with turquoise in objects such as buckles, bridles, belts, bracelets, rings, pins, earrings, and wrist guards. Both men and women adorn themselves with jewelry. Layers of silver and turquoise necklaces are especially striking on Navajo women dressed in their traditional velveteen blouses and long satin skirts.

C. Pottery

Although the Navajos do make pottery, they have not developed the art form as highly as they have developed weaving and silversmithing. Today a few Navajo potters make utilitarian objects such as bowls, drums, and cooking jars used in ceremonies and in the preparation of dyes for wool. Recently Navajo artists have also begun to make decorative pottery for sale outside the reservation.

D. Basketry

Like pottery, basketry is a minor art form within the culture. Baskets are usually made of sumac and dyed with the natural materials used for dyeing wool. Colors include red, indigo, black, and occasionally yellow. These baskets are shallow forms about 3 to 4 inches deep and 12 to 18 inches wide and are used in Navajo ceremonies.

E. Sandpainting

Sandpainting is both a ritualistic performance used in sacred ceremonies and an art form developed for commercial purposes. Sandpaintings created for sale are made from sand glued onto boards. Although the commercial designs are similar in style and subject matter to those of ritual sandpaintings, they do not replicate the sacred designs performed in ceremonies.

II. The Land and Its Effects on the Culture

A. Location of the Navajo Reservation

The Navajos live on the largest Native American reservation in the four corners area of the United States. The reservation encompasses 25,000 square miles, occupying areas in southeastern Utah, northeastern Arizona, and northwestern New Mexico, and bordering the southwestern corner of Colorado.

B. Characteristics of the Land

The land within the reservation can inspire awe. It has deep, colorful canyons, high mountains, prominent buttes, mesas, and vast open desert areas. Elevations range from 5,500 feet to 10,000 feet. Most areas receive little rain.

C. Influence of the Land on Navajo Housing

The traditional house is the hogan, an eight-sided structure made from logs held together with mud. It can be easily constructed from natural resources. The interior of the hogan is one large room 15 to 25 feet in diameter and serves as a living space for a Navajo family. The door faces east, in the direction of the rising sun.

D. Influence of the Land on Navajo Life

The beauty of the land has no doubt contributed to the Navajos' reverence for all of nature and to their spiritual beliefs. The Navajos see themselves as one aspect in the harmonious flow of the universe. Their lifestyle reflects this belief. Many Navajo people are sheep herders. Wool from sheep and dyes from the plants provide the raw materials from which to make weavings. In addition to tending sheep, Navajos may spend their days raising crops, developing their skills to make crafts for sale and for use in rituals and daily life, and participating in the spiritual ceremonies that are an integral part of their lives.

III. The Navajo People and Culture

A. The Navajo Family Structure

The Navajos have a matrilineal society in which the grandmother is viewed as the center of the family. Children born to her are members of her clan. When a daughter marries, she and her new husband build a hogan nearby so that their children can herd their grandmother's sheep. Although Navajo children may attend reservation schools, many are educated primarily by family members. Because their language is unwritten, the history and culture of the people are passed down orally from one generation to the next. Navajo children learn skills to create craft items from their elders and acquire knowledge about Navajo beliefs and rituals through the teachings and performances of the medicine men.

B. Beliefs, Ceremonies, and Rituals

The Navajos believe that the universe is full of powerful forces with potential for good and evil. These forces are in a delicate balance that can be upset by humankind. The Navajos perform blessing and healing ceremonies called *ways* to reinforce or restore balance. *Ways* are performed for everything—people, places, houses, crops, livestock, the opening of a store, mental and physical illnesses. Their purpose is to create *hozho*, the natural state of health and harmony within the supernatural and natural worlds, society, and individuals. These ceremonies combine prayers, chants, dances, and the performance of ritual art (sandpaintings).

C. Use of Art for Ceremonial Purposes: The Ritual of Sandpainting

Ritual sandpaintings are viewed not as "art objects" but as sacred activities performed within spiritual ceremonies (*ways*). These sandpaintings may be thought of as "visual prayers," used to "beautify the world." *Beautifying the world* means establishing and maintaining the condition of *hozho*. A sandpainting is performed by a medicine man who creates prescribed designs in sand on the ground inside a hogan. (Although the Navajos believe these designs were given to them by their deities, the Holy Ones, many ethnologists think the designs and practice were acquired hundreds of years ago from neighboring Pueblo tribes.)

IV. Similarities and Differences Between the Navajo People and People in Our Culture

SIMILARITIES	DIFFERENCES
A. Both live in family units with a person recognized as the head of the family.	The Navajos view the grandmother as the head of the family. In Western cultures the father is usually viewed as the family head.
B. Both have systems for educating children	Although many Navajo children attend reservation schools, much of their learning comes from knowledge and skills passed down through generations from one family member to the next. Education in our culture occurs primarily through formal schooling.

SIMILARITIES	DIFFERENCES
C. Both have spiritual beliefs, practices, leaders, and places of worship.	The religious leader of the Navajos is the medicine man, who performs spiritual ceremonies in special hogans. In our society religious leaders and doctors perform the functions of the medicine man in the Navajo culture.
D. Both use art to reflect ideas, beliefs, and values.	Navajo art reflects the culture's connectedness to the land and reverence for beauty and harmony through symbolic depictions of plants, animals, natural phenomena, and supernatural beings. Art in our culture reflects ideas, beliefs, and values of Western society.
E. Both value art as an expression of culture.	The Navajos value their art primarily for its function in rituals and daily life. The Navajo view of art as an integral aspect of life and spiritual practices reflects an "art for life's sake" philosophy. Westerners tend to perceive and value their art more as aesthetic expression created to enhance the environment. This kind of valuing reflects an "art for art's sake" philosophy.

NAVAJO SANDPAINTING

Introduction

As you can see from the map at the end of this packet (Figure 9.6), the Navajo reservation occupies parts of three of the four states in the four corners area of the United States (Nevada, Arizona, and New Mexico). The land, characterized by vast open deserts, high mountains, and colorful canyons, is exceptionally beautiful. One of the primary characteristics of the Navajo people is their reverence for the natural world. They view themselves as one aspect in the flow of a universe filled with powerful forces with the potential for good and evil. According to Navajo beliefs, these forces are in delicate balance and can easily be upset by humankind. To ensure balance and harmony within the universe and health and well-being among their people, the Navajos perform spiritual ceremonies called *ways*. These include prayers, chants, dances, and ritual sandpaintings.

Ritual Sandpaintings

Ritual sandpaintings are not considered "art" or even "objects" in Navajo culture. They are not created for decorative purposes. They are not intended to hang on walls to beautify Navajo dwellings. A ritual sandpainting is a performance done by a healer called the *hatathli* (medicine man) in ceremonial *ways*. A single *way* may take as long as eight days to perform and can consist of multiple sandpaintings recounting episodes of particular myths. Through these performances a medicine man transmits values, beliefs, and heritage of a culture that has no written language. A sandpainting functions as a "visual prayer," performed in the healing and/or blessing of a particular person, object, place, or event. Medicine men, viewed as healers and spiritual leaders of the tribe, are similar to our doctors and religious leaders. A sandpainting performance in Navajo culture may be compared to a ritual in a religious service in our own culture.

Before a sandpainting can be performed, sand must be prepared. This is done by traveling to secret locations to obtain rock of the appropriate kinds and colors. The rock is chipped loose, transported home, allowed to dry, and ground into various degrees of fineness. Once this preparation has been completed, the medicine man performs sandpaintings on the ground inside hogans (Navajo dwellings) that have been specially consecrated for ritual use. To produce the image, he holds sand within the palm of his hand and sprinkles it between his thumb and forefinger. The designs he makes are believed to have come from the Navajo deities or Holy Ones and are considered sacred. Performed as a ritual, a sandpainting must be reproduced in a prescribed manner, exactly replicate traditional designs, and be completed by sunset. In ceremonies involving the healing of a sick individual, the patient is seated on top of the completed sandpainting. The medicine man performs his healing by touching a portion of the sandpainting and then the patient. Through this act, he transfers the power of the sandpainting to the individual. The sickness leaves the patient and har-

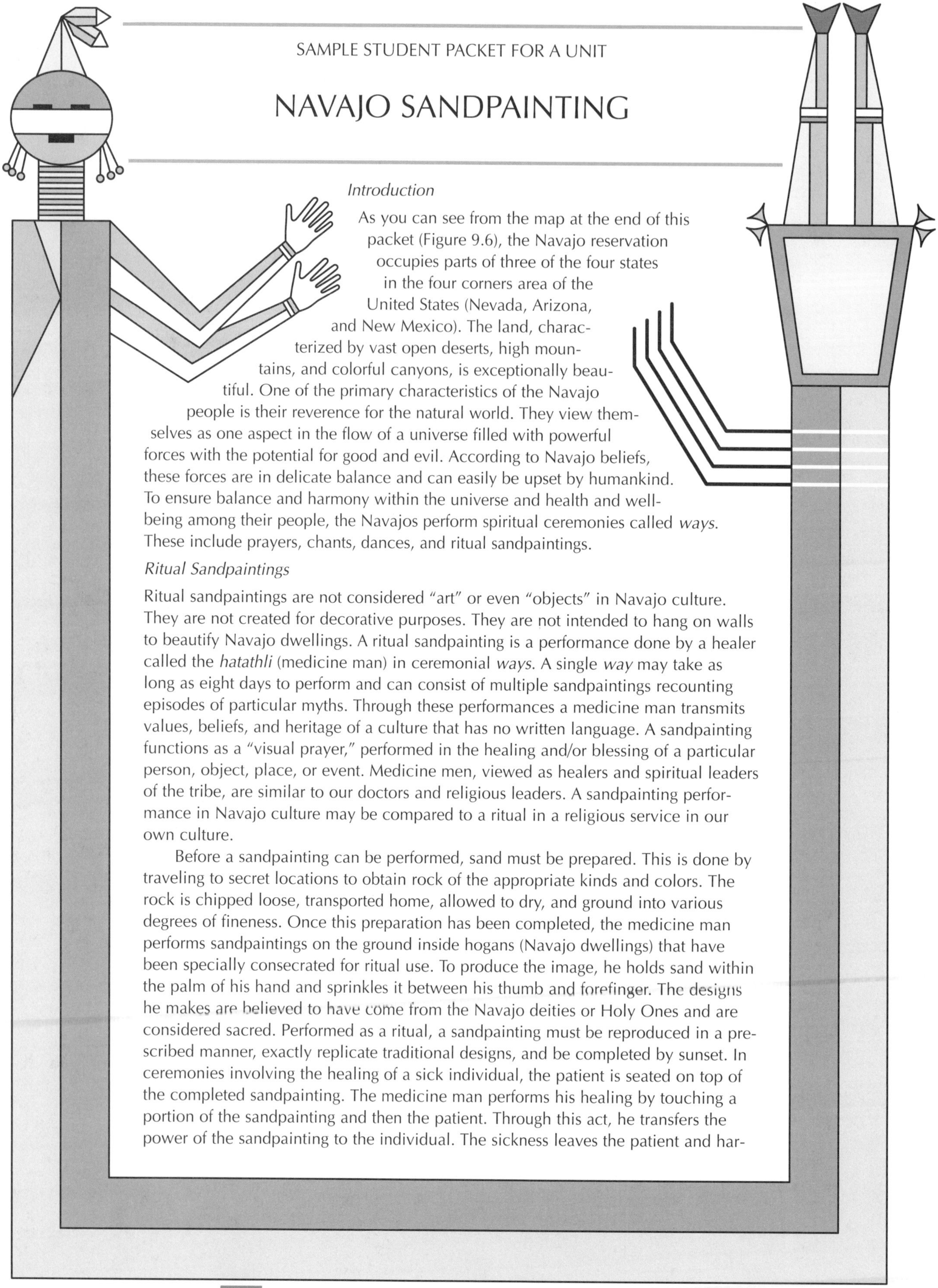

FIGURE 9.3
Rainbow Yei

mony in the universe is restored. Before the sun sets, the sand is erased with a sacred feather staff and swept onto a blanket to be carried outside, and returned to nature.

When a sandpainting is performed, it is designed with the opening facing east, from where evil may not easily enter. The other three more vulnerable sides must be protected from evil forces. In many sandpaintings protection is created through a pair of guardian figures flanking each side of the eastern entrance. In addition, a linear form often encircles the southern, western, and northern sides. The diagram on the first page of the student packet, Figure 9.3, the Rainbow Yei (god), illustrates the most frequently used protective motif. Besides the use of these figures, Navajo sandpaintings are characterized by a number of qualities:

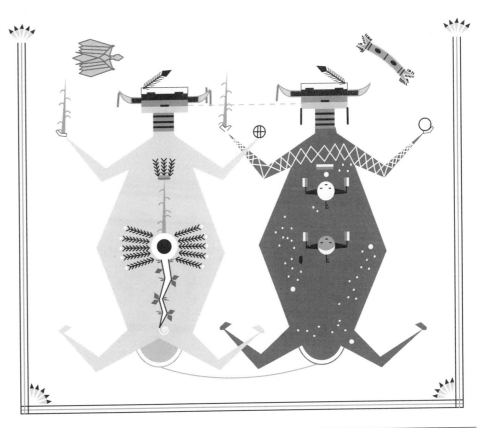

FIGURE 9.4
Navajo Sandpainting: Mother Earth, Father Sky

- Because of the manner in which they are performed, they are primarily linear.

- Color is used symbolically and is limited by availability of natural rock from which the sand is made.

- Objects such as animals, plants, gods, natural and supernatural forces are represented as simplified, stylized geometric and organic shapes.

- The content is symbolic, transmitting myths, which may be illustrated in a sequence of individual sandpaintings performed in *ways* lasting several days.

- Most sandpaintings are designed with radial or symmetrical balance. Asymmetrical balance is used less often.

The sandpainting shown in Figure 9.4 illustrates these characteristics. The top of the image is the eastern edge. Two guardian figures protect the opening. The line surrounding the other edges is a rainbow with feathered prayer plumes, providing additional protection. The figures are Mother Earth and Father Sky. Mother Earth contains a circle in the middle of her body, symbolizing the place from which the Navajo people emerged from the underworld into this plane of existence. Sprouting from this circle of water are the Navajos' four sacred plants: corn, bean, squash, and

tobacco. Mother Earth holds a sacred corn plant and a basket with corn pollen. Father Sky's body is the black night sky, with markings representing the Milky Way (the zigzag lines), crescent moon, stars, and constellations. He also holds a corn plant and a sacred tobacco pouch. A line of sacred pollen links their mouths. Together Mother Earth and Father Sky symbolize the two halves of creation—the ultimate in perfection and cosmic harmony. They appear in many *ways* because of their power and importance in Navajo mythology.

Commercial Sandpaintings

In the last few decades Navajos have engaged in increased commerce with people from outside the reservation. They have enhanced their economy through the sale of craft items such as rugs, jewelry, and pottery. They have also sold images made from sand glued onto boards. These permanent sandpaintings are similar in style and subject matter to ceremonial sandpaintings. Because they lack details incorporated into ceremonial sandpaintings and are not part of ritual performance, they have no power as instruments of healing. They are simply decorative items. In their making, some artists use traditional methods for gathering rock and grinding sand. Increasingly, however, artists use commercially colored sands or they color neutral sand using oil pigments. Many have also replaced the traditional mortar and pestle with hand-operated coffee grinders. The sand is adhered to particle or plywood boards by sprinkling it onto glued areas. Like many examples of ethnic art made for commercial purposes, the products vary in quality. The best are exquisitely designed and crafted and should not be considered as inferior to ritual sandpaintings. What may have begun as an imitation of the "real thing" has become highly developed into an art form of its own.

Your Assignment

Having explored an art form and belief system of another culture, we now turn to ourselves and our own culture to discover similarities:

1. Consider how the Navajos use an artistic expression (sandpainting) to reinforce a cultural belief (the potential to create a harmonious flow within society and the universe).

2. Think about the word *harmony* and what it might mean in our culture. Who helps to create harmony within your family, school environment, neighborhood? Do you know friends, relatives, teachers, religious or community leaders who help maintain harmonious relations in your life or environment? What symbols or designs might be used to represent harmony?

3. Think about how you might depict a person (yourself, someone you know, or a made-up being), a symbolic object, or a design to represent harmonious relations in your environment.

4. Translate your idea into a permanent sandpainting, as you follow these steps :

   a. Experiment with the process of "painting" with sand.
   b. Explore design possibilities using construction paper shapes.

FIGURE 9.5
Sandpainting Assignment: Teacher Example

c. Create your final sandpainting following these criteria:
   • Design an image representing harmony within your life, family, school, or community.
   • Use lines and simplified geometric and/or organic shapes to depict the image.
   • Incorporate symbols or use art elements symbolically.
   • Think about balance. You may use symmetrical, radial, or asymmetrical balance.
   • Think about color. You may use three or four colors that symbolize something you want to express. Strengthen your image by using contrasting colors.

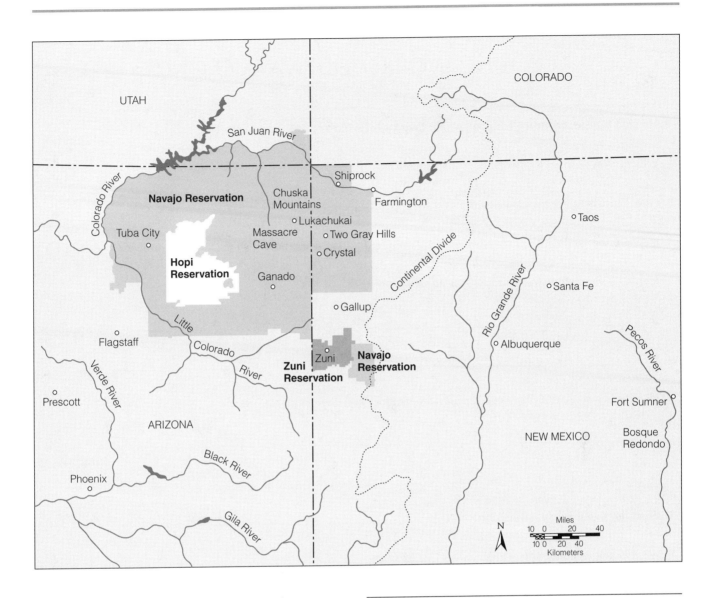

5. Write a paragraph interpreting your artwork. Discuss the meaning of the image and how you represented it, using the teacher's sample sandpainting and pinagraph as guides.

Teacher's Sample Paragraph Interpreting the Assignment

As I thought about the assignment, I realized that both as a teacher and as a parent, I nurture people and reinforce harmonious relationships. Therefore, I decided to create an image of myself. As you can see (Figure 9.5), I was influenced by Navajo design and especially inspired by the Rainbow Yei. My body encircles the central symbol, much as the Rainbow Yei protects a Navajo sandpainting. Other shapes and images reflect my function and qualities as a guide for my children and students (symbolized by the

FIGURE 9.6
Map of Navajo Reservation

vines). The spiraling circle, emphasized by the arrows, symbolizes ever expanding growth and wisdom. The spiral points to my head, out of which grow antennae (in the shape of feathers), through which I tune into potential problems. The diamond in the center symbolizes my ability to create solutions to problems that block harmonious relations. The butterfly symbolizes playfulness, a quality that contributes to harmony among people. The moon and diamond-shaped stars reflect a larger perspective of harmony beyond our lives into the world and the greater universe.

CLOSING WORKSHEET: NAVAJO UNIT

1. How do Navajos reinforce harmony within their culture, nature, and the universe?

2. Why do Navajos make sandpaintings for themselves?

3. How and where are these sandpaintings made?

4. How are the sandpaintings the Navajos make for sale different from those they make for themselves?

5. Identify 4 characteristics typical of Navajo sandpaintings:

   a. _____   c. _____

   b. _____   d. _____

6. Identify two similarities between Navajo sandpaintings and your sandpaintings:

   a. _____

   b. _____

7. What does your sandpainting represent? _____

8. What is unique about your sandpainting? _____

9. What do you like about your sandpainting? _____

10. Rate your success by giving yourself a 5 (highest) to 1 (lowest) score on each criterion below:

	Student Score	Teacher Score
a. Ability to interpret the assignment in your own way (creativity)	_____	_____
b. Design/composition	_____	_____
c. Craftsmanship	_____	_____
d. Overall assessment	_____	_____

FLEXIBLE APPROACHES TO PLANNING

The Navajo sandpainting unit progresses from the general to the specific, as diagrammed in Figure 9.7. This is simply one way to approach multicultural planning. Although it can work well with middle or high school students who attend art class five days a week, it may be too much for elementary students attending class once a week. Three alternative approaches include (1) presenting one art form of a culture, (2) presenting the work of one artist (or group of artists) representative of a culture, and (3) focusing on one art form in a cross-cultural investigation.

Overall view of art and culture of another people

↓

Presentation of several examples of one art form used as the cultural exemplar

↓

Focus on one work of art to illustrate theme, content, and style

↓

Use of artwork to motivate self-expressive interpretations of theme

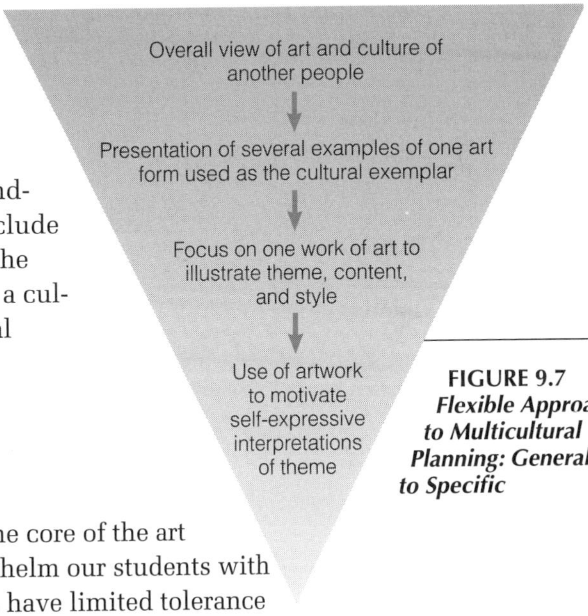

FIGURE 9.7
Flexible Approaches to Multicultural Planning: General to Specific

PRESENTING ONE ART FORM OF A CULTURE

Because our intent is to emphasize art making as the core of the art education experience, we must be careful not to overwhelm our students with academic study of the outside world. Young audiences have limited tolerance for viewing and discussing art. Eventually someone will have had enough and interrupt a presentation with "When are we going to make something?" Consider what is feasible within your time frame and developmentally appropriate for your population. Rather than presenting a culture through an overview of multiple artistic expressions, you may pare down to one art form presented as the exemplar. The assignment using Japanese carp kites as the cultural exemplar (presented in Chapter 7) illustrates this approach.

PRESENTING THE WORK OF A SINGLE ARTIST OR GROUP

A second alternative is to look to the work of a single artist or group of artists whose works reflect cultural themes, conditions, events, and/or values. Examples cited earlier in the chapter include the Mexican muralists Orozco, Rivera, and Siqueiros; the African-American artists Ringgold, Lawrence, Johnson, and Bearden; and multiethnic graffiti artists.

FOCUSING ON ONE ART FORM IN A CROSS-CULTURAL INVESTIGATION

A third option involves focusing on one form of art and examining various expressions, meanings, and functions within several different cultures. Masks are especially well suited for cross-cultural study. This is because masks are often created as ceremonial objects used by non-Western peoples in transformation rituals. As students view and discuss masks from Bali, Alaska, Oceania, and Mexico, for example, they may develop understanding of differences among cultural expressions of a universal theme. They may also develop knowledge and appreciation of art from the vast portion of the globe that is not Eurocentric.

You may choose to present (1) one culture in depth through a variety of representative art forms, (2) a specific aspect of a culture through one art form,

Theme	Cultural exemplar	Selected culture	Geographical location	Studio area	Productive experience
Ethnic pride	Jacob Lawrence's paintings/murals	African American	United States	Painting	Mural

Geographical location	Selected culture	Cultural exemplar	Theme	Studio area	Productive experience
Mexico	Mexican	Crafts related to festivals	"Making it special"	Crafts	Bread dough relief sculptures

Studio area	Productive experience	Theme	Cultural exemplar	Selected culture	Geographical location
Sculpture	Imaginary clay animal	Symbolic representation of personal qualities	Mythological animals	Various cross-cultural examples	Multiple locations

Cultural exemplar	Selected culture	Geographical location	Theme	Productive experience	Studio area
Transformation masks	Selected NW Coast Native American tribes	Canada/Alaska	Transformation	Papier-mâché masks	Sculpture

FIGURE 9.8
Generating Content in Multicultural Planning

(3) an aspect of a culture as reflected through the work of one or more artists, or (4) human connections through a cross-cultural investigation of one art form. Whichever approach you choose, you should select content that supports your student population. Because there is so much content, so many cultures and art forms from which to choose, selecting the most fitting can be challenging. Having a system for generating ideas and making selections can be helpful. Figure 9.8 lists thinking strategies and demonstrates that a number of different starting places (theme, geographical location, studio area, cultural exemplar) can serve as the initial motivation for planning.

S U M M A R Y

Multicultural art education is a vehicle to investigate universal and particular characteristics of art as culture. Through the study of various cultures and their art, students make discoveries about the connectedness of humankind. They learn to view their own lives as part of the human experience, reflected through art. They also discover the particularities that make themselves, other individuals, and cultures unique. We address multicultural art education as a way of leading students to explore who they are in a world that appears smaller and smaller, as contact among its inhabitants becomes greater and greater.

Multiculturalism within the context of art education makes connections between the "inside" world of the student and "outside" cultures. Issues in multicultural planning and teaching help to establish the following summarized guidelines:

- Select cultures and art forms relevant to your student population.
- Avoid the stereotyping that occurs when an entire area, such as "Africa," is presented as if all inhabitants belonged to one culture.
- Do adequate research to present accurate information on individual cultures.

- Present the art of other peoples within the contexts of their cultures.
- Guide students to understand relationships between universal and particular characteristics of peoples and their art expressions.
- Make connections between cultures and students' lives within their own culture.
- Use art of other cultures to motivate authentic self-expression.
- Keep in mind the primary focus: exploration and enhancement of the self through art-making experiences motivated by cultural exemplars from all over the world.

Putting this theory into practice suggests a strategy for multicultural planning modeled in a sample unit on Navajo sandpainting. The plan is supported by a teacher's outline for an introductory lesson and a student packet. The unit, providing an in-depth view of a culture, illustrates one way to plan multicultural units. Because of its broad scope and length it may not be suitable for all students.

Options for designing multicultural art experiences include presenting (1) one culture in depth through a variety of representative art forms, (2) a specific aspect of a culture through one art form, (3) an aspect of a culture as reflected through the work of one or more artists, or (4) human connections through a cross-cultural investigation of one art form. You may design these experiences by starting with a variety of motivations: a theme, a geographical location, a studio area, a culture, or an art form. Beginning from any one of these points, you can design appropriate, meaningful, multicultural experiences for all students at every grade level.

A. GENERATING IDEAS FOR MULTICULTURAL UNITS

Directions

Use the spaces below to generate ideas for four multicultural experiences. Demonstrate flexibility by progressing in the order indicated for each idea.

1. Theme ⟶ Cultural exemplar ⟶ Selected culture ⟶ Geographical location ⟶ Studio area ⟶ Productive experience

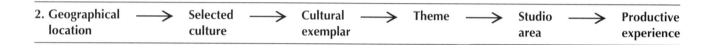

2. Geographical location ⟶ Selected culture ⟶ Cultural exemplar ⟶ Theme ⟶ Studio area ⟶ Productive experience

3. Studio area ⟶ Productive experience ⟶ Theme ⟶ Cultural exemplar ⟶ Selected culture ⟶ Geographical location

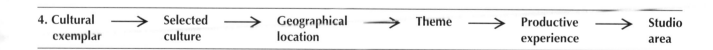

4. Cultural exemplar ⟶ Selected culture ⟶ Geographical location ⟶ Theme ⟶ Productive experience ⟶ Studio area

B. CONNECTING THE "INSIDE" TO THE "OUTSIDE"

Directions

1. Write a universal theme, a corresponding cultural exemplar, and a studio experience from the preceding exercise in the box below. 2. Use the compare-and-contrast web to demonstrate how a cultural exemplar and your teacher's example might be linked through the theme.

Theme:	**Cultural exemplar:**	**Studio experience defined by these criteria:**
_____	_____	_____
_____	_____	_____
_____	_____	_____
_____	_____	_____
_____	_____	_____

Compare-and-Contrast Web

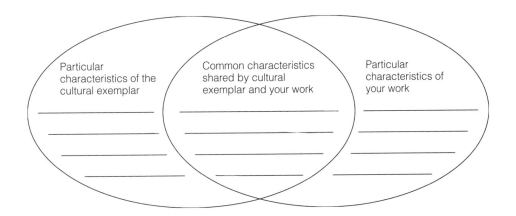

Particular characteristics of the cultural exemplar

Common characteristics shared by cultural exemplar and your work

Particular characteristics of your work

MAKING
INTERDISCIPLINARY
CONNECTIONS

Interdisciplinary education, like multicultural education, is a vehicle that can lead students to perceive art as an expression beyond themselves. Whereas in multicultural education we broaden students' visions of art by connecting with other cultures, in interdisciplinary experiences we broaden visions by connecting with other subjects. As students are led to see relationships between art and dance, music, drama, mathematics, social studies, the sciences, and language, they develop understanding of art's impact on all of life.

As an experiment to discover what connections students make between art and "real life," you might ask them to tell you what "art" is. You may be pleased by the diversity of responses or taken aback by their limited visions. Research has indicated that many children have a very narrow view of art: "Art is drawing and painting; artists are people who make pictures; art is found in museums." When thinking of art, children may in their minds represent the entire field by the painting hanging over the couch in the living room. One of our responsibilities as educators is to move students beyond narrow views of their immediate surroundings. In relating art to life, we promote understanding of these concepts:

- Everything in the human-made environment was designed and created by someone.

- Each day we make decisions involving art as we choose what to wear, what to buy, and how to design our living spaces.

- Art can be related to all of human existence.

To introduce concepts connecting art to life, you might ask these questions:

- What objects in your classroom, school environment, home, and community were designed by someone? (desks, chairs, playground equipment, appliances, traffic signs, movie posters, cars, buildings, video games, paintings)

- What do we call the people who designed and made these objects? (designers, draftspeople, engineers, architects, city planners, landscapers, painters, photographers, artists)

- How did they use art in the design and creation of these objects? What kinds of art skills did they use? What kinds of art decisions did they have to make? (choices about shape, color, size, composition, materials, construction, function, audience appeal, meaning)

- What skills and knowledge from other fields did they need to produce these objects? (reading, writing, measuring, physics, psychology)

- What are the subjects that provide these skills and knowledge? (English, mathematics, science)

Through this kind of exploration students learn that art is linked to a wide variety of objects, activities, and experiences that have connections to what they do and learn in other subjects. This chapter presents guidelines for integrating art with other subjects in interdisciplinary art experiences. Sections discuss (1) approaches to interdisciplinary education and (2) planning interdisciplinary units of study.

▼
APPROACHES TO INTERDISCIPLINARY EDUCATION

In response to research on learning, interdisciplinary education has become a strong movement in contemporary practices. As individuals progress through life, they have experiences that are multifaceted and result in a variety of learnings about one's self, others, and the world in general. These experiences provide opportunities to see relationships, make connections, and create contexts for meaning. They promote learning in a holistic way.

Formal education, in contrast, has traditionally been delivered in a *linear* way. In a six-hour day a student might move from math to art to social studies to physical education to science to English, as if each were a separate bin of information moving along a conveyor belt on an assembly line. Because students progress through a compartmentalized day never being asked to make connections between art and social studies, they don't. As a result, they tend to accumulate free-floating information that they readily forget because it has little meaning. The goal of interdisciplinary education is to provide an alternate path toward the acquisition of knowledge. The progression might look like that in Figure 10.1.

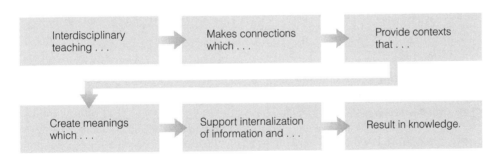

FIGURE 10.1
Interdisciplinary Flowchart

Today's emphasis on making connections is reflected in the number of terms referring to integration processes: *interdisciplinary, multidisciplinary, transdisciplinary, cross-curricular.* Although each has a particular meaning, all relate to teaching strategies and educational models intended to break down compartmentalization, to promote higher-level thinking skills, and to reflect the interrelatedness of all of life. Typically these approaches make connections in one of two ways: (1) They focus on what to teach, presenting thematic content that may be explored in a number of subject areas. Mexico, for example, may be addressed through its geography, history, politics, art, music, dance, literature, and religion. (2) They focus on how students learn, shifting the emphasis from content to processes common across disciplines. Students are presented with experiences involving decision making, problem solving, collaborative learning, research, and so forth. Through such experiences, regardless of whether they occur in math, social studies, science, or art, students develop thinking and expressive skills and learn how to acquire knowledge.

Although educational models designed to integrate content, learning processes, and life experiences may be relatively new, interdisciplinary education was introduced as long ago as the 1920s. It was pioneered in the Progressive Movement by John Dewey. Viewing the classroom as a microcosm of the real world, he designed educational experiences that were problem centered. Students, often working cooperatively, were encouraged to research, experiment, and use whatever information and materials they had available to them—in the areas of science, math, social studies, and the arts—to solve a given problem.

This interdisciplinary teaching strategy was initially viewed as an asset to art education, bringing art into everyday use in the classroom. The approach was called "correlated art" and involved students in using art materials and activities to visually represent and share information. Children made objects such as dioramas, charts, posters, table top displays, and puppets. Although correlated art was an improvement over previous practices (in which art may have been relegated to the 2:30–3:00 slot on Friday afternoons), it eventually was criticized for being used for its instrumental value rather than for its intrinsic worth. Art content was not actually *taught*; art activities were simply *used* to support teaching of other subjects.

Art education within this context became known as the "handmaiden" of the curriculum. To understand the metaphor, imagine a handmaiden holding a mirror up for a subject to view herself in its reflection. Art education provided the mirror that reflected the content of other subjects.

Because art can be used to motivate learning in other subjects, it continues to be used in this instrumental way. A common rationale for the integration of art with academic subjects is heightened interest resulting from hands-on experiences. Many educators, particularly on the elementary level, teach through art and approach art teachers with requests to correlate by having students make things.

MAKING BALLOON GLOBES

BETTY had been in her position as an elementary art teacher a short time when the fourth grade social studies teacher came to her with a request: Would she make papier-mâché globes (to be hung from the light fixtures during open house) as part of a unit on geography? The teacher assured her she would help. Betty had no idea what this meant, but wanting to look as if she fit in her new position, said yes. The following week the students arrived with a sack of assorted balloons. Some were round, some were oblong, some were pear shaped—in various sizes. The children fought over who got the big round ones and finally settled down to cover them with papier-mâché. Because some of the students did not finish a complete layer, the classroom teacher promised to complete the process in her class.

The following week Betty and her students spent half the period stuffing the collapsed shells on the balloons that had not been fully covered the week before (nor touched in the interim). In the next two sessions the students finished the papier-mâché process and painted their globes blue. On the last day the classroom teacher distributed dittoed reproductions of the continents. Students were to color and cut the dittos and glue them onto their globes. Betty watched, horrified, as the students completed the project by pasting the continents anywhere they could find spaces on their globes of differing sizes and shapes.

Betty might have benefited from the advice of art educator Edmund Burke Feldman, who cautioned, "You should think of yourself first as an art professional; your self-esteem ought to depend on your authenticity as an art professional; and your teaching should reflect the fact that art is your primary discipline." In addition to teaching *through* art, we have a greater commitment: to teach *in* art. We have a responsibility to inform administrators, faculty, and parents that we (1) follow a curriculum, (2) plan units of study, (3) teach content, and (4) assess growth just as teachers in any other discipline do. The message here is not to avoid interdisciplinary planning, but to present art education in ways that reveal its substance and to explore supportive integration strategies. Questions to consider before saying yes to the next request to make objects reflecting the study of math, science, or social studies are discussed next.

- *Why should art teachers become involved in interdisciplinary planning?* There are two reasons: (1) Art can be used to enhance study in other subjects, and (2) other subjects can be used to motivate study in art.

- *How can art be used to enhance study in other subjects?* (1) Because art involves visual design, it can be related to anything in the natural world. In a science unit, for example, a teacher might use art activities to explore the configuration of snowflakes and introduce symmetrical balance. To illustrate Fibonacci's mathematical sequence, a teacher might have students observe, draw, and analyze growth patterns in sunflowers, pinecones, and/or pineapples. (2) Because visual design is involved in the creation of all human-made objects, the history of our species can be chronicled through art. Teachers of all subjects can present cultural objects (objects made and used by individuals in cultures) as vehicles to convey information about human conditions, contributions, values, and aesthetic tastes. (3) Because art is a language, it can be used by any teacher to promote expression and to demonstrate learning. Students who are visually or kinesthetically-oriented may benefit most from expressing ideas and knowledge through art processes.

- *How can other subjects motivate study in art?* Other subject areas have their own content. It is often the same content we explore in art. The social sciences address culture; so does art. Math involves the study of relationships; so does art. Science looks at physical, emotional, and psychological characteristics; art reflects these same characteristics. Literature is based in expression and form; so is art. Music, dance, and drama celebrate the human spirit; so does art. Content from any subject area can be used to motivate art expression.

- *How can art teachers keep the focus on art in interdisciplinary planning and teaching?* Critics of interdisciplinary art education have directed us to look carefully at how the parts fit together. Art can be reduced to a small cog in a large machine (general education). In addressing this concern, we must remember that art can be used in a number of ways within different contexts to serve various purposes. The box on page 198 illustrates this idea in the presentation of three strategies for interdisciplinary planning: (1) art used to promote learning in other subjects, (2) art integrated on an equal basis with other subjects, and (3) art using other subjects as a vehicle to explore its own content and processes.

Interdisciplinary education in and of itself is neither good nor bad. It is simply an approach to organizing content and delivering instruction. At its best it can result in a synergy in which the parts come together in mutually supportive ways to promote connections, meaning, and knowledge. At its worst it can replace intrinsic worth with instrumental value, reducing some subjects to superficial roles in support of others. Art has been one of the subjects most visible for its supporting role. This has not won us an Oscar. It has resulted in our being viewed as an "ornament" or "frill." We must be especially mindful of how we

Art Used to Promote Learning in Other Subjects

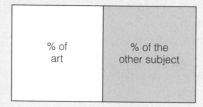

| % of art | % of the other subject |

Teachers in all subject areas may use this approach to design units of study involving the use of art materials, processes, and/ or concepts. Use of art activities in academic units may supplement instruction in art, but does not take its place. The purposes of this approach are to motivate through hands-on learning, to provide opportunities to express ideas and knowledge in nonverbal ways, and to integrate art into the total school curriculum and environment. Art teachers may serve as resources for academic subject area teachers.

Art Integrated on an Equal Basis with Other Subjects

| % of art | % of the other subject |

Teachers of art and one or more other subjects work as a team, coordinating planning for multiple units on a common theme. Each teacher addresses the theme from his or her particular area. Each subject stands on its own, resulting in a mutually supportive relationship. The art teacher may begin one step behind an introduction to an academic unit. For example, she might motivate students by asking what they learned about the Middle Ages in social studies. Responses can provide a cultural context for a unit on heraldry. This approach offers optimal opportunities for integration. However, it can be difficult to implement because of required planning time and coordination efforts.

Art Using Other Subjects as Vehicles to Explore Its Own Content and Processes

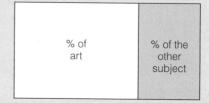

| % of art | % of the other subject |

Art teachers approach classroom teachers or academic subject area teachers prior to the beginning of a school year to discuss curricula and possible interdisciplinary links on which to base art units using content in other subject areas. This approach affords art teachers the most autonomy to (1) select content to promote learning in art, (2) sequence content in the most fitting ways, and (3) progress at a rate supporting the nature of art activities. (Art units can take longer to implement than academic units, particularly at the elementary level, wher classes only once a week.)

approach interdisciplinary education. Of the three approaches in the box above, the last may be best suited for our purposes. Guidelines for using this approach in the development of a unit of study follow.

▼ PLANNING INTERDISCIPLINARY UNITS OF STUDY

Whether you coordinate with other faculty or work on your own, you will need to do some preliminary work before designing any interdisciplinary art unit. This section provides a procedure you may follow and presents a sample interdisciplinary unit plan.

● SUGGESTIONS FOR INTERDISCIPLINARY PLANNING

Your initial challenges in designing interdisciplinary art units will be in selecting content from other subject areas that supports the teaching of art and generating planning strategies that reflect integration. Some suggestions follow:

1. *Explore themes that can link art to other subjects.* Identifying themes in art is not difficult. The challenge is in investigating content of other subjects to discover commonalities. You may research in a number of ways:

   a. Confer with other subject area teachers.
   b. Investigate resources such as curriculum guides, student text books, encyclopedias, and Web sites on the Internet.
   c. Talk to students.

2. *Choose a theme for your unit.* Make your selection on the basis of the theme's potential to support the teaching of art and to connect with another subject.

3. *Explore art content relevant to the theme. Explore content of the other subject that supports your art teaching.* The content of both subjects will appear in your unit plan as concepts. To ensure that you are addressing content in both areas, list concepts for both subjects separately (as illustrated next). The number of concepts in each area need not be equal. Because your emphasis is in art, the art side may be weighted more heavily.

ART CONCEPTS: **CONCEPTS OF OTHER SUBJECT:**

_____   _____

_____   _____

_____   _____

_____   _____

4. *Determine how content from the other subject will be integrated into the overall art experience.* Consider sequencing of the interrelated parts. An interdisciplinary scope and sequence can be structured in a variety of ways. These are some options:

   a. Begin with the content of the other subject, using it as a motivation for studio experiences.
   b. Conclude with the content of the other subject, discussing what students experienced in art and relating it to their learning in the other subject.
   c. Incorporate content from the other subject as part of the study of the cultural exemplar. (This strategy can work especially well in the integration of art and social studies.)
   d. Integrate other forms of expression, such as reading, writing, music, movement, and drama into units of study as motivation for and/or interpretation of art expressions. Draw parallels among visual, verbal, musical, and kinesthetic art forms.

5. *Move from brainstorming ideas, investigating content, and experimenting with sequencing to developing an integrated unit plan.* An integrated unit plan can be designed using the same basic structure as any other unit plan. Notice in the sample plan following that concepts for each subject have been listed separately, reflecting the procedure suggested in step 3. The scope and sequence illustrates the integration process. The closing reflection sheet addresses content in each subject area.

INVENTING INSECTS

I. Theme and General Description

Insects serve as the theme to connect art and science. Students investigate the anatomical structure of insects and invent new species of insects, using paper shapes. These are arranged in cooperatively created background murals.

A. Grade level: Third
B. Time: seven 60-minute sessions

II. Goals

A. To develop understanding of connections between artists and scientists (historical)
B. To demonstrate problem-solving skills in the invention of an anatomically correct insect (productive)
C. To demonstrate creativity in the design of a mural depicting insects in an environment (productive)
D. To demonstrate skills in the use of media and processes including cutting, gluing, printmaking, painting, and arranging parts in a composition (productive)
E. To demonstrate understanding of formal qualities, focusing on pattern, texture, and balance (productive/critical)
F. To develop understanding and appreciation of creative writing and book illustration (historical/aesthetic)
G. To demonstrate critical skills through oral and written discussion of artwork and book illustration (critical)

III. Concepts

ART	SCIENCE
A. Artists use a variety of objects as subject matter.	A. Scientists use art to study nature. They draw pictures to learn about shapes, colors, textures, and patterns in natural objects.
B. Artists study natural objects (such as insects) in order to represent them in artistic visualizations.	B. Insects are small six-legged animals that are part of the natural world.
C. Artists also invent new forms.	C. All insects have the following parts:
D. Texture is the way something feels—smooth, rough, scratchy, furry, slimy.	1. Head, which includes the mouth, eyes, and in most but not all insects a pair of antennae.
E. Pattern is a repeated design—stripes, spots, etc.	2. Thorax, the middle section of an insect's body, which includes three sets of legs—one pair connected to each section of the thorax—and in most but not all insects a pair of wings.
F. All natural objects have texture.	3. Abdomen, the back section of the body, containing internal organs.
G. Many natural objects have pattern.	D. All insects have colors (including black and white), shapes, forms, and textures.
H. Simple shapes can be combined to make more complicated shapes (in the design of invented insects).	E. Some insects have pattern
I. A balanced composition can be achieved by equally distributing the parts.	F. Insects live all over the earth. They exist on land, in the air, in water, underground.
J. Gerald McDermott is a writer/illustrator who tells stories about imaginary animals.	G. 99% of all insects are beneficial. They pollinate plants, serve as food for larger animals, help keep the landscape clean, feed on harmful insects, provide us with products like honey, wax, and silk.
	H. Appearances of insects reflect what they do and where they live.

IV. Cultural Exemplar

Illustrated storybook *Anansi the Spider,* by Gerald McDermott

V. Scope and Sequence of Experiences

Day 1: Introduction to interdisciplinary art–science connection

A. Teacher places large laminated insect parts randomly on the chalkboard (using masking tape or magnetic strips). A volunteer student arranges the parts into a correct insect image. This activity serves as a motivation to introduce (or review) insect parts and characteristics.

B. Students work cooperatively in small groups to create large imaginary insects with anatomically correct parts, using colored tagboard, scissors, glue, markers, crayons, and embellishing materials.

C. Students share products and discuss the interrelated work of artists and scientists.

Day 2: Insect textures and patterns

A. Students are provided with resources (encyclopedias, nature books, *National Geographic,* etc.) in which to investigate surfaces of insects. They discuss the difference between texture and pattern and identify examples of each in various insects.
B. Students are asked to imagine what insect textures and patterns might look like under a magnifying glass.
C. Through the process of vegetable, string, and gadget printing, students create patterned and textured surfaces on colored tagboard that will be used later to create invented insects.

Days 3–4: Insect forms

A. Students discuss a variety of insects, their functions, and habitats. They analyze relationships between forms and functions. (For example, giant water bugs have long, flat hind legs that work like oars.)
B. Working individually, each student draws designs for and creates an invented insect. Criteria for insect design are as follows:

1. The insect must be composed of cut paper shapes. Plain paper may be used in combination with printed papers made in the previous experience.
2. The insect must contain some pattern and some texture.
3. The insect must be anatomically correct.
4. Insect parts should be designed to reflect a specific function in a particular place (on the ground, on foliage, on water, in air).

Day 5: Insect environments

A. Environments in which insects are found are reviewed.
B. Students, working in their original cooperative groups, discuss the function of their insects and where each is likely to be found. As a team they paint an environment from an insect's perspective, in which to place each group member's creation.

Day 6: The integration process

A. Students complete painted backgrounds.
B. After a discussion of what makes a balanced composition, students glue insects into environments.
C. The teacher reads *Anansi the Spider* and shares illustrations with the class. Students are asked to comment on similarities and differences between their work and McDermott's illustrations.

1. Similarities:
   - Both have pattern, texture, and painted surfaces.
   - Anansi may have been designed with cut paper pieces like students' insects.
   - Both the students' insects and Anansi have bold simple shapes.
2. Differences:
   - The students' animals are designed to be anatomically correct insects with three body parts and six legs. Anansi has two body parts and eight legs. He is therefore not an insect, but an arachnid.
   - McDermott's background is more like design than environment for his characters.

Day 7: Verbal interpretation of the visual image

A. Working in their groups, students plan for a presentation (a story and/or description) of their murals. (This can be done orally or in written form.)
B. Each group shares its mural and story/description.
C. Students complete a closing reflection sheet to demonstrate learning.

VI. Evaluation Procedure

A. Reflection on planning and teaching
   1. Were art/science components integrated to support art as the primary focus?
   2. How effective was the sequencing of activities to support unit content and learning?
   3. Was time sufficient to explore processes and concepts?
B. Observation of student behaviors
   1. Were students motivated by science content?
   2. How well did students demonstrate understanding of concepts through oral, written, and studio processes?
   3. Were cooperative learning activities effective?
C. Assessment of products
   1. How successful was work in reflecting understanding of concepts and in fulfilling criteria?
   2. How successful was work in demonstrating fulfillment of goals (growth in problem-solving behaviors, use of media and processes, creative interpretation of science content, compositional skills)?

INVENTING INSECTS

1. How do scientists use art? _____
_____

2. How do artists use science? _____
_____
_____

3. Name the three body parts of an insect:

   a. _____ b. _____ c. _____

4. Is Anansi an insect?_____

   Why or why not? _____

5. Is your invented insect anatomically correct?

   Why or why not? _____

6. How have you used pattern? _____
_____
_____

7. How have you used texture? _____
_____
_____

8. What does your insect do? _____
_____
_____

9. Where does your insect live? _____
_____
_____

10. What do you like best about your insect? _____
_____
_____

11. Did your group achieve balance in the mural design?_____

    Why or why not? _____
_____

12. What do you like best about your group's mural? _____
_____
_____

13. Which group created the best mural? _____

    Why? _____

ANALYSIS OF THE INTEGRATION PROCESS

The integration process in interdisciplinary planning can be challenging even for veteran teachers. One way to facilitate your growth in this area is to analyze structures of model interdisciplinary units. As you review the plan presented here, notice these characteristics.

- The introduction is integrative in nature. While exploring science content (insects) students participate in an art activity (a visual problem-solving exercise involving the manipulation of shapes). This learning experience provides a first step toward fulfillment of a primary interdisciplinary goal: understanding of art's connection to other subjects and to life in general.

- The theme provides a vehicle to systematically explore content in both art and science:

ART	SCIENCE
Shape in visual design	Anatomical structure of insects
Pattern and texture in visual design	Surface qualities of insects
Relationship of form to function in visual design	Functions/habitats of insects

- The unit is long; however, its length can be justified because of the breadth of studio experiences:
  1. Drawing ideas for invented insects
  2. Printing textures and patterns
  3. Constructing insects with paper shapes
  4. Painting large background environments
  5. Arranging parts into balanced compositions

- The cultural exemplar, *Anansi the Spider*, is presented last. (The unit's subject, insects, cannot serve as the cultural exemplar because an insect is not a cultural object.) McDermott's illustrated book is the selected cultural object and is presented to show how a writer-artist used processes and created images related to the students' study within the unit.

- Because students are asked to respond in writing, as they interpret their murals through storytelling and/or complete the unit worksheet, they are involved in another interdisciplinary experience. Writing across the curriculum (WAC) has become an increasingly popular educational strategy. It can be used to (1) strengthen verbal abilities, (2) develop critical thinking and problem-solving skills, (3) demonstrate art knowledge in a nonvisual form, and (4) motivate studio activities. Many art teachers begin with "writing prompts" to help students generate ideas in studio activities. In this unit art was used to motivate writing/storytelling. Whether art experiences are used to motivate writing or the reverse, the result may be the same: an increased level of expression in one or both areas, resulting from heightened motivation. Any art unit can include an interdisciplinary component through reading and writing activities. The primary interdisciplinary connection in this unit focused on the relationship between art and science. The verbal–visual combination in McDermott's work was used to support this connection. A possible interdisciplinary follow-up unit might begin where we left off with McDermott, this time emphasizing the literature–art connection in the dual role of the writer-illustrator of children's books.

This unit provides one model for interdisciplinary planning. As you analyze other units, you will see variations in the structure of the scope and sequence, as well as in content. A key to interdisciplinary planning is flexibility.

One particular structure may be better suited than another to address specific content. You may explore a variety of possibilities in planning to find the most effective route toward a goal. Here are some questions you might use as guides:

1. What do I want students to know and do in art?
2. What content/processes in other subjects might I use to facilitate their learning?
3. Given the nature of content/processes in both subject areas, how can I integrate the components and sequence the experiences for optimal success?
4. In what ways might students demonstrate learning?

S U M M A R Y

Through interdisciplinary connections, we broaden students' perceptions of art and lead students to understand art's relevance to their own lives, art's relationship to other subjects, and art's impact on all existence. In addition, we support research on learning by replacing compartmentalized structuring with holistic approaches. Holistic strategies promote analysis of how the parts fit together, create contexts for meaning, and lead to the internalization of information and the acquisition of knowledge.

Although interdisciplinary education is a major movement in practices of today, it is not new. During the 1920s the Progressive Movement introduced correlated art to support learning of academic subjects through experiential activities. Art education within this context became known as a "handmaiden"—an instrument to reflect study in areas other than art. This use of art continues to the present day and is especially popular with classroom teachers at the elementary level. It can be viewed as a strategy to teach *through* art. As art specialists, we must recognize the purpose and place of this kind of instruction and the differences between it and teaching *in* art.

Interdisciplinary planning in art education can take a variety of forms. Three strategies are discussed here: (1) Art used to support teaching in other subjects presents the role of the art teacher as advisor to teachers in classroom settings. Experiences resulting from this approach supplement regularly scheduled instruction in art. (2) Art integrated on an equal basis with another subject involves the formation of an interdisciplinary team to plan and teach independent units in each subject area on a selected theme. (3) Using other subjects to motivate learning in art requires that art teachers have knowledge in other subject areas, but does not necessarily rely on collaboration with other subject area teachers to plan or teach.

In theory, interdisciplinary integration can appear to be an excellent approach to teaching. In practice it has been problematic. Teachers have little time to form interdisciplinary teams, plan together, and implement instruction within a common time frame. When one subject is addressed only instrumentally in support of another, it suffers. To avoid problems arising within interdisciplinary teaming efforts and to maintain integrity within art programs, many art educators are turning to the third interdisciplinary planning strategy.

Guidelines for implementing this approach and a sample interdisciplinary art/science unit convey these messages:

• Look to art education goals as guides in selection and integration of content in other subject areas.
• Prepare yourself to use content in another subject by doing adequate research.

- Select only content that supports what you are teaching in art. (Leave content that is not directly relevant to your unit to be addressed by the teacher of the other subject in his or her own unit of study.)
- Be flexible in structuring a scope and sequence to accommodate differences in interdisciplinary units of study.
- Avoid raising "bats" in the field of interdisciplinary education by emphasizing art content.

Teachers today have become more knowledgeable about the pitfalls of interdisciplinary planning/teaching. At the same time many view integration of content and/or processes as the optimal way to educate students. As we move forward in the twenty-first century, we are challenged to supply not only an increasingly growing body of information, but also instruction to enable students to understand it, to make connections, and to integrate their newly acquired knowledge into their lives. At its best, interdisciplinary education has the potential to fulfill these goals.

EXPLORING THE INTEGRATION PROCESS

Directions
1. Identify a subject you might use to motivate learning in an art unit.
2. Provide a brief description of the unit.
3. Generate concepts you would introduce within each subject area.
4. Design a scope and sequence for a 4-session unit.

An idea for an interdisciplinary unit integrating art and _____

Unit description:

Art Concepts
(list below):

_____ **Concepts**
(list below):

"EXPLORING THE INTEGRATION PROCESS" *(continued)*
UNIT SCOPE AND SEQUENCE

Day 1:

Day 2:

Day 3:

Day 4:

C H A P T E R

FOCUSING ON ART CRITICISM AND AESTHETICS

Art criticism, aesthetics, and art history are three domains that together constitute the "response" aspect of art education. Through instruction in these domains we guide students to respond as viewers to their own art (addressing the "inside" component of our model of art education) and to the art of others (the "outside" component). Art criticism deals with the development of perceptual and analytical skills required to make reasoned judgments about the quality of art objects. Aesthetics is a branch of philosophy that studies the nature of what is considered beautiful or valuable. Within art education the study of aesthetics guides students to develop personal tastes and presents reasons for appreciating and valuing art by individuals and cultures throughout time and place. Art history provides the cultural/historical contexts for understanding art as a reflection of visions, values, and experiences of humankind.

We have addressed these domains previously as aspects of art education used to support the focus of our art education model—art making. We have demonstrated how to integrate them into units of study by presenting cultural exemplars, critique sessions, and reflection sheets. This chapter and the next one shift our focus. Here we address these domains not as supports for art production, but for their own sake. The purpose is to increase your knowledge and skills in teaching them and to prepare you to intentionally address each one in comprehensive units of study.

This chapter presents two integrally linked domains—art criticism and aesthetics. They are addressed together to underscore their connectedness. It is not possible to lead students to understand why they themselves or anyone else in the outside world might appreciate art without having them view and discuss visual qualities. Art criticism is a vehicle for understanding aesthetics. The ultimate purpose of viewing and discussing art is to have an "Aha!" or "Oh, wow!" experience—an aesthetic experience so moving as to be life enhancing. We begin in the first half of the chapter by discussing art criticism within the context of art education and presenting the art criticism teaching model. The second half addresses aesthetics within the context of art education and provides a connection to studio production.

▼ ART CRITICISM WITHIN THE CONTEXT OF ART EDUCATION

Art criticism can be broadly defined as processes to develop perceptual, verbal, and judgment skills used to respond to the visual world. Students may use these skills to respond to their own art, the art of others, and design in their environments. Reasons for including art criticism within curricula vary, depending on philosophical perspectives. Many subject-centered art educators use art criticism along with aesthetics and art history as a vehicle to transmit cultural heritage. Emphasizing this aspect of art education, they point out that most students will not choose art as their life's work and may have little connection with art as *makers* once they leave school. They strive to develop students' skills, knowledge, and attitudes as *viewers* of art, as well as addressing the role of the art critic in contemporary society. Through this approach they encourage students to make lifelong connections with art. This perspective differs significantly from the view of those who define art as a species-centered behavior. These art educators view art making as a natural activity intrinsic to humankind. One of their goals is to encourage people to continue throughout their lives to make art for the pure pleasure of expressing themselves visually. Studio-centered teachers view art criticism as important in supporting art production. Returning to our model of art education, we are reminded that through art criticism students can address these issues:

- How do I understand and express myself?
- How can I experience and understand the art of others?
- What do I say through my art?
- What are others saying to me?
- How do I deliver my messages?
- How can I assess and learn from the art of others?
- How can I assess my work?

Loosely defining art criticism as oral and written communication about visual qualities of artwork and design in the human-made environment, we can identify an early instance of its use within a society-centered orientation. It occurred in the 1890s as "picture study," a practice in which teachers showed examples of "masterpieces" and discussed their subject matter (often depictions of Bible stories) in order to transmit moral values. An art educator who has significantly influenced our understanding of art criticism today is Edmund Burke Feldman. In *Varieties of Visual Experience* (1992), he presented these procedures:

Feldman's Art Criticism Processes

- *Description:* Viewing a work of art and taking a visual inventory of its parts, noting what is immediately visible (objects comprising the subject matter and/or art elements used within the composition)

- *Analysis:* Discovering the relationships among the parts by attending to design principles within the composition

- *Interpretation:* Discovering meaning within the work by focusing on content and expressive qualities

- *Judgment:* Evaluating quality by assessing the work on specific criteria and ranking it within the context of like works

The purposes of these procedures are to encourage students to look at a work of art long enough to really see, to keep students from making immediate judgments without having paid enough attention to a work's visual qualities, and to provide for powerful aesthetic experiences as viewers of art.

An organization of the 1970s also dedicated to this goal was the Central Midwestern Regional Education Laboratory (CEMREL). Its purpose was to develop strategies and training for elementary classroom instructors to teach critical processes related to aesthetic education. The work of this group, documented in *The Joyous Vision: A Source Book for Elementary Art Appreciation* by Al Hurwitz and Stanley Madeja (1977), was significant, but short-lived because of funding problems. Nevertheless, it influenced the field by providing a foundation for including art criticism, aesthetics, and art history as curricular content. What CEMREL began in the 1970s continued in the 1980s and 1990s as a major aspect of DBAE.

The art educator most often associated with art criticism within DBAE is Harry Broudy. He developed a procedure similar to Feldman's, in which students attend to visual qualities of an art object. His method, called "aesthetic scanning," is presented next:

Broudy's Aesthetic Scanning

- *Technical properties:* Focusing on a work to discover how it was made in terms of processes and media

- *Sensory properties:* Focusing on art elements, an aspect Feldman addresses as part of his description step

- *Formal properties:* Focusing on design principles, an aspect Feldman addresses in his analysis step

- *Expressive properties:* Focusing on those qualities having to do with mood, emotion, feeling—an aspect Feldman addresses in his interpretation step

▼
THE ART CRITICISM TEACHING MODEL

Just as the visual constructs we call "teaching models" can be designed to lead students through productive experiences, they can be designed to lead students through experiences within the response domains of art education. This section presents the art criticism teaching model, the first of three models addressing the teaching of art criticism, aesthetics, and art history. It combines Feldman and Broudy's approaches in a six-step procedure. This model, presented in Figure 11.1, is followed by (1) a description of each process, (2) an artwork used as a motivation, and (3) sample questions and answers to illustrate practical application.

FIGURE 11.1
The Art Criticism Teaching Model

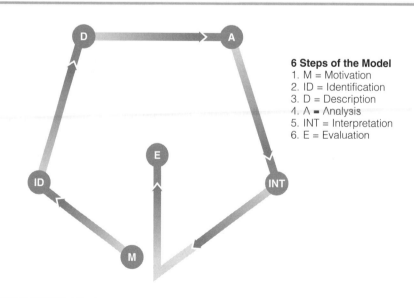

6 Steps of the Model
1. M = Motivation
2. ID = Identification
3. D = Description
4. A = Analysis
5. INT = Interpretation
6. E = Evaluation

STEPS AND APPLICATION OF THE ART CRITICISM TEACHING MODEL

The following two boxes provide guidelines in using each step of the model and an application. Notice the student–teacher interaction. The teacher does not *tell* the students about the visual qualities in an image, but uses questioning strategies to guide students to *discover* them.

Steps of the Art Criticism Teaching Model

1. M = Motivation—the presentation of an artwork

   The teacher presents an art object and asks questions pertaining to the following:
   a. What art form the object is (a painting, sculpture, print)
   b. What tools and media were used (paint brushes, air brush, oil paint, ink)
   c. What processes or techniques were used to create the artwork (impasto, wet on wet, etching)

2. ID = Identification of objects comprising the subject matter

   The teacher asks students to do the following:
   a. Identify the subject matter (portrait, still life, landscape)
   b. Take a visual inventory of the objects in the composition (house, tree, person)

3. D = Description of art elements

   The teacher asks questions to guide students through a description of the qualities of art elements:
   a. Qualities of colors (light, dark, cool, warm, bright, dull, blue-green)
   b. Qualities of lines (long, short, curved, straight, hard, soft, broken, jagged)
   c. Qualities of shapes, spaces, and forms (organic, geometric, flowing, angular, small, large, sharp)
   d. Qualities of textures (soft, hard, smooth, scratchy, shiny)

4. A = Analysis of design principles

   The teacher asks questions to guide students in analyzing the visual relationships within the composition. Students discuss how the parts have been arranged through these design principles:
   a. Balance/proportion
   b. Emphasis and subordination
   c. Contrast and transition
   d. Rhythm, repetition, pattern
   e. Unity/harmony

5. INT = Interpretation of meaning

   The teacher asks questions to lead students to discover personal meanings. Such questions might be
   a. What do you think this work is about?
   b. Does this work have meaning to you because it reminds you of experiences in your life?
   c. What emotions do you feel as you view this work?
   d. If you could become a person or object in the work, what might you tell us?
   e. What do you think the artist was trying to convey? What is he or she saying to you?

6. E = Evaluation of quality

The teacher presents criteria and other artwork with similar characteristics to provide standards by which to judge the quality of the work. Students evaluate quality by doing the following:

a. Referring to criteria on which to judge quality
b. Comparing the work with similar works on established criteria
c. Judging the quality of the work by ranking it (as first, second, third or most successful to least successful) with the other works on the specified criteria

---

Plate 11.1 illustrates a painting by Henri Rousseau entitled *The Merry Jesters* (1906), which is used as the motivation in the sample application of the model on the following pages. You may present the motivation in a number of ways—using large reproductions, slides, transparencies, Internet images, or pictures in student texts or magazines.

PLATE 11.1
Henri Rousseau, **The Merry Jesters** *(circa 1906)*

Philadelphia Museum of Art: Louise and Walter Arensberg Collection

ART CRITICISM STEP 1:
PRESENTATION OF THE MOTIVATION

Motivation: Explaining the Process

You can begin teaching art criticism in kindergarten as long as you select motivations that will appeal to a 5-year-old. As you choose an artwork, think about the ages, interests, and developmental levels of your students. Young children are very concrete. They relate most easily to objects. If you ask them to tell you what they see, they will identify things—houses, people, trees—rather than focusing on lines, shapes, or colors. As students gain skills in observing and discussing art, you can present more sophisticated motivations. This painting could be used as a motivation in kindergarten through twelfth grade. As you read the sample questions and anticipated responses (provided at the right), assume that the audience is at middle school level. Motivation questions relate to (1) the art form, (2) the media and tools, and (3) the processes.

Motivation: Sample Questions and Anticipated Responses

1. Q: What art form has the artist used to express his idea?
   A: This is a painting.
2. Q: What medium do you think the artist used to create this painting?
   A: Probably oil paint.
3. Q: How do you think the artist applied the paint?
   A: With paint brushes.

ART CRITICISM STEP 2:
IDENTIFYING OBJECTS IN THE SUBJECT MATTER

Identifying Objects in the Subject Matter:
Explaining the Process

In this step students identify the subject matter and take a visual inventory of the objects in the composition. Motivations that have realistic subject matter with clearly identifiable objects are easiest for students to discuss. When you introduce young children to this process, use motivations containing objects that students will be able to identify and find interesting. Motivations with abstract imagery will be more challenging. Nonobjective works do not lend themselves to the identification process, because they do not have identifiable subject matter. When you present nonobjective works, you may skip the identification step and move directly into description. As you read the discussions exemplifying each process, notice that key words have been italicized. In this discussion they are words pertaining to subject matter.

Identifying Objects in the Subject Matter: Sample Questions and Anticipated Responses

1. Q: What is the *subject matter* of this painting?
   A: It's a *landscape.*
2. Q: Where do you think the *scene* takes place?
   A: In a *jungle.*
3. Q: What *objects* do you see that lead you to identify this place as a jungle?
   A: *Monkeys,* some kind of *bird,* lots of different kinds of *plants.*

ART CRITICISM STEP 3: DESCRIBING ART ELEMENTS

Describing Art Elements: Explaining the Process

After students have identified objects in the composition, they can easily be led to see and discuss the visual qualities of the objects. As students describe these qualities, they focus on *art elements*. This step provides opportunities for students to discover the richness of colors, the expressiveness of lines, and the varieties of shapes and textures in a particular artwork. As they discuss these qualities, you can introduce new vocabulary and teach concepts about art. One decision you need to make is how much to include. If you are teaching a unit on color, you may focus on color only. You might also begin by asking students to list art elements in order of importance within the image and then guide them to discuss elements proceeding from the most to the least evident. Your choice of what to present will be determined by the goals, concepts, and cultural exemplar you include in the unit. You may structure a critical discussion in such a way that information provided in the identification step leads into the description step. The conversation on the right illustrates how to do this.

Describing Art Elements: Sample Questions and Anticipated Responses

1. Q: How do you know there are lots of different kinds of plants?
   A: They are different *shapes*.
2. Q: What do these shapes have in common? How are they alike?
   A: They are all shapes found in nature. They are *organic*.
3. Q: What else besides shape has the artist used to distinguish one plant from another?
   A: *Color*.
4. Q: Describe the *variations* in the color green.
   A: *Bright* greens and *dull* greens. *Brownish* greens. *Dark, medium,* and *light values* of green.
5. Q: Describe the *textural* quality.
   A: The surface of both the plants and animals looks *smooth*.
6. Q: How would you describe the quality of the *lines*?
   A: *Flowing*.

ART CRITICISM STEP 4: ANALYZING DESIGN PRINCIPLES

Analyzing Design Principles: Explaining the Process

The analysis step requires a shift in the way students view an artwork. When students identify objects and describe art elements, they focus on the parts of the composition. In the analysis step students discuss relationships. To see relationships, students must view the whole composition. As they discuss these relationships, they are analyzing design principles.

To introduce analysis, you might select a motivation in which a single design principle is clearly apparent. Once students gain understanding of one design principle, they can be led to see and discuss further in the analysis process. Analysis is more subjective than identification and description. If you ask students to find the focal point, for example, you might discover that individuals have different views. Different answers can be considered right as long as students can justify their opinions. As students gain analysis skills, you might present more ambiguous images that elicit multiple right answers. The discussion on the right illustrates how to move from description to analysis.

Analyzing Design Principles: Sample Questions and Anticipated Responses

1. Q: Focus on the flowing quality of lines. Instead of looking at each plant or each line, look at the *overall composition*. What is the effect of the lines?
   A: They create a *rhythm* flowing around and framing the monkeys.
2. Q: What is the effect of this framing?
   A: It makes the monkeys *stand out*.
3. Q: How else has the artist *emphasized* the monkeys?
   A: He has placed them in the *center of the composition* and *contrasted* them through their dark color against light leaves.
4. Q: How has the artist used *balance*?
   A: The painting is quite *symmetrical*. The white flower on one side is balanced by the bird on the other. The identically shaped leaves on each side also create *symmetry*.
5. Q: Does the composition seem *unified*? If so, how?
   A: Yes, *unity* is achieved primarily through *repetition* of shape and color and *balance* of objects.

ART CRITICISM STEP 5: INTERPRETING MEANING

Interpreting Meaning: Explaining the Process

Interpretation is the most subjective of all art criticism processes. In this step students talk about meaning—what the artwork means to each one personally. In sharing personal meanings, every student can make a contribution that is a right answer. Questions to promote the discovery of personal meanings include these:

- What do you think this artwork is about?
- How do you feel when you view this work?
- Does this remind you of any feelings, experiences, people, or places in your life?

After students have shared personal meanings, you might give them a chance to speculate on the artist's intent. We may or may not know the intent of an artist. Sometimes objects represent personal or cultural symbols that are known. Sometimes an artist purposefully uses ambiguity to elicit individual interpretations. Rousseau's paintings can be especially interesting to interpret because they are based on fantasy. The discussion at the right demonstrates how to move from description and analysis of formal properties to interpretation of meaning.

Interpreting Meaning: Sample Questions and Anticipated Responses

1. Q: We have established that the artist has achieved unity through a variety of art elements and design principles. The parts go together. Is there anything about this painting that doesn't seem to fit?
   A: There are some strange objects—a bottle of milk, a back scratcher, a pointer.
2. Q: What is the effect of those objects?
   A: They lend an unreal quality to the picture. They turn what might have been a representation of reality into fantasy.
3. Q: What is happening in this fantasy?
   A: Who knows? Perhaps these objects made for human use are all that remain after a struggle in which the monkeys won.
4. Q: What else could this picture be about?
   A: Nothing real. The space looks flat; the plants look fake; the animals look posed. Perhaps this is a stage set.
5. Q: If it were a stage set, what mood would it suggest?
   A: Comical and scary at the same time.
6. Q: Do you think the artist painted this as a serious representation of reality?
   A: No, I think he was having fun with his imagination . . . and with ours.

ART CRITICISM STEP 6: EVALUATING QUALITY

Evaluating Quality: Explaining the Process

In the evaluation step students judge the quality or success of a work. In order to make judgments, students need to have criteria to establish the "rules of the game." (What are we looking for? What is the artist trying to do or say?) Students also need other works that can be judged by the same criteria in order to tell how successful the work is when compared to others of its kind. Having established this painting as a fantasy, we might judge its quality by comparing it with paintings by other artists who created fantasy landscapes. Or we might compare it to another Rousseau painting, such as *Exotic Landscape* in Figure 11.2. The goal in evaluation is to provide opportunities for students to make judgments which they can defend as a result of working through the preceding five steps.

FIGURE 11.2
***Author's Drawing of Rousseau's* Exotic Landscape**

Evaluating Quality: Sample Questions and Anticipated Responses

1. Q: Look at the motivation, *The Merry Jesters,* and *Exotic Landscape.* These paintings are by the same artist and depict similar subject matter. If you were to assess them as fantasies, which one would you judge as superior?

   A: *The Merry Jesters* is definitely much weirder with those monkeys staring out at us and those strange objects. It is superior as a fantasy.

2. Q: Which one is better at evoking a mood?

   A: Once again *The Merry Jesters* wins. I don't think these are jesters or merry. This painting gives me the creeps. I don't like it, and that's exactly why I think it's a better painting. The other one seems kind of "Ho-hum, let's hang out in the trees" to me.

3. Q: Compositionally, which one do you think is a better painting?

   A: Although I like the rhythmic quality in *Exotic Landscape,* I am not drawn into its composition the way I am in *The Merry Jesters.* This painting rivets my attention to those monkeys. The power in this painting is achieved through emphasis. Because of this, I judge *The Merry Jesters* as superior.

FLEXIBLE IMPLEMENTATION OF THE MODEL

As you read through the explanation of each step and the sample questions, you may have felt overwhelmed by the complexity of the model. Typical questions include the following:

- "Do I have to include all the steps?"
- "Must I present the steps in the order in which they appear in the model?"
- "Do I need to include all the art elements and design principles?"
- "Do I have to lead students through the entire model in one period?"

The answer to each of these questions is no. A teaching model is like a road map. It presents a structure that lets you see the big picture and make your own decisions about how you want to traverse the land. The model is simply a theoretical construct, which you can implement to suit your needs. You can begin anywhere that seems most appropriate or will stimulate the most interest. You will select the steps of the model that relate to your lesson, and exclude what is irrelevant. When working with young children, you might go from identification to interpretation, skipping description and analysis. Some teachers prefer to begin with interpretation and then ask "why" questions to encourage identification, description, and analysis. These variations are illustrated in Figure 11.3.

Your ability to be flexible in using this model is important. When you lead students through art criticism experiences, you do so by asking more than by telling. Students may not always respond in the "correct" category. You may be more successful when you can "go with the flow." You will also enhance your success as you learn what your students are capable of doing and align your expectations with their abilities. Art criticism involves learning skills, just as studio production does. If your students have had little experience, you will need to begin wherever they are perceptually, regardless of their ages or grade levels.

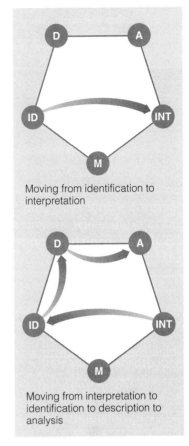

Moving from identification to interpretation

Moving from interpretation to identification to description to analysis

FIGURE 11.3
Two Ways to Flexibly Implement the Art Criticism Teaching Model

AESTHETICS WITHIN THE CONTEXT OF ART EDUCATION

Having explored art criticism processes, we are now ready to turn our attention to the end goal—the "Oh, wow!"—aesthetics. This is a branch of philosophy concerned with the study of what has been perceived to be of beauty, worth, and value—the study of the nature of art. As an aspect of art education, it has been presented as part of art criticism dealing with evaluation. In the past art criticism/aesthetics has been referred to as the "critical/appreciative" domain of art education. Since DBAE formalized art education into four areas of study, aesthetics is now often addressed as a separate domain. A goal of DBAE proponents is to promote a connection with art through the study of philosophical inquiry into its nature. (Aesthetics has thus been described as "the study of the study" of the nature of art.)

Aestheticians inquire about the nature of art by asking these questions:

- Why does an object qualify as a work of art?
- What makes an artwork different from objects we do not consider art?
- Why does a work of art have personal, cultural, or monetary value?
- Who establishes the value?

Children in a museum standing in front of a Pollock, DeKooning, or Rothko may ask these same questions in their own ways:

- "You call this art?"
- "What's so great about *that*?"
- "My little sister could make something this good!"
- "People pay money for this stuff?"

Here we address how to answer these questions and establish connections to art criticism and art production.

Trying to present an area of philosophical inquiry in terms students can understand, many teachers have defined aesthetics as the domain of art education dealing with appreciation. However, although aesthetics does deal with appreciation, it is not synonymous with appreciation. Appreciation is an attitude we promote through experiences in all domains of art education. As students learn to use tools, explore media and techniques, and develop ideas in studio activities, they gain appreciation for creation processes and for their own art products. They also further their appreciation of art as they learn through cultural and critical discussions. This appreciation can be considered as a by-product of productive, cultural/historical, and critical experiences. But teaching aesthetics goes beyond promoting attitudes of appreciation. It develops knowledge about the value of art through time in cultures all over the globe.

By studying aesthetics, students discover many reasons for appreciating art. They learn what particular artists, schools of art, periods in art history, and cultures value as "aesthetic" expressions. They learn that the term *aesthetic* applies to a wide variety of visual expressions, some of which may be considered "beautiful" whereas others may be seen as slick, humorous, outrageous, or even ugly. What we label "art" depends on the criteria we use to make judgments. Throughout history criteria have been established that reflect various beliefs and ideas about what is beautiful and valuable. The study of these beliefs and ideas addresses the "outside" aspect of aesthetics.

In addressing the "inside" aspect, we lead students to discover what they themselves find to be beautiful, pleasing, and valuable. We encourage them to develop personal tastes. We broaden their visions and enhance appreciations of their own and others' artwork. The attitudes and knowledge we develop through aesthetics enrich students' lives as viewers. They also promote growth in art production. In our model of art education we teach art criticism, aesthetics, and art history through the presentation of cultural exemplars. These serve as models with which students visually connect in studio experiences. By presenting a wide variety of images, we encourage students to experiment with and expand their own visual voices. We lead them to ask, "What do I like?" and "How might I reflect my personal tastes through my own content, style, and expressions?" This last question may be difficult to answer without exposure to art gained over a period of years. The first question, however, a kindergartner can answer, and you can use it as a starting point in teaching aesthetics.

AESTHETIC CONCEPTS

The key to teaching anything—including aesthetics—is starting where your students are and leading them gradually toward broader and deeper understandings. When we address aesthetics, we present activities in which students view and discuss objects to discover and share their appreciations of these objects. You might introduce aesthetics to young students by asking them what kinds of objects they like to look at or touch. You could record their responses on the chalkboard and then ask if students have collections of any objects listed (or not listed). Have them bring in and share objects from their collections—rocks, shells, coins, stamps, dolls, trains, books, CD packages, posters, etc. Sometimes these objects have real monetary worth and are expected to increase in value. Often, however, students collect such objects simply because they enjoy looking at them. Collectors of all ages are sensitive to the similarities and differences in the visual qualities of their objects. A first grader can tell you the differences in color, shape, and texture between two rocks in his collection. He can tell you which one is the "prettiest" and why he thinks so. A coin collector in middle school can tell you what symbols are on the front and back of various coins, which one is worth the most, and which one she prizes most highly. A high school math major can tell you why he chooses to decorate his room with works of M. C. Escher rather than those of Jackson Pollock.

As students are given opportunities to share their aesthetic tastes, they can be led to understand this concept: *People appreciate a wide variety of objects for many different reasons.* From this general idea students can move on to explore other aesthetic concepts. The following box provides additional concepts and activities to "concretize" them.

"Concretizing" Aesthetic Concepts

Concept: We may appreciate an art object because we like the material from which it was made.

Concretizing Activity: Show examples of furniture or craft items made from beautiful wood, sculptures carved from delicately colored stone, or jewelry made with highly polished gems and metals. Have students describe the qualities of the materials. Ask them what they find beautiful in the materials and why they might appreciate such objects.

Concept: We may appreciate an art object because we value the skill of the artist who created it.

Concretizing Activity: Present an artwork that shows great skill in using a process or medium, Michelangelo's *David,* for example. Ask students to describe the detail in a hand or foot. Ask them to imagine themselves carving *David* and to speculate on how many years of practice they might need to achieve Michelangelo's skill. Have them guess Michelangelo's age when he carved *David.* (He began the work when he was 26.)

Concept: We may appreciate an art object because we value the artist's process as an expression of creativity.

Concretizing Activity: Introduce the work of Jackson Pollock. Explain that Pollock was concerned with exploring novel processes to create art. Pollock walked around large boards on the floor dribbling house paint. The marks he made became records of his actions. Processes used by action painters include riding bicycles through painted surfaces to create lines, shooting at plastic bags of paint attached to boards to create explosive marks, and using large house paint brushes to record "dances" performed on canvases. After showing and discussing a variety of processes used in action painting, have students brainstorm novel processes to record actions. Have them try different processes—creating images by rolling marbles in paint, drawing with twigs, blowing on watercolor or ink blots to create a record of movement.

Concept: We may appreciate an art object because it represents an original idea.

Concretizing Activity: Show examples of minimal or conceptual art. For example, present slides of Christo's wrapped buildings and bridges. Explain that Christo came up with a unique idea—no one else had ever thought of making an artwork by wrapping a building. Lead students to discuss the impact the wrapped buildings have as objects in their environments. Show other examples of minimal or conceptual sculptures, focusing students on the visual and symbolic relationships between these human-made objects and their natural environments. Ask students to bring in photographs of landscapes, and have them design models for environmental sculptures to place in the landscapes. Instruct them to design images symbolizing *ideas* rather than representing objects.

Concept: We may appreciate art as a reflection of human expression and achievement.

Concretizing Activity: Show pictures of Simon Rodia's Watts Towers. Ask students to imagine themselves creating an environmental sculpture made from objects such as broken bottles, scrap metal, and junk found on the street. Show examples of "street art"—murals on buildings or window screen paintings in East Baltimore, for example. Ask students to design sculptures, murals, or window screen paintings reflecting life in their environment.

Concept: We may appreciate an art object because of the quality of the visual image.

Concretizing Activity: Ask your students to identify artwork or objects in the environment they find beautiful. Have them explain why they are attracted to these objects. Present an artwork that our society has judged as beautiful and have students speculate on the criteria used to judge beauty.

Concept: Ideas of beauty change over time.

Concretizing Activity: Select a particular subject matter—architecture, for example. Show photographs of urban centers that have a variety of architectural styles. Ask students to describe and analyze physical characteristics of the buildings. Then have them speculate on what "beauty" looked like at the time each building was designed.

Concept: Criteria for judging art change over time.

Concretizing Activity: Show examples of Van Gogh's paintings. Present historical background on Van Gogh's success as a painter during his lifetime. (He sold only one painting and that one was used for target practice.) Talk about the worth of Van Gogh's paintings today. Contrast the criteria used to judge Van Gogh's work during his lifetime with the criteria we use today.

Concept: A work does not have to be "beautiful" to be considered art.

Concretizing Activity: Show artwork that the average person may not consider "beautiful"—paintings by DeKooning, drawings by Kollwitz, or sculptures by Oldenberg, for example. Ask students to speculate on why these are valued as works of art. As students discuss these works, develop a list of reasons for valuing works intended to portray something other than "beauty" in a traditional sense.

Concept: Aesthetic expression and appreciation are universal.

Concretizing Activity: Select an art form such as masks and show examples from various periods and cultures. Include "masks" worn by Paleolithic man on a hunt, an actor in a classical Greek drama, a Native American shaman performing a healing, an American fashion model applying make up, a child dressed for Halloween. Talk about masks as a universal art form. Have students speculate on why these masks were valued by wearers and spectators in different cultures.

Concept: We can increase our appreciation for a work by understanding the intent of the artist or culture of origin.

Concretizing Activity: Present a work with which your students are not familiar (possibly one from a different culture). Lead them through the steps of the art criticism model without giving them any cultural information about the work. Ask them to rate their appreciation of the work on a scale of 1 to 10. Then provide historical information about the piece, its cultural significance, and the intent of the artist.

Ask students to rate their level of appreciation on a 1–10 scale again. Compare the first set of scores with the second set. Determine whether increased knowledge resulted in increased appreciation.

Concept: Reasons for creating and appreciating aesthetic expressions vary from culture to culture.

Concretizing Activity: Present a painting from Western culture and ask students why it may have been created and why they appreciate it. Then present an example of a non-Western work—a Navajo sandpainting, for example. Ask students to tell you why they appreciate it. Tell students what function sandpaintings serve in Navajo culture and why they are appreciated by Navajo people. Using a compare-and-contrast web, have students discuss similarities and differences in rationales for making and appreciating art in two cultures.

AESTHETIC THEORIES

As students are introduced to aesthetic concepts, artwork by Western and non-Western peoples, intentions of artists, and responses from viewers, they develop awareness of the range of objects we call *art.* This awareness can be heightened through knowledge of aesthetic theories—ideas explaining reasons for appreciating art. This section investigates a number of theories used to assign value.

THEORIES REFLECTING A WESTERN ORIENTATION

Cultures all over the globe have defined reasons for valuing their artistic expressions. Theories that have dominated our Western culture are concerned with valuing art because of the visual qualities of the work itself (not the meaning or function of an object within a cultural context). Three of these theories especially useful in understanding and assigning value to much of Western art are (1) imitationalism, (2) formalism, and (3) emotionalism.

IMITATIONALISM   Imitationalists are primarily concerned with imitating the natural world through realistic representation of subject matter. Imitationalism may have its roots as far back as Paleolithic times when hunters imitated animals in the caves of Altamira and Lascaux. Other examples of imitationalism include Roman busts, Dutch still life paintings, portraits of the Renaissance, landscapes of the Romantic period, and works of the Super-realists today. Historically imitationalism has been one of the strongest expressions in the Western world.

FORMALISM   Formalist theory reflects an interest in formal qualities—visual characteristics achieved through art elements (line, color, shape, texture) and design principles (balance, contrast, rhythm, emphasis, unity). A formalist is attracted to an artwork because of its design qualities and composition. Although artists from all periods have been concerned with composition, they may not have viewed formal qualities as their primary focus. Since the invention of the camera has provided an alternative to art as an imitator of nature, artists have become free to deviate from reality to explore design. The Impressionists (focusing on color), the Cubists (focusing on shape), and many of the works of the early twentieth-century American abstractionists were formalists. Exemplars of formalism include works by Braque, Brancusi, Arp, Mondrian, Dove, O'Keeffe, Sheeler, Demuth, Vasarely, Albers, and Escher.

It may be relatively easy to see and appreciate formal qualities in the works of these artists because they are all abstractionists. Because they were not concerned with realistically imitating subject matter, design qualities and structures of their compositions may be more apparent. It is also possible to appreciate realistic works from a formal point of view. For example, many people appreciate Andrew Wyeth not because of his imitationalism, but because of his compositions—his use of contrast, asymmetrical balance, space, and texture. Although an imitationalist may not appreciate abstract and non-objective works, a formalist may appreciate any type of work as long as he or she finds its design quality and composition pleasing.

EMOTIONALISM Emotionalism, also called expressivism, is a theory in which value is derived from the expressive or emotional content of the work. Many emotionalists use abstraction as a way to exaggerate reality and intensify emotional qualities. Their main concern is the expression of feelings rather than fidelity to nature. Examples of emotionalism include works of the Fauves (What could be more emotional than a group whose name translates to "Wild Beasts"?), the German Expressionists, and the Abstract Expressionists of the 1960s. Exemplars of emotionalism include works by DeKooning, Kollwitz, Bacon, Münch, and Scholder. Some people might also view a realistic artist such as Andrew Wyeth as an emotionalist because of the strong feelings he is able to elicit through a painting such as *Christina's World*. Emotionalists may express feelings through realistic, abstract, or nonobjective images.

One way to teach these theories is by presenting three works of art, each of which clearly represents one theory. The imitationalist work should be realistic, with much clearly defined detail. The formalist work might be a nonobjective piece with high impact because of its design. The emotionalist work could be a piece in which abstraction is used to intensify feelings. The following procedure is presented as a model you might use to introduce these theories.

A Procedure to Introduce Imitationalism, Formalism, and Emotionalism

1. Display three works of art, each of which clearly represents one of the three theories. Arrange the works in the following order: imitationalism (a Dutch still life painting, identified as number 1), formalism (a Vasarely print, identified as number 2), and emotionalism (a Fritz Scholder painting, identified as number 3).

2. Focus students' attention on number 1. Ask them to indicate who likes the work and why. Use the chalkboard to record responses that fit imitationalism ("I like it because it looks real." "The objects have lots of detail.")

3. Ask a student to come up to the work and point out examples of realistic detail (dew drops on petals, highlights on pewter jugs, fuzz on peaches, insects on plants, and so forth).

4. Tell students that *imitationalism* is a theory that explains why we appreciate art. People who value imitationalism appreciate art that realistically imitates the natural world. Artists and viewers who appreciate such artwork are called *imitationalists*.

5. Direct students' attention to work number 2. Ask for a show of hands to indicate who likes it.

6. Ask students if the work is a realistic representation of nature. After they respond with a no, ask students why they like the work. Students may respond with "I like

the colors." "I like the pattern and the contrast." "The design is neat." Record responses on the chalkboard.

7. Explain that these are all good reasons for appreciating art. Many people appreciate works of art because they like the design of the composition. Ask for a show of hands indicating who likes the work because of its design. Explain that the design or composition of a work is created by its formal qualities—art elements and design principles.

8. Ask students to name the art elements and design principles they see in the work (color, line, shape, pattern, emphasis, etc.). Tell them that *formalism* is another aesthetic theory conveying the idea that we appreciate a work because of its design or composition. Artists and viewers who are primarily concerned with formal qualities are called *formalists*.

9. Direct students' attention to work number 3. Ask for a show of hands to indicate who likes it.

10. Ask students if the work is realistic. (By selecting an abstract work, you will elicit a no response.) Then ask students if they like the work because of its design. If the answer is no, go on to the next question: "Why do you like this work?" As students respond with answers appropriate to emotionalism, write them on the chalkboard: "I like the strong feeling of the Indian." "He looks so powerful." "This picture reminds me of _____ or makes me feel like _____."

11. Tell students that a third aesthetic theory explaining why we appreciate art is *emotionalism.* Emotionalism has to do with the emotional or expressive quality of a work.

12. Ask student to share moods or emotions they feel as they look at the work. Write their responses on the board and tell them that artists and viewers who are primarily concerned with portraying feelings and emotions are called *emotionalists.*

The purpose of this exercise is to expand awareness. As students realize they can view art from several perspectives, they may enhance their appreciation for a wider variety of artwork. They may also develop skill in communicating their awareness and appreciations to others. When students discuss an imitationalist work, they identify realistically rendered objects in the subject matter. When they discuss a formalist work, they describe qualities of the art elements and analyze the composition. When they discuss an emotionalist work, they interpret meaning and discuss emotional impact. Do the words *identify, describe, analyze,* and *interpret* sound familiar? These are *art criticism* processes. By going through the steps of identification, description, analysis, and interpretation, students move toward a goal—expanded appreciation. John Dewey called this heightened state an "aesthetic experience." We might refer to it as a "Wow" experience, diagrammed as follows:

Identification	Description	Analysis	Interpretation	WOW

The "Wow" is a result of having taken in through the senses, heart, and mind something of significance, something of value. It occurs in the evaluation step, in which quality, success, and merit of a work are determined. Art criticism is not simply about learning to see or to make reasoned judgments—it is about providing processes for attending to art in order to be profoundly affected by its delicacy or strength or beauty or rawness. Art criticism is a vehicle through which we deepen aesthetic experiences and understanding of aesthetic theories. These theories—imitationalism, formalism, and emotionalism—provide criteria for judging works of art.

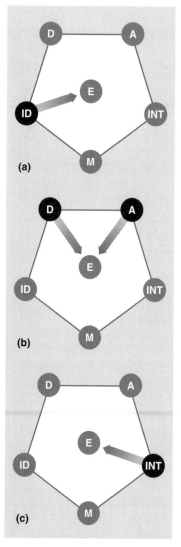

FIGURE 11.4
The Aesthetics Teaching Model

DETERMINING AESTHETIC PREFERENCES VIA THE AESTHETICS TEACHING MODEL

The aesthetics teaching model (see Figure 11.4) illustrates the relationship between aesthetics and art criticism. It includes three aesthetic theories—imitationalism, formalism, and emotionalism—and shows how aesthetic quality is evaluated from the three points of view. The key to understanding how aesthetic preferences are formed through the processes of art criticism lies in knowing what steps are important to whom. An imitationalist, a formalist, and an emotionalist may all work through each step of the art criticism model to determine aesthetic quality. However, each would emphasize a different section of the model. Figure 11.5 illustrates how each might use the model.

FIGURE 11.5
Determining Aesthetic Preferences Based Solely on Observation of the Artwork Itself

1. An Imitationalist's Perspective
An imitationalist might work through all steps, labeling the motivation as a particular art form, identifying the objects in the subject matter, describing the art elements, analyzing the design principles, interpreting meaning, and evaluating quality. However, his or her number 1 criterion for relating to the work and judging it as an aesthetic expression is its realistic quality. The step of the model that is most important to an imitationalist is *identification*. This is the step in which he or she takes a visual inventory of the objects. The more clearly defined and detailed the objects are and the greater the fidelity to the natural world, the better an imitationalist considers the work to be.

2. A Formalist's Perspective
A formalist values design. Therefore, for such a person the most important processes of art criticism are *description* and *analysis*. In focusing on these steps, he or she learns how the art elements and design principles were used to construct the composition. A formalist would evaluate a work primarily on the aesthetic quality of the design, regardless of whether the work were realistic, abstract, or nonobjective.

3. An Emotionalist's Perspective
An emotionalist, in contrast, may have little concern for realistic imitation of life or harmonious balance in a composition. He or she goes for emotional impact. Such a person values the power of a work to express feelings, stimulate the imagination, and elicit emotions. The step most important to an emotionalist is *interpretation*. It is the interpretation process that moves him or her from objective perception to subjective meaning. An emotionalist would evaluate a work primarily on its emotional/expressive qualities.

The variations in the model can help explain why different types of works ranging from realism to minimalism to action painting are all considered art. Once students have been introduced to these three theories and understand their relationships to art criticism processes, they can participate in role-playing activities to reinforce their knowledge. The boxed "Gallery Opening" is an exercise you might use to actively involve students in oral and/or written discussions.

Gallery Opening

Directions:

To present this aesthetics activity, use the following procedure:

1. Choose a theme (portraits, animals, landscape, interiors, architecture, etc.) for artwork to be displayed in a mock gallery ope
2. Select reproductions that fit the theme and te each of these theories—imitationalism, formalism, and emo
3. Exhibit the works in the art room.
4. Divide students into groups of three, e st, a formalist, and an emotionalist.
5. Have each group select one artwork cuss from each member's perspective (totaling three
6. After each member has commented background.
7. Continue this process until all grou s, each illustrating a theory. (This activity can also be done as using the following discussions as a model.)

Response from an imitationalist viewer (discussing Portrait of a Merchant, Plate 11.2*):*

Wow! What a painting. I love it. It is so realistic. I want to walk up to those papers tacked to the wall and smooth them down. I don't know who this person is, but I'm certain that he was real, that he worked in this crowded space and that he had an important job. From his clothing I would guess that he lived around the sixteenth century. Judging by his jewelry, his coat, the fur collar, I believe he had some money. The artist has portrayed every detail of this man and his environment. I am awed by the artist's skill, his attention to detail, and his ability to create the illusion of reality—of depth and form and human substance—on this flat piece of canvas. He is a master!

Response from a formalist viewer:

I can understand why as an imitationalist you respond so favorably to this painting. I do not share your enthusiasm, however. I am not as interested in the accuracy with which the artist depicted *what* is in the painting (objects on the table, papers on the wall) as I am in *how* the artist presents the image using visual language (color, value, balance, contrast). I agree that the sitter is probably a real and important person. He is the focal point. I wish the artist had not distracted me with those two stacks of papers. I find both the proximity of the papers to the sitter's face and their high contrast against the dark wall very jarring. I wish the background were lighter so that the figure stood out more. I would like to see more intermediate values, some use of transition. I also find the overall image cluttered. Less detail and more space would improve it. There is just too much for this to be a good composition.

Response from an emotionalist viewer:

I don't know where you went to school but you missed the point entirely. This isn't a bad composition—it's a great composition. The artist has made you feel exactly the way he wanted you to feel—claustrophobic, cluttered, cramped. What do you think

PLATE 11.2
Jan Gossaert, Portrait of a Merchant *(circa 1530). Oil on wood
panel, 25" × 18 3/4"*

National Gallery of Art, Washington, D.C.,
Mellon Bank Fund

this painting is about? Realistically portraying the sitter? Creating a pleasing composition in which the figure clearly stands out from the background? No. This is not a portrait of a man; this is a portrait of a man's *life*—his daily existence in this stuffy space.
Look at the expression on his face. He's looking out at the viewer with those furtive little eyes and those tightly pursed lips, as if to say, "I dare you to intrude, to challenge
me." The artist intended to distract you with those white sheets crowding in around the
sitter's head. The clutter of objects is purposeful and conveys feeling and meaning.
Both the composition and objects themselves are used in a symbolic way to portray
the emotional quality of this man's state of being and life. I think he communicated his
message very well indeed!

Background information:

This picture, entitled *Portrait of a Merchant,* was painted in 1530 by the Netherlands
painter Jan Gossaert. It depicts a merchant seated at a table on which are scattered the

PLATE 11.3
Helen Hardin, **Looking Within Myself I Am Many Parts** *(1976)*

© CRADOC BAGSHAW 2000

tools of his trade—a talc shaker used to dry ink, an ink pot, quill pens, paper, a metal receptacle for sealing wax, and a pair of scales for testing the weight of coins. Attached to the wall are balls of twine and batches of paper labeled "miscellaneous letters" and "miscellaneous drafts." Tentatively identified by the monogram on his hat pin and index finger, the sitter is believed to be Jerome Sandelin, a tax collector in Zeeland (on the southern coast of present-day Holland).

Response from an imitationalist viewer (discussing Looking Within Myself I Am Many Parts, Plate 11.3*):*

Do I like this? I'm the one who wants to smooth the ruffled pages back down onto the wall in the other painting, remember? What's there to smooth in this? The image is entirely flat and abstract. I can recognize designs that look Native American, the suggestion of hair, and a turquoise necklace. However, the image does not seem to be about portraying these details. It seems to be more about patterns, colors, and shapes.

Although this may be a good painting to some, it is so far removed from my concept of art that I can't even make a judgment. I don't like it and I don't think it's art.

Response from a formalist viewer:

This piece has the qualities the first one lacked. My eye flows throughout the composition. The linear quality is especially strong and rhythmical. The curved lines and shapes juxtaposed against the angular shapes of eyes and mouth create an effective contrast. The colors are almost complementary, and variation is achieved more through intensity than value. The limited use of color emphasizes the use of shape.

Although some of these shapes look as though they may have been drawn mechanically, the overall design has an organic flow. The balance is also interesting. I see this image as both symmetrical and asymmetrical, organic and geometric, warm and cool, full of fluidity and tension—one element against the other creating a unity from opposites. I love the play of elements in this composition. I love this painting.

Response from an emotionalist viewer:

I am not particularly drawn in to images that are so meticulously and precisely rendered. I prefer more spontaneously created marks. However, certain qualities in this painting appeal to me. I agree that the message is about contrast, the lines running upward from the nose and downward from the mouth split the image in two, implying duality. The color may imply light and shadow aspects of the personality. The eyes are shaped and placed in such a way as to suggest sadness. The image conveys a heaviness, perhaps contemplation or introspection. This painting does not touch me because of its composition, but because of what I read into the expression.

Background information:

This picture, entitled *Looking Within Myself I Am Many Parts,* was created in 1976 by Helen Hardin. The painter was a Native American whose mother, Pablita Veralde, was herself an accomplished artist from the Santa Clara Pueblo in New Mexico. This is one of many self-portraits reflecting Hardin's inner feelings and outward life. Hardin struggled with embracing her Native American heritage at the same time she was breaking away from the traditional Native American painting style for which her mother was famous. Both her father and husband were Anglos. She moved between two worlds— that of her native people and that of the outside culture of the art world. Throughout her life, which ended in a bout with cancer in 1984, she felt there was no place in which she fit. She described herself as "always on the outside looking in."

Response from an imitationalist viewer (discussing Head Surrounded by Sides of Beef, Plate 11.4):

You've got to be kidding! I was willing to concede on the second painting that maybe there was something I just didn't get. In that picture I was at least able to appreciate the precision with which the image had been drawn. But this! What is it? The man's face looks as if it has been scraped away. The hands are just blobs of color. And what is that thing in the background? Is it part of the chair? It looks like sides of beef! Whatever it is, it doesn't fit, and it's too sloppily rendered to be recognizable. The paint has been applied quickly without any attention to detail. The image is dark, ugly, and weird. Furthermore, it's badly painted. I think it's awful.

Response from a formalist viewer:

Yes, the picture is dark, ugly, menacing, and sloppily painted. I don't much like it either. But I'm seeing something really interesting. Do you notice any similarities between this and the realistically painted portrait? Look at the compositions. Each figure is placed in a frontal position, emerging from a dark background. In both paintings the head is framed by symmetrically shaped and placed light-colored objects that seem to compete for attention with the sitter himself. I was really bothered by the white papers in the first painting. I am equally bothered by the meatlike forms in this painting. But I learned something from our emotionalist friend. Maybe I'm supposed to be bothered. Maybe

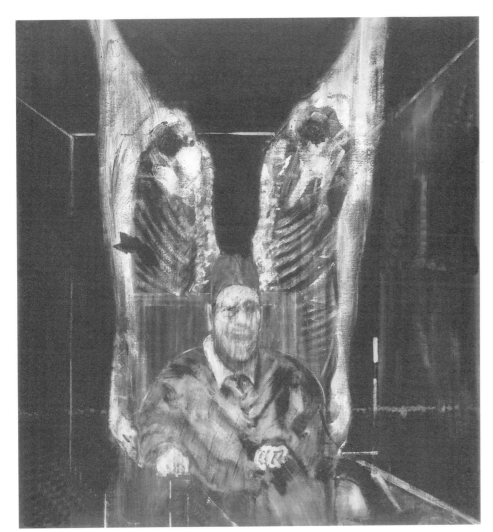

PLATE 11.4
Francis Bacon, **Head Surrounded by Sides of Beef** *(1954). Oil on canvas, 50 3/4" × 48"*

Art Institute of Chicago, Harriet A. Fox Fund. © 1999, The Art Institute of Chicago. All rights reserved. Estate of Francis Bacon/ Artists Rights Society (ARS), New York

those sides of beef against the dark background are supposed to create tension. The converging lines, the symmetrical balance, the use of contrast all draw us in to the focal point in the center. Although I do not like this painting, and I'm not sure what the artist is trying to say, I can appreciate the way in which the artist has led us into the composition.

Response from an emotionalist viewer:

At last a picture I can really relate to! I don't get excited over paintings in which every brushstroke has been eliminated. I'd rather look at a good photograph than a realistically rendered scene. I like to see paint, brushstrokes, the energy of the artist recorded in the expressiveness of the mark. I don't like nice, clean, clear, pretty pictures. I like ambiguity; I like strong emotions. I like this painting for all the reasons you don't like it—its darkness, weirdness, "sloppiness," emotion. The other two paintings also have expressive qualities I admire. In the realistically painted portrait the artist conveyed feeling through the use of subject matter and composition. In the second painting the artist expressed emotion through the juxtaposition of colors, shapes, and lines. Neither can begin to compare to this last painting, however, in terms of emotional impact. Here the artist has used subject matter to elicit emotional responses. We see a figure who might be a pope or a king grimacing or screaming out at us. He sits tightly clutching the arms of something that might be a throne—or an electric chair—on which hangs part of a slaughtered animal. The scene reeks of death. The dark space is small, compressed, confining. The figure, appearing even smaller, seems trapped and terrified. The compositional qualities serve to intensify the image. Additionally, the quality of the marks themselves are violent and scary. The artist has integrated medium, process, composition, and subject matter in an incredibly expressive statement. This painting is a masterpiece!

Background information:

This picture, entitled *Head Surrounded by Sides of Beef,* painted in 1954 by the English artist Francis Bacon, is an example of an appropriated image. Using Velazquez's painting *Pope Innocent X* as his inspiration, Bacon recreated the Velazquez image using his own expressive style and imagery. Bacon's paintings are intentionally dark, shocking, and morbid. What he sought to achieve in his work were images that "unlock the deeper possibilities of sensation."

THEORIES REFLECTING A GLOBAL PERSPECTIVE

The conversations presented in the preceding activity illustrate how you may lead students to demonstrate a working knowledge of art criticism, aesthetics, and the connection between them. Although these theories of aesthetics may be applicable in viewing and discussing many works of art from all over the world, they represent particular perspectives defining the nature of art. These views may or may not fit all the cultural exemplars we present to students. Looking back to Chapter 9, we are reminded of the emphasis on global perspectives. Widening our vision of art and culture, we may explore peoples whose art has nothing to do with (1) imitating nature, (2) organizing design elements, or (3) expressing personal emotions or meanings. A visit back to the Navajo reservation to view the artwork in Plate 11.5 illustrates the point.

PLATE 11.5
Pollen Boy on the Sun, *Navajo sandpainting from the Blessing-way ceremony.*

This image is a computer-generated design by the author illustrating the content and composition of a traditional sandpainting performed in a ritual by a medicine man. It has been handed down from one generation to the next and is not attributable to a specific artist.

Pollen Boy on the Sun is a sandpainting performed in the Blessingway ceremony. The rays of the sun are symbolically depicted as feathers. There are four groups of different-colored feathers, each group representing individual songs from the ceremony. The feathers, organized according to the four directions, are divided by sacred plants. The sandpainting when performed with the sacred plants is used in the blessing of a boy. When performed without including the sacred plants, the ritual is done to bless a man or a hunter. Sandpaintings such as this one are used to bless or cure individuals of an illness, as well as to transmit cultural heritage through visual stories and myths. Their use and value exemplify a non-Western aesthetic, further illustrated in the conversation in Table 11.1.

TABLE 11.1
A Conversation Contrasting Western and Non-Western Views of Art

WESTERN ANTHROPOLOGIST:	NAVAJO MEDICINE MAN:
"I have come to your reservation to learn about how your people express themselves through art. What can you tell me about the art of your people?"	"Much of what you call 'art' we view as part of everyday life. For example, our sandpaintings are not viewed by us as 'art' but as rituals to restore and maintain the harmony of nature."
"Tell me about your sandpaintings. How are they created?"	"Medicine men perform ritual sandpaintings by recreating designs they received from the Holy Ones. Each sandpainting must exactly replicate these designs."
"In our culture that would be considered copying. Art works that are copied have little value. We value creativity—novel ideas, new thoughts."	"We are not interested in creativity when we perform sandpaintings. Our intent is to perform a ceremony in a prescribed way. Since it is a ritual, it is begun and finished within a certain time."
"I understand that in your culture production time is important because it is part of the ritual. Emphasis on production time is not so important to us."	"Yes, timing within the ritual is important. However, when the ritual is over, the painting is destroyed. Our sandpaintings are not created to last forever."
"One of the things we value is longevity. We prize works that have lasted for centuries."	"Objects are often made by Native American peoples to serve them in their rituals. Many 'works of art' that have been made for specific ceremonies are of no value when the event is over."
"Since we value longevity, we also appreciate materials that will last a long time."	"We value materials also. We take great care to select and grind the perfect rocks for our sandpaintings. But when the sandpainting is finished, we return the sand to nature. This is part of the ritual symbolizing our connectedness with the earth.
"Artists in our culture create art for its own sake. Collectors display paintings, drawings, and sculptures in their homes and offices."	"Yes, I know. We make permanent sandpaintings on particle boards to sell to tourists. They take these small replicas home and hang them on their walls. We don't use sandpaintings for decoration."
"Western philosophers have theories to explain why we appreciate certain kinds of art. Some people in our culture appreciate art that looks real and imitates nature."	"We are not concerned with realistic interpretation of nature. The images in our paintings are symbols of nature and natural phenomena, not realistic representations."

(continued)

TABLE 11.1 *(continued)*

WESTERN ANTHROPOLOGIST:		NAVAJO MEDICINE MAN:
"We also value artworks because of their design qualities—things like balance, contrast, and repetition."	→	"When we recreate the designs that were handed down from the Holy Ones, we use the design principles of which you speak. However, we are more concerned with the performance of the ritual, not with the creation of the composition."
"We also value artworks because of their emotional qualities and the feelings they evoke within us."	→	"Our sandpaintings do not look like emotional works of art by Western standards. They are very precise and may seem stiff to you. However, we believe they have curative powers. As our people learn the meanings of the symbols and the stories and experience the rituals, they may feel certain emotions."
"What would you say is the primary purpose of your artwork?"	→	"That's easy to answer. The purpose of art in the Navajo culture is to beautify the world."
"One of our purposes for creating art is also to beautify our environment."	→	"Yes, but your meaning of 'beautify' is different from ours. When we say *beauty* we are talking about *harmony* between the natural and the supernatural and among all things on earth and in the universe. Your idea of beauty seems more like decoration."
"Perhaps. It seem that art serves a function in both our cultures. As I hear you explain your art and how it serves you, I understand that your people use and appreciate art in different ways from my people."	→	"That is as it should be. If we were all the same, there would be no need for harmony. Harmony is the peaceful relationship among things that are different from one another."
"Good explanation."	→	"Thank you."

This dialogue illustrates two different valuing systems. In one an artwork is viewed as an object having worth in and of itself, reflecting an "art for art's sake" philosophy. In the other an artwork is valued for the function it serves within a culture, reflecting what Dissanayake called an "art for life's sake" view. Much of the art produced in the world—by non-Western peoples, tribal societies, and folk artists everywhere—is made, used, and valued as an instrument serving societal living.

In addition to these examples of art, entirely different kinds of art expressions are growing out of the postmodern age. Postmodern expressions challenge people to expand their definitions of art. These expressions may not fit into categories used to define "art" in a traditional sense. They may have very little to do with "composition," focusing instead on presenting content, delivering a message, and engaging the viewer to actively participate and interpret meaning. They may be parodying the art of the past by altering appropriated images. They may take the form of installations, performances, collaborations, and interactive art. Often they cannot be understood or appreciated by walking through art criticism processes designed to understand more traditional art expressions. In addressing a postmodern piece, one might ask,

- What is the artist's message?
- Is the piece a comment on societal beliefs, values, or norms?
- How has the artist conveyed meaning?

- What is the relationship between the form (medium) of the presentation and the content (meaning)?

- Is the form itself part of the meaning, or is it simply a vehicle to express content?

- If this message were expressed through another more traditional art form, would the impact be as strong?

- What do you feel or think as you view this piece?

- How does the piece impact you?

When we view the breadth of expression we classify as "art" today—a Renaissance painting, a ritual mask, a quilt created by an "outsider" artist (a self-taught artist outside the mainstream of art and often society), and a piece of performance art—we may conclude that we need more than one system for exploring the meaning and value of art. We may use the processes of identification, description, analysis, and interpretation to help students connect with art objects and encourage "Wow" experiences through attention to visual qualities. At the same time, however, we must be sensitive to what these works are about beyond their visual qualities. When we present works in which meaning and value are derived from cultural contexts, both within and outside our culture, we must find additional ways to promote understanding and appreciation. Two aesthetic theories especially suitable for exploring art from a broader perspective are contextualism and instrumentalism.

CONTEXTUALISM   Contextualism is a Western aesthetic theory that has emerged recently in our history. It was introduced in the 1960s by the philosopher Nelson Goodman. It is a belief that the meaning and worth of art can only be determined in the context in which it is made and used. Contextualists view art as a social communication system, requiring knowledge of a shared code that is transmitted from the maker of the object to the receiver. When we view objects such as Navajo sandpaintings, Mexican "Day of the Dead" sculptures, Tibetan mandalas, or Chinese landscape paintings, we may see how fitting this aesthetic theory can be. It can be equally fitting to address an installation of television monitors projecting images about a social issue. These examples of "art" are significant not only as objects, but as instruments used to visually communicate beliefs, values, and cultural heritage.

INSTRUMENTALISM   The aesthetic theory instrumentalism (also called *pragmatism*) is a branch of contextualism. Instrumentalists believe that art serves a purpose and leads to some thought, action, or activity beyond itself. An instrumentalist might ask, "What is the purpose of this object?" "How well does it fulfill its function within the culture?" "How effective is it in moving people to respond to its message?" Worth is determined on the basis of an object's instrumental value to society.

Art within all cultures has been made to serve particular functions, including these:

- To support spiritual beliefs and practices (sandpaintings, masks, ceremonial blankets)

- To transmit social and political messages (World War II propaganda posters)

- To serve daily living (vessels, utensils, clothing, jewelry)

In many non-Western cultures these functions merge into one. Spiritual practices, transmission of culture, and daily activities are interrelated aspects of the whole. Objects created for these purposes are often made and viewed as "special" because their intent is to serve a special function. As such they are instruments through which their makers and users elevate life from the mundane to the special. A jar becomes more than a vessel for storing liquid; a garment becomes more than clothing to cover the body. These objects, transcending their functionality and used as symbols in the celebration of life, reflect the view, not only that art is for life's sake, but that *art makes things special.*

"Art for art's sake" and "art for life's sake" provide different reasons for assigning value. The first perspective focuses on the visual qualities of the art object. Those using this system assume that visual language is universal and that an art object can therefore be understood and appreciated by all. An object is valued in and of itself and need not be concerned with serving a function within a culture. The second perspective focuses on contextual meanings and functions. Contextualists believe that art is not a universal language but an idiosyncratic symbolic communication system used in the service of particular cultures. As such it is understood only as we explore its cultural contexts. (To understand and appreciate *Pollen Boy on the Sun,* for example, we needed to look beyond its visual qualities to its symbolism and ceremonial significance.) Cultural context, then, not the form of the object itself, is what gives meaning and value to a work. Faced with what appear to be polar opposites, we might ask, "Can we use both these perspectives to support our model of art education?" The answer is yes.

▼ CONNECTING AESTHETICS TO STUDIO PRODUCTION

How can we use these theories to support studio practice? We might begin by reviewing the groundwork we have already laid in art production. We could then turn to each aesthetic theory to discover a fit for various types of studio activities. Conversely, to motivate different productive experiences we might begin by looking at each theory and at a variety of artwork exemplifying each. Where we start is not important; that we make fitting connections is. For purposes of this discussion, we will use aesthetic theories as a framework.

IMITATIONALISM

Imitationalist works reveal a level of skill in observation and use of tools, media, and techniques to realistically represent objects. Some of what we do as art educators is to lead students to see and to reproduce what they see through observational drawing, painting, or sculpting activities. These experiences may be closed-ended exercises to learn how to represent an object in contour line, achieve volume in a drawing through shading, or create the illusion of depth through linear perspective. Whom might you select to exemplify these skills—Leonardo, Raphael, a contemporary photorealist? The works of these and other imitationalists may be used not only to illustrate skills we build in closed-ended exercises, but to model creative self-expression in products oriented toward realism.

FORMALISM

Formalists are primarily concerned with visual qualities created through art elements and design principles. We present art elements and design principles as components of "visual language." The "concretizing" activities in Chapter 6 are open-ended exercises intended to build visual language skills and are oriented toward formalism. The unit on Georgia O'Keeffe in Chapter 4 is also oriented toward formalism, focusing on visual problem solving through the use of art elements.

Since subject-centered art education was introduced in the 1960s, many art educators, in their emphasis on art elements and design principles, present formalist theory. The value these teachers place on formalism (consciously or not) is evident in the criteria they establish for making and assessing art—use of contrast, emphasis, symmetry, balance, unity, and so on. This focus is appropriate when assignments are intended to promote visual problem solving through the use of art elements and design principles. An emphasis on formal qualities may be misplaced, however, in assignments that lead in other directions—exploring a universal theme through personal narrative, for example. When we design a studio activity, we need to ask ourselves, "What is the purpose of this experience?" If the answer is "form," then formalist criteria are fitting. If the focus is on content, expressive criteria are better suited for framing assignments and making judgments.

EMOTIONALISM

Emotionalists value meaning, content, and expressive qualities revealed through choice of subject matter, media, and processes. Questions you may ask students to contemplate as viewers and creators of emotionalist works are "How does a work speak to me?" "What do I want to say through my own work?" "What subject matter, medium, process, style shall I choose to convey my message?" Students will have neither the insight nor the skill to make these choices and act on them without substantial background in art. We provide that background. Laissez-faire experiences, oriented toward exploration of media and techniques, can be especially useful in building this kind of knowledge. Through experimentation students learn about qualities of media and possibilities and limitations of processes. They develop their own visual vocabularies, which they can file away for future use in assignments involving the expression of emotional content.

Once students have been introduced to these theories, they might be challenged to consciously embrace one or more in self-expressive ways. The following assignments may be used to provide direction and help students build their visual repertoires.

BEAUTIFUL BILLBOARD CONTEST To structure this activity, ask students to divide themselves into groups identified as imitationalists, formalists, and emotionalists. (A class of 24 students might have six groups, two in each aesthetic category.) Present the following scenario:

Your school is in competition with other schools to win the "(name of your town) Beautiful Billboard Contest." This billboard will be used to advertise your town. Because you don't know what styles of art the judges like, you decide to play it safe. You divide into groups—imitationalists, formalists, and emotionalists. Each group brainstorms by talking, writing, and creating thumbnail sketches for billboard designs using a selected aesthetic theory. Groups make sketches of their final ideas and enlarge them on banner paper. Completed "billboards" are shared, discussed in terms of aesthetic theories, judged using the criteria appropriate for each theory, and displayed in the school.

CREATE AN ARTWORK IN THE STYLE OF . . . This experience might be most successful with a group of advanced high school students that is working independently on self-determined studio problems. The assignment involves creating an artwork in the style of a particular school of art or artist that fits an aesthetic theory. To structure the assignment put aesthetic theories on the board and ask students what school of art or artists fit each theory. The list might look like this:

Imitationalism	*Formalism*	*Emotionalism*
Dutch still life	Cubists	Fauves
N. C. Wyeth	Stuart Davis	German Expressionists
Leonardo	O'Keeffe	DeKooning
Richard Estes	Monet	Van Gogh

Ask each student to then choose a theme or subject matter typical of the artist or school of art and create a work in the style of his or her chosen exemplar. As part of the critique, have students (1) display their works and reproductions of the cultural exemplars, (2) share what attracted them to the exemplars and how they used them to motivate their own work, (3) discuss similarities and differences between their works and the cultural exemplar, (4) identify criteria that are most applicable for evaluation, and (5) critique the student work on the established criteria.

CONTEXTUALISM

Educators have identified contextualism as particularly fitting in the study of a variety of expressions. The discussion in this chapter on Navajo sand-painting presents a non-Western art form and the use of contextualist theory. The studio approach suggested in Chapter 9 involves a process in which students are led to (1) investigate the particularities of an art object within its culture, (2) view the object as one example of a universal theme, and (3) look to their own lives and cultures for motivation to interpret the theme in self-expressive ways. Art educators embracing contextualism have tended to turn their attention away from formalism. Rather than defining studio problems focusing on composition (the use of art elements and design principles), they define problems in terms of thematic content—a fitting approach for addressing multicultural, folk, and postmodern art expressions. Themes may be explored by students individually or collaboratively in assignments oriented toward personal narratives, social issues, and fundamental human concerns. They are about something relevant within the students' experiences and reflect an "art for life's sake" view.

INSTRUMENTALISM

All cultures have created art for instrumental purposes. These objects are made to transmit messages about political and social conditions, to serve in spiritual practices, to cure the ill, to elevate everyday existence from the mundane to the special. You may use instrumentalism to motivate various kinds of studio experiences. In the area of graphics, for example, you might ask students to design billboards or posters reflecting social themes—environmental concerns, pollution, crime, poverty, substance abuse. You might also have students create drawings, paintings, or sculptures reflecting community, home, and family values. Or you might have students explore crafts—textiles, jewelry, and ceramics—for the purpose of creating "special objects" to serve "special purposes." A motivation for such an assignment might be as follows: Tell students that they are preparing for a gathering to honor the eldest relative in their own family. This is to be a celebration in which every one brings a hand-made gift. The gift must be very special, symbolizing the significance of the elder in each person's life. The object must be crafted with the utmost care and reflect the expressiveness and creativity of the maker. Present cross-cultural examples that reflect instrumentalism and the idea of "making it special." Have students point out the unique characteristics of each one to "concretize" their understanding of "making it special." The goal is to lead students to see beyond what they are making to the potential power of these objects to visually communicate something about their culture, their families, themselves, and values.

A HOLISTIC VIEW

Our intention here is to be as inclusive as possible. As we view each of these aesthetic theories, we may see them not as exclusive of one another, but as mutually supportive. Imitationalism provides a framework for the study and creation of works that reflect direct observation of the real world. Formalism provides structure for developing visual composition. Emotionalism creates contexts for exploring meaning, content, and expressive qualities. Contextualism offers opportunities to connect with others through universal themes defining human experience. Instrumentalism presents a perspective that transcends the object and focuses on art's potential to transmit messages. These theories and the studio experiences they support are integrally connected. They build the foundation for the diverse body of experiences advocated in art education today.

S U M M A R Y

Art criticism and aesthetics are two interrelated domains of art education dealing with perception and appreciation of art. Art criticism is a combination of processes through which we lead students to observe and discuss visual qualities. Aesthetics is a branch of philosophy dealing with the study of what is considered to be beautiful or valuable. As a domain of art education, it reflects a goal of art criticism—the "Aha!" the "Oh, wow!"—the heightened awareness and appreciation gained from working through art criticism processes.

Both art criticism and aesthetics have an "inside" and an "outside" component relevant to our model of art education. "Inside" aspects deal with how we lead students through discussions, reflection sheets, and critique sessions to focus on the nature and quality of their own work. This chapter addresses the "outside" aspect. *The Merry Jesters* is presented as a motivation for working through the steps of the art criticism teaching model, listed as follows:

1. M = looking at the *motivation* (an artwork) and defining its form (painting, drawing, sculpture, etc.), materials, and processes used in fabrication

2. I = *identifying* the subject matter and taking a visual inventory of the objects comprising that subject matter

3. D = *describing* the characteristics of the art elements used to portray subject matter

4. A = *analyzing* visual relationships creating the composition by focusing on design principles

5. I = *interpreting* the meaning of the work by focusing on content and expressive qualities

6. E = *evaluating* the quality of the work by ranking it with like works on specified criteria

Aesthetic theories, reasons for valuing art, grow out of perception and thinking related to these art criticism processes. Three theories emerging from our Western tradition are imitationalism, formalism, and emotionalism. Imitationalists value art that imitates the natural world through realistic rendering of subject matter. Formalists value art for its formal qualities—art elements and design principles used to create visual composition. Emotionalists emphasize expressive qualities and content over subject matter or composition. In all three theories, value is determined by focusing on the art object itself. Through the art criticism processes of identification, description, analysis, and interpretation, the viewer may connect with the object and use one or more of these steps to determine quality and assign value. This perspective has been called "art for art's sake."

Although art criticism processes can be used to connect with any work of art, they may be insufficient by themselves to lead to understanding and appreciation. Postmodern works challenge the viewer to go beyond traditional concepts of art. People in other cultures may have reasons for producing and valuing art that are different from ours. Two aesthetic theories fitting for exploring global expressions are contextualism and instrumentalism. Contextualists believe that art objects can only be understood and appreciated by investigating their cultural contexts. Often these objects are not considered to be "art" by their makers and users. They are made to serve specific functions within a society and are used and appreciated as instruments transmitting values, beliefs, and traditions. Instrumentalism is a branch of contextualism that explains this view of art and valuing system. This perspective has been called "art for life's sake."

As we analyze how we assign value and learn about how value is assigned by others, we see connections between aesthetics and art criticism and art history. Critical processes help us to perceive visual qualities and develop appreciation. Study of art within cultural contexts enables us to understand intentions of artists and value assigned by particular peoples. Aesthetics is also connected to art production. The relationship between aesthetics and art production is especially important from the perspective of this text. We have embraced a studio-centered approach, identifying art making as the primary focus. When we consider how we promote growth—through exploration of media and processes, skill-oriented exercises, visual problem-solving activities, motivations to encourage self-expression—we focus on studio experiences directed toward the "inside." These experiences occur within the contexts of units that also contain "outside" aspects. The "inside" and the "outside" are integrally connected: Cultural exemplars motivate and mirror what we intend to develop in our own students—productive skill, visual literacy, creativity, authenticity, meaning. These exemplars are models of aesthetic expression. Viewed in this light, aesthetics becomes far more than the study of a branch of philosophy. It drives our curricular choices and provides substance and meaning in studio-centered art education.

A. USING THE ART CRITICISM TEACHING MODEL

Directions

Demonstrate your knowledge of art criticism by selecting an artwork and working through the steps of the model.

Title of Artwork: _____ **Artist:** _____

1. Discuss the motivation: (a) What art form is it? (b) What medium was used? (c) What techniques were used?

    a.

    b.

    c.

2. Identify the subject matter and list the objects portrayed. (If the motivation is a nonobjective work, proceed to the next step.)

    a. Subject matter:

    b. List objects:

3. Select the strongest art element and describe its qualities.

    a. Art element:

    b. Describe qualities:

4. Select the strongest design principle and analyze how it contributes to the composition.

    a. Design principle:

    b. Analyze its use in the composition:

5. Interpret the work by discussing what you think it is about and how you feel as you look at it.

    a. I think this work is about . . .

    b. As I look at this work, I feel . . .

6. If you were to evaluate the work, what three criteria would you select for judging quality?

    a.

    b.

    c.

B. CONNECTING AESTHETICS TO STUDIO PRODUCTION

Directions
Use the structure below to support studio production through aesthetics.

Imitationalism: **Cultural Exemplar:** _____ **Grade Level:** _____

Studio Assignment:

Formalism: **Cultural Exemplar:** _____ **Grade Level:** _____

Studio Assignment:

Emotionalism: **Cultural Exemplar:** _____ **Grade Level:** _____

Studio Assignment:

Contextualism: **Cultural Exemplar:** _____ **Grade Level:** _____

Studio Assignment:

12

PRESENTING ART HISTORY

Art history completes our presentation of response domains. It is integrally connected to art criticism and aesthetics, providing the cultural contexts to support understanding of these areas of art education. Although it focuses on the "outside," art history has the potential to enhance understanding of the "inside." As students compare their own ideas, values, and expressions to those of others, they may be encouraged to ask, "Who am I, and how do I fit into the broad picture of humanity?" In this book we have been exploring the teaching of art history all along through cultural exemplars. The purpose of this chapter is to deepen your understanding of how to address art history. Sections include (1) strategies for teaching art history and (2) the art history teaching model.

▼ STRATEGIES FOR TEACHING ART HISTORY

Art history was not addressed in a systematic way until subject-centered teachers began responding to the criticism that art education lacked substance. As we have seen, the 1960s reflected a more academic approach to the teaching of art, mirroring a back-to-basics orientation, and an interest in multiculturalism, motivated by the civil rights and the women's liberation movements. Then history began to be integrated into programs on a more regular basis in more visible ways. In general, art education today reflects a wide variety of approaches, ranging from child centered, focusing almost exclusively on the "inside," to DBAE, placing major emphasis on history and culture. Because national and state guidelines for art education urge teachers to address art history, we see a number of strategies used in presenting historical content.

● PRESENTING ART HISTORY THROUGH OSMOSIS

One approach to teaching history—through osmosis, as if art history could just seep into students' consciousness without being explicitly taught—can be seen in the rooms of some art teachers trained before the subject-centered movement. For these instructors, art education may be defined exclusively as studio production. Often cultural exemplars are nonexistent. Art history is "included" through reproductions permanently displayed around the room. In some cases these displays are never mentioned. Their function is to provide an "aesthetic environment" and "exposure to art." Although students may be impressed when they first enter these rooms, eventually they become numb to the visual impact. They stop noticing and learn nothing. Art history does not teach itself.

TAKING YOUR STUDENTS TO ART

One of the better ways to "expose students to art" is through museum trips. Many museums employ educators who work with art teachers to provide experiences for students. Some museums send pretour packets to schools, and teachers use these materials to motivate and prepare students for trips. When students arrive at a museum, they may be greeted by docents, volunteers who have been trained to conduct museum tours. Often a museum will offer a selection of tours for various grade levels. Themes for tours may include the following:

1. *A particular subject matter.* Students may be shown a variety of art forms using a particular subject matter—animals, for example—and presented with cultural/historical information about how different artists or cultures depict this subject. This type of presentation is typically designed for primary-level students.

2. *Formal properties of art.* As docents ask questions that call for description and analysis of art elements and design principles, students learn to "read" artwork. These tours sharpen students' critical skills and provide cultural/historical information about artwork. Museums may gear this type of presentation toward students in upper elementary and middle school grades.

3. *A comparison of different cultures through art.* Because many museums group artwork in galleries (rooms) according to culture, some tours focus on similarities and differences among cultures. Museums that house non-Western collections may offer tours that compare and contrast a non-Western culture with Western art and society.

4. *Art styles explored through "-isms."* Museums also display artworks according to periods in art history and schools of art. This organization lends itself to tours that focus on "-isms." For example, students may learn about the development of Impressionism, Expressionism, or Cubism. These experiences may reinforce understanding of the relationship between art styles and aesthetic theories. Tours of this nature are often geared toward high school students.

You can coordinate what you teach with museum visits in several ways. You can select a preexisting tour to reinforce a unit. You can also design a unit expressly to accompany a particular exhibit in a museum. Docents, when given enough time, may design special tours. Museum educators can also help you design self-guided tours. They may assist you in researching cultural/historical information, provide library services, and reproduce slides. Do not assume that the museum gift shop is the only place to acquire materials. Museum education departments exist to provide services to you. To acquaint yourself with these services and resources, make an appointment with a museum educator and ask questions such as these:

1. What kinds of tours do you offer?

2. Do you send out previsit materials to prepare teachers and students? How long may I keep the materials?

3. What kinds of worksheets do you have for students to use during a visit?

4. Do you have posttour materials to reinforce learning through classroom activities after the visit?

5. Are docents available to give tours?

6. Will docents design special tours if I explain what I want students to see and learn?

7. How do I arrange to take my students on a self-guided tour?

8. Do you have a library available for my use?

9. Will a museum educator help me research a particular topic, artist, or period?

10. May I have slides made of artwork in your permanent collection? How much do they cost?

11. Do real museum pieces or reproductions ever travel to schools? How is this arranged?

12. Do museum educators offer workshops for teachers?

13. How can I be invited to museum workshops?

These questions may open doors to possibilities you did not know existed. You should learn how to use museum facilities and to access information as part of your continued development as an art educator. Many museums, private galleries, and individual artists have Web sites on the Internet, which can be used to research historical and contemporary art expressions. Resources for students and teachers have expanded significantly as discipline-based art education and museum education have come together to support one another. Ideally, students at all grade levels should visit a museum through school tours at least once a year. Unfortunately, constraints such as funding, availability of museums and buses, substitute teachers, and time often prohibit the realization of this vision.

BRINGING ART TO YOUR STUDENTS

If you can't take your students to art, perhaps you can arrange for art to be brought to your students. Picture Parent Programs may be funded through a PTA (Parent Teacher Association), a school district office, or grants. These programs provide resources and training for volunteer parents to present reproductions of art (and sometimes even real pieces) to students in art and academic classrooms on a regular basis. You may choose to work with a parent volunteer in a number of ways: (1) team-teach a lesson, (2) rely solely on the expertise of the parent volunteer, or (3) let a parent introduce cultural information that you will expand on later. Regardless of how you use a volunteer, you need to provide guidelines to ensure educationally sound experiences that relate to units of study you are presenting to students.

On a more sophisticated level, technology has made it possible to bring art to students in a variety of forms. These include videos, CD-ROMs, Digital Video Discs, and Internet Web sites. Nowadays computers are standard equipment in many classrooms, including art rooms. Through the World Wide Web students may view artwork all over the globe.

PRESENTING ART IN THE DARK

"Art in the dark" refers to slide presentations that could last a few minutes, a whole period, several days, or an entire semester. This approach is especially popular in high school art appreciation courses. Teachers of these courses often rely on the showing of slides as a method for presenting information and involving students in historical, critical, and aesthetic discussions. The quality of these slide lectures may vary widely. The poorest may never go beyond the bare facts: the work's title, the artist, the date, and the location. The best may include information about the time and culture in which the piece was produced, the artist's life and circumstances under which he or she created the work, the relationship of the work to other works in art history, and the reception of the work during the time it was created. Although "art in the dark" has a negative connotation, it is simply a method of presenting information. Showing slides is not a poor teaching strategy. What may be poor or excellent is the way in which slides are presented and integrated into a unit. The key to presenting slide lectures well is careful selection of images and design of questions to motivate active participation. (Can anything be more boring than a presentation of fifty slides accompanied by information to answer Trivial Pursuit questions?) One way to promote active participation is to encourage students to compare and contrast artwork as they view different images projected simultaneously. Another strategy is to design worksheets on which students record responses. You might also group students to discuss what they have seen and to share ideas and appreciations.

USING CULTURAL EXEMPLARS

The presentation of cultural exemplars within units of study is the strategy for teaching art history proposed in this text and embraced by many art educators. Teachers use this method because a synergistic relationship occurs through integration of the parts. As students learn in each domain, they build one activity on the next and experience heightened motivation. Knowledge of art history inspires ideas in art production. Exploration of media, processes, and ideas in studio activities whets the appetite for knowledge of art history. Art criticism is a natural lead in to cultural information. Historical information sets the stage for the study of aesthetics. A cultural exemplar can be thought of as the glue that binds the components of a unit together. Through the exemplar we teach art history, criticism, and aesthetics. The cultural exemplar also helps define the productive component, as we make choices about presenting art forms, processes, media, styles, and content in studio assignments. In addition to using cultural exemplars to design units, teachers can also use them to structure curriculum. Some different approaches are listed next.

1. *Chronological approach:* A teacher might begin with Paleolithic humankind, and sequence units along a timeline. The drawback is that this tends to provide a linear progression of Western art, while excluding non-Western cultures.

2. *Thematic approach:* A teacher might select a series of themes, such as landscape, architecture, the figure, family, human relationships, transformation, through which to explore the universal and the particular.

3. *Cultural approach:* A teacher might design curriculum through units exploring various cultures. This approach can be advantageous because Western and non-Western art and cultures can be compared and art and social studies can be readily integrated.

4. *Studio approach:* A teacher might select studio areas—drawing, painting, print making, sculpture, crafts—and present artists working with particular art forms, processes, media, or styles within each area.

These approaches offer a variety of ways to shape curriculum. Because content is packaged differently in each approach, strategies used to organize information may vary. You have already been introduced to one strategy in Chapter 9 (on multiculturalism). In this approach we began by embracing an entire culture, progressing from the general to the specific. We can also progress from a narrow focus (one artwork) to broader cultural contexts. These two strategies are compared in the diagrams at the top of the next page.

Progressing from the General to the Particular in the Presentation of Historical Content
Overview of art and culture of a people ⟶ Presentation of several examples of one art form used as the cultural exemplar ⟶ Focus on one work of art to illustrate theme, content, and style

Progressing from the General to the Particular in Presenting Historical Content

Progressing from the Particular to the General in the Presentation of Historical Content
Presentation of one artwork ⟶ Cultural/historical information to guide students in understanding the work as an expression of its time and culture ⟶ Additional artwork and information to help students understand the significance of the work in the continuum of art history

Progressing from the Particular to the General in Presenting Historical Content

Having already explored the first approach, we turn our attention to the second. By using the art history teaching model, you will be guided to develop a system that progresses from a single work of art to a broad cultural context.

▼ THE ART HISTORY TEACHING MODEL

This model is designed to parallel the art criticism and aesthetics teaching models. Like them, it provides processes used to focus on particular aspects of an artwork. The purpose of this model is to lead students in a systematic way to understand cultural/historical dimensions of a work. This section presents (1) the model (Figure 12.1), (2) an explanation of the steps, and (3) a practical application.

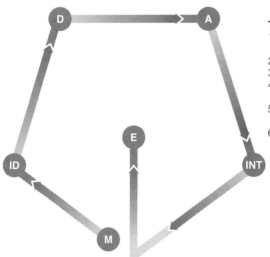

The Six Steps of the Model
1. M = Motivation—presentation of the art object
2. ID = Identification of factual information
3. D = Description of cultural contexts
4. A = Analysis of relationships of the art object to other works in time and place
5. INT = Interpretation of the work by the artist and/or culture of origin
6. E = Evaluation of the work by the artist and/or culture of origin

FIGURE 12.1
The Art History Teaching Model

STEPS OF THE ART HISTORY TEACHING MODEL

As you can see in Figure 12.1, the steps of the art history teaching model — motivation, identification, analysis, interpretation, and evaluation—are identical to those of the art criticism teaching model. The difference is that the steps of the art criticism teaching model refer to processes engaged in by students, whereas the steps of the art history model refer to content addressed by the teacher. The information in the following box illustrates this difference and describes how a teacher might use the art history teaching model to present a large amount of cultural and historical information in smaller, understandable bits.

The Steps of the Art History Teaching Model

1. M = Motivation—the presentation of an artwork

   The motivation step engages students in looking at the art object. It is identical to the motivation step in the art criticism teaching model. The teacher questions students or provides information about the following:

   a. The art form (painting, drawing, print, sculpture)

   b. Tools and media used (paint brushes, air brush, oil paint, ink)

   c. Processes used to create the work (impasto, wet on wet, etching)

2. ID = Identification of facts used to catalogue the object

   The identification step introduces basic factual information to answer *what, who, when,* and *where* questions. You might think of identification in this context as the step that provides information to identify an object in a catalogue or art exhibit:

   a. Title of the work

   b. Artist

   c. Date the work was made

   d. Present location of the work

3. D = Description of cultural/historical context

   The description step provides information to guide students in understanding and appreciating the object as an expression of culture. This is the most important step of the model and possibly the most challenging to present. Cultural/historical contexts include so much information and can mean many different things. You will make choices about what will be interesting and relevant to your students and units. As you present cultural contexts to students in first, seventh, or twelfth grade, you will need to decide how much to include and where to focus. The nature of the cultural exemplar can help you make these decisions. The illustrations following indicate where you might place your focus using exemplars such as

   * *A narrative work depicting a historical event.* Focus on the subject matter of the work as a record of history. The paintings in the Frederick Douglass and Harriet Tubman series by Jacob Lawrence are examples of works that need explanations of the stories to be understood and appreciated as cultural expressions.

   * *The work of an artist who depicted scenes and events in his own life.* Focus on the artist's life as reflected through his or her works. For example, a presentation on the paintings of Van Gogh could include some details of his life and the environment in which he lived.

   * *The work of an artist who is known for his or her style.* Focus on how the artist developed his or her *style.* In presenting the work of Monet, for example, you might explain how Monet broke away from traditional salon painting, took his easel outside, began a new art style, and painted a picture derogatorily referred

to as *impressionistic*—a label providing a name for a school of art—the French Impressionists.

- *An object that reflects social conditions and values.* Focus on cultural significance. In a presentation of Pop Art, for example, explain the intent of the artists. What were they saying? How did they reflect their culture? Were they humorous? Were they serious? Were they taken seriously?

- *An object that symbolically represents an event or condition.* Focus on the symbols and their meanings. Identifying the subject matter of *Guernica,* for example, is not enough. To understand the painting as an outcry against war, students must know specifically what Picasso was reacting against.

- *An object that has a ceremonial function in a culture.* Focus on the *function.* If you present a ceremonial object—a sandpainting, for example—include information about how the object was made, its use and symbolic significance in the ceremony, and what happened to the object when the ceremony was over.

When you think about all the information you could include in cultural contexts, you might feel overwhelmed. The questions that follow can help you decide where to place your focus in a specific presentation:

a. Why did the artist create this work?

b. How did the artist create it? (How was he living? Where was he living? What were the circumstances under which he worked?)

c. Is the subject matter significant? Does it tell a story?

d. Does the work serve a function?

e. Does the work reflect cultural events, beliefs, or values? Does it embrace or react against society's norms?

f. Does it reflect the personal journey of an individual artist?

g. What cultural/historical information would be most interesting to my students and relevant to my unit?

h. How much time have I allotted to present the information? Should I present it in one long session or in several short intervals within the unit?

As you think about each question, ask yourself, "Do I need to address this?" Some of your answers may be no. You can then provide focus by addressing the questions to which you answered yes.

4. A = Analysis of relationships between the work and other works in time and place

Remember that the term *analysis* refers to relationships. The analysis step promotes understanding of the influences artists and cultures have had on one another. As you discuss how a single work of art relates to other works in time and place, students learn that artists work together, share ideas, borrow from one another, look to other times and cultures for inspiration, and have impact on artists of the future. In this study of relationships you may choose a narrow or wide focus of artworks with which to compare the piece you have selected as the motivation. For example, you may present the following:

- *One of Monet's haystack paintings with other haystack paintings.* Discuss Monet's interest in capturing light qualities in a series of paintings created at different times of day, as you compare and contrast paintings within this series.

- *One of Monet's paintings in a context of other works that represent his progression from realism to greater and greater degrees of abstraction.* Talk about the development of Monet's impressionistic style and where the selected painting falls along the continuum.

- *An early painting by Monet along with paintings by artists who influenced him.* Discuss how artists Manet and Turner contributed to Monet's development.

- *A Monet along with works of other French Impressionists.* Discuss the stylistic similarities and differences among Monet, Renoir, and Sisley, for example.

- *A Monet along with examples of Postimpressionists.* Discuss Monet's impact on Van Gogh's early work. Explain how Monet paved the way for the Post-impressionists in their depiction of landscape images and use of color, texture, and abstraction to achieve formal and emotional qualities.

- *A Monet along with examples of American Impressionists.* Discuss the impact Monet and other French Impressionists had not only in time, but in place (another continent).

As you can see, analysis of relationships among artworks can be complex. You may present a piece within the context of the artist's own work or within the context of a school of art, a style, a time period, a culture, or a geographic location. The questions that follow can help you to decide what to include:

a. When the artist created this work, who or what influenced him or her?

b. Is this work significant in the development of the artist's own style, career, or life? How was it influential in the artist's development? How does it relate to works the artist created later?

c. Did the work influence the development of other artists? How does this work relate to the works of other artists?

d. Did this work influence artists in other locations or cultures? What is the relationship of this work to works in other areas or cultures?

e. Where does this work fit along a time continuum of historical periods and styles?

5. Int = Interpretation of meaning to the artist and culture of origin

The interpretation step provides information about how the work was interpreted by the artist and within the culture of origin. The difference between the interpretation steps in the art history teaching model and the art criticism teaching model is point of view. In the art criticism teaching model, students are asked to make interpretations from their own point of view. In the art history teaching model, the emphasis shifts from a student-centered view to an artist/culture-centered perspective.

Questions to help you select information about cultural/historical interpretations include these:

a. Did the work have personal meaning to the artist? What was it?

b. Does the work have cultural significance? What is it?

c. Did members of the culture agree about its meaning?

d. Have interpretations of the work changed over time?

e. How does our culture today interpret the work?

6. E = Evaluation of quality

The evaluation step provides information to guide students in understanding how the work was assessed as an art object by the artist and the culture of origin. It includes criteria used by the artist and culture to evaluate the work. Although the evaluation steps in the art criticism and art history teaching models are similar, the difference again is point of view. When we use the art criticism teaching model, we lead students to establish their own criteria and make their own judgments about the quality of a work. When we use the art history teaching model, we focus on judgments made by the artist and culture of origin. The following questions can guide you in presenting this information:

a. What criteria did the artist use to determine his or her success?

b. What criteria did the culture of origin use to judge the work?

c. Were the criteria used by the artist the same as those used by the culture?

d. Was the piece judged as a successful artwork by the artist and/or culture when it was created?

e. Is the piece viewed as high-quality art today?

f. What criteria or standards do we use today to judge the work?

APPLICATION OF THE ART HISTORY TEACHING MODEL

The art history teaching model guides you in selecting and sequencing cultural/historical information. You may use as little or as much of the structure as is applicable to your students and unit. Presenting too much information at one time can be as ineffective as teaching art history through osmosis. Students learn very little when they are overwhelmed. However, superficial art history presentations in which the only memorable detail is that "Van Gogh cut off his ear" rank only one step above "art history through osmosis." Using the art history teaching model, you will learn what is too much to present in a single class period. You may need to build students' interests in cultural presentations by starting with ten-minute segments. As students become used to having art experiences that are not studio oriented, they can become involved in longer cultural presentations. Table 12.1 that follows illustrates how each step of the model may be used to explore the work of Jacob Lawrence (see Plate 12.1).

PLATE 12.1
Jacob Lawrence, Frederick Douglass Series No. 12 (1938–1939). Casein tempera on gessoed hardboard, 17 7/8″ × 12″

Hampton University Museum, Hampton, Virginia

Use of the Art History Teaching Model to Select, Organize, and Discuss Information Pertaining to Panel 12 from the *Frederick Douglass* series by Jacob Lawrence

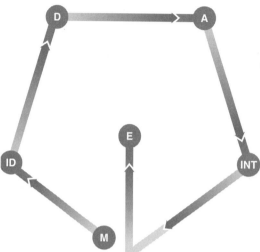

The Six Steps of the Model
1. M = Motivation—presentation of the art object
2. ID = Identification of factual information
3. D = Description of cultural contexts
4. A = Analysis of relationships of the art object to other works in time and place
5. INT = Interpretation of the work by the artist and/or culture of origin
6. E = Evaluation of the work by the artist and/or culture of origin

---

1. Motivation

What art form, medium, and process were used?

This is a painting done with casein tempera on a gessoed hardboard panel measuring 12″ × 17 7/8″.

---

2. Identification of Facts Used to Catalogue the Object

Identify the artist, title of the work, date the work was created, and present location.

a. The painting was done by Jacob Lawrence.

b. This painting is Panel 12 of the *Frederick Douglass* series, which consists of 32 panels recording the life of an escaped slave named Frederick Douglass. Each panel depicts a significant episode in the life of Douglass.

c. Lawrence painted the series between 1938 and 1939, when he was 21 years old.

d. The series now belongs to Hampton University Museum in Virginia.

---

3. Description of Cultural Contexts

a. Who is Jacob Lawrence?

Jacob Lawrence is an African-American artist who was born in Atlantic City, New Jersey, in 1917. In 1930 he moved to Harlem, where he was influenced by the Harlem Renaissance of the 1920s–1930s. During this time of heightened racial consciousness, Lawrence was encouraged to use black people as subject matter. He researched the lives of two famous escaped slaves and painted their life stories In the *Frederick Douglass* and *Harriet Tubman* series. These gave Lawrence his start as a visual story teller and series painter. He became a highly respected artist, painting individual pictures, murals, and series. In 1990 he completed his fifteenth series and received the National Medal of Arts from President Bush. Today he lives in Seattle, Washington, where he continues to work as an artist.

b. Why did Lawrence select Frederick Douglass as the subject of his story?

In 1940 Lawrence remarked, in regard to this series,

I've always been interested in history, but they never taught Negro history in public schools . . . . I don't see how a history of the United States can be written honestly without including the Negro. I didn't do it just as a historical thing, but because I believe these things tie up with the Negro today. We don't have physical slavery, but an economic slavery. If these people, who were so much worse off than the people today, could conquer their slavery, we could certainly do the same thing. They had to liberate themselves without any education. Today we can't go about it in the same way. Any leadership would have to be a type of Frederick Douglass. . . . How will it come about? I don't know. I'm not a politician. I'm an artist, just trying to do my part to bring this thing about. . . .

c. How did Lawrence create the Frederick Douglass series?

Lawrence began with library research he had done on the life of Douglass. He selected written passages that described important events in Douglass's life. He decided that each passage would be visually represented in a painting. He made drawings depicting each passage on 32 gessoed panels and then laid them out in sequence. He mixed one color at a time and filled areas of each panel where that color was to appear. He organized the series into three parts, following the three parts of Douglass's autobiography: "The Slave," "The Fugitive," and "The Free Man." Panel 12 is part of the "Slave" section.

d. Who was Frederick Douglass?

Frederick Douglass was born Frederick Bailey to a white man and an enslaved black woman in 1818. He never knew his father's identity and was separated from his mother at infancy. His early years were spent in Talbot County, Maryland, where he experienced the hardships of slavery. When Douglass was 8, he was sent to Baltimore to work as a houseboy in the home of a woman who taught him to read. In 1833 he was returned to Talbot County to work as a plantation laborer. Panel 12 shows him plotting to escape. The caption accompanying the panel states,

> *It was in 1836 that Douglass conceived a plan of escape, also influencing several slaves around him. He told his co-conspirators what had been done, dared, and suffered by men to obtain the inestimable boon of liberty.*

He was caught and sent to Baltimore to work in the shipyards. In 1838 he escaped to New York City. From there he moved to Massachusetts, where he adopted his new name, Douglass. He joined the Antislavery Society and became a public speaker and writer. In 1845 he published his life story. Fearing the details would lead to his capture and return to slavery, he fled to England. English Quaker abolitionists bought his freedom, and he returned to the United States as a free man in 1847. During the remainder of his life, Douglass continued to be a powerful advocate for freedom. He was a major figure in the Underground Railroad, attended the first women's rights convention in 1848, and held political positions under the leadership of several presidents. Douglass died of a heart attack in 1895 in his home in Washington, D.C., after attending a women's rights meeting.

4. Analysis of the Relationship of the Work to Other Works in Time and Place

a. Whom did Lawrence study to develop his direction as an artist?

Lawrence was trained at the Harlem Artworkshops, where he studied the old masters. He was especially drawn to figurative artists who made social/political statements—Pieter Breughel the Elder, Honoré Daumier, Käthe Kollwitz, Francisco Goya, George Grosz, and Mexican muralists.

b. Who influenced Lawrence in his own environment?

Lawrence's early influences were provided by the Social Realism Movement of the 1930s. Harlem community artists Charles Alston, Augusta Savage, and Henry Bannarn encouraged Lawrence with their ethnic themes.

c. How has Lawrence's style developed since he painted the Frederick Douglass series?

Lawrence developed his style further in the Harriet Tubman series, increasing his use of exaggeration, simplification, angular shapes, and symbolism. As Lawrence matured as an artist, he continued to use more intense color and imagery and flat, simplified shapes in narrative images. Lawrence has continued to produce individual canvases and series to the present day. In 1990 he completed his fifteenth series, entitled Eight Sermons of the Creation from the Book of Genesis.

d. How has Lawrence influenced other artists?

For more than fifty years Jacob Lawrence has influenced other artists through his style and subject matter. His greatest contribution is seen as his ability to portray authentic, vivid, historical narratives. His style is characterized by flat colors, simplified shapes, exaggerated gestures, and ethnic scenes. These characteristics, which he began to develop in the *Frederick Douglass* series, are also shared by a number of other contemporary African-American artists such as Robert Gwathmey, Varnette Honeywood, William Johnson, and Charles Searles. Not only is Lawrence an important contributor to the development of African-American art, but because of his narrative subject matter, he offers a significant link in the traditions of American history painting and American scene painting.

5. Interpretation of Meaning to the Artist and Culture of Origin

Lawrence created the *Frederick Douglass* series to have meaning on several levels. On the literal level Lawrence's intent was to document the life of Frederick Douglass. As people viewed his work when it was produced, they may have seen only a visual record of the story. Looking at Panel 12, they may have said, "This picture is about Douglass's plotting to escape." For Lawrence and many others, the painting has meanings that go beyond the story. Lawrence used the same images over and over. These images are not literal; they are symbolic. Through colors, shapes, size relationships, and objects, Lawrence implied meanings. The color brown suggested the slaves' connection with the earth. Lawrence used that brown in the interior of the log cabin. He intensified the oppressiveness of the color by contrasting it with some areas of bright color. He also used size relationships to imply oppression and fear. Although the interior of the cabin looks small, the figures look even smaller, huddled in the lower portion of the composition. Notice how the shapes of the these huddled figures form a unit. They are one as they plot their escape. These soft shapes are contrasted with the spiky shapes of the trees. Lawrence used these spiky trees as a symbol of danger in the outside world. He also used a red flower as a symbol of hope. As Lawrence matured as an artist, he intensified his imagery through the use of symbolism, abstraction, and formal qualities. As viewers learn to read his works, their interpretations may expand from the superficial level of the story into deeper psychological meanings. Lawrence has helped us understand his work through his own interpretation: "If at times my productions do not express the conventionally beautiful, there is always an effort to express the universal beauty of man's continuous struggle to lift his social position and to add dimension to his spiritual being."

6. Evaluation of Quality as Determined by the Artist and Culture of Origin

The *Frederick Douglass* series was generally well received by the art community in which Lawrence worked. He found support in the culture of the Harlem Renaissance. This culture understood the worth of the narrative image to transmit history and values. The real test of a work or a body of works, however, is how its image as art survives over time. Will the work still be judged as high quality fifty or more years after it was created? In a 1988 interview with Ellen Harkins Wheat (published in *Jacob Lawrence: The Frederick Douglass and Harriet Tubman Series of 1938–1940*), Lawrence remarked, "They [the paintings in the series] are some of the most successful statements I have made in my life."

Jacob Lawrence may be considered as a non-Westerner because he is African American. Nevertheless, he was influenced by both Western and non-Western artists and has taken a place in the art world today as a major painter in America. The art history teaching model provides fitting steps through which to explore his work. The model can also be used to investigate works of tribal peoples whose lives and artistic expressions may have little in common with ours. Table 12.2 illustrates how the model might be used to reflect differences between Western and non-Western cultures and works.

TABLE 12.2
Use of the Art History Teaching Model with Western and Non-Western Exemplars

WESTERN EXEMPLARS	NON-WESTERN EXEMPLARS
Motivation	
The art form, media, and processes are likely to be known.	The work can be classified as a specific art form. Media and processes may not be readily apparent or known.
Identifying Factual Information	
Who made the work is important information in Western culture. Factual information is likely to be known (except in the case of anonymously produced folk art).	Who made the work may not be important. Artists are often unknown. Works may not be signed, dated, or titled, and exact whereabouts may be unknown.
Describing Cultural Contexts	
Information may focus on an *individual artist* as the creator of the object and on the *subject* of the work.	Information may focus on *customs, rituals, and beliefs of the culture* in which the work was produced and on the object's *function* in societal use.
Analyzing Relationship of the Piece to Other Works	
Relationships may foucus on *time.* Who influenced the work? Who was influenced by the work? What school of art or period in art history does it fit? Where does the work fit in a chronological progression?	Relationships may focus on *place.* How does the work compare to works in other places and cultures? Has the work influenced art of other peoples?
Interpreting Meaning	
Focus may be on the meaning assigned by the *artist* who created the work. (What was his or her intended message?)	Focus may be on the meaning assigned by an *entire culture.* (How does the object transmit cultural beliefs and values?)
Evaluating Quality	
Criteria and judgments about the quality of a piece may *change,* as different styles and aesthetic theories emerge in the Western tradition.	Criteria and judgments may *remain constant,* as traditional art expressions continue to be valued and handed down from one generation to the next.

You may view the art history teaching model as a tool to guide you in selecting and presenting information. Whether you include content pertaining to all six steps or limit content to selected steps, you should provide information that gives a work meaning within the context of the unit of study. This involves going beyond the motivation and identification steps to determine what cultural/historical information is most relevant and age appropriate. Teaching art history, like teaching any other domain of art education, entails decision making. Some of the decisions you need to make will be about where to start (with a broad cultural view or a single work of art), what to present, how much to present, how to sequence content, and how to connect to the lives of your students. Think of the art history teaching model not as a formula but as a reminder of the many choices you have available to you.

S U M M A R Y

Art history was not systematically integrated into curricula until subject-centered advocates began doing so in the 1960s. The back-to-basics movement, causing an academization of art education, and the civil rights and women's liberation movements, inspiring an interest in multiculturalism, laid the groundwork. Since then art educators have become increasingly involved in teaching art history. A growing alliance between DBAE proponents and museum educators, as well as increased access to cultural content through the Internet, have also helped establish art history as an integral component of art education.

The strategy for integration suggested here is the use of cultural exemplars, presented in all fully developed units of study. An in-depth look at a sample exemplar, a painting by Jacob Lawrence is provided using the structure of the art history teaching model. This model, which parallels the art criticism and aesthetics teaching models, consists of these steps:

- Motivation—presenting an artwork and providing information about the art form, tools, media, and process
- Identification of facts used to catalogue the object—providing information to answer *what, who, when,* and *where* questions (title, artist, date, and location)
- Description of cultural/historical contexts—presenting background about the work, the artist, and/or the culture of origin
- Analysis of relationships between the work and other works—providing connections among artwork, artists, and cultures in time and place
- Interpretation of meaning—revealing intentions of artists and meanings assigned by cultures of origin
- Evaluation of quality—discussing criteria and judgments made by the artist and/or culture of origin

This structure models a way to progress from the particular (a single work of art) to the general (broad cultural contexts). It provides one approach to teaching art history. Another approach involves progressing from a broad cultural context to a single work of art (modeled in Chapter 9 in presenting Navajo sandpainting). These two strategies illustrate a point: There is no one way to teach art history. How you present historical content will depend on what you are teaching, why you are teaching it, to whom you are teaching, and how the content will be used to promote learning. Flexibility, as always, is the key to designing and presenting content.

STRUCTURING A CULTURAL/HISTORICAL PRESENTATION

Directions
Use the categories of the art history teaching model, presented below, to structure a historical presentation designed for a specific grade level.

Grade Level: _____

1. Presentation of the motivation:

   a. Art form_____

   b. Processes/techniques _____

   c. Tools/media _____

2. Identification of facts:

   a. Title _____

   b. Artist _____

   c. Date _____

   d. Present location _____

3. Description of cultural/historical context:

4. Analysis of the relationship between the work and other works in time and place:

5. Interpretation of meaning assigned by the artist and/or culture of origin:

6. Evaluation of quality as reflected by the artist and/or culture of origin:

P A R T

4

SEEING THE BIG PICTURE

PART IV concludes the text with an overall view of where we have been. It is intended to help you synthesize your learning and make the transition into teachers of art. Chapter 13, "Integrating the Components," addresses integration on four levels: (1) integrating art criticism, aesthetics, and art history in presentations of cultural exemplars; (2) integrating response and productive aspects in a scope and sequence; (3) integrating all four domains of art education in comprehensive unit plans; and (4) integrating units in yearly plans. Chapter 14, "Addressing Standards, Assessment, and Accountability," presents the National Visual Arts Standards and analyzes how the contents of this book have prepared students to address them. Chapter 15, "Demonstrating Teacher Competencies," presents strategies for creating art education portfolios, interviewing for positions, and stepping into the field as fully prepared art educators.

C H A P T E R

13

INTEGRATING
THE COMPONENTS

Stepping back and viewing the big picture, you can see how much territory you have covered. This chapter is intended to help you integrate and fine-tune aspects of art education previously presented and to extend your thinking from designing individual units to sequencing units in long-range planning. Four levels of integration are explored: (1) integrating art criticism, aesthetics, and art history in discussions of cultural exemplars; (2) integrating response and productive aspects in a scope and sequence; (3) integrating all four domains of art education in a unit plan; and (4) integrating units in a yearly plan.

▼
INTEGRATING ART CRITICISM, AESTHETICS, AND ART HISTORY

As we have seen in the last two chapters, art criticism, aesthetics, and art history are discrete areas of art education. Some art educators working within a DBAE framework present these domains as separate entities. They address the functions of art critics, aestheticians, and art historians, leading students to understand their roles in society. Within this text we define these domains as three integrated aspects dealing with viewing, discussing, understanding, and appreciating one's own and others' art. Having presented each domain separately to promote understanding of processes and content within each, we now provide strategies for integration. This section (1) compares each of the three teaching models dealing with the response aspect of art education and (2) provides a sample dialogue integrating the three domains.

As you look at these models together (as shown in Figure 13.1), you can imagine how steps from all three might be integrated to mutually support each domain in the presentation of a cultural exemplar. A discussion can begin with any domain. Some art educators believe that beginning with art criticism whets the appetite for historical information. Ask yourself which domain seems most logical or interesting, given the nature of the motivation and situation. Then simply use your common sense to develop a presentation that integrates the others. The boxed sample presentation extends the discussion begun in the last chapter, integrating art criticism and aesthetics with historical information on Lawrence's *Frederick Douglass* series. Each step within the presentation has been identified by domain—history (HIST), criticism (CRIT), or aesthetics (AES). The particular step of each model is also indicated. The first step is identified as HIST:id. This indicates the use of the art history teaching model and the identification step. Step 2 is the description process in the art history teaching model; step 3 is the identification process in the art criticism teaching model, and so on.

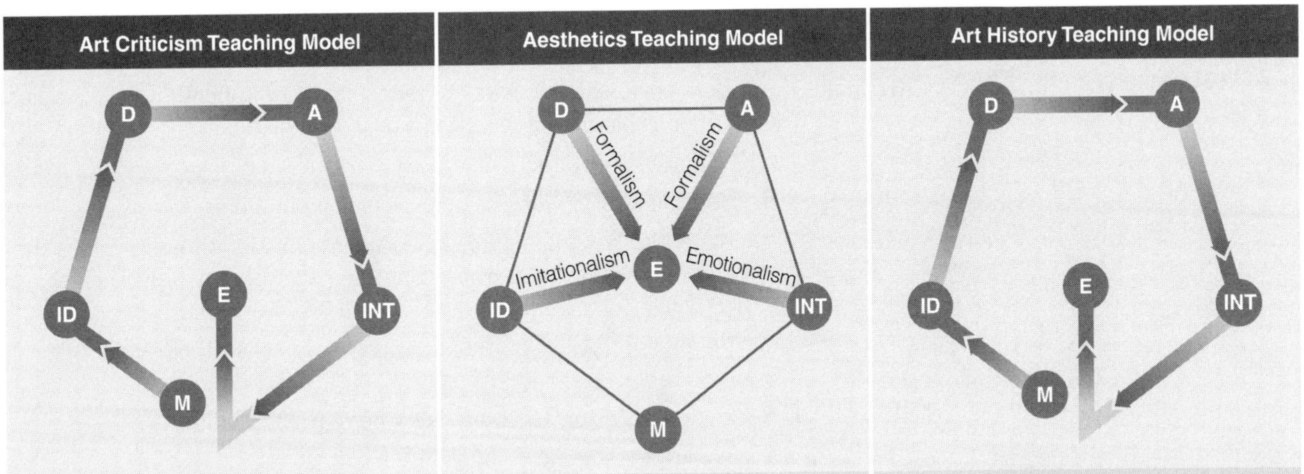

Art Criticism Teaching Model	Aesthetics Teaching Model	Art History Teaching Model

M = Motivation (artwork)

ID = Identification of objects in subject matter

D = Description of art elements

A = Analysis of design principles

INT = Interpretation of meaning by students

E = Evaluation of quality as determined by student assessment

M = Motivation (artwork)

ID = Identification of objects in subject matter = step used to assess worth on the basis of imitational qualities

D = Description of art elements

A = Analysis of design principles = two steps used by formalists to determine quality on the basis of design and composition

INT = Interpretation of meaning = step used to assess worth on the basis of emotional/expressive qualities

E = Evaluation of quality as determined from one or more of the three aesthetic points of view

M = Motivation (artwork)

ID = Identification of facts (who, what, when, where)

D = Description of cultural contexts

A = Analysis of the relationship of work to other works in time and place

INT = Interpretation of meaning by the artist and/or culture of origin

E = Evaluation of quality as determined by the artist and/or culture of origin

FIGURE 13.1
Comparison of the Art Criticism, Aesthetics, and Art History Teaching Models

Integrating Art History, Art Criticism, and Aesthetics in a Presentation on Panel 12 from the *Frederick Douglass* series by Jacob Lawrence

HIST:id 1. Show Panel 12 and identify the artist, time it was painted, title of the work and subject of the series.

HIST:d 2. Present historical information to address these questions:

    a. Who was Jacob Lawrence?

    b. Why did he paint the story of Frederick Douglass?

    c. How did he paint the series?

    d. Who was Frederick Douglass?

CRIT:id 3. Ask students to identify what they see in Panel 12.

CRIT:int 4. Have students interpret what is happening in the scene.

HIST:d 5. Tell students what the painting depicts.

HIST:d 6. Show panels 1–11 of the *Frederick Douglass* series from the book *Jacob Lawrence: The Frederick Douglass and Harriet Tubman Series of 1938–1940,* by Ellen Harkins Wheat. Use the paintings to tell the story of Douglass's life to the point where he plots his escape (shown in Panel 12).

CRIT:int 7. Ask students why they think you chose to focus on this particular panel to represent Douglass's life.

HIST:int 8. Explain that this panel reflects an important decision about how Douglass chose to lead his life, and it symbolizes what he stood for.

CRIT:anal 9. Ask students to tell you how Lawrence has drawn attention to Douglass in this composition and record responses on the board:

    a. "Douglass is wearing white."

    b. "He is facing out with the other figures around him."

    c. "The entire group of figures has been emphasized through color—the bright red, yellow, and white contrasted against dark brown, green, and black."

    d. "The organic shapes of the figures stand out against the straight lines of the cabin."

CRIT:int 10. Ask students if Douglass looks like a hero in this picture.

    a. "No. His eyes are wide open. He looks scared."

    b. "He also looks hunched over and small in comparison to the log cabin."

HIST:d 11. Ask students what they think happened next. Then show the next painting in the series, of Douglass being captured. Complete the story by showing and discussing his life through the remaining panels in the series.

CRIT:d 12. Ask students if Lawrence told the story through realistic imagery. Have them describe how Lawrence used colors and shapes. Record the responses on the board:

    a. "He used flat, simplified shapes."

    b. "He used minimal detail."

    c. "He used some bright colors, such as yellow, red, blue, and white, and a lot of dark brown and dull green."

    d. "The shapes, colors, and details are so simple that his paintings look like a child might have done them."

CRIT:int 13. Ask students to speculate on why Lawrence painted the way he did.

    a. "Maybe he didn't know how to draw and paint very well yet."

    b. "Maybe he made things intentionally simple so that we would concentrate on the story."

    c. "Maybe he didn't intend the figures and objects to look real. Maybe they're more like symbols of what happened, how people were treated, how they were feeling."

HIST:int 14. Tell students about Lawrence's use of symbolism—the red flower to signify hope, the spiky trees to symbolize fear of the outside world, the color brown to reflect the slaves' connection with the land, the small huddled figures to imply oppression.

AES: 15. Ask students to speculate about how (a) an imitationalist, (b) a formalist, (c) an emotionalist, and (d) an instrumentalist might respond to Lawrence's painting:

    a. "An imitationalist might like the subject matter because it tells a story. He or she probably would not like the way the subject matter is painted because it is not detailed and realistic. He or she might miss the symbolism and think Lawrence didn't know how to draw or paint."

    b. "A formalist would like this painting. Lawrence has done a great job of drawing our attention to the huddled group and Douglass as the main figure. The shapes of the windows and the steps on the lower left provide good asymmetrical balance. The repetition of the boards helps unify the composition. The yellow moon behind the dark tree draws our attention to the tree as a symbol of danger. I think Lawrence is really a master at designing composition."

c. "An emotionalist would probably like this painting because of the symbolism. He or she would also like it because of the emotional qualities Lawrence was able to convey. The figures really look scared and secretive. The space is oppressive. The mood is ominous."

d. "Of all the aesthetic theories, instrumentalism might be the most fitting for this work. Instrumentalists believe that art serves a purpose and leads to some thought, action, or activity beyond itself. I think Lawrence approached this series from the standpoint of an instrumentalist, speaking as a member of the African-American community, and sending a message to his people about strength, courage, and action."

AES: 16. Ask students to share their perceptions of the work and their reasons for appreciating it.

HIST:anal 17. Discuss how Lawrence developed his style. Show works of some of the artists Lawrence studied (Pieter Breughel the Elder, Honoré Daumier, Diego Rivera).

HIST:anal 18. Show examples of Lawrence's contemporaries—African-American artists to whom he is stylistically related—Robert Gwathmey, Varnette Honeywood, William Johnson, and Charles Searles.

HIST:anal 19. Discuss how Lawrence's style developed over a period of years and show examples of Lawrence's later works.

CRIT:e 20. Ask students to compare the paintings in the *Frederick Douglass* series with Lawrence's most recent works. Have them evaluate which paintings are the best. Ask them to give reasons for their judgments.

HIST:e 21. Tell students how Lawrence views the paintings in the *Frederick Douglass* series: "They are some of the most successful statements I have made in my life."

HIST:d 22. Tell students about Lawrence's life today:

a. He has had a full career as an artist and educator.

b. In 1987 he retired as professor emeritus from the School of Art at the University of Washington.

c. In 1990 he completed his fifteenth series, *English Sermons* of the *Creation from the Book of Genesis,* and received the National Medal of Arts from President George Bush.

d. Today he lives in Seattle, Washington, where he continues to work as an artist.

AES: 23. Have students write letters to a friend or to Lawrence himself expressing their appreciation of him as an artist.

This presentation is targeted for the high school level and, because of its scope, may be presented over two periods. The first day might focus on Lawrence and the *Frederick Douglass* series, taking students through step 16. The next period might continue the discussion with historical analysis, beginning with step 17. Through this kind of investigation, teachers can lead students to go beyond historical facts to develop a deeper relationship with Douglass, Lawrence, and their messages about humanity. Tailoring this presentation to primary-level students, we may also send messages about humanity. Narrowing our focus, we might do the following:

- Introduce children to Frederick Douglass through a presentation of selected panels in the series (art history)
- Lead students to understand art as visual storytelling, encouraging them to become involved in identification and interpretation (art criticism)
- Encourage students to share their appreciations of the work (aesthetics)

▼ INTEGRATING RESPONSE AND PRODUCTIVE COMPONENTS

Having explored how to integrate art history, art criticism, and aesthetics in the response component, we are ready to address the use of this component to support our primary emphasis: art making. Before doing so, however, we will take one last look at teaching models to sequence productive experiences. Figure 13.2 provides a comparison of the three presented in this book.

Regardless of which productive model you use to structure a unit of study, you will design units that integrate productive and response components. There is no "right" or "best" way to do this; and by adhering to a specific integration model, you will restrict your flexibility. As discussed in Chapter 3, a cultural exemplar may be introduced at the beginning, middle, or end of a unit. You may start with the "inside" (the experiences, thoughts, feelings of the individual child) or with the "outside" (an aspect of art exemplified through the work of a master artist). In addition to addressing placement of a cultural exemplar within a unit, you should also consider what the art object has the potential to exemplify. A cultural exemplar may be used to illustrate any number of things—a theme, subject matter, style, formal qualities, medium, and/or techniques. We can, therefore, present one exemplar to students in a wide range of grade levels, addressing different aspects of the work in multiple units of study. Many teachers present an individual artist, school of art, style, or culture to students at several grade levels, focusing on particular aspects most appropriate for each level. Questions you might consider when using a single exemplar in multiple units are these:

- How can I use this exemplar to teach a number of different concepts?
- Who is my target audience for each concept?

FIGURE 3.2
A Comparison of Three Teaching Models Used to Sequence Productive Experiences

Product-Oriented Model	Process-Oriented Model	Creative Problem-Solving Model
M = Motivation: Stimulus to engage learning	M = Motivation: Stimulus to engage learning	P = Problem: Presented as the motivation
A = Activity step: Process-oriented exercises done in preparation to create final product	A1, A2, A3 = Activities: Process-oriented experiences related by a common theme—not intended to be final products, but exercises to explore aspects of art and art-making behaviors	CPS = Creative Problem-Solving Activity: Brainstorming of multiple solutions to problem
P = Product: Creation of final product based on learning gained in activity step		S = Solution: Final product—synthesis of ideas generated in CPS step
E = Evaluation: Judgment based on criteria defining problem for final assignment	E = Evaluation: Judgment based on fulfillment of objectives defining the experiences	(E = Evaluation): Not stated but implied through criteria defining the problem

- What presentation strategies are most appropriate for students at various levels?
- How might I most effectively connect this information with the "inside," as students participate in studio activities?
- Where is the best place to begin—with the "outside" or the "inside"?
- How can I use the response component in a supporting role, placing primary emphasis on art-making experiences?

The sample experiences in Tables 13.1, 13.2, and 13.3 use model planning strategies to help answer these questions. They demonstrate how to use the *Frederick Douglass* series in the scope and sequence for three units of study designed for use at the second grade, seventh grade, and advanced high school levels. As you study these examples, note the following:

- The shift in the focus of the cultural exemplar as it is presented from one sequence to the next
- The position of the response component related to the productive component in each sequence
- The emphasis on art making as reflected in time allotted to the productive component

---

TABLE 13.1
Sample Scope and Sequence 1: Jacob Lawrence, Storyteller (2 sessions, second grade)

PRODUCTIVE ASPECT

(day 1)   1. Introduce the motivation: a discussion in which students share memorable events in their lives (birthday parties, holidays, trips, the first day of school, shopping for something special, getting a new pet).

(days 1–2)   2. Using the process-oriented teaching model, lead students through studio activities in which they explore painting in a series of pictures depicting memorable experiences.

RESPONSE ASPECT

(closure of day 2)
(art history)   3. Explain that artists often tell stories through pictures they paint and introduce Jacob Lawrence as an artist who tells stories through his paintings. Show selected panels from the *Frederick Douglass* series.

(art criticism) 4. Ask students to tell you what they see and to guess what the paintings represent.

(art history)   5. Tell Frederick Douglass's story through selected paintings.

(art criticism/ art history) 6. Have students share their own paintings and contents. Lead students to see and discuss similarities and differences between their own and Lawrence's work.

(aesthetics)   7. Have students share appreciations of their own, classmates, and Lawrence's work.

(art history)   8. Ask questions that encourage students to share what they learned about Jacob Lawrence and Frederick Douglass.

TABLE 13.2
Sample Scope and Sequence 2: Jacob Lawrence, Abstractionist (8 sessions, seventh grade)

RESPONSE ASPECT

(day 1)
(art history)
1. Relate the story of Frederick Douglass through a presentation of selected panels. Introduce Jacob Lawrence, and discuss his background and intent in painting the narrative.

(art criticism)
2. Contrast Lawrence's style with Norman Rockwell's, presenting selected paintings of each artist. Discuss Lawrence's use of simplified, exaggerated shapes as a form of abstraction used to create impact.

(aesthetics)
3. Relate Lawrence's style to formalism and Rockwell's style to imitationalism.

PRODUCTIVE ASPECT

(day 2)
4. Have students make a series of sketches illustrating memorable events in their personal lives or in their community—holiday gatherings, trips, cultural celebrations, fairs, circuses, concerts, sports activities, parties, vacations, etc. Ask students to select one idea to use as subject matter of a poster celebrating the event.

(days 3–7)
5. Lead students through a sequence of processes in which they do the following:
   a. Illustrate the event in a drawing.
   b. Enlarge, simplify, and exaggerate shapes to create emotional impact.
   c. Use fadeless colored paper to create posters.

RESPONSE ASPECT

(day 8)
6. Have students share posters and discuss content, meaning, and use of simplification and exaggeration in their designs.

(art criticism)
7. Have students compare content, meaning, and stylistic qualities of their works with Lawrence's.

(aesthetics)
8. Have students discuss orally or on written worksheets:
   a. Impact of formalism in their own and Lawrence's work
   b. Information demonstrating knowledge of Frederick Douglass and understanding of Lawrence's intent in painting the series

TABLE 13.3
Sample Scope and Sequence 3: Jacob Lawrence, Symbolist (15 sessions, high school)

RESPONSE ASPECT

(day 1)
(art criticism)
1. Show the complete *Frederick Douglass* series through a slide presentation without giving any historical background. Ask students to comment on the work in terms of quality, content, and meaning.

(art history)
2. Show the series again, this time supplying cultural/historical information about Lawrence, Douglass, and symbolic content within the series.

(art criticism)
3. Ask students to again share perceptions of the work, after having learned historical information.

(aesthetics)
4. Introduce contextualism as a theory that meaning of an artwork can only be determined in the context in which it is made and used. Discuss the series as a visual communication system requiring knowledge of a shared code (symbols).

PRODUCTIVE ASPECT

(days 2–4)
5. Have students imagine that they, like Lawrence, are visual biographers who communicate on a symbolic level. Ask them to create a series of sketches documenting their own lives or significant experiences through symbolic content.

(days 5–13)
6. Have students work from one or more sketches to create a "symbolic autobiography." Include in the motivation and criteria the use of mixed media, resulting in an integration of drawn and painted images, photographs, and three-dimensional objects used as symbols.

RESPONSE ASPECT

(days 14–15)
(art criticism/
aesthetics)
7. Have students share work, content, meanings, appreciations.

(art history/
art criticism/
aesthetics)
8. In a writing assignment, have students analyze their own work and Lawrence's work in the light of contextualism.

INTEGRATING THE FOUR ART EDUCATION DOMAINS IN A UNIT PLAN

Our next step is to create a context within which to place an integrated scope and sequence—an integrated unit plan. The format for this plan is identical to the one to which you have already been introduced with the exception of one narrow column on the left-hand side. This area is to record the domain(s)—*P* for production, *C* for criticism, *A* for aesthetics, and *H* for history—within the unit components: goals, concepts, scope and sequence, and evaluation procedure. As you can see from Table 13.4, each domain can be addressed separately or in combination. What is most important is that each domain is addressed at least once in each unit plan component. Thus a goal in production will be supported by a concept, an activity, and an evaluation procedure relating to production. Likewise, goals in art criticism, aesthetics, and art history will be supported by related concepts, activities, and evaluation procedures pertaining to each domain.

TABLE 13.4
Telling Stories Through Pictures

DOMAIN(S)	
	I. Theme and General Description
	A. The theme "memorable experiences" is presented in a class discussion. Students participate in a painting experience, creating a series on "Memorable Experiences in My Life." They are introduced to Jacob Lawrence as a visual storyteller and compare their art and stories with his.
	B. Grade level: Second
	C. Time: Two 60–minute sessions
	II. Goals
P	A. To demonstrate ability to communicate experiences and values in visual form
P	B. To develop psychomotor and expressive skills through a painting experience
C	C. To develop skill in "reading" visual stories through the processes of identification and interpretation
H/A	D. To develop understanding and appreciation of narrative paintings as visual stories
H/A	E. To gain understanding and appreciation for Jacob Lawrence and Frederick Douglass
A	F. To develop appreciation for one's own life experiences and artistic expressions
	III. Concepts
P	A. We can tell stories about our lives by painting pictures.
H/C	B. Artists tell stories through pictures: Jacob Lawrence told the story of Frederick Douglass through his paintings.
A	C. People like Lawrence's paintings because they tell the story of a hero.
A	D. We may like our own paintings because they tell something about us.
	IV. Exemplar
	Selected examples from the *Frederick Douglass* series to illustrate Douglass's life
	V. Scope and Sequence of Experiences
P	A. Introduce the motivation: a discussion in which students share memorable events in their lives. Lead students through a studio activity in which they explore painting in a series of pictures depicting memorable experiences (days 1–2).

H	B. Introduce Jacob Lawrence as an artist who tells stories through his paintings. Show selected panels from the Frederick Douglass series (second half of day 2).
C	C. Ask students to tell you what they see and to guess what the paintings represents.
H	D. Tell Douglass's story through selected paintings.
C/H	E. Have selected students share their own paintings and discuss meanings. Have students compare and contrast their art and stories with Lawrence's.
A	F. Have students share appreciations of their own, classmates', and Lawrence's work.
H	G. Have students demonstrate knowledge of Lawrence and Douglass by responding to closing questions.

VI. Evaluation Procedure

P	A. Observation of studio behaviors and art products, focusing on the following:
	1. Ability to express an idea in visual form
	2. Skill in using the process of painting
	B. Observation of discussions to ascertain the following:
C	1. Students' ability to "read" visual images through processes of identification and interpretation
C/A	2. Students' willingness and ability to comment on their own and others' work
H	3. Students' ability to answer closing questions about Lawrence and Douglass

▼ INTEGRATING UNITS IN A YEARLY PLAN

The unit presented in Table 13.4 illustrates that even in an experience as short as two sessions taught to children at the primary level you can integrate all four domains of art education. This is true whether the unit begins with the "inside" or the "outside." It is true in multicultural and interdisciplinary units. It is true in units that deal with drawing, painting, sculpture, or any other studio area. Whether we present one work of art as a cultural exemplar or an entire period in art history, it is true. By beginning with the design of "comprehensive units"—those integrating art production, art criticism, aesthetics, and art history—we lay the foundation for comprehensive programs. We define "comprehensive program" as one that integrates the four domains of art education. There are many ways to do this. In our model of art education, we have integrated the domains through a studio-centered approach. In this section we provide content for our model, as we move from sequencing *within* to sequencing *of* units of study.

IDEAS FOR LONG-RANGE PLANNING

At this point on your path you may have well-developed understandings of art education content and instructional strategies. If you were asked to design a unit on a particular theme, culture, interdisciplinary connection, or art process, you could. How confident do you feel about your ability to generate a sequence of plans spanning an entire year? Students of art education can make abrupt transitions into teachers of art when faced with their first planning challenge: an outline of content (unit plans) for what they intend to teach every class all year long—due in the principal's office a week before school starts. Although this may sound like your worst nightmare, it may in fact come true. Many administrators require teachers to submit yearly plans. Without a strategy for selection and integration of content, the task can be overwhelming.

F RESH out of college, Nancy had just been hired as a new art teacher. She spent a week at an in-service workshop, where one of the assignments was to design a yearly plan. Nancy prepared for this in the following way:

- First she reread all her notes from her art education courses.
- Then she reviewed all her unit and lesson plans from field experiences and student teaching.
- Next she read the district art curriculum guide from cover to cover.
- Following this, she made a list of what she needed to include in her plan.

At last Nancy felt ready. She began by writing what she intended to do with all her classes on the first day of school and progressed day by day to the last hour. When she shared her plan at the workshop, her colleagues sat in stunned amazement. Finally one of them said, "Nancy, you've planned for every day of the year. What happens if school is closed because of snow?" Looking blankly into space, Nancy mumbled, "Snow . . . ?"

Schools do occasionally close because of snow, heat waves, bomb threats, and other assorted disturbances that throw your carefully planned schedule off track. These general rules will help you keep your perspective:

- Know what you are expected to accomplish in terms of general content.
- Look to your students as guides in selecting specific content.
- Create a framework that accommodates snow days, fire drills, and spontaneous happenings.

Knowing what you are expected to accomplish is important. Many states have guidelines drawn from national standards (addressed in the next chapter), which are used to formulate district guidelines and curricula. Today's curriculum guides can be quite comprehensive, including philosophy statements, goals, content for each grade level or course, sample unit plans, and teaching strategies. These have been viewed as both a blessing and a hindrance. The best such guides provide a vision of educational effectiveness without creating molds into which all programs must fit. They may present the four art education domains without specifying particular content. They may require that teachers address art elements and design principles without dictating which should be taught at each grade level. They may encourage the inclusion of multicultural exemplars without mandating specific peoples or places. They present teachers with strategies for "fishing" rather than supplying them with "fish."

In some districts, however, curriculum developers have felt the need to supply the metaphorical fish themselves, requiring that teachers address particular formal properties, artists, schools of art, and/or cultures at specific grade levels. Thus, Van Gogh may not be presented in fourth grade because he is on the sixth grade list. Students move through a lockstep progression in the study of design principles until they arrive at *unity* in grade five. Although this is done to ensure that content is presented in an orderly sequence, this system can inhibit inventive teachers.

You may find yourself in a district with curriculum guidelines written in general terms to encourage flexible implementation and creative thinking; guidelines specifying *the* path to follow in each grade level; or no guidelines at all. Regardless of the situation, you will be faced with long-range planning. Where do you start? You may look to your students to determine the most fitting experiences to support their particularities. At the same time you must also address art content. The challenge is to create appropriate links between students and content. One way to begin the school year is to (1) meet your students, (2) present an open-ended activity designed to initiate a conversation in which students tell you about themselves through visual language, and (3) respond to this conversation through the presentation of units specifically designed to support their needs and interests. The guided visualization "A Trip into Space" (Chapter 5) is intended to initiate such a conversation.

Waiting until the first day of school so you can meet your students before you begin planning may cause tremendous anxiety, however. It can also irritate your principal, who may be waiting for your long-range outline. An answer to where to stand between a student-centered orientation and a content-centered orientation is this: Begin your thinking process at the level of generalities, which can be fine-tuned as you progress through the year to accommodate the particularities of your students. The generalities with which you begin can be content-oriented. Your first step might be to list categories, such as the following:

- Studio areas (art forms, media, processes)
- Subject matter/themes
- Formal properties
- Art criticism, aesthetics, art history

The next step is to continue brainstorming by generating ideas, content, and/or processes within each category. Tables 13.5, 13.6, and 13.7 illustrate a format you might use for this procedure. They divide into productive and response aspects, into which the preceding categories have been placed.

TABLE 13.5
Content for long range planning: Productive aspect—Studio areas

Drawing and Two-Dimensional Design	*Painting*	*Print Making/Photography/Film Making/Computer Art*

• *Drawing media:* crayons, markers, colored pencils, brushes, pastels, chalk, charcoal, conté crayon, pen and ink
 • *Drawing processes:* drawing from imagination, drawing from observation, gesture drawing, contour drawing, shading, hatching, stippling, mechanical drawing
 • *Two-dimensional design processes* using construction paper, tissue paper, mixed media
	• Finger painting
	 • Easel painting
	 • *Painting with different media:*
	   Tempera paints
	   Watercolors
	   Gouache
	   Egg tempera
	   Acrylics
	   Oils
	   Encaustics
	   Colored inks
	   Mixed media
	 • *Techniques involving the use of*
	   Modeling
	   Hard-edge
	   Impasto
	   Glazing
	   Dry brush
	   Wash
	   Stippling
		• *Planographic methods* (print is created from images on a flat printing plate or surface)
		   Monoprinting
		   Silk screening (serigraphy)
		   Stencil printing
		 • *Relief methods* (print is created from areas in relief on plates in which portions are either built up or carved away)
		   Printing from relief plates made with string, cardboard, Styrofoam, inner tubes, etc. (collographs)
		   Wood and linoleum block
		   Gadget and vegetable printing
		 • *Intaglio methods* (print is created from ink in recessed areas of a plate) Plexiglas etching
		 • Fine art approaches to photography, film, and computer art

(continued)

TABLE 13.5 (*continued*)
Content for long range planning: Productive aspect—Studio areas

Sculpture and Three-Dimensional Design	Crafts	Graphic/Industrial/ Environmental Design

• *Additive processes*
  Paper sculpture
  Relief sculpture with paper, wood,
  Styrofoam, clay, cardboard, found
  objects
  Assemblage
  Wire sculpture
  Mobiles
  Stabiles
  Papier-mâché
  Soft sculpture
• *Subtractive processes*
  Soap carving
  Plaster carving
  Wood carving
  Stone carving
• *Modeling* (employing both additive and
  subtractive techniques)
	• *Ceramics*
	  Modeling/pinch method
	  Coil method
	  Slab method
	  Wheel throwing
	• *Jewelry*
	  Clay
	  Paper
	  Plastic
	  Metals (copper, brass, silver)
	  Natural materials (shells, bones,
	  feathers, etc.)
	  Lapidary
	  Found objects
	• *Textiles* (use of fabrics and fibers such as
	  cloth, paper, yarn, thread, raffia, beads)
	  Weaving, stitchery, applique
	  Quilting
	  Paper making, felt making
	  Tie-dyeing, batiking
		• Lettering
		• Illustration
		• Posters, banners, murals
		• Packaging
		• Architecture
		• Industrial design
		• Environmental planning
		• Fashion design
		• Approaches to photography, video, film
		  making, and computer graphics in
		  applied art fields

TABLE 13.6
Content for long-range planning: Productive aspect—Subject matter, Styles, Formal properties

Subject Matter	Styles	Formal Properties

• Seasons
• Holidays
• Figure (self, family, friends, comic book
  characters, portraits of real or imaginary
  people)
• Landscape (cityscapes, ocean scenes,
  desert scenes, jungle scenes)
• Nature (plants, animals, shells, bones,
  feathers, rocks)
• Architecture
• Interiors
• Human-made objects and environments
• Experiences, special events, celebrations
• Universal themes—love, brotherhood,
  war, peace, ecology, conservation of the
  planet
• Still life
• Fantasy, myth
	• *Representational:*
	  Pop Art
	  Photorealism
	  Dutch still life painting
	• *Abstract:*
	  Impressionism
	  Cubism
	  Surrealism
	  German Expressionism
	• *Nonobjective:*
	  Hard-edge
	  Color field
	  Action painting
	  Op Art
		• *Art elements*
		  Line
		  Shape, space,
		  Form
		  Color
		  Texture
		• *Design principles*
		  Balance
		  Contrast
		  Rhythm
		  Pattern
		  Emphasis
		  Unity

(continued)

TABLE 13.7
Content for long range planning: Response Aspect, Criticism, Aesthetics, History

Art Criticism	Aesthetics	Art History

• Critical processes:
  Identification of subject matter
  Description of art elements
  Analysis of design principles
  Interpretation of meaning
  Evaluation of quality
• Discussions of cultural exemplars
• Critiques of one's own works and works of fellow students
	• Aesthetic concepts (ideas about the value of art)
	• Personal reasons for appreciating art
	• Criteria for judging art in different times, places, and cultures
	• Aesthetic theories:
	  Imitationalism
	  Formalism
	  Emotionalism
	  Contextualism
	  Instrumentalism
		• Discussions about human-made objects as reflections of culture:
		  Everyday utilitarian objects
		  Craft items
		  Ceremonial art and artifacts
		  "Fine art" objects (drawings, paintings, sculptures, photographs)
		• Discussions about who creates art in various times, places, and cultures
		• Careers in art
		• The progression of art through time (focusing on chronological development)
		• The study of art through place (focusing on similarities and differences in various locations)
		• The study of individual artworks, artists, styles, schools of art, and periods in art history

DEVELOPING A YEARLY PLAN

Tables 13.5, 13.6, and 13.7 can be thought of as a menu, containing options from which to select. The challenge is to integrate the parts in ways that make sense. This can be done through a framework for sequencing units. The steps that follow outline a procedure for designing a framework and using it to develop a yearly plan.

1. *Select the components that will comprise your framework.* Determine what components you want to include in your framework. The content of your "menu" can help you formulate categories, such as these:

   a. Unit description
   b. Studio process/medium
   c. Subject matter/theme
   d. Formal properties
   e. Cultural exemplar
   f. Aesthetic orientation

2. *Design a matrix.* Structure the selected categories into a matrix that can be used to sequence units of study, similar to the following:

Unit	Unit Description	Studio Process/Medium	Subject Matter/Theme	Formal Properties	Cultural Exemplar	Aesthetic Orientation
1.						
2.						
3.						

This framework allows you to see the big picture at a glance. By looking at a completed matrix, you can quickly determine whether you have addressed multiple aesthetic theories or have given inordinate attention to imitationalism. Of course, you may intend to focus on imitationalism because you are teaching observational drawing. In this case you might look to see that you have included a range of media, subject matter, and cultural exemplars. The purpose of the framework is to help you select and sequence content to support whatever goals and objectives are appropriate in a given situation.

3. *Divide the year into segments.* Determine the time frame for the school year and divide it into segments according to grading periods—number of weeks per quarter, trimester, or semester. Reproduce a separate matrix for each grading period.

4. *Select one grade level or course for which to generate a sequence of units for one grading period.*

5. *Provide a focus for the sequence by selecting a theme for the first time segment.* The following themes might be used:

   a. One or more studio areas (drawing and printmaking)
   b. One or more cultures (selected Native American tribes)
   c. A time period (Renaissance)
   d. A geographical location (Mexico)
   e. One or more schools of art (Impressionism and Postimpressionism)
   f. One or more aesthetic orientations (imitationalism)
   g. One or more formal properties (emphasis through shape and color)
   h. Subject matter (interiors and exteriors)
   i. Interdisciplinary connections with other subjects (art/math, art/science, art/music)

6. *Generate ideas for units focusing on the theme for the first segment.*

7. *Think about timing.* How many units can you teach in one segment? Your timing depends on a number of variables:

   a. Consider the ages and developmental levels of your students. Younger students will do better with shorter units spanning two to three class sessions. You might plan three or four units in one 9-week quarter for primary-level students and one or two units for students at upper elementary, middle, or high school levels.
   b. Consider the nature of productive experiences. Process-oriented units may take less time than product-oriented units. Some processes, such as papier-mâché and plaster carving, require extended periods of time. Skill-oriented activities require more time than laissez-faire experimentation. Open-ended assignments require time to explore ideas and to solve problems.
   c. Consider the number of process-oriented activity steps necessary to prepare students for the creation of final products.
   d. Consider strategies for presenting historical/critical/aesthetic content. Will you involve students through discussions, games, or worksheets? Will you present all the information on one day, or in segments over several periods?
   e. Consider the amount of time required for critiques of work in progress and completed products.

8. *Narrow your ideas for units to what you think you can reasonably accomplish in the first time segment.* Allow yourself an extra day here and there for snow days.

9. *Establish a sequence for the units.* To determine what to present first, ask yourself these questions:

   a. Are prior skills and knowledge necessary for students to accomplish goals and objectives? If so, what are they?

   b. Do students have these skills and knowledge?

   c. If they do not, what do I need to present before I teach this unit?

   The answers to these questions can lead you to discover two types of sequencing: *independent* and *dependent*. In independent sequencing ideas and skills can be presented in any order because understanding does not depend on prior

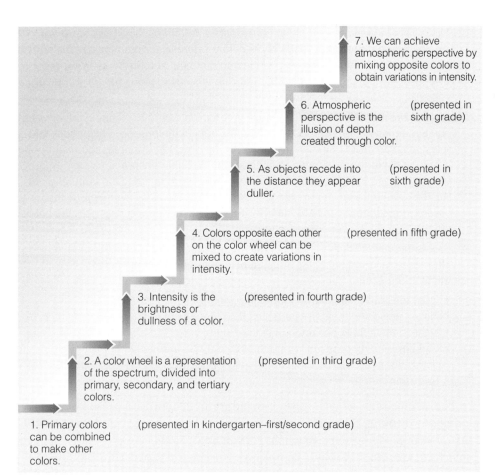

7. We can achieve atmospheric perspective by mixing opposite colors to obtain variations in intensity.

6. Atmospheric perspective is the illusion of depth created through color. (presented in sixth grade)

5. As objects recede into the distance they appear duller. (presented in sixth grade)

4. Colors opposite each other on the color wheel can be mixed to create variations in intensity. (presented in fifth grade)

3. Intensity is the brightness or dullness of a color. (presented in fourth grade)

2. A color wheel is a representation of the spectrum, divided into primary, secondary, and tertiary colors. (presented in third grade)

1. Primary colors can be combined to make other colors. (presented in kindergarten–first/second grade)

knowledge. For example, if you select art elements as your focus for a quarter with first graders, you can begin with a unit on any one art element—color, shape, line, or texture. The order in which you present each element may not matter. First graders can understand differences in color without being able to name shapes or draw lines. Suppose, however, you wish to start out the year teaching incoming middle schoolers a unit on color and decide to have students do paintings using atmospheric perspective. Will they be able to do this? Their ability depends on the degree to which their experiences in elementary art education prepared them. They must have acquired previous knowledge and skills to be ready for this assignment. Figure 13.3 shows how concepts and learning experiences build on one another in a dependent sequence.

The steps in Figure 13.3 illustrate that students must understand one concept before they can move on to the next. Before you ask your students to create paintings using atmospheric perspective, you need to find out what they already know about color. If they have had no previous art education in their elementary backgrounds, you may need to revise your thinking and design a unit around what you consider to be a "first grade" concept: Primary colors can be combined to make other colors in the spectrum. A student's level of artistic development may not correspond to what we think is "normal" for his or her chronological age if he or she has not had opportunities to learn and express in art. You may need to look to your students rather than to your curriculum guide to determine what is most fitting for specific populations.

10. *Define the units decided on by filling in the matrix.* Check to see that you have planned for the breadth you intended to embrace. Modify as needed to improve selection of content and/or sequencing.

11. *Repeat this process with other grade levels or courses, designing sequences for the first grading period.*

12. *Move from the matrices for one marking period to unit plans, if possible.* If you are not required to submit yearly plans before school starts, you may at this point move from these matrices to unit and lesson planning and teaching. What you learn from experiencing your students during this first marking period will help you design matrices for the rest of the year.

13. *Plan for the following marking periods.* If you must continue planning for subsequent marking periods before school begins, repeat the process. The themes you select can vary from one marking period to the next. For example, you might plan a year by exploring media and techniques the first quarter, formal properties the second quarter, interdisciplinary connections the third quarter, and cultural diversity the fourth quarter. You might also include all these aspects under one theme used throughout the year. The sample yearly plan that follows illustrates the latter approach, using *studio areas* as a unifying theme.

14. *Assess the plan.* Whether you plan one marking period at a time or an entire year all at once, you should assess the plan before you begin implementing it. You might address these questions:

   • Does the plan reflect curriculum guidelines/content?
   • Have I neglected to address aspects? If so, how can I modify to include them?
   • Is the content fitting for my population?
   • Can I present this content within the allotted time frame? What might I eliminate, add, modify to build flexibility into this plan?
   • Does this plan reflect my program and serve my students' needs?

These questions, as well as the procedure in general, are presented to guide your thinking. They do not address *what to teach;* they address *how to make decisions* about what to teach. As you analyze the sample yearly plan in Table 13.8, keep this in mind. Its purpose is to model a structure capable of reflecting decisions about what to include and the order in which to progress.

TABLE 13.8
Sample Yearly Plan for Seventh Grade (50 minutes twice weekly)

FIRST QUARTER: DRAWING/TWO-DIMENSIONAL DESIGN

Unit Description	Studio Processes/Media	Subject Matter/Theme	Formal Properties	Cultural Exemplar	Aesthetic Orientation
Unit 1A (1 week) Symbolic representation of the self, motivated by the guided visualization "A Trip into Space" (process oriented)	*Visual problem solving:* assorted two-dimensional media and processes, including drawing and collage	Symbolic representation of the self	Line Color Shape Texture	A variety of works that could be interpreted as "symbolic self-portraits"	Contextualism (dealing with symbolic content unique to each person)
Unit 1B (2 weeks) Exploration of contour drawing in a series of exercises designed to build perceptual and drawing skills (process oriented)	*Contour drawing:* pencils Flair pens, newsprint, white drawing paper	Shoes, hands, heads, assorted objects in the classroom environment	Line	Works illustrating linear quality by artists such as Matisse, Calder, Da Vinci	Imitationalism (dealing with observation)
Unit 1C (3 weeks) Exploration of abstraction using the O'Keeffe unit presented in Chapter 4 (product oriented)	*Contour drawing—abstracting:* pencils, paper, watercolor, oil pastels	Small natural objects—shells, seed pods, leaves, feathers, twigs, bark, etc.	Line Shape Color Texture	Selected works by Georgia O'Keeffe	Imitationalism (dealing with observational drawing) formalism (dealing with use of art elements in abstraction)
Unit 1D (3 weeks) Exploration of instrumentalism through the design of a poster intended to convey a social/cultural message (product oriented)	*Drawing ideas:* simplifying images for purposes of intensification, designing with cut paper shapes	Social/cultural issues	Shape Color Emphasis	Selected paintings and posters by Jacob Lawrence and graphic designer Lance Hidy	Formalism (dealing with composition) instrumentalism (dealing with intent and message)

(continued)

TABLE 13.8 (continued)
Sample Yearly Plan for Seventh Grade (50 minutes twice weekly)

SECOND QUARTER: PRINT MAKING/PAINTING

Unit Description	Studio Processes/Media	Subject Matter/Theme	Formal Properties	Cultural Exemplar	Aesthetic Orientation
Unit 2A (2 weeks) Exploration of mono-printing in a series of expressionistic self-portraits (process oriented)	*Mono-printing:* water-based printing inks, Plexiglas printing plates, brayers, assorted papers	Expressionistic self-portrait	Color Shape Line Texture	Expressionistic representations of the head/figure by Münch German Expressionists Fauves	Emotionalism (dealing with feeling quality)
Unit 2B (2 weeks) Exploration of color to depict mood, emotional qualities in a series of landscape sketches (process oriented)	*Painting:* tempera paints, bristle brushes, assorted colored/white paper	Mood as depicted in landscape images	Color Contrast Transition	Selected paintings by the Impressionists (focusing particularly on Monet) and Postimpressionists	Formalism (dealing with use of color) emotionalism (dealing with mood)
Unit 2C (4 weeks) Symbolic representation of a state of mind as depicted through an interior scene (product oriented)	*Drawing ideas:* paper/pencil, mixed media, combining tempera paint, oil pastels, and text as part of the image	Fantasy/symbolic interior scene reflecting a state of mind, issue, feeling	Color Shape Texture Pattern Unity	Hollis Zigler's paintings/oil pastels reflecting her verbal/visual documentation of her life and battle with cancer	Emotionalism (dealing with feeling quality) contextualism (dealing with meaning)
Unit 2D (1 week) Exploration of relationships between musical and visual expression through the creation of nonobjective paintings, inspired by music (process oriented)	A combination of painting, drawing, and printed images using gadgets and vegetables in mixed media (tempera paint, chalk, oil pastel, markers)	Musical mood and rhythm translated into visual mood and rhythm/movement	Line Color Shape Texture Rhythm/movement Contrast Unity	Selected works by Kandinsky Various types of music	Formalism (dealing with use of elements and principles in visual interpretation) emotionalism (dealing with feeling quality)

TABLE 13.8 (continued)
Sample Yearly Plan for Seventh Grade (50 minutes twice weekly)

THIRD QUARTER: SCULPTURE/THREE-DIMENSIONAL DESIGN

Unit Description	Studio Processes/Media	Subject Matter/Theme	Formal Properties	Cultural Exemplar	Aesthetic Orientation
Unit 3A (2 weeks) Exploration of line used to create form in wire sculpture (product oriented)	*Manipulation of wire to create form:* wires, pliers, wire cutters	Human head or animal head/ full body	Line Form Movement	Selected works by Alexander Calder	Formalism (dealing with the use of line to create form) emotionalism (dealing with expression of a particular quality, emotion, or gesture)
Unit 3B (4 weeks) Satirical representation of a well-known person or group in the culture, created from scrap materials, in a cooperative learning experience (product oriented)	*Sculptural processes involved in the creation of an assemblage:* mixed media including wood scraps, paper, fabric, found objects, photographs, drawn and painted images	Human figure	Form Texture Emphasis (exaggeration for the purpose of satire)	Selected sculptures by Marisol Escobar	Formalism (dealing with selection and combination of materials to create form) emotionalism (dealing with satire)
Unit 3C (3 weeks) Representation of an aspect of one's personal life or life in one's culture through the creation of a shadow box containing symbolic objects (product oriented)	*Sculpture processes involved in the creation of a relief sculpture:* mixed media including real objects, drawn or painted images, photographs, scrap materials	An aspect of one's own life or life within one's culture	Form Shape/space Balance Unity	Shadow boxes of Joseph Cornell	Formalism (dealing with shape and space in arrangement of objects) contextualism (dealing with personal/cultural meaning)

TABLE 13.8 (continued)
Sample Yearly Plan for Seventh Grade (50 minutes twice weekly)

FOURTH QUARTER: CRAFTS

Unit Description	Studio Processes/Media	Subject Matter/Theme	Formal Properties	Cultural Exemplar	Aesthetic Orientation
Unit 4A (3 weeks) Exploration of hand-building processes in the creation of "Storyteller" figures (product oriented)	*Pinch, coil, and slab hand-building methods:* clay, tools, clay boards	Relationships as portrayed through mother/father and child using human, animal, or plant forms	Form Texture Repetition Unity	Selected storyteller figures from various Pueblo (Southwestern Native American) cultures	Formalism (dealing with form, texture, and use of repetition through inclusion of multiple children) emotionalism (dealing with feeling quality)
Unit 4B (6 weeks) Exploration of papier-mâché in the creation of transformation masks (product oriented)	*Processes used to construct armatures, papier-mâché and embellish masks:* armature, wallpaper paste, paint, embellishing materials (feathers, yarn, raffia, etc.)	Transformation from one state, condition, or frame of mind to another	Form Color Shape Texture Balance Contrast Unity	Art and artifacts from Northwest Coast tribal cultures, focusing particularly on transformation masks	Contextualism (dealing with specific meanings of masks) instrumentalism (dealing with purpose) formalism (dealing with design qualities) emotionalism (dealing with emotional impact)

SUMMARY

Integration can be addressed on four levels: (1) integrating art criticism, aesthetics, and art history within the response aspect of a unit; (2) integrating response and productive aspects in a scope and sequence; (3) integrating all four art education domains within the component parts of a unit plan; and (4) integrating units in long-range planning. Content of the first three levels reviews concepts and processes presented previously and helps you to synthesize and fine-tune your understanding and planning processes.

Moving from sequencing within units of study to sequencing of units of study is a new challenge. Strategies for long-range planning can help in making decisions that support district and/or state guidelines, programs, and students. The first step involves brainstorming for what to include within the four domains of art education.

The second step involves moving from the menu generated in brainstorming to the design of a framework for long-range planning. This framework provides a matrix for selecting and sequencing content presented over several weeks in multiple units of study. The components of the matrix can be whatever you choose. Those presented here are (1) unit description, (2) studio process/medium, (3) subject matter/theme, (4) formal properties, (5) cultural exemplar, and (6) aesthetic orientation.

These six categories, displayed horizontally across the framework, can be used to generate and analyze content *within* units of study. The vertical axis of the framework provides information about sequencing *among* units of study. Sequencing among units is just as important as sequencing within units, because in each domain we build one skill and/or concept on the next. We may present color, for example, in every grade, addressing it at higher and higher levels as we progress. Thus, the activities and concepts we present about color in fifth grade depend on prior learning in grades 1 through 4. Sequences that build on prior learning are called *dependent.* Much planning both within a course or grade level and from one grade level to the next involves dependent sequencing. In some instances, however, the order in which we sequence units does not matter because prior knowledge or skill development is not a factor. In these cases we may use *independent* sequencing to reflect the independent rather than the connected nature of the units.

Whether you are involved in the sequencing of two or three units in a student teaching situation, sequencing for a single grading period, or sequencing for an entire year, you will deal with relationships. You will make choices about what to present within units and how to progress from one unit to the next. A sample framework provides a structure to support you in generating ideas, selecting content, and sequencing experiences within all four domains of art education. Your attention to these processes will serve you in your long-range planning and prepare you to attend to issues presented in the next chapter, dealing with standards and accountability.

A. INTEGRATING THE FOUR DOMAINS OF ART EDUCATION IN A UNIT SCOPE AND SEQUENCE

Directions

Design a sample scope and sequence, using the examples in this chapter as guides. Identify a cultural exemplar and specify a grade level. Divide the scope and sequence into response and productive aspects, as previously modeled. Indicate under response aspect whether procedures fall into the category of criticism (C), aesthetics (A), and/or history (H). (A single procedure may encompass multiple domains.)

Aspect (Response or Productive):	Cultural Exemplar: _____ Grade Level: _____
	Sample Scope and Sequence

B. SEQUENCING UNITS OF STUDY

Directions

Select a theme and grade level for two dependently sequenced units of study. Use the framework below to plan their content and progression.

Theme: _____ **Grade Level:** _____

	Unit Description:	Studio Process/Medium:	Subject Matter/Theme:
Unit 1			
	Formal Properties:	Cultural Exemplar:	Aesthetic Orientation:
Unit 2	Unit Description:	Studio Process/Medium:	Subject Matter/Theme:
	Formal Properties:	Cultural Exemplar:	Aesthetic Orientation:

CHAPTER

14

ADDRESSING STANDARDS, ASSESSMENT, AND ACCOUNTABILITY

Contemplating the breadth and depth of content we present and the experiences we foster in just one year through art education, you may be stunned to discover that our field continues to be viewed by some as a "frill." Artists continue to be stereotyped as "right-brained fluffheads" and art teachers continue to be viewed as keepers of the "dull," "disturbed," and "dysfunctional." This perception is caused by ignorance, which we ourselves may have helped perpetuate. Because art teachers of the past often did not define content, set standards, and assess outcomes in ways embraced within academics, art education was not viewed as being accountable. Subjects in which accountability was not demonstrated were not taken seriously. This chapter challenges the view of art education as a frill, addressing standards, assessment, and accountability. Sections include (1) investigating National Visual Arts Standards, (2) relating national standards to the contents of this book, and (3) demonstrating accountability.

▼ INVESTIGATING NATIONAL VISUAL ARTS STANDARDS

Both general education and art education have come a long way in the 1980s and 1990s to provide standards and demonstrate accountability. This change was in part prompted by a wakeup call in the form of the 1983 publication *A Nation at Risk,* by the National Commission on Excellence in Education. In response to a call for educational reform, national goals for general education were announced in 1990 by the U.S. Department of Education. They defined knowledge and skills all students must have in all subjects to fulfill their personal potentials, become productive and competitive workers in a global economy, and take their places as adult citizens. These goals became law with the passing of the Goals 2000: Educate America Act. The act identified the arts as core subjects of equal importance in education as the academics. The Consortium of National Arts Education Associations responded by developing national standards in the arts specifying what students should know and be able to do on completion of high school:

1. Communicate at a basic level in the four arts disciplines—dance, music, theater, and visual arts.

2. Communicate proficiently in at least one art form.

3. Develop and present analyses of works of art.

4. Have an informed acquaintance with exemplary works of art from a variety of cultures and historical periods.

5. Relate various types of art knowledge and skills within and across disciplines.

In addition to these general arts standards, specific standards for each art discipline have been developed. They have been divided into two categories:

content and achievement. *Content standards* specify what students should know and be able to do and may be viewed as *goals or outcomes*. *Achievement standards* form a subcategory of content standards, specifying expected levels of achievement for students in grades K–4, 5–8, and 9–12. Within the 9–12 grades, two levels have been specified: proficient (for the general high school student) and advanced (for the art major). Achievement standards may be thought of as *objectives or indicators*. Table 14.1 identifies the six content standards and related achievement standards for each level in visual art.

TABLE 14.1
K–12 National Content and Achievement Standards for Art Education

CONTENT STANDARD 1: UNDERSTANDING AND APPLYING MEDIA, TECHNIQUES, AND PROCESSES

K–4 *Achievement* *Standards*	**Students** • Know the differences between materials, techniques, and processes • Describe how different materials, techniques, and processes cause different responses • Use different media, techniques, and processes to communicate ideas, experiences, and stories • Use art materials and tools in a safe and responsible manner
5–8 *Achievement* *Standards*	**Students** • Select media, techniques, and processes; analyze what makes them effective or not effective in communicating ideas; and reflect upon the effectiveness of their choices • Intentionally take advantage of the qualities and characteristics of art media, techniques, and processes to enhance ideas • Use different media, techniques, and processes to communicate ideas, experiences, and stories
9–12 *Achievement* *Standards* *(Proficient)*	**Students** • Apply media, techniques, and processes with sufficient skill, confidence, and sensitivity that their intentions are carried out in their artworks • Conceive and create works of visual art that demonstrate an understanding of how the communication of their ideas relates to the media, techniques, and processes they use • Use art materials and tools in a safe and responsible manner
9–12 *Achievement* *Standards* *(Advanced)*	**Students** • Communicate ideas regularly at a high level of effectiveness in at least one visual arts medium • Initiate, define, and solve challenging visual arts problems independently using intellectual skills such as analysis, synthesis, and evaluation • Use art materials and tools in a responsible manner

CONTENT STANDARD 2: USING KNOWLEDGE OF STRUCTURES AND FUNCTIONS

K–4 *Achievement* *Standards*	**Students** • Know the difference among visual characteristics and purposes of art in order to convey ideas • Describe how different expressive features and organizational principles cause different responses • Use visual structures and functions of art to communicate ideas
5–8 *Achievement* *Standards*	**Students** • Generalize about the effects of visual structures and functions and reflect upon these effects in their own work • Employ organizational structures and analyze what makes them effective or not effective in the communication of ideas • Select and use the qualities of structures and functions of art to improve communication of their ideas
9–12 *Achievement* *Standards* *(Proficient)*	**Students** • Demonstrate the ability to form and defend judgments about the characteristics and structures to accomplish commercial, personal, communal, or other purposes of art • Evaluate the effectiveness of artworks in terms of organizational structures and functions • Create artworks that use organizational principles and functions to solve specific visual arts problems
9–12 *Achievement* *Standards* *(Advanced)*	**Students** • Demonstrate the ability to compare two or more perspectives about the use of organizational principles and functions in artwork and to defend personal evaluations of these perspectives • Create multiple solutions to specific visual arts problems that demonstrate competence in producing effective relationships between structural choices and artistic functions • Create artworks that use organizational principles and functions to solve specific visual arts problems

(continued)

CONTENT STANDARD 3: CHOOSING AND EVALUATING A RANGE OF SUBJECT MATTER

K–4 *Achievement* *Standards*	**Students** • Explore and understand prospective content for works of art • Select and use subject matter, symbols, and ideas to communicate meaning
5–8 *Achievement* *Standards*	**Students** • Integrate visual, spatial, and temporal concepts with content to communicate intended meaning in their artwork • Use subjects, themes, and symbols that demonstrate knowledge of contexts, values, and aesthetics that communicate intended meaning in artworks
9–12 *Achievement* *Standards* *(Proficient)*	**Students** • Reflect on how artworks differ visually, spatially, temporally, and functionally, and describe how these are related to history and culture • Apply subjects, symbols, and ideas in their artworks and use the skills gained to solve problems in daily life
9–12 *Achievement* *Standards* *(Advanced)*	**Students** • Describe the origins of specific images and ideas and explain why they are of value in their artwork and in the work of others • Evaluate and defend the validity of sources for content and the manner in which subject matter, symbols, and images are used in the students' work and in significant work by others

CONTENT STANDARD 4: UNDERSTANDING THE VISUAL ARTS IN RELATION TO HISTORY AND CULTURE

K–4 *Achievement* *Standards*	**Students** • Know that the visual arts have both a history and specific relationships to various cultures • Identify specific works of art as belonging to particular cultures, times, and places • Demonstrate how history, culture, and the visual arts can influence each other in making and studying works of art
5–8 *Achievement* *Standards*	**Students** • Know and compare the characteristics of artworks in various eras and cultures • Describe and place a variety of art objects in historical and cultural contexts • Analyze, describe, and demonstrate how factors of time and place (such as climate, resources, ideas, and technology) influence visual characteristics that give meaning and value to a work of art
9–12 *Achievement* *Standards* *(Proficient)*	**Students** • Differentiate among a variety of historical and cultural contexts in terms of characteristics and purpose of works of art • Describe the function and explore the meaning of specific art objects within varied cultures, times, and places • Analyze relationships of works of art to one another in terms of history, aesthetics, and culture, justifying conclusions made in the analysis and using such conclusions to inform their own art making
9–12 *Achievement* *Standards* *(Advanced)*	**Students** • Analyze and interpret artworks for relationships among form, context, purpose, and critical models, showing understanding of the work of critics, historians, aestheticians, and artists • Analyze common characteristics of visual art evident across time and among cultural/ethnic groups to formulate analyses, evaluations, and interpretations of meaning • Analyze relationships of works of art to one another in terms of history, aesthetics, and culture, justifying conclusions made in the analysis and using such conclusions to inform their own art making

CONTENT STANDARD 5: REFLECTING UPON AND ASSESSING THE CHARACTERISTICS AND MERITS OF THEIR WORK AND THE WORK OF OTHERS

K–4 *Achievement* *Standards*	**Students** • Understand there are various purposes for creating works of visual art • Describe how people's experiences influence the development of specific artworks • Understand there are different responses to specific artworks
5–8 *Achievement* *Standards*	**Students** • Compare multiple purposes for creating works of art • Analyze contemporary and historic meanings in specific artworks through cultural and aesthetic inquiry • Describe and compare a variety of individual responses to their own artworks and from various eras and cultures

9–12 *Achievement* *Standards* *(Proficient)*	**Students** • Identify intentions of those creating artworks, explore the implications of various purposes, and justify their analyses of purposes in particular works • Describe meanings of artworks by analyzing how specific works are created and how they relate to historical and cultural context • Reflect analytically on various interpretations as a means for understanding and evaluating works of visual art
9–12 *Achievement* *Standards* *(Advanced)*	**Students** • Correlate responses to works of art with various techniques for communicating meanings, ideas, attitudes, views, and intentions • Describe meanings of artworks by analyzing how specific works are created and how they relate to historical and cultural contexts • Reflect analytically on various interpretations as a means for understanding and evaluating works of visual art

CONTENT STANDARD 6: MAKING CONNECTIONS BETWEEN VISUAL ARTS AND OTHER DISCIPLINES

K–4 *Achievement* *Standards*	**Students** • Understand and use similarities and differences between characteristics of visual arts and other arts disciplines • Identify connections between visual arts and other disciplines in the curriculum
5–8 *Achievement* *Standards*	**Students** • Compare the characteristics of works in two or more art forms that share similar subject matter, historical periods, or cultural context • Describe ways in which the principles and subject matter of other disciplines taught in the school are interrelated with the visual arts
9–12 *Achievement* *Standards* *(Proficient)*	**Students** • Compare the materials, technology, media, and processes of the visual arts with those of other arts disciplines as they are used in creation and types of analysis • Compare characteristics of visual arts within a particular period or style with ideas, issues, or themes in the humanities or sciences
9–12 *Achievement* *Standards* *(Advanced)*	**Students** • Synthesize the creative and analytical principles and techniques of the visual arts and selected other arts disciplines, the humanities, or the sciences • Compare the materials, technology, media, and processes of the visual arts with those of other art disciplines as they are used in creation and types of analysis

▼
RELATING THE NATIONAL STANDARDS TO THE CONTENTS OF THIS BOOK

These standards have been advanced as a remedy to deal with lack of standardized expectations and lack of standardized evaluation instruments. In them art educators hope to present a consensual voice to speak to governing bodies. The standards are intended to provide a clear statement of the mission of art education, a vision of common expectations, and their ensuing rewards.

By now you are familiar with a variety of voices, rationales, and visions that have shaped our field. You may ask, "Is it possible to speak in a consensual voice? Whose voice is it? Is it wise to assume that what is fitting for one is fitting for all?" These are questions with which art educators are currently grappling. Those who align themselves with subject-centered art education, focusing on content as the stuff of curriculum, are generally supportive of the standards. Those who embrace a child-centered orientation, developing curriculum from the needs and values of individual populations, tend to view the standards more skeptically.

Noteworthy as a dissenting voice is Peter London, who has championed community-based art education. In a 1997 lecture at the National Art Education Convention, he presented this idea: Rather than developing standards by which art learners across the nation will be judged, we might allow standards to emerge from the particulars of locale. As an alternative to national standards, he suggested "the creation of indigenous standards, local standards, standards that arise from the particular circumstances of particular people in their particular moment and place in history." He asked,

> Have you examined the different functions that art can serve so as to employ the powers of the creative process to the best advantage of the students, school, and community at large? I.e., art can serve as decoration, enhancing the look of people, places and things. Art can serve to heal and give comfort. Art can serve to build community by gathering people together to celebrate their common and unique fortunes. Art can serve as a hammer for social justice. Art can serve as a spiritual exercise, elevating consciousness, refining and extending our Being. Art can serve so many functions. Which are best for your students, your community?

The point in presenting a dissenting view is not to give you permission to dismiss the National Visual Arts Standards. On the contrary, the message is to encourage you to examine them, as we have examined other issues, with a critical eye. There are always those who enthusiastically jump on the bandwagon and those who say, "Wait a minute—let's take a closer look." London was urging us to be discerning, to see the "patches" in the "patchwork quilt." In taking a closer look, you must (1) know the standards exist, (2) know what they say, (3) move them from the level of "information" to a level of understanding and knowledge within yourself, and (4) make reasoned decisions, depending on who you and your students are, about how you will address standards in your program. The placement of the National Visual Arts Standards toward the end of this text is purposeful. Had you encountered these in Chapter 1, you might have run screaming off in the opposite direction, claiming you could not possibly address all this. Now you can. The boxed discussion reviews each standard, translates the terminology into language used within this book, and directs you to particular chapters addressing each.

Viewing the National Visual Arts Standards in the Light of This Book

Standard 1: *Students will be able to understand and apply media, techniques, and processes.* This standard focuses on art making. Content that addresses abilities to make and reflect on one's own art is presented in Chapter 2, "Emphasizing Art Making," Chapter 7, "Promoting Creativity," and Chapter 8, "Encouraging Reflection."

Standard 2: *Students will use knowledge of structures and functions.* "Structures" is defined as means of organizing the components of a work into a cohesive and meaningful whole, such as sensory qualities, organizational principles, and expressive features. "Functions" are the use of structures to achieve intended effects or to serve specific purposes. This knowledge refers to understanding of visual language for the purpose of producing and responding to art. Visual language, as defined by sensory qualities (art elements) and organizational principles (design principles), is addressed from the perspective of the art maker in Chapter 6, "Teaching the Language of Vision." Sensory qualities, organizational principles, expressive features, and functions are addressed from the perspective of the art viewer in Chapter 8, "Encouraging Reflection," and Chapter 11, "Focusing on Art Criticism and Aesthetics."

Standard 3: *Students will choose and evaluate a range of subject matter, symbols, and ideas.* This standard moves students beyond an understanding of visual qualities into a comprehension of content and meaning. Like the previous standard, it encompasses both productive and response aspects. Chapter 7, "Promoting Creativity," and Chapter 9, "Embracing Diversity," address self-expression, authenticity, content, and meaning from the perspective of the art maker. Chapter 11, "Focusing on Art Criticism and Aesthetics," and Chapter 12, "Presenting Art History," explore meaning from the standpoint of the viewer. In addition, all the chapters in Part I, "Preparing for Teaching," and Chapter 13, "Integrating the Components," prepare you to develop programs embracing a wide range of curriculum content.

Standard 4: *Students will understand the visual arts in relation to history and culture.* This standard is addressed through the use of cultural exemplars, presented in every sample unit of study. In addition, Chapters 9, 11, and 12, "Embracing Diversity," "Focusing on Art Criticism and Aesthetics," and "Presenting Art History," focus specifically on relationships between art and cultural/ historical contexts.

Standard 5: *Students will reflect on and assess the characteristics and merits of their work and the works of others.* This standard is addressed in Chapters 8 and 11, "Encouraging Reflection," and "Focusing on Art Criticism and Aesthetics," as well as through critical discussions in sample units of study.

Standard 6: *Students will make connections between visual arts and other disciplines.* This standard reflects art's relationship to other subjects and to life in general and is addressed in Chapter 10, "Making Interdisciplinary Connections."

To determine how to apply the standards in daily teaching, you might use a system similar to the one presented here: We (1) identified the standards, (2) defined them in our own words, and (3) reviewed the contents of this book to ascertain whether we had addressed each. Having progressed to this point in your education, you may be well prepared to address these standards. You simply need to view them in light of what you already know and do. The following box provides suggestions for how to do this.

Addressing the National Visual Arts Standards

1. Familiarize yourself with the standards.
2. Use a long-range planning framework (such as the yearly planning matrix presented in Chapter 13) to ensure that you address all six standards at each grade level or course within a given year.
3. Develop unit plans in which content standards are reflected in the goals.
4. Design lesson plans in which achievement standards are reflected in the objectives.
5. Make sure you provide ways for students to demonstrate meeting of goals and objectives through studio behavior and products, written work, and oral discussions.
6. Determine levels of achievement through assessment procedures. Assessment procedures include the following:
   a. Responding to the evaluation section at the end of lesson and unit plans
   b. Evaluating studio work in critique sessions, on reflection forms, and through the use of portfolios (discussed in the next section of this chapter)
   c. Evaluating written work—closing worksheets and assignments addressing productive, critical, historical, and/or aesthetic content
   d. Observing behaviors of students engaged in studio work and oral discussions
7. Compare achievement levels of your students with achievement expectations specified in the National Visual Arts Standards.

▼ DEMONSTRATING ACCOUNTABILITY

Accountability may be defined as "proof" that we teach what we claim to teach. We demonstrate accountability in long-range, unit, and lesson plans. These reflect our awareness of content and achievement standards and our intent to address them. We demonstrate accountability through our classroom environments, teaching visuals, and personal artwork. We also demonstrate accountability through the achievements of our students. In academic subjects, student achievement is measured through written performance. Because records of learning in art are primarily visual, art teachers have had difficulty demonstrating accountability within a system valuing verbal over visual expression. This section addresses this issue, discussing (1) using portfolios to demonstrate learning, (2) assessing outcomes, and (3) designing a grading system.

● USING PORTFOLIOS TO DEMONSTRATE LEARNING

In Chapter 5, "Preparing for Your Students," we touched on the use of portfolios as an organizational strategy. Portfolios can be more than containers for storing work. Today the word *portfolio* has a much broader connotation and is used by teachers in all subject areas to refer to a packet of materials documenting achievement. Two types of portfolios are used in art education. The *application/competition portfolio* is used primarily by high school students seeking scholarships, admission into higher education programs, and employment opportunities. Typically such a portfolio contains selected examples of one's highest quality work. The other type, our focus here, is a *personal growth portfolio*. This, as its name implies, is a record of growth. It can be used in kindergarten through twelfth grade to track progress of individual students. It reflects curriculum content, instructional strategies, and student achievement. It can also provide concrete evidence of accountability.

To investigate how to implement personal growth portfolios in teaching practice, we will draw parallels between a unit of study and its reflection in a portfolio. Every unit of study, regardless of content, length, or intended grade level, contains a productive component (which includes at least one process-oriented activity and possibly a product-oriented experience) and a response component (which includes opportunities to demonstrate through oral discussions and written assignments skills, knowledge, and attitudes pertaining to art criticism, aesthetics, and art history). Both studio and written work become content of the portfolio. Work can be organized in an order reflecting the sequence within a unit. To illustrate this, let's return to two previously presented units. Under each unit is a list of works that might comprise portfolio content:

1. "The Abstraction of Georgia O'Keeffe" (Chapter 4)

   - Contour drawing exercise
   - Reflection sheet on contour drawing (Chapter 8)
   - Abstraction worksheet (Chapter 4)
   - Abstraction reflection sheet (Chapter 8)
   - Experimentation with oil pastel and watercolor
   - Laissez-faire reflection sheet focusing on experimentation process (Chapter 8)
   - Preliminary sketches for final assignment

- Completed abstraction
- Closing worksheet (Chapter 8)

2. "Navajo Sandpainting" (Chapter 9)
   - Practice exercise "painting" with sand
   - Cut paper activity to generate ideas for final product
   - Preliminary sketches for final product
   - Completed sandpainting
   - Paragraph interpreting sandpainting
   - Closing worksheet

In reviewing a portfolio of this work, a teacher might look for evidence of growth as reflected in abilities to do the following:

- Use sensory properties (art elements) to achieve intended effects
- Use structures (design principles) to effectively organize composition
- Solve problems in visual form
- Interpret themes in self-expressive ways
- Reflect on one's work through processes of identification, description, analysis, interpretation, and evaluation
- Make connections between one's own work and the work of others
- Demonstrate knowledge and appreciation of art in and as culture

These achievements, as demonstrated through studio and written work, reflect students' abilities to meet the National Visual Arts Standards.

As you consider national standards, units of study, portfolios, and accountability, you might be overwhelmed; or you might begin to see how the pieces fit together to form a whole. The procedure shown in the box is provided to help you move from an overwhelmed to a calm state, in which to understand relationships within the whole.

Suggestions for Using Portfolios to Assess Growth in Art

1. Refer to your long-range plan to review units comprising a single marking period. Work from these units will be the content of one portfolio.

2. As work is completed for the first unit of study, have each student place it in his or her individual folder.

3. Review the contents of each folder to determine whether goals and objectives have been met by each student.

4. Have students put work from each subsequent unit in separate unit folders. Review work at the conclusion of each unit.

5. At the conclusion of a marking period, have each student place his or her unit folders into an individual portfolio. Review the portfolio of each student, looking for evidence of growth.

6. Have students keep separate portfolios for each marking period.

7. At the end of the year put these portfolios (four if marking periods are divided by quarters) into one larger portfolio for each student. Review contents to determine yearly progress and meeting of standards.

8. Be flexible in implementing the system. It is intended to help you use portfolios to demonstrate educational content, learning outcomes, growth, and accountability. You can demonstrate all these aspects of art education even if the portfolios don't reflect everything you taught and students did. A work may not become part of a portfolio because of a number of reasons: It may be too big, a group project, three-dimensional, hanging in the cafeteria, at home, in the wastebasket. What is important is not that you save each and every scrap of paper, but that you have a system for tracking the progress of individual students and the class as a whole.

ASSESSING OUTCOMES

A portfolio in and of itself is simply evidence that work was done. The level at which the work was accomplished is a judgment you must make. Although we touched on assessment in Chapter 8, "Encouraging Reflection," the focus was on strategies to lead students to self-assess. Here we present assessment as a procedure to ensure that we meet standards. We can assess a student's work in one of two ways: (1) We can view it in the context of works produced by other students and rank it within that body of work; (2) we can view a student's work within the context of his or her previous works to determine growth.

MAKING COMPARISONS WITHIN THE CONTEXT OF WHOLE CLASS PERFORMANCE

This method is common among art teachers and is reflected in the way we conduct critique sessions: We display work of all students. Based on specific and general criteria and quality of work demonstrated by the group as a whole, we judge each work as being superior, good, acceptable, or unacceptable. The system can be used advantageously with homogeneous groups of students who can be motivated by competition with one another (such as high school art majors competing for art scholarships). It also helps teachers establish norms for particular classes. What is normal (average) for one class may not be normal for another. Some groups may perform at consistently high levels, mid-levels, or low levels of achievement. Other groups may reflect a wide range of abilities at all levels.

As a teacher views a body of work produced by an entire class, determining both the level and the range, she (or he) can establish class norms. She may also be able to identify works of "special students" because they are so different from the norm. "Special students" can be viewed simply as those who for some reason do not fit the norm—either because they are superior or because they are challenged in ways normal students are not. These students can be inhibited in a system in which their work is continually compared with others. The work of an artistically "gifted" student, when compared to works by "average" classmates, may always appear superior. This student may always receive *A* grades, cease to be challenged, lose motivation, and become complacent. Work of the "challenged" student, in contrast, may appear inferior to the norm and never be viewed as worth more than a *C* grade. To meet the needs of such a student, a teacher might use the second assessment system.

MAKING COMPARISONS WITHIN THE CONTEXT OF A STUDENT'S PREVIOUS PERFORMANCE

All students can benefit from this method, which may be used in conjunction with the first. Students who are most likely to benefit, however, are those least likely to gain by a comparison to a class norm. The most effective strategy to support students who do not fit within the artistic norm of a class is to avoid comparing them to it. Rather than tracking these students with other students, put each one on his or her own track. Use personal growth portfolios to assess progress by comparing them at any given point with where they were in past performance. Students compete only against themselves, progressing on a path that supports their needs, working at whatever level and speed they are able. The value of personal growth portfolios as assessment measures is that they can be used to track individual performances of "gifted," "normal," and "challenged" learners—any and all students you will ever teach. These portfolios can be used to identify strengths, pinpoint weaknesses, set individual norms and standards, and provide direction for where to go next with a specific student or an entire class.

DESIGNING A GRADING SYSTEM

Portfolios eventually go home with your students. You are left with a record in a grade book. This is an important document that should be carefully structured to reflect contents of units and student achievement within various experiences comprising each unit. The following guidelines show how to do this:

1. *Use a grading system to reflect both productive and response aspects of every unit.* Give marks for both making art and responding to one's own and others' art.

2. *Determine what is most important in a unit and reflect that emphasis through a weighted grading system.* Decide which experiences are central to the unit and which activities play supporting roles. The primary focus should be worth a greater percentage in the overall assessment. Those who support a studio-centered orientation reflect their emphasis by assigning more grades to the productive than to the response aspect. Teachers embracing a DBAE approach in which studio production is used to support understanding of art objects may assign more grades to the response aspect. Through a weighted grading system, you reflect your orientation and values.

3. *Reflect the importance of process-oriented activities in all units by grading work resulting from them.* You may give separate grades for performance in each activity or calculate an average for performance in several. Analyze the role of these activities in relationship to the whole unit to determine their importance and the number of grades to assign.

4. *Reflect the importance and amount of time spent on product-oriented assignments through the grading system.* In short units you may give one grade for process and one grade for product-oriented assignments. The longer a unit is, the longer students are likely to spend in the creation of final products. To reflect importance and time spent, record multiple grades based on fulfillment of several criteria—both specific to the assignment and general (content, creativity, composition, and craftsmanship).

5. *Reflect the response aspect of a unit by assessing both written and oral responses.* Written responses can be assessed by grading reflection sheets; unit worksheets calling for demonstration of critical, aesthetic, and/or historical knowledge; interpretive writings; reports; and/or tests. Depending on the importance of written assignments, each may be graded separately, or they may be combined and given a grade based on an average. You may also use a check system to reflect oral responses. Each time a student volunteers and/or supplies an appropriate response, you might note his or her willingness and ability to think or demonstrate knowledge with a mark in a grade book.

6. *Reflect the importance and length of time spent on units through the number of grades recorded for each.* Decide how many grades you will need to accurately reflect achievements within units spanning two sessions, four sessions, ten sessions, etc. A ten-session experience should be weighted more heavily than a two-session experience. Some teachers give a minimum of one grade per week. This system can work on the high school level, where students may spend an extended period of weeks working on a single piece of art. A number of grades on multiple criteria can be given on one artwork over the

period of weeks required for completion. This system may not lend itself to shorter units in which grades are given for process-oriented work, product-oriented work, and response activities. Two or three grades per week may better reflect the content of short units.

7. Consider giving additional marks at the end of each grading period for aspects such as effort, behavior, work habits, attendance, and overall progress as demonstrated through growth portfolios. These marks can be especially helpful in determining grades of students who are on a border line between one grade and another.

8. Average all grades of each student to determine a grade for a marking period. This is a simple method for calculating grades. Because you have weighted the most important assignments by giving them more than one mark, you avoid dealing with percentages. The sample grade sheet in Figure 14.1 models a system for recording grades for one 9-week marking period, the first marking period for the hypothetical yearly plan presented in the last chapter.

S U M M A R Y

The National Standards for Visual Arts serve as a framework through which we can view the contents of this book. These standards emerged as a result of the Goals 2000: Educate America Act, which provided a law mandating the teaching of art in grades K–12. Six content standards, which may be viewed as goals, specify what students should know and be able to do in art. Achievement standards, which may be viewed as objectives, specify levels of achievement within the K–4, 5–8, and 9–12 grades. Like every issue or trend in art education, the move to standardize art education through the National Visual Arts Standards has been controversial. Those who embrace the standards tend to come from a subject-centered orientation. Those who question them are generally more closely aligned with child-centered education, pointing out that standards emerging from the particulars of specific populations or locales might serve us better. Regardless of where you stand philosophically, as an informed art educator, you should understand these standards:

1. Understanding and applying media, techniques, and processes
2. Using knowledge of structures and functions
3. Choosing and evaluating a range of subject matter
4. Understanding the visual arts in relation to history and culture
5. Reflecting on and assessing the characteristics and merits of one's own work and the work of others
6. Making connections between visual arts and other disciplines

Accountability, or proof that we teach what we claim to teach, can be demonstrated in a number of ways. One of the most effective is personal growth portfolios. These are records of the content and processes we address, as reflected by student achievement within each unit. Unlike application/competition portfolios, in which only a select number of the highest quality final products are exhibited, personal growth portfolios contain as much documentation as possible. Process-oriented work, product-oriented work, reflection sheets, and any other written assignments all become the content of this portfolio. Its purpose is to provide a systematic way to collect work and assess progress of individual students and entire classes.

Grade Sheet—First 9-Week Marking Period—Grade 7—Period 2

Criteria for Grading Units of Study	Unit (Assignment)	Week	1. Adam, John	2. Bark, Bob	3. Carroll, Fran	etc.
Creative interpretation of assignment	Unit 1 — "A trip into space" (1 week)	Week 1	C	A	D	
Observation/drawing skills as demonstrated by folder of drawings from week 1 of unit	Unit 2 — Contour Drawing (2 weeks)	Week 2	A	B	C	
Observation/drawing skills as demonstrated by folder of drawings from week 2 of unit	Unit 2	Week 3	A	B	C	
Meeting response goals as demonstrated in written work/oral contributions	Unit 3 — "The Abstraction of Georgia O'Keeffe" (3 weeks)	Week 4	B	B	C	
Overall aesthetic quality of final product	Unit 3	Week 5	C	A	C	
Average of grades for process-oriented activities (contour drawing; abstraction worksheet)	Unit 3	Week 6	B	B	C	
Meeting response goals as demonstrated in written work/oral contributions	Unit 4 — Poster inspired by Jacob Lawrence (3 weeks)	Week 7	B	A	B	
Understanding/use of formal properties, as demonstrated in final product	Unit 4	Week 8	B	A	B	
Idea, creativity, interpretation of social/cultural issues	Unit 4	Week 9	B	A	B	
General behavior/overall performance						
Behavior/work habits			B	A	C	
Personal growth portfolio			B	A	B	
Attendance (absences and/or tardies)			0	0	3	
Grade for quarter			B	A	C	

FIGURE 14.1
Sample Grade Sheet

Assessment is a process in which we continually engage, as we observe behaviors and products to determine whether they reflect learning and growth. We can assess behaviors and products in one of two ways: (1) We can view an individual's work within the context of works produced by other students and rank it within that body of work; (2) we can view a student's work within the context of his or her previous works to determine growth. The first method can be advantageous in establishing class norms and in promoting healthy competition. The second supports students along their individual paths and is especially effective with students who do not fit within the "artistic norm" of a particular class. Because personal growth portfolios are vehicles for tracking the progress of individual students, they are especially valuable as assessment measures. They can be used to evaluate the work of "gifted," "average," and "challenged" students, and to demonstrate achievement levels of an entire class.

Grading is the process we use to reflect assessment. Although teachers use a variety of systems, the results are usually marks in a grade book (or computer-generated grade sheet). Because a grade book demonstrates assessment procedures, it is an important document. It should be carefully structured to reflect experiences within units and achievement levels of each student participating in experiences. Meeting standards and demonstrating accountability are not easy. Processes involve long-range, unit, and lesson planning; teaching; and collecting, assessing, and documenting the results of that teaching.

ADDRESSING THE NATIONAL VISUAL ARTS STANDARDS

Directions

Review the six content standards for art education. In the space under each list activities you have actually presented and/or those you might develop to lead students at a particular grade level to meet the National Visual Arts Standards.

Grade Level: _____

1. Understanding and applying media, techniques, and processes:

2. Using knowledge of structures and functions:

3. Choosing and evaluating a range of subject matter, symbols, and ideas:

4. Understanding the visual arts in relation to history and culture:

5. Reflecting on and assessing the characteristics and merits of one's own work and the work of others:

6. Making connections between visual arts and other disciplines:

C H A P T E R

DEMONSTRATING TEACHER COMPETENCIES

15

In our last step we move from demonstrating student competencies to demonstrating teacher competencies. Whether you are completing student teaching and about to enter the field, or you are already a member of the profession, you might consider how to best showcase yourself and your accomplishments. This chapter addresses this concern, providing guidelines for (1) articulating a philosophy of education, (2) developing an art education portfolio, and (3) presenting yourself at an interview.

▼ ARTICULATING A PHILOSOPHY OF ART EDUCATION

Your initial contact with an educational institution or a school district may be through a written application sent to a personnel office. You may begin your transition from student to teacher as nothing more than a name in a file drawer. What you include in that application might be your ticket to progress from a dark drawer to a chair in a sun lit office facing an interviewer. Typically application forms ask for educational background—college transcripts, letters of recommendation, scores on the Praxis tests (national examinations for teachers), a résumé, and a philosophy statement. Among all these documents, the one affording the best opportunity to showcase yourself may be the philosophy statement. Even if one is not required in a written application, eventually you will be asked about your philosophical orientation. Make sure you have one that can be articulated in a short period of time or in the space of one or two paragraphs.

Articulating a philosophical orientation is more easily said than done. You might begin by reflecting on the educational experiences, people, and learnings that have most influenced you. You can ask yourself these questions:

- Who am I?
- What do I value?
- How do I define myself as an art educator?
- What is my vision of art education?
- How does it serve individuals and society?
- How might it be implemented?

By contemplating these questions, you can formulate a belief system, a philosophy, to reflect your ideas, your intentions, the paths you are likely to take, and paths you are likely to avoid. You may define yourself as studio-centered, community-based, a proponent of DBAE, or "holistic." You may define art education through interdisciplinary connections, global perspectives, problem-solving experiences, or all of the above.

The purpose of defining yourself to others is not to demonstrate that you have the "right" answers. It is to help them and you decide whether or not a fitting match can be made between you and the needs and values of a particular educational system. As you read the sample philosophy statement in the box, analyze its contents from the perspective of an art supervisor investigating teacher candidates.

A Sample Philosophy Statement

"What are my beliefs about art education? What does art education do? What should it look like?" In considering these questions, I am struck by the realization that art education has been primarily defined by conditions, needs, and values of twentieth-century society. Yet, on entering the teaching profession, we, the products of twentieth-century education, will be teaching children of the twenty-first century. What will these students need to develop into healthy adults who will give form to the future? They will need to be able to think, to solve problems, and to function in a technological age. They will exist on a planet that seems smaller than it appeared to the inhabitants of the last century. They should have knowledge of the peoples of this planet. As advances are made in the sciences and humanities, people are likely to explore connections among body, mind, and spirit. They will need experiences to develop these dimensions. They may also have more free time. They will want to find fulfilling ways to experience themselves as participants and observers in their world.

If a single subject in the educational curriculum can meet these needs, that subject is art. Through experiences in art, students do learn to think, to solve problems, and to give aesthetic form to their ideas. They develop an appreciation of themselves and an ability to communicate with others through the sharing of forms and ideas. They also develop knowledge and appreciation of others. *Art* as a noun is a universal human expression that binds all people together. *Art* as a verb is a process through which every person can express his or her unique make up of body, mind, and spirit. Art education provides experiences to help all students develop to their fullest potentials as individuals who think, feel, know, appreciate, and creatively express themselves.

The art education programs of today and tomorrow should be designed to meet the needs of all students at every grade and developmental level. These programs should be delivered through organized, sequential units of study in which art production is primary. Production should be supported through the study of cultural exemplars, which integrate the making of art with criticism, aesthetics, and history. Goals, content, and experiential teaching strategies should promote understanding of art's impact on the cultures of this planet, on everyday experiences, and on the lives of each and every student in our classrooms. Art education is not a frill: It is a must.

Reading this statement, a supervisor might infer that this applicant

- Is interested in the quality of life now and in the future
- Is imaginative and able to speculate about what might be
- Cares about individuals and society
- Believes that art education can be of value to all people
- Sees art education as a necessary part of the curriculum
- Believes in sequential programs that include all four domains of art education in integrated units of study
- Advocates a studio-centered approach
- Embraces global perspectives
- Is enthusiastic about art education as a field and a profession
- Can express ideas in written language

This initial impression may lead to the next step, an interview in which an applicant can support beliefs through tangible evidence: an art education portfolio.

▼ DEVELOPING AN ART EDUCATION PORTFOLIO

An art education portfolio is a package that represents you as a teacher. You should consider content, structure, and aesthetic appeal in its design. Through your portfolio, you will

- Demonstrate your ability to translate your philosophy into practical application
- Illustrate your ability to present information in an organized manner
- Send psychological messages
- Impact viewers through visual images and overall aesthetic expression

A clearly delineated structure and careful integration of written and visual material can influence an interviewer to consider your portfolio as something special, rather than just another notebook among many. The form in which you present information should impress the logical mind and appeal to the creative spirit. This section suggests how to do both, and includes three boxes: (1) suggestions for developing an art education portfolio, (2) a sample table of contents, and (3) a sample résumé.

Suggestions for Developing an Art Education Portfolio

1. *Consider the initial impact of a document reflecting your achievements.* Decide what kind of visual statement you want to represent you. You might choose a three-ringed binder with a sheet of clear acetate over the cover, under which you can slip your own design. Many students select these because of the psychological messages they can send through the imagery. You might, for example, do the following:

   a. Create a design perhaps in primary colors suggesting expressions of young children to convey interest in teaching on the elementary level.

   b. Design a computer-generated image to signal a focus on art and technology on the high school level.

   c. Suggest an orientation toward DBAE though images and words such as *production, criticism, aesthetics,* and *history.*

   d. Reflect a thematic approach suggestive of interdisciplinary or multicultural emphases.

   e. Present experiential aspects of art education through a montage of photographs illustrating children in art activities.

   f. Focus on the developmental aspect of art education by including images by students at various grade levels.

   Or you may wish to make a statement through a plain, leather-bound portfolio.

2. *Devise a system for organizing the contents of the portfolio.* You may wish to include these items in the following order: (a) a title page, (b) a table of contents (and divider tabs separating the sections), (c) your résumé, (d) your philosophy statement, (e) a sequence of individual unit packages reflecting your teaching experience, (f) examples of studio work representing you as an artist, (g) additional written material documenting educational accomplishments.

3. *Select a number of units (four to six can provide a representative sample) to illustrate the breadth of your teaching experiences.* In selecting units, consider the following:

   a. Range of grade and/or developmental levels

   b. Diversity of student populations

   c. Diversity of experiences, cultural exemplars, teaching strategies

4. *Sequence the units to reflect a logical progression.* Units may be sequenced in a variety of ways:

   a. By grade level, progressing from the lowest to the highest (or vice versa)

   b. By experience, reflecting a chronological progression from the first field experience to the last student teaching experience (or vice versa)

   c. By categories such as two-dimensional, three-dimensional, interdisciplinary, or multicultural experiences

5. *Design unit packages to reflect content, teaching, and student achievement.* A "package" is a collection of materials documenting a unit of study. The Georgia O'Keeffe unit presented in Chapter 4 illustrates one way to document unit, lesson, and visual planning. The procedure suggested here is similar and involves these steps:

   a. Begin the presentation with one or two pages of photographs of students working during unit activities. This introduction serves as a motivation, piquing viewers' interests and encouraging them to ask questions. In addition, it provides a prompt you can use in discussing experiences.

   b. Follow with additional documentation of studio work, which can be represented in actual form, photographic prints, or slides.

   c. Follow the visual introduction with the unit plan, illustrating your ability to envision an entire experience in writing.

   d. Follow the unit plan with one representational lesson plan, illustrating your ability to plan for daily experiences. Select the plan that most effectively illustrates unit content.

   e. Include unit materials such as reflection forms, student worksheets, written assignments, and student packets. You may also include the following:

   (1) The sequence of visuals you created to teach the unit

   (2) Visuals of the cultural exemplar

   (3) Student examples of process-oriented activities leading to final assignments

   (4) Representative final products

   (5) Bulletin boards and/or showcase displays

6. *Consider whether you wish to use this document to present yourself as an artist.* You can include a separate section within this portfolio that showcases your personal work through slides and/or prints. You can also present your artwork separately in a studio portfolio. Whichever method you select, provide an indication of the breadth of studio experiences you have had, and include only your highest quality work.

7. *Conclude the portfolio with materials that illustrate your educational achievements.* These may include the following:

   a. Awards and certificates of recognition

   b. College transcripts

   c. Scores on the Praxis tests

   d. Letters of recommendation

Once you have decided on the content (units of study) you will include and the structure you will use, you can begin designing the individual parts of your portfolio. The box that follows illustrates a sample table of contents you can use as a model.

Sample Table of Contents for an Art Education Portfolio

Contents

1. Résumé

2. Philosophy Statement

3. Units Representative of Teaching Experience

    A. Elementary experience
        1. "Telling Stories Through Pictures," a narrative painting unit presented at the first grade level involving visual storytelling and showcasing the work of Jacob Lawrence
        2. "Invented Insects," an interdisciplinary art/science unit presented at the third grade level involving the design of imaginary insects, placed in cooperatively made murals
        3. "My Family," a sculpture unit presented at the fifth grade level involving assemblage constructions motivated by the works of Marisol Escobar

    B. Middle school experience
        1. "The Abstraction of Georgia O'Keeffe," a two-dimensional design unit presented at the sixth grade level illustrating a strategy to teach abstraction
        2. "Symbols, Meanings, and Mandalas," an interdisciplinary art/math unit presented at the seventh grade level, involving an investigation of the circle as a mathematical construct and a shape used across cultures in mandala designs
        3. "Transformation Masks," a mask-making unit on the eighth grade level motivated by Northwest Coast tribal cultures' transformation masks

4. Studio Work

    A. Personal artwork
    B. Professional artwork from previous work experiences

5. Additional Documents

    A. Awards
    B. Transcripts
    C. Scores on Praxis tests
    D. Letters of recommendation

There are a number of ways to design résumés. As a general rule, your résumé should be one to two pages long and should be limited to those experiences applicable to the position you seek (teaching art). A typical résumé of a student who has just completed student teaching might look like the sample in the following box.

Jean Jones
52 First Avenue
Baltimore, Maryland 21339
(410) 280-5679

Career Objective A position teaching art in grades K–12

Education Bachelor of Science in Art Education,
May 1999, Towson University
Towson, Maryland 21204

Student Teaching
April–May 1999 Dumbarton Middle School
Baltimore, Maryland
Under supervision, planned and taught units of study in grades 6–8

Februrary–March 1999 Pot Spring Elementary School
Baltimore, Maryland
Under supervision, planned and taught units of study in grades 1–5

Field Experience
December 1998 St. Agnes School
Baltimore, Maryland
Under supervision, team planned and taught a five-lesson unit on the second grade level

November 1998 Cedar Avenue Middle School
Baltimore, Maryland
Under supervision, team planned and taught a five-lesson math/art interdisciplinary unit on the sixth grade level

Related Work Experience
Summer 1995, 1996, 1997 Directed arts and crafts activities for elementary-age students at Camp Bravo, Baltimore, Maryland

Fall 1993 Taught crafts course at Mt. Vernon Senior Center
Designed window displays for Hecht's Department Store

Community Activities Taught Junior High Sunday School at Unity Church
Conducted arts and crafts workshops for Boy Scouts of America

Memberships Maryland Art Education Association
National Art Education Association

References (List names, addresses, and telephone numbers of references here.)

PRESENTING YOURSELF AT AN INTERVIEW

Although a well-organized, aesthetic art education portfolio can be an extremely influential document in an interview, it is not sufficient in itself. The most important criterion by which you will be judged may not be how you look on paper, but how you appear in person. Candidates are often assessed on a point system, in which a predetermined number of points is awarded for the portfolio, grade point average, and oral interview. In many school districts the oral interview is weighted most heavily. As you sit before an interviewer, you might be assessed in these areas:

- Verbal communication (clarity, grammar, presentation, organization)
- Nonverbal communication (expression, eye contact, body language)
- Knowledge of subject matter
- Knowledge of children and their developmental stages
- Problem-solving skills (ability to imagine and give answers to "what if" situations)
- Interviewing skills (ability to "think on your feet")
- Motivation (energy level, assertiveness)
- Personal characteristics (friendly, positive, confident, sincere)

Interviewing strategies vary. In one district you may be required to answer twenty-five questions in 45 minutes. In another, you may be asked to explore six questions in an hour. Some interviewers ask broad, open-ended questions, such as "What is your philosophy of art education?" Others ask more specific questions, such as "What characterizes students' artwork in the schematic stage of development?" Some interviewers take the lead by working from a predetermined list of questions. Others may let you lead them as they use your responses to formulate questions and pursue a particular direction. At the conclusion of a session an interviewer may ask if you have any questions or things to share. If you have not yet found an opportunity to present your portfolio, this is the time to say, "I've brought my art education portfolio. May I share it with you?" This sharing can be what influences an interviewer to offer you a contract.

PRESENTING PORTFOLIOS AS AN INTERVIEWING STRATEGY

MANDY had just completed her student teaching experience. Since her performance had been outstanding, the district art supervisor called her to interview for a position. Mandy was well prepared with her art education portfolio and her portfolio of personal artwork. She was also very nervous. During the interview, she sat in a poised, nearly motionless manner, answering each question with what sounded like textbook responses. She was obviously knowledgeable, but seemed stiff and unenthusiastic. At the end of the interview, the supervisor asked if she had anything else to share. Mandy took out her art education portfolio, and the supervisor began mechanically turning pages. When he came to the photographs introducing her first unit, he perked up and said, "Tell me about this!" Mandy relaxed, forgot about textbook definitions, and began sharing herself and her experiences. At this point the real interview began—and subsequently Mandy was offered a contract.

Interviewing can be anxiety-provoking. Anticipating what to expect and being prepared can help. The boxed exercise and suggestions that follow may help you progress toward your goal—a position as an art teacher.

Interviewing Exercise

1. Prepare to interview for the teaching position you know should be yours by role-playing the parts of an interviewer and an interviewee with a partner, alternating roles.

2. On a sheet of paper, generate questions an interviewer might ask an interviewee. Questions may be drawn from the following categories:
   - Knowledge of the history and/or philosophy of art education
   - Knowledge of art education content
   - Ability to apply knowledge in teaching situations
   - Interdisciplinary approaches to teaching
   - Multicultural content and teaching strategies
   - Designing lessons, units, and programs
   - Assessment strategies
   - Knowledge of children
   - Motivational devices
   - Strategies to promote creativity
   - Discipline techniques
   - Organization and management skills
   - Rationales for teaching art
   - Personal experiences relevant to art
   - Your own artwork
   - Interests and strengths as a teacher

3. Interview your partner.

4. Switch roles and respond to your partner's questions.

5. Consider the questions you had difficulty generating and/or answering and what to do to better prepare yourself.

The preceding exercise illustrates a point: Ultimately you must take responsibility for your level of preparedness. You must do whatever you deem necessary to be a competitive candidate. Sharing with your classmates can be an excellent strategy to help you reach your goal. The box that follows provides additional suggestions.

How to Get a Job Teaching Art

1. Be clear within yourself about who you are as an art educator. (Those who are not clear may find themselves following any teacher, policy, or educational trend that comes across their paths without considering purpose, relevance, or value.) Ask yourself these questions:
   - Who am I?
   - What do I value?
   - How do I define myself as an art educator?
   - What is my vision of art education?

2. Formulate your philosophy of art education based on your answers to these questions. Put your ideas in writing. Rework the form and content to create a succinct statement.

3. Introduce yourself through this statement in an application form and/or an art education portfolio.

4. Provide evidence in your art education portfolio that you can translate theory (your philosophy statement) into practice (what you reflect in planning and teaching through your unit presentations).

5. Present yourself through your portfolio in an assertive way. The portfolio is not only a documentation of your achievements; it is also a visual aid you can use in discussing your experiences.

6. Be as prepared as possible for an interview. To prepare yourself, consider doing the following:

   • Reflect on questions you might be asked about children, art education content, planning, teaching, organizing a classroom, maintaining discipline, motivating behavior, assessing work. Practice interviewing with a classmate.

   • Bring representative examples of teaching and studio work to an interview even if your art education portfolio is not yet complete.

   • Wear clothes that (1) you can afford to buy, (2) you feel comfortable wearing because they reflect your individuality, and (3) look professional.

   • Get a good night's sleep.

7. Know that if you have progressed to this point, you are a well prepared, competitive candidate, capable of securing a position as teacher.

S U M M A R Y

Your last step is securing a position as an art educator, as you demonstrate your competencies in visual, written, and oral form. It is important to articulate a philosophy of art education. Strategies to reflect on yourself, formulate values, and express ideas in written form are crucial processes, not only because they help you to be in touch with yourself, but because they help you to present yourself to others. Who are you?

This question can be answered not only by what you write in a philosophy statement or what you say at an interview, but also by what you present in an art education portfolio. This is a vehicle through which you can creatively present yourself and demonstrate planning and teaching competencies. It should include a table of contents, your résumé, your philosophy statement, selected units of study reflecting your teaching experience, and additional materials documenting your educational achievements. Some students today are putting their portfolios on compact discs. The disc can be sent before a meeting, allowing an interviewer to preview a candidate. Once at an interview, however, many candidates prefer to show the actual portfolio because it may allow greater interaction with a prospective employer.

As you review this chapter, you might note that although you may now be at "the end of the road," you have also come full circle. Do you remember where you were when you began in Chapter 1? You started by considering rationales for teaching art. These rationales form your art education philosophy. Where were you then? Where have you been in the interim? Where are you now?

PREPARING TO WRITE A PHILOSOPHY STATEMENT

Directions

As a preliminary exercise to writing a philosophy statement, complete the phrases in the boxes below.

1. I believe the purposes of education in general are . . .

2. I believe art education serves these purposes because . . .

3. In order to serve these functions, I would design an art education program characterized by . . .

4. An example of my vision translated into practical application is . . .

FROM AVOIDING BATS
TO WHOLE-BRAINED
FUNCTIONING

Do you remember when you discovered "bats"? Your first step may have been learning what you should not do. For a while you may have defined yourself by what you were rejecting. You can go only a short distance by defining who you are not. Eventually you must identify who you are.

The intent of this text has been to help you formulate your vision and translate it into action. As you learned to do this, you transformed from a maker of art into someone who is also capable of teaching students to make and understand art. To explore the transformational process, consider the stereotypical view of an "artist": He or she may have well-developed affective, intuitive, creative capacities and attributes we associate with the right hemisphere of the brain. Are you one of these people? To determine how "right-brained" you are, answer the questions below:

- Do you become so engrossed in activities that you lose track of time?
- Do you act on ideas and explore possibilities without considering the order in which you do things?
- Do multiple ideas and images come to you at once rather than in a sequential progression?
- Are you capable of dealing with multiple ideas and visions at one time?
- Do you create images by progressing from the parts to the whole?
- Are you comfortable not knowing the appearance of the whole when you begin a process?
- Does ambiguity appeal to you?
- Can you deal with multiple right answers?
- Do you prefer to interpret and imply rather than to define through exact measures?

If you answered "yes" to most of these questions, you may have highly developed capacities associated with right-brained functioning. As an artist you may be able to do well using primarily the right hemisphere. Imagine, for example, that you are in a studio, working without time constraints. You are exploring media and ideas without knowing where you are going or what the next step will be. You trust your intuition. For the moment you just let things happen without needing to control anything, without making judgments. The outside world seems to vanish as you become one with your materials and process. You are totally absorbed in the act of creation.

Now imagine yourself as an art teacher in a room with thirty children. You are just letting things happen. You have no need to worry about time or to know what your next step will be. You trust that you will be guided to do the right thing at the right time. How is your vision progressing? Has pandemonium occurred yet? You cannot function as a teacher without the ability to create order, to sequence steps, to lead students through activities in predetermined time frames, to analyze situations, and to make judgments. These are skills you develop as you activate the left hemisphere of your brain. Because many students enter art education programs as "artists" with well-developed right-brained capacities, much of this book has been concerned with the development of left-brained skills. A key word, presented over and over in this book, is *structure*. Consider these theoretical constructs as examples of structure:

- Closed-ended to open-ended to laissez-faire continuum
- Teaching models
- Formats for lesson, unit, and yearly plans
- Concept, process, and product visuals
- Task analysis
- Sequential webs
- Dependent sequencing
- Assessment forms
- Grading systems

These tools have one thing in common: They structure processes for planning, delivering, and/or evaluating instruction. Their function is not to present art teaching as left-brained. They are not meant to transform you from predominantly "right-brained" to predominantly "left-brained." Rather they are offered as a means to achieve balance in "whole-brained" functioning. Whole-brained functioning is demonstrated through ways of thinking, ways of knowing, ways of being and doing that integrate all behavioral domains—physical, cognitive, and affective. When we understand both hemispheres, we can promote whole-brained functioning in our students. Table PS.1 provides sample activities to develop abilities associated with both hemispheres.

TABLE PS.1
Activities to Promote Whole-Brained Functioning

RIGHT HEMISPHERE	LEFT HEMISPHERE
• Play with materials and processes in laissez-faire experiences.	• Participate in closed-ended experiences to develop abilities to follow directions.
• Use oral, verbal, and visual brainstorming techniques to generate ideas.	• Classify information into categories.
• Use creative problem-solving strategies to develop fluency, flexibility, originality, and elaboration.	• Write task analyses and use sequential webs to order processes.
• Visualize and fantasize in guided imagery exercises.	• Use writing exercises to demonstrate knowledge of historical, critical, aesthetic, and productive information.
• Interpret meanings in your own and others' artwork.	• Research cultural and historical information.
• Use artwork as motivations for writing. Use poems and stories as motivations for art production.	• Analyze art's relationships to math, science, language, and social studies.
• Use music to block out stimuli in the outside world and to focus on the creative process.	• Analyze connections among art, literature, music, and dance.
• Explore the senses by describing visual qualities, feeling textures, smelling aromas, tasting foods, and discussing sensations. Intensify the ability to perceive through a particular sense by blocking other senses. (For example, with eyes closed describe how surfaces feel.)	• Discuss how the everyday environment reflects visual design.
	• Enhance verbal communication through art exercises designed to develop reading, writing, and spelling skills.
• Do studio activities in which color, shape, line, and texture are used to convey feelings rather than to define objects.	• Use writing exercises to describe how art elements have been used to express feelings and emotions.
• Use balance, rhythm, contrast, and emphasis to suggest moods and emotions.	• Analyze how design principles have been used to create composition.
• Enhance perceptual skills through exercises such as drawing negative areas in still life setups, copying paintings turned upside down, and making contour drawings of objects.	• Enhance evaluation skills through the use of oral and written critiques.
• Communicate ideas in visual form.	• Explain how artists convey ideas in visual form.

If a single word can convey the essence of what we are about as art educators today, *balance* is it. Consider how art education has developed, beginning with the teaching of mechanical drawing and progressing toward the rich tapestry that now exists. Consider how the pendulum has swung back and forth, reflecting changes in rationales and practices. Consider the art educators who have defined the field. Some of them point in the same direction and some do not. Their signposts may say,

- Art to Support the Social Order
- Art to Promote Self-Expression
- Art to Gain Cultural Capital
- Art to Develop Visual Literacy
- Art to Enhance Creative Thinking
- Art to Intensify Experience and to Uplift the Human Spirit
- Art as an Intrinsic Species-Centered Behavior

These ideas are not mutually exclusive. You may view them as potential puzzle pieces to use in ways most fitting for you and your students. Now at the end of this book (and possibly the end of a program in teacher preparation), remember that there are no pat answers in the field of teaching. The words and ideas that work for one may not work for another. Who are you as an art educator, and what words or ideas might you choose as support along your journey?

R E F E R E N C E S

References Pertaining to Art Education

Anderson, T., & McRorie, S. (1997). A role for aesthetics in centering the K–12 art curriculum. *Art Education, 50*(3), 6–14. Goodman's aesthetic theory contextualism contrasted with formalism; using aesthetics to define curriculum.

Arnheim, R. (1989). *Thoughts on art education.* Los Angeles: The Getty Education Institute for the Arts. A distillation of Arnheim's contributions to the field of art education.

Bang, M. (1991). *Picture this.* Boston: Bulfinch Press. Use of visual language, focusing on shape, color, and composition to convey nonverbal messages.

Broudy, H. (1987). *The role of imagery in learning.* Los Angeles: The Getty Center for Education in the Arts. Broudy's art criticism model, Aesthetic Scanning.

Chalmers, F. G. (1996). *Celebrating pluralism: Art education and cultural diversity.* Los Angeles: The Getty Education Institute for the Arts. Approaches to multiculturalism within art education.

Dewey, J. (1934). *Art as experience.* New York: Perigree. Relationship between art and humanity in a child-centered orientation to art education.

Dissanayake, E. (1988). *What is art for?* Seattle: University of Washington Press. Art defined as "species-centered" behavior; an anthropological view of art and art making.

Dissanayake, E. (1991). "Art for Life's Sake." Keynote address, 1991 National Art Educators Association convention, Atlanta, Georgia, March 22, 1991.

Dissanayake, E. (1992). *Homo aestheticus: Where art comes from and why.* New York: Free Press. Art defined as "species-centered" behavior; an anthropological view of art and art making.

Dow, A. W. (1899). *Composition.* Boston: J.M. Bowles. Art elements, design principles, and composition as defined by Dow.

Efland, A. D. (1990). *A history of art education.* New York: Teachers College Press. Philosophical and historical frames of reference for art education from the classical Greek era through the 1980s.

Eisner, E. (1972). *Educating artistic vision.* New York: Macmillan. Art education text integrating philosophical, historical, and practical aspects of teaching.

Eisner, E. (1987). The role of discipline-based art education in American schools. *Art Education, 40*(5), 4–45. Philosophical/theoretical presentation of DBAE.

Feldman, E. B. (1992). *Varieties of visual experience.* Englewood Cliffs, NJ: Prentice Hall. College-level text on art appreciation containing Feldman's model of art criticism.

Feldman, E. B. (1993). Best advice and counsel to teachers. *Art Education, 46*(5), 58–59. Comments by Feldman on interdisciplinary teaching and other issues in art education.

Feldman, E. B. (1994). *Practical art criticism.* Englewood Cliffs, NJ: Prentice Hall. Feldman's approach to art criticism.

Gardner, H. (1980). *Artful scribbles: The significance of children's drawings.* New York: Basic Books. Analysis of children's artistic development as demonstrated through drawings.

Gardner, H. (1983a). Artistic intelligences. *Art Education, 36,* 47–49. Gardner's theory of multiple intelligences.

Gardner, H. (1983b). *Frames of mind: The theory of multiple intelligences.* New York: Basic Books. Gardner's theory of multiple intelligences.

Gardner, H. (1990). *Art education and human development.* Los Angeles: The Getty Center for Education in the Arts. Use of symbol systems in human development; work of Nelson Goodman; Arts PROPEL.

Goodman, N. (1968). *Languages of art: An approach to a theory of symbols.* Indianapolis: Bobbs-Merrill. Investigation of symbol systems and symbol-using skills relevant to arts education.

Greh, D. (1990). *Computers in the art room.* Worcester, MA: Davis. Guide to using technology in the art room.

Hurwitz, A., & Madeja, S. S. (1977). *The joyous vision.* Englewood Cliffs, NJ: Prentice-Hall. Documentation of work of CEMREL in aesthetic education.

Hurwitz, A., & Day, M. (1991). *Children and their art.* San Diego: Harcourt Brace Jovanovich. Developmental stages in cross-culture examples of children's drawings.

Itten, J. (1963). *Design and form: The basic course at the Bauhaus.* J. Maas, Trans. New York: Reinhold. Description of Bauhaus curriculum and teaching.

Lazear, D. (1991). *Seven ways of knowing: Teaching for multiple intelligences.* Arlington Heights, IL: IRI Skylight. Investigation of multiple intelligences (as defined by Gardner) and teaching strategies to promote them.

Lippard, L. (1990). *Mixed blessings: New art in multicultural America.* New York: Pantheon Books. View of multiculturalism within America as reflected through art.

London, P. (1989). *No more secondhand art: Awakening the artist within.* Boston: Shambala. Approaches to teaching and exercises to promote authentic artistic expression.

London, P. (1994). *Step outside: Community-based art education.* Portsmouth, NH: Heinemann. Theory and practical application of community-based art education.

London, P. (1997, December). National standards, no: Genius of place, yes. *CBAE News,* 1–3. Excerpts from London's 1996 address at the NAEA Convention presenting an alternative to the National Visual Arts Standards.

London, P. (1998). Lowenfeld verbatim. *Art Education,* 51(3), 56–61. Excerpts from London's 1998 address at the NAEA Convention promoting Lowenfeld and child-centered art education.

Lowenfeld, V. (1957). *Creative and mental growth.* 3rd ed. New York: Macmillan. Early edition of Lowenfeld's book containing information on visual and haptic types excluded from more recent editions.

Lowenfeld, V., & Brittan, L. (1982). *Creative and mental growth.* 7th ed. New York: Macmillan. Later edition of Lowenfeld's book containing illustrated summary charts of artistic stages of development; characteristics of creativity.

Mittler, G. A. (1986). *Art in focus.* Encino, CA: Bennett and McKnight. A discipline-based text for high school students presenting models for teaching art criticism, aesthetics, and art history, and strategies for studio production.

National Art Education Association. (1994). *The National Visual Arts Standards.* Reston, VA: Author. Standards identifying what every student should know and be able to do in art from grades K to 12.

Szekely, G. (1988). *Encouraging creativity in art lessons.* New York: Teachers College Press. Promoting creativity through classroom environment, planning, and teaching.

Schuman, J. M. (1981). *Art from many hands.* Worcester, MA: Davis. Practically oriented multicultural crafts text including cultural/historical bibliography.

Thompson, K. M. (1995). Maintaining artistic integrity in an interdisciplinary setting. *Art Education,* 48(6), 38–45. Issues concerning integrating art with other subjects in interdisciplinary planning.

Torrance, E. P. (1986). The nature of creativity as manifested in testing. In R. Sternberg, ed., *The nature of creativity.* New York: Cambridge University Press. Characteristics of creativity.

References Pertaining to General Education/Teaching

Hunter, M. (1982). *Mastery teaching.* El Segundo, CA: Tipps Publications. Strategies for effective teaching in any classroom setting.

Hurst, B., Wilson, C., & Carmen, G. (1998). Professional teaching portfolios. *Kappan,* 79(8), 578–582. Definition and use of teaching portfolios.

Palmer, P. J. (1998). *The courage to teach.* San Francisco: Jossey-Bass. Philosophical/theoretical views on the art of teaching from the perspective of the author.

Von Oech, R. (1986). *A kick in the side of the head.* New York: Harper & Row. Strategies for promoting creative problem solving across disciplines.

References for Selected Cultural Exemplars Discussed in This Book

Bearden, R., & Henderson, H. (1993). *A history of African-American artists from 1720 to the present.* New York: Pantheon Books. Chapter 9, "Embracing Diversity."

Courtney-Clarke, M. (1986). *Ndebele.* New York: Rizzoli. Chapter 9, "Embracing Diversity."

Joe, E. B., and Bahti, M. (1978). *Navajo Sandpainting.* Marceline, MO: Walsworth. Chapter 9, "Embracing Diversity."

McDermott, G. (1972). *Anansi the spider.* New York: Holt. Chapter 10, "Making Interdisciplinary Connections."

O'Keeffe, G. (1976). *Georgia O'Keeffe.* New York: The Viking Press. Chapter 3, "Planning Visually and Verbally," and Chapter 4, "Progressing Through Planning Toward Teaching."

Scott, J. (1989). *Changing woman: The life and art of Helen Hardin.* Flagstaff, AZ: Northland. Chapter 11, "Focusing on Art Criticism and Aesthetics."

Wheat, E. H. (1991). *Jacob Lawrence: The Frederick Douglass and Harriet Tubman series of 1938–1940.* Seattle: University of Washington Press. Chapter 12, "Presenting Art History."

REFERENCES